Welfare and the State

SOCIOLOGY FOR A CHANGING WORLD
Series Editors: Janet Finch and Graham Allan
Founding Editor: Roger King

This series, published in conjunction with the British Sociological Association, evaluates and reflects major developments in contemporary sociology. The books will focus on key changes in social and economic life in recent years and on the ways in which the discipline of sociology has analysed those changes. The books will reflect the state of the art in contemporary British sociology, while at the same time drawing upon comparative material to set debates in an international perspective.

Published

Rosamund Billington, Annette Fitzsimons, Leonore Greensides
and Sheelagh Strawbridge, *Culture and Society*
Lois Bryson, *Welfare and the State: Who Benefits?*
Frances Heidensohn, *Crime and Society*
Glenn Morgan, *Organisations in Society*
Mike Savage and Alan Warde, *Urban Sociology, Capitalism and Modernity*
Andrew Webster, *Science, Technology and Society*

Forthcoming

Prue Chamberlayne, Brian Darling and Michael Rustin, *A Sociology of
Contemporary Europe*
Angela Glasner, *Life and Labour in Contemporary Society*
Marilyn Porter, *Gender Relations*
John Solomos and Les Back, *Racism in Society*
Claire Wallace, *Youth and Society*

Series Standing Order
If you would like to receive future titles in this series as they are published, you can make use of our standing order facility. To place astanding order please contact your bookseller or, in case of difficulty,write to us at the address below with your name and address and the name of the series. Please state with which title you wish to begin yourstanding order. (If you live outside the United Kingdom we may not have the rights for your area, in which case we will forward your order to the publisher concerned.)

Customer Services Department, Macmillan Distribution Ltd
Houndmills, Basingstoke, Hampshire RG21 2XS, England

WELFARE AND THE STATE

Who Benefits?

Lois Bryson

MACMILLAN

First published 1992 by
THE MACMILLAN PRESS LTD
Houndmills, Basingstoke, Hampshire RG21 2XS
and London
Companies and representatives
throughout the world

ISBN 0–333–48825–3 hardcover
ISBN 0–333–48826–1 paperback

A catalogue record for this book is available
from the British Library.

Printed in Hong Kong

Reprinted 1993

Contents

List of Tables and Figures   viii
Acknowledgements   ix

Introduction – Who Benefits?   1

1 The Sociological Context   9
   A crisis of the welfare state?   9
   Moving in a market-orientated direction   12
   The political tussle over the welfare state   15
   The global context   17
   Limits of sociological definitions of welfare   19
   Limits of sociological approaches – gender and race   23
   Broadening the discourse   25
   Conclusion   29

**2 Conventional Welfare Discourses: Their Relevance
   in the 1990s**   30
   The duality of the discourse   30
   Conventional approaches to defining key terms   33
      (i) Social welfare   33
      (ii) Social policy   34
      (iii) Social wage   34
      (iv) Welfare state   36
   Data collection and the scope of definitions   36
   Normative/political classifications of welfare discourses   39
   Classifying perspectives   42
      (i) Individualist/anti-collectivist discourses   43
      (ii) Social reformist perspectives   45
      (iii) Political economic perspectives   46

(iv) Feminist perspectives 47
(v) Anti-racist perspectives 49
Limits of the perspectives 52
Revisiting basic issues 55
   (i) Residual versus institutional welfare 55
   (ii) Absolute versus relative poverty 57
   (iii) Selective versus universal provision 59
   (iv) Horizontal versus vertical equity 63
Welfare and citizenship 65
Conclusion 67

3   Cross-national Trends in Welfare State Development   69
Broad national approaches to welfare 70
The British welfare state – from Poor Laws to the
New Right 77
The Australian experience – a wage earners'
welfare state 89
The USA – the traditional laggard 99
Japan – welfare state or welfare society? 106
The Nordic countries – model welfare states 110
Conclusion 119

4   The Distribution of State Welfare   121
I.   Who benefits from social welfare? 124
   Social security 124
   Health and other services 125
   Housing 126
   Education 128
   The better-off and social welfare:
   universal versus selective provisions 129
II. Who benefits from occupational welfare? 131
   Occupational welfare and the political context 131
   The extent of occupational welfare 133
   Occupation and social security 134
   Occupation and private pensions 135
   Other forms of occupational welfare 139
III. Who benefits from fiscal welfare? 143
   Defining fiscal welfare 143
   Levying taxation 143
   Progressivity in the tax system 145
   Tax exemptions/expenditure 146

Defining income for taxation purposes 148
Opportunities for tax exemptions 149
Housing and taxation 151
Tax allowances for dependants 152
Deductibility of gifts to charitable organisations 153
IV. Who benefits from government intervention? 154

5 Men's Welfare State **159**
Liberal theory and the patriarchal welfare state 161
Men and social welfare 164
The family wage 167
Male workers and the usurpation of advantage 170
Men and state power 175
Men and caring 177
Corporatism and citizenship 180
Welfare and the role of the state 185
Conclusion 188

6 Women's Welfare State **190**
Women's economic position **192**
Women's role – from legitimate dependence to
proletarianisation? 196
Education and training 200
Women and employment 201
  (i) Unemployment 204
  (ii) Relative economic disadvantages of women's
    employment 205
Child care 207
Women and caring 211
Women and power in the welfare state 215
Equality policies 217
Threats to recent gains 222
Conclusion 223

**Conclusion: The Welfare State in the Twenty-first
Century** **226**

Recommended Reading 235
References 236
Index 253

List of Tables and Figures

Tables

3.1 Government receipts as a percentage of Gross
   Domestic Product – 1984 or 1985   74
4.1 Non-wage labour costs as a percentage of wages and
   salaries, 1978   134
5.1 Women's dependency in Sweden and the USA   174
6.1 Women's economic dependency in several Western
   societies   195
6.2 Forgone total earnings at age 60 from different
   education and child-bearing scenarios   208

Figure

5.1 Gender-structuring of state apparatus   176

Acknowledgements

Many people have provided assistance, support and inspiration during the process of the writing of this book. There are too many for it to be practical to thank them all individually. Nonetheless there are some who have made a very direct contribution to the project and I am keen to acknowledge this contribution and express my thanks.

My greatest debt is to Professor Janet Finch, who proposed the writing of this book on a visit to Australia in 1987. Later, during the research phase, she not only provided advice but also the hospitality of her department and her home in Lancaster. She has been unstinting in her assistance.

People in a number of countries helped me as I moved around collecting data and informed opinions. Others acted as researchers at various stages of the project. Still others have undertaken, with admirable good humour, the tedious task of reading drafts. I have been provided with much helpful and insightful comment. In these varying capacities I am indebted too: Sabina Berloge, Julia Brannen, Drude Dahlerup, Anne Edwards, Annette Felahey, Ian Gough, Dulcie Groves, Beatrice Halsaa, Barbara Hobson, Donald Horne, Cathie Jensen-Lee, Wuokko Knocke, Arnlaug Leira, Inge Maerkedahl, Frauke Meyer-Gosau, David Morgan, Martin Mowbray, Ron Parsler, Kathy Ruane, Diane Sainsbury, Peter Taylor-Gooby, Steve Tomsen, Lorraine Wheeler and Anna Yeatman.

I want also to take the traditional opportunity to express my gratitude to my deceased parents for encouraging my interest in matters political, and to my children, Frances and Matthew, for their supportive attitudes over the years. Finally I want to take the

opportunity to thank Geoff Sharp, the teacher who originally fired
my interest in critical sociological analysis.

LOIS BRYSON

Introduction: Who Benefits?

The task of understanding and defending welfare policies has taken on a new urgency as state provisions have come under attack in the advanced industrial societies. Until quite recently we routinely referred to these societies as welfare states, but this term no longer fits as comfortably. We have witnessed a significant change of political direction by both conservative and non-conservative governments. The change involves a stated intention to rely more on the market and to reduce state interventions. The emphasis is on cost-cutting, something which is evocatively phrased, 'rolling back the state'. The changes have produced a prolific crop of writings of all political hues. Theorising to date, however, has not proved adequate to underpin a comprehensive answer to the classic sociological question of 'Who benefits?' from these new directions in policy. The theory is lacking, as are expansive research programmes, though the evidence is gradually accumulating. There is no shortage of general and composite evidence, however, from any number of countries, that the poor and most disadvantaged are falling behind.

The aim of this book is to explore the nature of sociological perspectives on the welfare state and assess their utility for both understanding the recent changes and for facilitating the achievement of greater equality. My analysis should be seen as part of the ongoing sociological project of developing theory to inform our understanding of the world around us, particularly its inequalities in the distribution of power and resources.

The 'welfare state' is a feature of twentieth-century social and economic development which promised to deliver economic security to those who are at a disadvantage within the market economy

1

of capitalist societies. As we shall see, this promise has, to an extent, been fulfilled. The most drastic features of early, unbridled industrial development, of the sort that the novelist Charles Dickens so graphically portrayed, have been ameliorated. Countries as widely dispersed as Britain, the Scandinavian nations and Australia cater far better for the economic and social needs of their poorer citizens than is imaginable without the 'welfare state'. Not that the welfare state is a simple and uniform phenomenon. As will become very clear, there are significant differences between the provisions available in each of the advanced capitalist societies. Indeed there are such significant differences between the measures adopted that it can be questioned whether they are all best called welfare states at all.

While there are undoubted benefits from the way the welfare state modifies the market, it is also very obvious, as critics have persistently pointed out, that the more ambitious aim of social equality via the welfare state is far from achieved. There are still very significant inequalities between rich and poor; men's interests are generally better served than women's; many racial groups are oppressed and other groups are still disadvantaged. Nor is the development of the welfare state proving a continuous and seamless process ultimately leading to a more just and uniform post-industrial society. The prediction of continuous progress, the Whiggish view of history and one subscribed to by Marx, had a revival during the period of post-Second World War economic boom (Bell, 1974). However, in the less expansionary economic circumstances of the seventies and eighties, once again the falsity of this promise was exposed. Once again it has become clear that the notion of inexorable progress is a myth which can merely mask the need for constant critical appraisal of the effects of the unequal power distribution.

The analysis undertaken here aims to unravel these limitations and conflicting effects of the welfare state in order to shed light on the question of whose interests are being served. There is a vast sociological literature on welfare. Indeed in researching for this book I could not but ask myself whether the topic could stand the weight of another volume. Within this vast literature, it is not surprising that there is a great deal of diversity in emphasis. There are volumes about the philosophy of welfare, the economics of welfare, the politics and histories of welfare, the practicalities of a range of social policies, discussion of the role of welfare in society more generally and, over recent times, a focus on welfare and women. Despite the volume of this literature, much of it suffers from a narrow treatment of the topic. This means that certain issues of key importance are effectively excluded. This in turn seriously limits the way in which the question 'Who benefits'? is approached.

The nature of any analysis of social phenomena is always of fundamental importance. It is not as if 'truth will out' and the evidence will speak for itself. Our understanding is itself moulded by the intellectual frameworks that we use. Language and concepts are never neutral; they do not provide a ready-made conduit through which messages are simply transferred. The language and form of analysis are themselves part of the political process, and help determine the nature of the discussion. Social analysis, in turn informed by social theory and multiple assumptions, is produced by and produces what social theorists call discourses. These are essentially conventional conversational and analytic structures which channel meaning in specific directions.

When we discuss any topic, certain elements are identified as central and become the focus of attention. This process of specification also determines what is *not* the object of discussion. Sociological analysis at its best has always been concerned with the effect of our processes of analysing, theorising and understanding. Terms such as demystification, debunking, deconstruction and ideology, which have been central to the sociological enterprise, indicate a concern with what falls outside the domain delimited by dominant conversations or discourses.

In political science, terms such as hidden agenda and non-decision express a similar concern to identify what lies behind the obvious and taken-for-granted. Anthropologist Edward Ardener expressed a similar theoretical concern as the process through which the dominant model (or models) of a society will suppress or mute the models of 'subdominant' groups. Such groups, who are usefully referred to as 'muted groups', will struggle to generate 'counterpart models' (Ardener, 1975, p. xii).

Over recent years, the work of French theorist Michel Foucault has been influential in directing far greater attention to the political nature of discourses.

Discourse is not simply that which translates struggles . . . but is the thing for which there is struggle, discourse is the power which is to be seized. (Foucault, 1984, p. 110)

Feminist theory and class theory represent attempts to develop discourses which better serve the interests of powerless or 'muted groups', in this case, women and the working class. As Yeatman puts it, 'contests over concepts like patriarchy, class, multicultural-ism etc. constitute the *politics* of patriarchy, class and multicultural-ism' (Yeatman, 1990, p. 162).

What I am interested in here are discourses which shape the nature of the welfare state and the contests over these which form a politics of the state. A complaint I make about much of the literature – that it constrains the discussion of welfare – is therefore simultaneously a complaint about intellectual constriction and pol-itical constriction. The interests of some, the already-powerful, are persistently privileged to the disadvantage of the interests of others, those muted groups, who remain those who are traditionally oppressed.

Limitations of current sociological approaches

There are two common ways discussions of the welfare state are restricted. First, and quite basically, definitions of welfare tend to focus too narrowly on 'welfare'. They are often only, or at best, mainly concerned with those forms of assistance that are provided by the state and by benevolent institutions to those who are at an economic disadvantage in the society. The focus is on groups that have been traditionally referred to as poor. This has the effect of ignoring the benefits that those who are better-off receive from the state and through state activity. This quarantines these benefits from scrutiny and comparative analysis. To make a full judgement about how much the poor get from the state, and whether it can be afforded in the 1990s and the twenty-first century, we need also to know how much and what those who are better-off receive.

A second limitation of much of the literature is that it is often written from the stance of white males. Thus the analysis serves best this group's interests. Little attention is paid to competing interests, such as those of women, people of non-dominant races and ethnic groups or other minority groups. The neglect of women is not the case with the feminist literature, of course, though it often ignores issues of race, ethnicity and other axes of inequality. Feminist analysis tends also to represent a discourse of its own; it is rarely integrated into other analyses, and this can limit its impact.

What is this book about?

My aim in writing this book is to develop a very broad critical perspective which can deal with the relative advantages of the rich, the poor and those in between. I also want to encompass the interests of various muted groups, particularly women and oppressed racial and ethnic groups. In assessing the effect of state intervention on the 'welfare' of people, *all* outlays, *all* policies and *all* state activities are taken, at least hypothetically, to be relevant. This broad approach to state intervention is made the broader because, as a matter of definition, such intervention also incorporates the negative instance; that is, the case of non-intervention. What the state fails to do, or indeed fails to recognise, is of as much potential concern as the more obvious examples of positive interventions. This point has been recognised by political scientists in their concern, in interest group politics, for the 'non-decision'; that is, how things are actually kept off the agenda and sheltered from public scrutiny and debate. Study of the non-decision-making process has highlighted its importance and shown how difficult coming to grips with these negative instances can be.

In summary, the position I adopt is that the state is generally interventionist and that *all* interventions, including non-interventions, in principle must be assessed in order to address the question 'Who benefits?' Clearly this approach calls for a comprehensiveness which is not achievable; selection of instances has to be made. However, acknowledging the theoretical desirability of such comprehensiveness has a crucial alerting effect and has significant consequences for the analysis that is undertaken.

In taking this broad perspective I will be concerned with a range of competing approaches to the welfare state, both historical and contemporary. I will draw on illustrative data from a number of countries, as an international perspective can highlight and expose more general processes. Nonetheless, my intention is neither to make exhaustive international comparisons between particular countries, nor to provide a comprehensive historical account. This would result in a very different and much larger book and one which goes beyond my particular concern. My task is to contribute a discourse which challenges orthodox and narrower sociological perspectives and to expose where conventional discourses act effectively to support the status quo. I will be concerned largely with the prosperous liberal democratic capitalist societies, looked at within a limited historical framework which concentrates on social welfare. Clearly one could be concerned with welfare in states with other forms, such as communist, fascist or militaristic states. While this would be a fascinating exercise, it is outside my brief and these states are not normally considered 'welfare states'.

The British welfare state provides one pivotal focus of the book. This is partly because this publication forms part of a British series, but also because Britain has a special place in both the rise and fall of the welfare state. Australia also receives regular attention, both because it is the country with which I am most familiar and because it is a welfare state of a different kind to the European style. As will be discussed in some detail in Chapter 3, to the extent that Australia can be called a welfare state, this was achieved through securing protection for male wage-earners and their families, rather than through a social democratic emphasis on citizenship and universal income-security measures and the social wage. Castles has concluded that Australia and New Zealand have wage earners' welfare states (1985, p. 103). This concept provides a useful source of insight.

The Nordic countries, particularly Sweden, will also regularly be drawn into the discussion, because these countries are looked to as providing a model for other welfare states. The USA will also receive attention because, in addition to its prominent role in the international scene, it is usually placed at the opposite end of the spectrum to Sweden in terms of welfare state development. Other countries, such as Japan, will be considered where such illustration throws light on issues of concern.

Looking now to the plan of the book, Chapter 1 sets the scene by looking to the current sociological and social context in which the book has been written. A consideration of the social environment highlights why it has proved necessary to defend gains made towards greater equality over recent decades. An overview of the gaps in the sociological literature exposes major problems for dealing effectively with this new context and sets out the aims of the approach adopted here. In Chapter 2, a more detailed discussion of a range of discourses about welfare is undertaken. This includes consideration of key concepts and the major theoretical schools that have contributed to the scholarly literature on the welfare state. The political philosophies which underlie them are of particular importance. The chapter is also concerned with more recent debates, particularly about the New Right and the state of the world economy, and the implications of these debates for social welfare.

Chapter 3 takes a look at the details of selected national welfare systems. The early part of the chapter compares the commitment to the welfare state of the major advanced capitalist societies. The rest of the chapter is focused on the development of the social welfare state in Britain, Australia, the USA, Japan and the Nordic countries. Particular attention is paid to the development of specific discourses, the interests served by these and their relevance today. Chapter 4 deals specifically with other forms of welfare, picking up on a broader approach proposed by Richard Titmuss, that occupational and fiscal welfare, as well as social welfare, must be of central concern. Occupational and fiscal welfare are specifically discussed in order to help reveal who is privileged. An attempt is also made to broaden the picture to include consideration of state interventions defined in the widest manner to include both action and inaction.

In Chapters 5 and 6 the conventional gender definitions are challenged. In Chapter 5 we turn to an analysis of men's welfare state which revolves around the employment role and the monopolisation of positions of power in each society by men from dominant groups. Women's welfare state (Chapter 6) has very different parameters. As has traditionally been the case, it revolves around women's positions as wives and mothers, even when they work outside the home. The nature of women's work, both inside and outside the home, involves responsibility for caring and a general lack of representation in positions of power. The conclusion draws out the implications of a broad approach to defining welfare and assessing its effects. An attempt is made to identify a framework which facilitates a more comprehensive approach to the beneficiary question. Such a framework should better support discourses which allow muted groups not only to be heard but also to achieve greater equality.

1 The Sociological Context

A crisis of the welfare state?

Changes to the economic and political circumstances of advanced capitalist societies over recent years make a reassessment of our way of theorising about welfare an urgent matter. These changes consist of a complex of factors, but important among them is an increasing reluctance on the part of governments to finance the welfare state. Governments in the liberal democracies are attempting to reverse the expansion of state provisions, that universal trend of the postwar decades which led theorists to coin the term 'interventionist state'. The aim of this reversal was, very broadly, to strengthen the market and reduce the directly distributive role of the state.

While welfare provisions continued to expand at least roughly in step with economic growth, the standard of living of the poorer members of most of the advanced capitalist societies did gradually improve. Not that this necessarily meant an improvement in comparative or relative equality: the gap between rich and poor did not necessarily decrease. Even though there was an increase in the general standard of living, groups largely remained in their original position in the social hierarchy. It was as if people were standing on a slowly-moving escalator. Such upward movement readily gave people the impression of greater equality; they recognised they had 'moved up', even though relative positions were maintained.

Over recent years, however, more limited economic growth precipitated significant changes in the direction of social policy. The 1990s offer few signs of expansion of welfare state provisions worldwide. Indeed, in many countries there has been talk of a backlash against the cost of the provisions of the welfare state and a revolt against high tax rates. Established provisions were reduced or threatened as governments pursued policies aimed at reducing spending and reducing tax rates (Henderson, 1989; Ministry of Finance, Sweden, 1989, p. 27). What had seemed to be a consensus about the necessity for, or at least inevitability of, the state guaranteeing social entitlements for their citizens, came under attack. The voice of private marketeers who emphasised conservative economics and denigrated welfare, gained a strategic place in policy debates. The strength and importance of this trend was underlined by the use of broadly similar rhetoric in relation to the Eastern European non-capitalist nations as they discussed the possibilities of restructuring their economies in the 1990s. Although their intentions developed in vastly different circumstances and the enterprise of changing from a command economy is of a very different nature, a similar discourse focused on a reduction in state activity and the promotion of the market was used.

Reluctance to support the welfare state in capitalist societies represented part of a trend, encompassed by the popular phrase a 'swing to the political right' (Coser and Howe, 1977; Sawer, 1982; Levitas, 1986). The effects of this swing of political opinion, together with changing and more problematic economic conditions, were interpreted by some·as creating 'a crisis of the welfare state' (Offe, 1984; Mishra, 1984). This 'crisis' was recognisable in some countries over two decades ago, but became very widely evident throughout the eighties. Indeed, in 1980 a conference entitled 'The Crisis of the Welfare State' was sponsored by the Organisation for Economic Cooperation and Development (OECD). As we will see, the OECD, an agency which provides strategic economic policy advice to its advanced capitalist nation members, plays a key role in relation to the policy trends with which this book is concerned.

The OECD was established under a Convention signed in Paris in 1960. Its objective is to

promote policies designed:
– to achieve the highest sustainable economic growth and employment and a rising living in Member countries, while

maintaining financial stability, and thus to contribute to the development of the world economy;

– to contribute to sound economic expansion in Member as well as non-member countries in the process of economic development; and

– to contribute to the expansion of world trade on a multilateral, non-discriminatory basis in accordance with international obligations.

(OECD, 1987, p. 2)

There were 20 original signatories to the Convention: Austria, Belgium, Canada, Denmark, France, the Federal Republic of Germany, Greece, Iceland, Ireland, Italy, Luxembourg, the Netherlands, Norway, Portugal, Spain, Sweden, Switzerland, Turkey, the United Kingdom and the United States. Four countries joined later – Japan, Finland, New Zealand and Australia, while, from the outset, there was an agreement that the Socialist Republic of Yugoslavia would participate in some of the OECD's work (OECD, 1987, p. 2).

The context of the 'crisis of the welfare state' has been identified by some commentators as a more general 'crisis of the capitalist state'. In the light of events in Eastern Europe and the Soviet Union from the late 1980s, it became clear that there was not only a crisis of the capitalist state. Nonetheless, the literature concerned with crisis has not generally attempted to link the stresses of the two political systems. They are certainly of a different nature, therefore I will direct my analysis almost exclusively to the advanced capitalist states.

The crisis of the capitalist state is seen to involve significant stress on governments as they juggle conflicting pressures. These pressures are to maintain a viable economy and the conditions for capital accumulation at the same time as they retain electoral legitimacy with voters who have come to expect a certain level of social provisions and relatively high levels of government expenditure (O'Connor, 1973, 1984; Habermas, 1975; Offe, 1984). Governments the world over have wrestled with politico-economic problems, particularly those concerning inflation, unemployment and reduced economic growth. Longer-term strategies to restructure their countries' economies were adopted in an attempt to deal with these problems. Against a background of pronouncements that there was an economic 'crisis of the capitalist state', traditional social welfare expenditure was readily redefined as something of a luxury.

Moving in a market–orientated direction

Waning enthusiasm for state welfare has been part of a more general attempt to reduce government activity. The OECD has been encouraging countries to move in a 'market-oriented direction' (Henderson, 1989, p. 32) in order to strengthen the commercial and business sectors. Privatisation, the moving of state functions into the private sector, has been a highly-visible strategy which encapsulates this trend. Duke and Edgell (1987, p. 279) see a commitment to privatisation as the policy which most clearly distinguished the British Conservative government, in power from 1979, from the previous Labour government. The Labour government had, from 1974, shared a similar commitment to government austerity, but not to privatisation (Kerr, 1981). Britain was a world-leader in promoting privatisation, though the extent to which the rhetoric was translated into practice varied from area to area of the economy. In the social welfare sphere, housing led in the privatisation stakes (Le Grand and Robinson, 1984; Papadakis and Taylor-Gooby, 1987).

Other countries certainly have privatisation on the agenda, though as in Britain, it has been a contentious issue (Wiltshire, 1987). In these countries, government enterprises were sold to private companies and the market was encouraged to become involved in areas which, at least since the development of the welfare state, had been largely the monopoly of government agencies. The formerly 'public' tasks that increasingly involved private business, included child care, care for the aged, the provision of pensions, education and even custody of prisoners, as well as a host of general maintenance tasks such as cleaning, laundry, waste disposal and building upkeep (Le Grand and Robinson, 1984; Evatt Research Centre, 1988). Even in the Scandinavian countries, where state provisions were under relatively little threat, the issue of privatisation was on the agenda (Esping-Andersen and Korpi, 1987).

At a *prima facie* level, these trends must be interpreted as a reversal of earlier moves towards greater equality. The development of certain public services and welfare measures, as well as the nationalisation of some industries, were variously claimed as methods to gradually modify the direct effects of market forces. However, governments interested in promoting privatisation point to a failure of government services to meet the needs of the public adequately. When this is done, even ardent supporters of public welfare must agree that there have often been problems with government provisions. Services have been unresponsive, inflexible, slow and unfriendly as well as costly. The goals of democracy, equity and efficiency have not necessarily been achieved. Nonetheless a re-emphasis on the market has not rectified this and at times has clearly promoted *greater* inequality. This has happened, for example, with the privatisation of public housing in Britain (Papadakis and Taylor-Gooby, 1987, chapter 5) and Sweden (Esping-Andersen and Korpi, 1987). The connection between collectivisation, privatisation and equality is a complex matter, as the economic and social crises in Eastern European countries dramatically remind us. Some of the complexities of the privatisation debte in capitalist societies will be addressed in later chapters.

While the details of current policies vary from one country to another, and the differences between them may be increasing, some form of 'crisis' of the state is recognised by virtually all OECD countries (Henderson, 1989), not to mention Eastern European societies. The conservative political direction that is evident in the advanced capitalist countries has been variously referred to as monetarism, economic rationalism, economic liberalism, neo-conservatism, the New Right (Levitas, 1986, pp. 1–24) or simply as dealing with economic realities. Throughout the book I will favour the term economic liberalism, though not use it exclusively, because it emphasises the lineage connecting this form of economic policy with earlier forms of liberalism of the *laissez-faire* variety (see Chapter 2). However, it must be recognised that, in the age of the interventionist state, traditional notions of *laissez-faire* can no longer be applied. The cries for small government by the New Right do not really envisage the removal of government intervention, but rather a redistribution of its efforts.

Under Margaret Thatcher the British government pursued economic liberalism most flamboyantly and represented one of the most conservative versions. The USA has not been far behind. It has not only been described as 'in full retreat' in respect of welfare state provisions (Glazer, 1986, p. 40), but also as exhibiting the strongest moral attacks on those broader citizenship rights won by the 'new left' during the sixties, particularly in relation to women (Levitas, 1986, p. 23). It is important to note though, that in the USA in the 1980s, Reagan did not so much cut government spending, despite his rhetoric, as divert it to military purposes (Jordan, 1987, p. 6); a trend inevitably continued by the Bush administration to meet the costs of military confrontation with Iraq. This element of militarism, while undoubtedly of major international importance, is beyond the scope of my analysis.

While the political directions pursued by many countries may be broadly similar, the strength of the trend varies between countries. The Nordic states, starting from a well-developed base, are suffering something less of a crisis than many others. They are by no means unscathed, however, and there are variations between the Nordic nations, with Denmark showing the greatest signs of pressures (Olsson, 1988; Vandenberg, 1990), as will be discussed later. Japan, still at the stage of developing its basic provisions (and arguably not a 'welfare state' at all), was perhaps the least affected by the swing to the right. Even so, the question of whether the cost of welfare provisions could be borne by the economy became a current issue (Noguchi, 1986).

In some countries, for example the United Kingdom and the United States, changes in policy direction occurred under conservative party governments. In others, including Australia, New Zealand, Sweden, Spain and France (before its change to a right-wing government), broadly similar directions were pursued by governments traditionally seen as being on the political left (Lawson, 1988; Henderson, 1989). Responses to similar macro-economic pressures, as will be explored, are affected not only by more immediate local economic and social circumstances, but also by a country's unique history. Government strategies are nonetheless made more uniform by the increasingly global structures that regulate the world economy (for example, the International Monetary Fund and the Organisation of Petroleum Exporting Countries) and those that provide policy advice to governments, such as the OECD.

The political tussle over the welfare state

When we consider the conflict over the welfare state and the ideas of the New Right, we can see much of the commentary about 'crisis' and 'backlash' as being too dramatic and certainly ahistorical. It is often more ideological than analytic. The ideas of the 'new' right are hardly new, though their precise form is very much shaped by the current context which involves the form of hightly interventionist state of the late twentieth century (Mishra, 1984). Because the state has developed such an extensive role, this provides a ready basis for insistent calls for the minimisation of government as a means of priming the economy. Government intervention is decried though, paradoxically, coercive activities focused on law and order or the military may be expanded. At the same time, an idealised conception of the market as the fundamental guarantor of freedom is propounded. This market element of New Right beliefs does utilise similar rhetoric to the *laissez-faire* doctrine of the nineteenth century (Sawer, 1982, p. 20). Such views are accompanied by residualist attitudes to welfare and negative attitudes to the 'undeserving' poor, another familiar theme in welfare history. As we shall see in Chapter 2, such attitudes can be traced back at least to the fourteenth century.

Whatever its distinctive features, the 'crisis' of the welfare state must be seen as part of the ongoing struggle over the distribution of power and resources in the various advanced capitalist societies. The state, with its institutionalised power relationships, represents one site for struggle. Over the past twenty or thirty years, in almost all these countries, some important gains were made by a number of previously quite powerless, muted groups, including minority racial and ethnic groups, women, gays, people with disabilities and others (Castells, 1983; Altman, 1982; Banks, 1981; Pierson, 1982). The conservatising trends in social and economic policies can be viewed as the product of a fight back by those who lost some ground in this continuing struggle over distribution (Wilenski, 1986: chapter 1; Levitas, 1986). John Kenneth Galbraith has termed this swing to the right, 'the revolt of the rich' (Sawer, 1982, p. viii).

If we look to history we can find evidence of earlier versions of similar power-conflicts. Flora and Heidenheimer record two examples of attitudes to the welfare state ('*Wohlfahrtstaat*') within

German politics in 1932, which quite graphically match up with left/right positions today. Revisiting Germany of the thirties, from whence it is claimed the term 'welfare state' originated, suggests that certain political tensions are endemic. Flora and Heidenheimer record the words of a war veteran, clearly a supporter of a socialist welfare state, who predicted a swing to conservatism partly because 'liberalism [as against socialist principles] has so eviscer-atetd this *Wohlfahrtstat* that it will surely break up in the hard times ahead' (Flora and Heidenheimer, 1984, p. 33). This view is contrasted with that of the Chancellor of the time, von Papen, who accused his predecessors of inducing the 'moral exhaustion' of the German people by 'creating a kind of welfare state' that burdened 'the state with tasks which were beyond its capability' (Flora and Heidenheimer, 1984, p. 19). The resemblance to con-temporary New Right ideology, as expressed by the likes of Mar-garet Thatcher, is palpable.

Those on the political right have offered reasons why the welfare state is the cause of modern ills (Thatcher's 'nanny state') and claimed the market must be reinstated as the distributor of resources, both social and economic (Harris and Seldon, 1987; Minford, 1987; Lawson, 1988). Those taking a centrist position have offered some defence of the welfare state, but have largely accepted that extensive provisions are no longer affordable. They have puzzled about how limited funds could be more effectively targeted to meet the needs of the most severely disadvantaged (Mishra, 1984; Deleeck, 1985). Economic salvation even so was sought at least partly through the market, and goals such as equity, democracy and participation, ceased to be stressed because they were not seen as affordable or realistic (Yeatman, 1990, chapter 7).

Left-wing theorists have debated how to deal with both the theoretical and practical implications of the shift to the political right. Those associated with the British journal *Marxism Today*, for example, identified the need for a project which creatively addresses current problems, a project they entitled 'new times' (Hall and Jacques, 1989). The Australian left's contemplation of the issue was a significant factor in the establishment of two new political parties; a number of alternative economic and social strat-egies were also proposed (Evatt Research Centre, 1988).

Feminists have been particularly concerned about the swing to the right because the gains made towards greater equality for women were achieved largely through government intervention and the implementation of universalist principles (Hernes, 1987a; Franzway, Court, Connell, 1989, p. 14). As we shall see, women as well as the poor, those of non-dominant racial and ethnic groups and other disadvantaged sections of the population have benefited from the extension of state action over recent decades. The interests of these groups are likely to be poorly served by a minimal market-oriented state (Sawer, 1983; Wilenski, 1986, chapter 1). Over recent years, those committed to extending the welfare state have been described by those on the political right as unrealistic and irrelevant, where previously they would have been accused of being subversive. Even those taking a centrist political position took to judging avid defenders of the welfare state as unrealistic.

The global context

I started this project with the problem of the 'crisis of the welfare state' at centre stage, intending to consider the situation in a number of First World countries. Very quickly I was forced to confront a veritable international epidemic of significant changes in social organisation. These ranged from developments in the European Economic Community, to the virtual collapse of the economies of a number of Second and Third World countries, and the recolouring of the political map of Eastern Europe. It quickly became apparent that an understanding of the current situation of 'the welfare state' is relevant for many countries beyond those capitalist nations which created and expanded the concept. Even for these countries its form will inevitably change to accommodate new international alliances, such as the European Community, which will develop their own social forms.

Understanding the welfare state is also relevant, though somewhat indirectly, to those Third World countries which provide the resources which allow the First World states their high standard of living and their highly-developed welfare provisions. There is too little recognition of this form of exploitation, muted as it is by distance. To focus on one nation, or the First World only, precludes the assessment of cross-national forms of inequality. It prohibits the analysis of the benefits that accrue to nationals of one country through the exploitation of resources, particularly cheap labour, available in another. To limit the analysis in this manner offers tacit comfort to First World nationals through absolving them from having to confront the plight of those in the countries whose resources are exploited. While traditionally the analysis of primary production has had a global profile, today all production needs to be located within a global framework. This is another element which can be dealt with only in a very partial way here. A thorough analysis would require a book of its own.

An understanding of the potential and limitations of the welfare state as a social form anchored in capitalism, is also relevant to Eastern European countries, as many of their leaders look to Western advanced capitalist states for ideas for the restructuring of their economic systems. The degree to which these states can maintain their current state welfare systems if they move to a profit-orientated economy, is yet to be established. Tensions quickly emerged between the former East and West Germanies over issues such as the right to abortion and universal child care because comprehensive provisions were available in East but not in West Germany (Kerschgens, 1990).

The world of the twenty-first century promises to be very different from the world of the 1980s and our sociological perspectives will need to be modified accordingly. With change continuing to occur though, the development of an adequate global perspective presents significant difficulties. Despite the difficulties of capturing such a fast-moving picture, I modified my original intention, which was to focus only on First World countries. The analysis now is undertaken with a new awareness of a backdrop of rapid global change. The broader context is approached with greater sensitivity, though, for practical reasons, it is not dealt with in any detail. The pace of change in world events cannot but reinforce the conviction that there is an urgent need for an international – a global – perspective at the same time as this speed of change renders such a perspective difficult to achieve.

International comparison also facilitates our capacity to isolate the links between policy and outcome. While this was the case in the past, it will hold even more for the future. Not that I am suggesting something at all revolutionary or new, the essence of effective sociological analysis has been recognised throughout the history of the discipline to involve both comparative and historical perspectives (Giddens, 1986).

Limits of sociological definitions of welfare

As well as limitations caused by a focus that is national and ahistor-ical, I have already noted that conventional discourses are often limited by a failure to define the notion of welfare sufficiently broadly and by a failure to give a central place to issues of gender and race. I shall expand a little on these limitations in order to more precisely uncover the implications of such omissions for our understanding of issues of equality.

When we consider the issue of breadth, the major problem is that much of the analysis is too narrowly focused on 'welfare'. This may seem a strange criticism when the topic is the welfare state. However, it is by no means a novel criticism. The renowned British commentator Richard Titmuss made such a criticism in the 1950s in an attempt to extend the range of the discourse. Similar pleas for a broader perspective have been periodically registered since (Sinfield, 1978; Rose, 1981; Keens and Cass, 1982; Jamrozik, 1983; Jordan, 1987). Nonetheless, the main body of research and analysis still tends to stick to narrower definitons, targeting con-ventional social problems and poorer groups. This has the effect of maintaining a bias in favour of the status quo.

In a much-quoted paper published in 1958, Titmuss advocated the extension of our conception of welfare beyond the traditional elements, which he identified as 'social welfare'. He pointed out that benefits were distributed in society increasingly in respect of states of 'dependency', something which receives clear recognition when it comes to pensions, and some other benefits. However, Titmuss was impressed by the relative arbitrariness with which the classifications 'social service' and 'social welfare' were applied. He suggested that state interventions recognised as 'social' existed alongside a much broader area of intervention not thought of in such terms but which shares similar objectives (1974, p. 42).

He likened 'social welfare' to the visible tip of the iceberg with two other forms of welfare, the equivalent of the part hidden below the waterline. The two parts of Titmuss's submerged welfare are benefits achieved through the taxation system, termed 'fiscal wel-fare' and benefits distributed through the employment system, termed 'occupational welfare'. As examples of fiscal welfare he included taxation allowances in respect of dependent children, and exemptions in respect of education. He suggested that even though fiscal benefits represent only another method of making transfers, they are perceived differently from social welfare benefits. Reactions to 'occupational welfare' are similarly different. As examples of occupational welfare Titmuss cited a long list of benefits including, 'death benefits; entertainment, dress and equipment; meal vouchers; cheap meals; motor cars and season tickets' (1974, p. 51).

Titmuss made a strong case for considering all three forms of welfare when assessing the equity effects of a nation's welfare state. Yet despite the merit of his argument and the fact that it has been widely accepted, most discourse still directs attention to those issues which are encompassed by Titmuss's 'social welfare' or, to use Sinfield's (1978) preferred term, 'public welfare'.

The focus in the sociological literature on the welfare state is largely confined to institutions such as social security, personal welfare services, health, public housing and education (Wilensky and Lebeaux, 1965; Gough, 1979; Thane, 1982; Edwards, 1988, p. 242). Even when the taxation system is recognised as a mechanism for the distribution of 'welfare', analysis is likely not to deal with its full scope. Discussion tends to focus on categories of taxation that parallel traditional social welfare provisions, such as tax concessions in respect of superannuation (which in effect is a private form of age pension) or concessions in respect of dependent children, spouses or people with disabilities. Concessions that are paid in respect of the purchase of private housing may also receive attention.

Most analyses have not taken a broad approch to taxation and equality. They rarely raise, for example, the manner in which the better-off may be favoured by the very structures of the tax system. As will be discussed in Chapter 4, this is probably because the benefits from such fiscal policies are not readily translatable into benefits for individuals. If the government fails to tax certain items, provides money at cheap interest rates to encourage the development of selected industries, fails to charge for the use of resources or picks up the tab for the pollution caused by a manufacturer, it is not always easy to see precisely to whom the benefits accrue. Nonetheless benefits do accrue and these are relevant to an analysis concerned with issues of state contributions to personal well-being and issues of equality.

One analytic approach to the welfare state which does offer

breadth of discursive framework is a political economic approach such as was developed in the ground-breaking work of Ian Gough (1979). Following on from O'Connor's analysis of *The Fiscal Crisis of the State* (1973), Gough considered the contribution of welfare, traditionally defined, to the interests of capital. He identified three functions of welfare within capitalism – accumulation, repro- duction of the workforce, and legitimation and control (1979, chapter 1). This framework has become well-recognised today, though the insights were only emergent at the time he was writing.

Gough proposed a number of ways in which welfare services contribute to the accumulation of capital, seeing this occurring both directly and indirectly. The contribution is direct, for exam- ple, when opportunities for private profit-making are provided to business through the letting of government contracts. The contri- bution is indirect in the case of welfare payments which allow otherwise poor citizens to be consumers of privately-provided goods and services. He notes that the function of reproduction of a reasonably healthy and appropriately trained workforce is accomplished, for example, through provisions for the family, particularly in respect of a dependent wife who then provides day- to-day family care, as well as through services such as health, housing and education.

The provision of social welfare services is also important for the maintenance of the legitimacy of the capitalist system and for the maintenance of social control. Welfare represents the 'human face' of capitalism, without which workers might be unprepared to contract their labour and might actively work for the overthrow of the system. Welfare provisions not only damp down discontent but, at the same time, have a controlling effect. For example, provisions tend to reinforce the sexual division of labour. This supports the gender status quo with the production of the labour force continuing within the home, making use of women's unpaid caring labour. The education system contributes too. Not only are skills taught but 'appropriate' attitudes to work are transmitted as well. This means that employers have a reasonably tractable workforce. Income support may be either tied to employment through individual insurance contributions or kept at a relatively low rate and stigmatised to ensure that social welfare will hardly ever be preferred to a job.

Gough does not see the welfare state as a form of automatic

response by capitalist interests and thus he avoids the problem of adopting a functionalist position and seeing welfare provisions as introduced simply to support capital accumulation. He recognises the welfare state as brought into existence and maintained by the struggle of the working class (Gough, 1979, pp. 58–62). He also accepts that even though welfare tends to support capital's interests, it has also improved the lot of workers and is partly a result of their own claims.

This form of analysis, which focuses essentially on the tension between certain functions of the state and the demands of citizens (usually male workers) has been extended over recent years (Habermas, 1975; O'Connor, 1984; Cawson, 1982; Offe, 1984; George and Wilding, 1984). The fact that certain measures have been achieved through struggle is seen to provide impetus for more change. Spurred by earlier success, pressure for the extension of such benefits is exerted by workers and other constituencies (George and Wilding, 1976, p. 84). This pressure ultimately is the dynamic behind the so-called 'fiscal crisis of the state' (O'Connor, 1973) when continuing demands to extend welfare provisions start to impinge too much on the interests of the dominant group. Mishra is particularly pessimistic about this dynamic. He doubts the liberal democratic state's capacity to maintain welfare provisions and accede to the claims made upon it. He claims that 'both the practice and the rationale of the welfare state are in jeopardy' (1984, p. xiii).

Offe has further analysed the way that welfare contributes to the maintenance of the legitimacy of capitalism. Because the economy is based on market exchange which inevitably involves conflicts of interest, he suggests there must be systems other than the economy to by-pass the market in order to contain these inherent contradictions. He proposes that the welfare state acts as such a mechanism, becoming a pacifier, the major 'peace formula of advanced capitalist democracies' (1984, p. 147). The welfare state acts as a 'flanking subsystem' (1984, p. 38) and the peace is kept in two ways. First, through providing, 'as a matter of legal claims', for those people who cannot make their way in the market economy. Second, through co-opting the labour unions by providing formal recognition of their corporate role 'both in collective bargaining and the formulation of public policy' (1984, p. 147). Offe's thesis expands our insight into the foundation and development of the welfare state, particularly its corporate nature. However, his argument does not readily account for the differing strength of unions in different countries. Why, for example, have labour unions been relatively so weak as advocates of public welfare in the USA? Also, given the pressure that was exerted on unions during the 1980s by the Thatcher and other governments, it remains to be seen whether their corporate role will be maintained alongside the pursuit of economic rationalist policies.

Because the role of the state has become so extensive in the advanced industrial societies, this focus on political economy has provided a broad and valuable theoretical framework. Previous analyses of welfare had lacked the underpinning of a theory of the role of the state, despite its obvious and increasing importance. Nonetheless, while this form of discourse on the state, class relations and social welfare offers many insights, it has the major limitation that it does not readily direct our attention to issues of equality which cannot be analysed in class terms, as is the case with gender and race (Williams, 1989).

Limits of sociological approaches – gender and race

The second area of limitation of the more conventional literature on welfare and the welfare state is its lack of a systematic perspective on gender and race. Apparently general analyses, such as those of Mishra (1977, 1984), Room (1979), George and Wilding (1976, 1984) and Wilensky (1975) have routinely assumed the subjects of their analyses to be genderless. They have ignored the valuable theoretical perspectives offered by feminism. Their analyses also imply racial and ethnic homogeneity.

Edwards has analysed British and Australian social policy texts published beween 1975 and 1988, for their treatment of issues of gender. She developed a 'feminist awareness typology' and found that recognition of gender issues has been left essentially to female writers. No book authored solely by male writers made it into the highest category of awareness. In the more recent male-authored literature it was more likely that some attention was directed to the interests of women in a separate section or as part of recurrent commentaries on the interests of various disadvantaged groups

(Edwards, 1988). Works of this nature are really not general analyses; they are at best almost exclusively concerned with class interests and then mainly masculine class interests. In the process they analyse the welfare state from the point of view of less than half the population.

To take only one example, in their summing up of *The Impact of Social Policy*, George and Wilding claim that 'on the whole social policy expenditure has been fairly successful in establishing minimum standards of living below which people do not fall' (1984, p. 251). Nowhere in their conclusion do George and Wilding suggest that different categories of people systematically occupy different levels of economic well-being, with women poorer than men and certain racial groups persistently deprived and oppressed. Indeed, throughout the whole book gender and racial inequalities are rarely mentioned. In his 1987 monograph *Freedom, Equality and the Market*, Hindess acknowledged the importance of the feminist contribution to social policy analysis but still felt able flippantly to recognise that had he taken the feminist literature into account 'it would have made for a different, more complex kind of book and perhaps a better one. It would certainly have been longer' (1987, p. 8). It is not necessarily that these analysts are unsympathetic to feminist or race issues it is just that, as Hilary Rose expressed it, they 'stand outside of their explanations' (1981, p. 477). As Edwards observes, at best 'they treat gender and sexism as theoretically unproblematic, as simply an extra dimension to the analysis of welfare' (1988, p. 211).

There are now many valuable works by women which analyse welfare issues and the welfare state directly from a feminist theoretical point of view (Wilson, 1977; Baldock and Cass, 1983; Dale and Foster, 1986; Pascall, 1986; Abramovitz, 1988; Williams, 1989). The feminist material has, however, often been so busy filling the gaps about women, or being specifically policy-orientated that it has not until very recently been directly concerned with a theory of the gendered state as such (Franzway, Court and Connell, 1989; Connell, 1990).

The dimension of race is still rarely dealt with at all in the literature on welfare and the welfare state. Feminists must be included with those guilty of ignoring race, though this exclusion has been increasingly recognised over recent years (Barrett and McIntosh, 1985; Williams, 1989). Black feminists have made clear the way in which bourgeois women may represent a 'muted' group in relation to dominant men, but they have been dominant in relation to other women and particularly Black women (Hooks, 1982; Mama, 1984, 1989).

Fiona Williams (1989) has developed a framework which does attempt systematically to deal with class, race and gender, despite the complexity of these interrelationships. Her approach is to associate 'organising principles' or themes with each dimension to facilitate analysis. She links 'work' with 'class' and acknowledges that excellent analyses of welfare and work within the context of capitalism have been undertaken. The problem, though, is that the analyses usually stop there. To encompass a 'patriarchal and racially structured capitalism', she adds 'family' as a critical site for gender relations, and 'nation' as the key organising principle of race. Nations are constructed in the likeness of dominant groups. In colonised societies, such as the USA and Australia, settlers (invaders) overwhelmed and discounted the cultures of the indigenous peoples, as well as usurping all or a major part of their territory. In these societies, indigenous peoples were left with little option but to be redefined by the colonisers. The effect can be similar for some groups of immigrants and 'guest workers'. They may similarly face an exclusionary culture and social structure developed to serve the interests of dominant groups. The form of Williams's approach has the potential to be broadened to allow for an understanding of the processes of exclusion on other grounds, for example disability, sexual preference and age. Capitalist societies clearly favour the able-bodied, they are heterosexual, and, western capitalist societies at least, are ageist. The old and the young are at least partially excluded, though this dimension is perhaps less problematic from the point of view of equity in so far as the age cycle itself is universally experienced.

Broadening the discourse

As already discussed, discourses must be treated as structures through which power is exercised and through which it can be challenged (Foucault, 1984). Social theory and social policy can also be understood as discourse, and social policy represents an especially strategic form of discourse as the state ultimately operates

> as much through the production of 'dominant discourses' – that is ways of symbolising and talking about the world – as it does through naked force' (Franzway, Court and Connell, 1989, p. 18).

Giddens has pointed out that dominant discourses are likely to involve three ideological elements to which we need to be alert. The first is that they represent 'sectional interests as universal ones' (1979, p. 193) or, as Connolly puts it, they present 'universal rhetoric to protect provincial practices' (Connolly, 1983, p. 226). Here a perennial example is the way that the interests of men of dominant groups are taken as applicable to women and to men from non-dominant groups. Much feminist literature can likewise be criticised for representing the interests of white middle-class women as universal (Hooks, 1982; Amos and Parmar, 1984).

A second ideological element of dominant discourses is that they deny, or at least de-emphasise, contradictions. This in turn means that those adversely affected may not readily recognise these contradictions (Giddens, 1979, p. 194). This de-emphasis of contradictions is the reason consciousness-raising programmes were necessary during the sixties and seventies to help women to question the taken-for-granted. This demystification was necessary so that women could come to clearly recognise where their interests lay.

A third important effect of dominant discourses to be watched for is the manner in which they 'naturalise' or reify the present. Things are made to seem natural and immutable rather than issues with a history and which are changeable (Giddens, 1979, p. 195). Again to use a gender example, women's subordinate position is frequently attributed to biological factors, despite an overwhelming amount of evidence that gender roles and gendered personality traits differ greatly between societies and between groups in any one society, which means they must be acquired. A similar situation applies to the attribution of characteristics on the basis of race.

A mere change of discourse will not, of course, inevitably lead people to recognise the false claims embedded in the original discourse. Feminist discourses have certainly raised debate but cannot yet be counted as fully successful in achieving the change they call for. The same applies in the case of class. There has been a consistent stream of research which has investigated the relationship beween class and social welfare. In the 1980s Goodin and Le Grand joined a distinguished line of scholars who have established that welfare benefits 'not only the poor' (1987). Nonetheless, even in the teeth of a vast quantity of evidence, a view is maintained by many that 'welfare' goes to the poor and lazy and the rest of the 'taxpayers' are burdened with these costs.

A persistent focus on 'social welfare', rather than on other forms of state support, forms part of an ideological process which protects the advantages of the better-off. There is an obvious contradiction involved in calling some government assistance 'social welfare' while failing to identify other forms of assistance as welfare. The advantages that are received by the more powerful members of the society are quietly ignored, or are identified as in the 'public interest'. Often they are excluded by being defined as part of economic policy and termed tariff protection, subsidy, taxation rebate, industry allowance, export incentive or the like. These are terms which quarantine benefits not only from the social stigma historically connected with social welfare, but also from the public scrutiny which is deemed warranted to safeguard public monies handed out as social welfare (Pond, 1980, p. 50).

At present much sociological analysis of the effects of social policies colludes with this selective definition of welfare. It is implied that conventional definitions are universal and, as is only 'natural', the poor receive most benefits as their need is greatest. This focus on the poorer members of society is maintained despite the fact that class analysis, which has been such a major force in sociology, demands comparison between rich and poor, powerful and powerless.

My analysis is based on the proposition that government outlays (direct and indirect) and other state activities (and failure to act) provide benefits and disbenefits for members of a society. When I use the word benefit here, I am not restricting my meaning to that technical usage in which benefit refers to a form of income security in respect of, for example, unemployment or sickness. By benefit I mean to indicate advantage in the widest sense. I include both tangible advantages, in the form of money (which includes welfare benefits in the narrow sense) or kind, and intangible advantages such as access to opportunities, enjoyment, power or status.

Disbenefits are the reverse. These may also be tangible, such as requiring money outlays, or outlays in terms of time or effort. For example a person with little capital to outlay on a house may be forced to buy or rent in an inexpensive location. This may well be on the outskirts of a large city, and in turn force long journeys to work involving costs in both money and time.

Intangible disbenefits involve lack of access to opportunities, enjoyment, power and status and restrictions on freedom, lifestyle and movement. Women suffer intangible disbenefits from their association with home, caring and the private sphere, because these activities are not valued as highly as those in the public sphere. Indeed the very dichotomy of public and private acts to disadvantage women because it implies that the spheres are separate and this allows the public domain, where men are dominant, to be seen as the more important (Pateman, 1987). Members of non-dominant racial groups also suffer intangible but very real disbenefits of oppression. They also suffer from the manner in which the dominant group provides the yardstick by which value is assessed.

As already indicated, much welfare state analysis colludes with dominant view not only by failing to interrogate for bias in distribution along class lines, but also by assuming gender and race neutrality. Here I will interpolate both gender and race as fundamental axes of inequality and oppression. In dealing with the concepts of both gender and race I am essentially concerned with social relations and more specifically power relations. I am not in the first instance concerned with substantive issues of what we mean by gender and race. Gender in fact has not proved impossibly problematic to define, since a binary classification of male and female is readily accepted. It is the causes and consequences of the distinction that are hotly contested. Definitions of race and the allied concept ethnicity, however, have been and remain the subject of much debate. Classifications have been generally based on either biological or cultural criteria, though over recent years there has been increasing recognition that it is only through power relations that these concepts take on their potency in social life. Certainly a person's physical characteristics, place of origin or culture only become issues of equity when these form a basis for discrimination.

In speaking of race and racism I am not concerned with the real or imagined characteristics of any particular group. Rather, I am concerned with the relationships between groups. Therefore the issue of the distinction of race from ethnicity is not taken to be a substantive issue but one of power. Where there is no oppression, the concepts of race and ethnicity become irrelevant, at least for the purposes of my analysis. Racism here refers to an extreme end of a continuum of oppression and inequality linked to notions of both race and ethnicity. In a similar manner, poverty can be seen as the extreme end of a continuum of socio-economic inequality.

Conclusion

The broad framework that I adopt opens up a vast range of issues which must be addressed if we are to confront the 'crisis of the welfare state' and answer the question 'who benefits' while paying attention to the systematic way class, gender and race relations are acted out. It is clearly not possible to deal with all the relevant questions in one book. Indeed, because the gaze of most social analysts has been so restricted in the past, the information to answer many key questions is not readily available. Nonetheless we can find valuable insights if we scan the literature and consider trends. Ultimately this text can only claim to be a contribution to what is essentially an enterprise of formidable proportions.

To proceed with a piecing-together of both the current social and sociological pictures we now turn to a consideration of conventional discourses on welfare and the welfare state. It is these which provide the framework within which most of the debate has been cast. The discussion is therefore concerned with both description and critique of the way the relevant concepts have been used.

2 Conventional Welfare Discourses: Their Relevance in the 1990s

This chapter is concerned with key concepts and perspectives that form the framework of conventional analyses of welfare and of welfare states. These are important because they provide the terms within which welfare as a social phenomenon is comprehended. I am particularly concerned with the political implications of conventional discourses because, as has already been indicated, the frame and form of social analysis is itself part of the political process. The way we talk about issues and the way we conceptualise them are fundamental to the outcome of social policy and to the issue of 'Who benefits?' 'Discourse is the power to create reality by naming and giving it meaning' (Yeatman, 1990, p. 155), something which Marx grappled with via the concept ideology and later Gramsci through the concept of hegemony.

The duality of the discourse

In unpacking conventional discourses we need first to return to fundamentals and consider just how welfare and its associated terms are used. At its most basic, the word welfare merely means well-being. A perfectly serviceable logical opposite is the word ilfare, yet curiously this is not in popular currency. In his book *Keywords*, Raymond Williams points out that ilfare was used between the fourteenth and seventeenth centuries and underwent a brief revival in the nineteenth and early twentieth centuries (1976, p. 281). The opposite to the term well-being, ill-being, is another term which is noteworthy for its lack of popular usage, and similarly worsement in relation to betterment. Nor are the words disbenefit and diswelfare, in general currency, though they are used more widely than ilfare or ill-being. Titmuss deliberately drew attention to the opposing concept when he exhorted people to ask not only 'whose "welfare state" ' but also 'whose "diswelfare state"' (1968, p. 133).

We should be wary of those words which direct our attention almost exclusively to positive elements. Feminists have exposed the concept of motherhood as involving ideology which hides its repressive side in a warm glow of sentiment which in turn mystifies social issues of power and inequality (Barrett and McIntosh, 1982). Community is another term which is rarely associated with negatives and which has the capacity to obscure issues of power (Plant, 1974, p. 23, Bryson and Mowbray, 1981). Similar cases have been made about democracy and participation. This is ideology in action. These terms are usually taken to have meanings which are descriptive and unproblematic. In reality they are both descriptive and evaluative or ideological. Unless the evaluative element is clearly exposed, the positive aura of terms like motherhood, community, democracy and participation has the capacity to mystify discussion of social issues, particularly issues of power (Plant, 1974, p. 23). Welfare is one of those terms which has a propensity to spread a warm glow that can then get in the way of clear-sighted analysis.

Not that there has been any absence of political opponents to the development of social welfare measures. The negative view that providing welfare only encourages idleness, demoralisation and profligacy is a hardy perennial. In itself it is a narrow view which contributes to a dichotomy between supporters and detractors. Proponents, too, contribute to this dichotomisation by often failing to recognise complexities and failing to scrutinise the taken-for-granted. Clearly, the capacity to highlight the problematic nature of welfare measures and focus on benefits and disbenefits within the same discourse is crucial. Most, if not all, social provisions have contradictory effects. It is therefore necessary to be aware constantly of indirect advantages and disadvantages of all interventions, as well as to consider the more obvious direct effects.

Let us take two straightforward illustrations, the first from the area of employment, the second from traditional social welfare. If a group of already reasonably well-paid workers (often well-organized male workers) receives a pay-rise, this will actually increase the group's relative advantage over others who are less well-paid (often female and unorganised male workers) and thus increase inequality. This can only be countered by a compensatory pay-rise for the more poorly-paid workers. The subtleties of such increases in inequality are commonly ignored.

A second example relates to pensions for single parents. Such pensions provide financial support and this is advantageous in a quite straightforward material manner. It is clearly better to have money than to starve. However, it is usual that at the same time, eligibility requirements have to be met, and these act as a measure of social control over recipients' freedom of action. For example, there is likely to be a limit to paid work that can be undertaken. Or there may be a requirement that any work that is offered *must* be taken (as in a work test or the 'workfare' programme of the USA and some other countries). In the area of private life it may be, as is the case of Britain and Australia, that if a pensioner lives with an employed person of the opposite sex this person is deemed to be supporting them. This particular rule has at times led to 'bedroom snooping', a common practice within the welfare state, to discover the nature of the recipient's personal relationships.

Apart from the restriction of eligibility rules, publicly-provided support may be stigmatised. Thus, to a greater or lesser degree, being in receipt of social welfare can diminish the social esteem afforded a beneficiary. In most countries social welfare is still seen as an inferior form of support to that provided through the labour market. It is virtually always overlooked that sections of the market economy are also in receipt of government support, as is the case where, for example, primary production or industry are subsidised or tax concessions are made to defray costs (see Chapter 4). Such subsidies and a range of other government support do not carry the stigma of welfare. Indeed they may actually carry a seal of approval which enhances the standing of the recipient. This lack of equivalent treatment is itself one of the unrecognised corollaries of government intervention.

Exclusive emphasis on the positive side of welfare not only diverts attention from its negative dimensions; it often also implies an uncritically optimistic view of history and an implicit faith in 'progress' or modernity and current solutions to probems. This is part of a very broad tendency to see circumstances as inevitably improving, a view which supports the status quo by implying that events are broadly on course. Such a view diverts attention from the question 'Who benefits?' It minimises issues of power and conflicting interests. Those developments that serve the interests of the powerful are likely to be accepted as 'progress', even when there may be catastrophic repercussions such as the environmental movement has exposed. Particularly stark illustrations of the contradictions embedded in the notion of progress can also be taken from colonial history and here too the consequences are still very much felt. Colonising nations such as Britain, France, Germany, Spain, Portugal and the Netherlands cast their roles as civilising ones, particularly through the introduction of Christianity, as they invaded other people's lands and exploited their resources. The colonising nations represented their economic and cultural dominance as progressive and paid little or no attention to the social and cultural suffering of the indigenous people.

Conventional approaches to defining key terms

A core of key concepts have been pivotal to discourses on welfare. The concepts of social welfare, social policy, social wage and welfare state are fundamental and need to be reviewed here. After considering them in turn, the discussion will focus on the political anchoring of the major analytic approaches.

(i) Social welfare

While the term welfare can merely mean well-being, most frequently today, together with *social welfare*, it is co-opted to refer to specific measures of public policy. The policy areas most frequently encompassed by the terms include income security, health, public housing, education and the social services provided through social work and related professions. I will refer to this constellation of social welfare provisions as the classical or traditional form.

The range of areas conventionally encompassed by the concept social welfare does, however, differ somewhat from country to country. In Sweden, the designation 'welfare ministries' applies to health and social affairs, labour, housing, education and cultural affairs. This takes in a wider range of areas than is typical for countries such as Britain, the USA, Australia and Japan where labour and cultural affairs would not be included. As will be discussed in more detail in Chapter 3, a hallmark of the Swedish welfare state over recent years has been this integration of a range of policy areas (Olsson, 1989, p. 273).

(ii) Social policy

The term *social policy* is sometimes used interchangeably with social welfare. More often, though, it is used rather more broadly. Social policy makes the distinction between the 'social' and other 'non-social' areas such as economic, defence and foreign policy. In this usage, social policy embraces all that is normally covered by social welfare, and more. Generally it also includes areas such as transport, town planning, the physical environment, consumer protection, anti-discrimination and affirmative action. Despite its somewhat broader scope than social welfare, social policy still usually encompasses the classic forms of welfare.

Feminist writers have been instrumental in broadening the focus of the analysis of social policy over recent years, as well as pointing to the limitations of the traditional boundaries. They have pointed to the relevance of the connections between home and work, reproduction and production, and the artificiality of separating other areas from social policy (Wilson, 1977; Williams, 1989; Waring, 1988; see Chapter 6).

(iii) Social wage

The sum of the collective benefits which are transferred to individuals or families in both cash and kind via the state, can be referred to as the *social wage*. This is distinguished from the 'private or personal wage which comes from employment' (Gough, 1979, p. 108). The social wage, at a minimum, encompasses benefits from the classic social welfare provisions, that is, social security, health, education, housing and the personal social services. While the variation between countries is considerable, the social wage generally also takes into account benefits that accrue from the taxation system where these can readily be equated with traditional social welfare benefits. For example, tax concessions for dependants, concessions in respect of interest payments on mortgages and allowances in respect of educational and health expenses (see Chapter 4).

National calculations of expenditure on the social wage are made readily enough by summating all items deemed to be relevant. The figure is usually expressed as a percentage of government outlays or Gross Domestic Product. For example, for Britain in the financial year 1986/87 social (wage) expenditures represented 24 per cent of Gross Domestic Product (Gough, 1990, p. 34). In Australia the equivalent figure was about 22 per cent for 1985 (EPAC, 1987, p. 15). Calculations for individuals and families are made on the basis of data obtained from income and expenditure surveys. Cash benefits received from the state (pensions and allowances) are apportioned and an estimation made of the cash value of services such as health and education that are used. The amount paid in income taxation is first deducted from the private wage and then an assessment is made of the net contribution of the social wage to the living standard of particular types of household. Issues of equity and distribution are then addressed statistically by comparing the social wage share that is received by various income groups. Gough uses such information, for example, in showing that, during the 1980s, income distribution in the United Kingdom became more unequal. This occurred through a number of processes, including a reduction in the social wage which can act to compensate those in receipt of low personal wages (Gouch, 1990, p. 39).

The items actually included in national calculations vary. In Sweden (Olsson, 1989, p. 273) and Belgium (Deleeck, 1985, p. 40), for example, cultural and recreational provisions are also included. However, the concept social wage rarely, if ever, encompasses all occupational and fiscal welfare. In Australia, for example, even tax concessions for private pensions were not counted until the late 1980s (EPAC, 1987). From time to time comment is made that virtually all government expenditure might be included under this heading, but the comments have neither been followed up in social analysis nor in public policy (Harding, 1984, p. 13; Graycar and Jamrozik, 1989, p. 64). The concept also has the problem that it suggests that people receive a social wage in addition to their economic wage. However, it is clear that the cost of the social wage first comes from conventional income and is then returned in a reconstituted form (Mishra, 1984, p. 85).

(iv) Welfare state

The term *welfare state* is used when a nation has at least a minimum level of institutionalized provisions for meeting the basic economic and social requirements of its citizens. When a nation is defined as a welfare state the major emphasis is on the provision of the classic forms of social welfare. However, regulation of the labour force and working conditions, general public health measures and some active intervention to at least partially redress inequality is usually implied as well. As Mishra notes, the concept refers both to intention (that is, 'the idea of state responsibility for welfare') and the state mechanisms, the 'institutions and practices', for delivering services and provisions (1984, p. xi). As will be discussed throughout the book, there is a great deal of cultural variation in the extent to which liberal democratic capitalist societies measure up in terms of welfare state criteria. Some, such as the USA and Japan, have a weak form which is often referred to as residual. In contrast, the well-developed welfare states of the Scandinavian countries are referred to as taking an institutional form. As well as there being variation between countries in state provisions, within countries different groups have their welfare catered for to varying degrees. In particular those of non-dominant races and women are likely to receive fewer general societal benefits, even though they may be well over-represented as recipients of state support.

Data collection and the scope of definitions

The scope of definitions of social welfare, social policy, social wage and welfare state is systematically affected by the way in which relevant information is collected and interpreted. This shows up very clearly when we consider fiscal and occupational welfare in Chapter 4. As the discussion of the social wage indicates, studies which assess the redistributional effects of various welfare measures rely on a limited range of collective expenditures. These are the figures that are routinely taken into account by formal government bureaus of statistics and those organisations such as the OECD which are concerned with economic analysis internationally. The data collected generally reflect the classical forms of social welfare (Kahn and Kamerman, 1975; Le Grand, 1982; Harding, 1984;

EPAC, 1987) with attention also paid to some specific forms of taxation and taxation exemptions. There are, from time to time, studies of occupational and fiscal welfare, but these have emerged intermittently and indices of these forms of welfare have rarely been incorporated into the routine data collection processes of governments or research agencies (Sinfield, 1978; Keens and Cass, 1982; Jamrozik *et al.*, 1981).

Many expenditure items such as those devoted to defence, roads and highways, public administration, law and order, and public safety are almost always excluded from calculations of the social wage. The problem is dismissed, by suggesting these items to be 'indivisible' (Graycar and Jamrozik, 1989, p. 64) or 'non-excludable', meaning that no one can be seen not to receive their benefits (EPAC, 1987, p. 8). However, it is not enough just to dismiss the matter as an administrative problem, which implies neutrality. Groups are very likely to benefit differentially from each form of government activity. Le Grand has drawn attention to this problem, calling it one of 'externalities'. As an example, he points to the potential for money devoted to the development of roads, indirectly to affect property values. Most studies of the benefits of money spent on roads are restricted to a consideration of effects on direct users rather than indirect effects and the gains and losses that accrue from these effects (Le Grand, 1987, p. 30).

A hypothetical example relating to law and order is useful to demonstrate the point about invisible benefits and disbenefits. If we take a phenomenon such as football hooliganism in Britain, we can very schematically consider the costs of government activity which attempts to control it. When we do so we are forced to the conclusion that the resources that are channelled into its control, be they policing, the building of barricades and other prophylaxis, conducting court cases, enquiries or publicity campaigns, essentially transfer resources to men, as workers in the law and order system and as professional beneficiaries of the game itself and the industry it supports. Soccer itself is a male activity. While I will not attempt to calculate precisely the resources involved, in principle it is easy enough to see how this could be done.

Next we might contemplate what other activities might be supported from the funds were they available for other purposes. Let us consider channelling the outlays towards women, though such

resources could be channelled to any other interests. Clearly services such as child care might be provided, but let us stick to
activities that have some similarity to the policing function. Efforts
could be directed to making the environment safer for women to
be abroad at night. Issues of domestic violence and rape might be
more effectively addressed. One fundamental issue here is the racist
nature of much policing. Law enforcement is likely to have a
differential impact on Black women and their families, so a simple
increase in policing is not implied. What I am trying to illustrate
is how a different use of resources could contribute to women's
interests rather than largely to men's.

Essentially, what such an exercise does is assess not only who
directly benefits from government activity and expenditure, it also
assesses the associated opportunity costs. It is certainly possible to
see how opportunity cost could be more explicitly considered;
they are not always and irrevocably 'indivisible'. But the public
discourses do not encourage us to ask these questions.

The importance of systems of public accounting should not be
underestimated. This is illustrated by considering one of the key
international accounting systems, the United Nations System of
National Accounts. Waring has demonstrated how, like most
accounting systems, it ignores women's reproductive labour and
their labour in the household and informal economies. In Third
World countries women's role as agricultural producers is ignored
as well, even when they are the major producers. This reinforces
women's general invisibility. The environment too is largely
ignored and for essentially the same reason. Where no economic
value is explicitly assigned, there is a wider implication of no direct
value. Within the dominant discourse such elements are largely
treated as worthless (Waring, 1988).

The major statistical concepts for assessing national economic
well-being, such as Gross Domestic Product, likewise focus on
production for exchange and consequently also exclude all aspects
of householding. This leaves us with the oft-quoted anomaly that
if the vicar married his housekeeper the Gross Domestic product
would be reduced by the amount of her former wages even though
she may perform the same, or more, domestic labour but without
wages. Similarly a cake baked at home is reckoned in the national
accounts only by way of the ingredients which have been purchased. A cake baked commercially has a labour component

attached. There is official interest in household production where undeclared cash transactions are involved. Such transactions are recognised as part of the underground economy. Official interest is aroused by the possibility of retrieving the taxation which informal transactions often evade. Interest in the taxability of goods and services underscores the strength of the focus on cash value.

Women undertake about 75 per cent of the household labour that is ignored by the national and international statistics (Iron-monger, 1989, p. x). This bias towards that which is priced, reinforces a lack of concern for 'women's work'. Indeed it diverts attention away from issues of outcomes, in this case particularly the well-being of people, but also other unpriced outcomes such as effects on the environment. Indices such as GDP essentially measure throughput – that is, how much income, capital and expenditure is used and produced. There has been an almost irres-istable tendency to see growth in this throughput as an automatic good. To merely assign a monetary value to household work is therefore not the answer, as this would merely reinforce the hegemony of exchange value as the unit of worth in economic discourse. Essentially, 'the household economy needs to be con-sidered not only in terms of non-market concepts of economic value but also in terms of a different social philosophy' (Jamrozik, 1989, p. 77).

Normative/political classifications of welfare discourses

The definitions that have just been discussed are inevitably norma-tive and political. However, the dimensions of their value base are more readily comprehended in the context of a discussion of the major perspectives that have been used in the analysis of the welfare state. These perspectives or discourses involve prescriptions, both explicit and implicit, about what ought to be. In fact a key element which distinguishes various discourses about the welfare state from each other, is the nature of the good society which they propose, particularly the role of the state in achieving this. There is wide acceptance that some basic minimum standard of living should be available to all citizens. That is, people should not live in dire poverty. Beyond this, views differ across the political spectrum about what is accepted as the appropriate role for the state and what people identify as poverty and inequality.

It is standard practice in the literature which takes an overview of approaches to welfare and social policy, to identity three or four major perspectives or discursive positions. The schools of thought identified in this manner are most often distinguished by their political stance. Room, for example, identifies three positions: neo-Marxist, social democrat and liberal. He further divides the liberals into market and political liberals, always an important distinction, but the more so today when economic liberalism is such a vocal position and one which is often in clear opposition to political liberalism (1979, chapter 3).

Political liberalism incorporates a humanism which leads its neo-conservative protagonists towards a 'reluctant collectivism' (George and Wilding, 1976). That is, they hesitantly accept a considerable amount of state (collective) action as necessary, though ideally they would prefer it otherwise. This is a position exemplified by Beveridge, commonly acknowledged as the architect of the modern British welfare state. He believed that

> liberty means more than freedom from arbitrary power of governments. It means freedom from economic servitude to Want and Squalor and other social evils (George and Wilding, 1976, p. 44)

A quality of humanism, often referred to as 'small-l' liberalism, is still a key factor which distinguishes political liberals from market or economic liberals. The difference is embodied in the classification of more humanist conservatives as wet (political liberals) and the anti-humanists as dry (economic liberals). However, even the most water-logggged tends to fall short of the more developed forms of humanism and concern for equality, particularly economic equality, which is common in varying degrees to political positions to the left of these classic liberal/conservative positions.

Subscription to humanist values does form a link between political liberals and social democrats. The two positions are, however, to be distinguished by the social democrats' emphasis on equality. The social democratic project explicitly aims to create greater equality within capitalist societies; it is essentially concerned with promoting equality of opportunity. This goal must be distinguished from that of Marxists, even though both share a humanistic tradition. Social democrats accept that capitalism can be gradually transformed into a society in which citizens are equal. For Marxists and neo-Marxists, equality can only be achieved within a different economic system, because the relationship between owners of the means of production and their employees is taken as inherently exploitative. The employers expropriate part of the worker's labour. Politically, social democrats take a left-centrist position while Marxists and neo-Marxists take a left radical position.

Given the political nature of the exercise, it should come as little surprise that, when we attempt to classify perspectives on the welfare state, the straightforward use of political terminology has its advantages. In analysing various schools of thought, Mishra has used the popular directional terms for the political spectrum, right (which he also calls *laisser-faire*), centre (social democracy) and left (Marxism) (Mishra, 1984). Parker similarly used the right, centre and left distinction, additionally referring to the positions as *laissez-faire*, liberal and socialist (Parker, 1975, pp.4–5). Her classification highlights the problematic nature of the term liberal, since for Parker this is a centrist position while for Room it represents the right position on the political spectrum. Parker's liberals do, however, overlap with Room's more moderate political liberals. To complicate the issue of classification further, it must be recognised that liberal values of freedom and concern for individual rights are an irreducible, if not necessarily the definitive, part of virtually all of the more radical movements devoted to greater equality.

The term economic liberalism, which equates with Room's market liberalism, is frequently used in relation to New Right economics. The *laissez-faire* categorisation, though having an old-fashioned ring to it, would probably be less confusing and does encapsulate part of New Right rhetoric. But the rhetoric does not equate with the reality. For many years there has been an acceptance across the political spectrum of high levels of state intervention, but conflict about what sort of state intervention. The New Right ostensibly rejects government intervention but in practice tends to selectively encourage it. For example, extension of law and order functions are frequently called for. Thus the term *laissez-faire* is not appropriate. To try to avoid confusion of terminology, I will avoid the term liberalism when referring to these major political division, though it is sometimes useful to be able to refer to political or economic liberals. This usage has the advantage of leaving the unqualified use of the term available to refer, not to a particular point on the political spectrum, but to a constellation of values concerned with human and social rights. These values, which have very general currency in the advanced capitalist societies, and are referred to as liberal, are what is flagged when societies are referred to as 'liberal democratic'.

In classifying the perspectives, recent work by Pascall (1986) and Williams (1989) proves particularly useful. Their approaches will broadly be followed here. Not surprisingly, they show a continuity with the categorisation of earlier writers (George and Wilding, 1976; Room, 1979; Mishra, 1984), but also incorporate important differences, which solve a number of problems. Pascall identifies the right position as individualist while Williams terms it anti-collectivist. Both identify the centrist positions as social reformist and the left positions as political economic, though they make it clear that the divisions are far from water-tight, indeed Williams formally identifies three sub-types of social reformism. Pascall and Williams each also nominate a fourth perspective – feminist – which is missing from all the other classificatory systems. Each recognises a range of feminist positions. Feminist perspectives are, at minimum, further categorisable as social reformist or political economic. Historically the feminist enterprise has been collectivist, so classification as individualist is unlikely.

Williams makes an important departure by adding a fifth perspective, entitled 'anti-racist critique'. This focuses on issues of race, including internationalist and anti-imperialist dimensions, as well as incorporating a feminist dimension. It is a radical left position, involving positions that can be classified as Black radicalism, socialism, Marxism and Black feminism. As Williams observes, an 'anti-racist critique' can hardly be said currently to exist as a coherent perspective, rather it is emergent (1989, p. 17). Nonetheless it is crucial to recognise the singularity of the position of oppressed racial groups and their resistance to this oppression.

Classifying perspectives

A fivefold categorisation – individualist, social reformist, political economic, feminist and anti-racist – has a number of valuable

features. One is the mere inclusion of gender and race\
serious omissions from the earlier classifications. A sec
tage is that the categorisation of the right political
individualist (or anti-collectivist) pinpoints the political e.
most import for our analysis of the welfare state. This set.
positions in clear opposition to others which embrace, to a greater
or lesser extent, collectivist principles on which the welfare state
is inevitably based. A third advantage for my purposes lies in the
designation of the centrist positions as social reformist rather than
social democratic, or in George and Wilding's (1976) terms, Fabian
Socialist. This makes the classification more readily applicable
internationally, in particular to those societies such as the USA,
Canada, Japan and Australia in which the term social democratic
is not in popular currency. The following brief overview of five
perspectives is intended to set the stage for the more detailed
analysis of welfare state developments in the rest of the book.

(i) *Individualist/anti-collectivist discourses*

The individualist position involves the espousal of market or economic liberalism. Politically this position is at the far right of the
political spectrum and is alternatively termed New Right or conservative. However, if we are to be precise about the use of words
we must recognise that the New Right position is not new nor is
it conservative, in the terms of the Oxford Engish Dictionary. The
core dictionary definition of conservative is, 'preservative, keeping
or tending to keep unchanged'. It is more accurate, as Thatcher
was wont to claim, to see the New Right project as radical, as
aiming to go back to selected 'roots', to values of an earlier period.
Those committed to economic liberalism, as they are quick to
point out, want to do more than conserve the status quo (Friedman
and Friedman, 1980; Harris and Seldon, 1987). They are anxious
to have governments withdraw from the collectivised provisions
of the welfare state and restore as many services as possible to the
market. This effectively means reneging on, rather than conserving
the 'settlement' which was achieved in the postwar period between
conservative and non-conservative political forces in respect of the
welfare state (see Chapter 3).

The individualist arguments which question the acceptability of
state intervention represent a return to an earlier form of liberalism

in which the state is seen as 'itself a threat to freedom'. The state should ideally be kept minimal because the competitive market is seen as 'the real guarantor of basic rights and freedoms' (Sawer, 1983, p. 27). This sentiment is forcefully expressed by Milton Friedman and Rose Friedman in their choice of an introductory quotation for their book *Free to Choose*. The extract is from a judgement made by Justice Louis Brandeis in a US court in 1928:

> Experience should teach us to be on our guard to protect liberty when the government's purposes are beneficial. Men born free are naturally alert to repel invasion of their liberty by evil-minded rulers. The greater dangers to liberty lurk in insidious encroachment by men of zeal, well-meaning but without understanding. (Friedman and Friedman, 1980, p. xiii)

It is this revival of a free market version of liberalism which makes the use of the term liberal confusing. This is because a competing meaning of liberal which has had some currency for at least two centuries, is to refer to moderates who advocate the use of state power to achieve a more just society. This meaning injects a humanistic element, viewing the state as an instrument which can be used in a neutral way to promote liberty. This view has dominated centrist politics in most advanced industrial societies, as least since the thirties and has underpinned Fabian and other social democratic views including New Deal liberalism in the USA. Such a position underpinned the Liberal reforms in the United Kingdom towards the end of the nineteenth century and early in the twentieth.

The recent history of the Australian conservative party (officially called the Liberal Party) provides a useful illustration of the recent reassertion of forms of economic liberalism. During the post-Second World War era, when there was a period of over twenty years of conservative government, the platform of the Liberal Party was discernibly more politically liberal. The Party accepted the role of government as to 'encourage', 'stabilise', 'maintain', 'promote', 'stimulate', and 'assist'. While 'there is no sense of any great originating role . . . neither is anything portrayed as "not the government's business"' (White, 1978, p. 45). To keep up with the appeal of the Whitlam Labor government (Australia's labour movement party is the Australian Labor Party), elected in 1972, the Liberal Party (Australia's major conservative party) platform was revised to include more collectivist goals. The new Platform recognised that 'the state had important obligations in relation to . . . quality of life, social equity and meeting the . . . ecological challenge . . . full employment, and the maintenance of comprehensive social welfare services' (Sawer, 1983, p. 27). However, this expansive mood was shortlived. Less than a decade later, the 1982 revisions called for 'reduction of government intervention'. Responsiveness to 'market signals' took precedence over such goals as full employment. Welfare was to be targeted only to those in most need. To the earlier equal opportunity goal of 'equality of opportunities, liberties and status for men and women' (White, 1978, p. 47), was added that this be pursued only in so far as it did not limit 'individual initiative, achievement or reward' (Sawer, 1983, p. 27).

In a recent article, Patrick Minford drew attention to conflicting elements of individualist and social reformist positions, using terminology strongly coloured by his political ideology. He firmly places himself among the New Right. He suggested that two major concepts of welfare have been in competition in Britain. The first is the 'safety net' concept which aims to ensure that people 'do not drop below a certain minimum living standard due to personal misfortune'. A second approach he terms 'paternalistic egalitarianism' (1987, p. 70). While his terminology is chosen to be disparaging to a position he rejects, the choice of the word paternalistic does highlight problems of virtually all social reformist analysis and policy formation, notably its sexism and ageism. Not that it is likely that Minford chose the term 'paternalistic' deliberately to expose these problems. He does not mention them directly and individualism, his favoured position, is particularly problematic for women and other oppressed groups. The fact that he nominates a safety-net approach to welfare shows the generality of an acceptance that some societal responsibility is necessary. In the latter part of the twentieth century, individualism has been more honoured in rhetoric than in practice. Individualists, however, notoriously recommend safety-nets of very open weave and flimsy quality.

(ii) Social reformist perspectives

The architects of the British post-Second World War welfare state, worked from a social reformist perspective. This position relied on Keynesian economics with its attempt to ensure, through government action, full employment – though, it must be noted, only for male workers. A more equitable distribution of basic income was sought through the social wage, through income security measures, the national health scheme, public housing and other services. Among the leading British social reformers we must count Beveridge, Marshall and Titmuss. These social reformers, and particularly the Keynesian economics on which they relied heavily, had a significant international as well as local influence. This can be partly attributed to the fact that social reformers, unlike Marxists, did not threaten the status quo. They did not extend their demands to call for a fundamental change of economic structure. Despite his relatively radical stance on many issues, Titmuss, for example, took for granted 'liberal capitalism . . . as the framework within which the see-sawing battle between capitalistic and welfare orientated values is to be waged perpetually' (Mishra, 1977, p. 15).

The social reformist perspective stresses individual needs and individual development but collective solutions. At the same time social reformers accept the notion that there are societal needs and goals, but these are seen as general needs that apply to all. Some groups are recognised as disadvantaged (though not usually women or those of non-dominant races) but intractable conflicts of interests are not recognised. A consensual view of society is thus taken and it is broadly assumed that all interests can be reconciled. The development of the good society is seen largely in administrative and technical terms. People must be insured against the uncertainty of the market and services must be adequate and universally available as of right. As we will see, these principles have been taken farthest in the Scandinavian countries.

(iii) Political economic perspectives

A political economic position on the other hand questions the structure of society. It does not accept that the goals of equality are achievable within the capitalist framework. The interests of capitalists and workers are not seen as ultimately reconcilable. As has been discussed briefly in relation to the theoretical position of Gough (1979), welfare itself is seen as furthering the interests of the capitalist class, even at the same time as it provides benefits to workers. Class elements and conflict of interests are stressed, rather than consensus, though the class interests that are identified are largely those of males of the dominant race.

Unlike social reformers, Marxist theorists have been at pains to demystify discourses that cast the capitalist state as a neutral administrative agency. Over recent years while many Marxists have recognised a certain 'relative autonomy' (Poulantzas, 1973a) of the state, they do not accept that this can override the state's basic support for capitalist interests. While the details of the various Marxist theoretical positions vary considerably, O'Connor's (1973) postulation of two major functions the state performs for capital – capital accumulation and legitimation – are accepted as a minimum. These are acknowledged as often in conflict. As Cawson's puts it, 'The state is trapped between producer power and consumer pressure via the electoral mechanism' (1982, p. 45). Welfare measures are interpreted as resulting from this complex conflict. The legitimation function of the state was what the radical British parliamentarian Joseph Chamberlain was recognising in a celebrated speech made in 1885 when he identified increased welfare as an element of the ransom that 'property will pay for the security it enjoys' (Digby, 1989, p. 43).

(iv) Feminist perspectives

Feminists, like political economists, also stress collective interests and conflict, rather than consensus, but the primary focus is on sex-based rather than class-based interests. Because of their family responsibiities and lack of easy access to their own resources, women have often been poor. For this reason feminists have a long history of concern with welfare issues. However, it was not really until the 1970s that we find emerging a body of literature of any size which systematically attempts to interpret the specific relationship of women to the welfare state. Since then a great deal has been written on the subject.

When relevant feminist theory is classified in terms of the left/centre/right political scale, we find a significant difference from the dominant malestream perspectives. The gender scales overlap in terms of the categories centre and left, with radical feminisms representing an extreme left position. There are no feminist perspectives that could be assigned to the far political right. By definition, a feminist is not concerned with conserving the status quo, nor returning to a more *laissez-faire* situation. There are, however, politically conservative feminists ('right-wing feminists') whose goal is largely limited to achieving equal access to society's rewards of money, status and power for a few privileged women. And the political situation is fluid. For the USA, Zillah Eisenstein has warned against a strand of 'revisionist' liberal feminism, which reemphasises the role of mother and could, she suggests, readily become anti-feminist (1984).

Liberal feminism, or liberal-reformist feminism, as Dale and Foster (1986) refer to the welfare-focused version, takes a centrist political position, accepting the broad basis of the social structure. Women's position in society is measured against universal definitions of citizenship and equality to point up the systematic subordination of women. This tradition provides a continuity with nineteenth- and early twentieth-century feminism, which was concerned with extending equal rights to women, through campaigns for property rights, the vote, equal educational opportunity and in the USA the still-unachieved Equal Rights Amendment (Banks, 1981). This has been the tradition which has underpinned late twentieth-century action resulting in anti-discrimination legislation, equal opportunity and affirmative action programmes as well as programmes to deal with women's poverty (Wilson, 1977; Sawer, 1985; Banks, 1981; Eisenstein, H., 1984; Holter, 1984).

Socialist feminism occupies a left position on the political spectrum. This perspective was originally referred to as Marxist feminism and reflected traditional Marxist concerns. Gradually a separate perspective has been developed because Marxism was found not to readily encompass sex as well as class as a fundamental basis of oppression (Hartmann, 1979; Eisenstein, Z., 1979; Barrett, 1980; Sargent, 1981). The early work within this tradition was concerned with the relationship of housework to the system of production. Marxism has traditionally relegated all work outside the capitalist mode of production to a position of unimportance and has never satisfactorily dealt with domestic labour. Socialist feminism still accepts the fundamental importance of the economic system, thus maintaining a materialist theoretical position, and still accepts that equality cannot be achieved within capitalism. However, notions of patriarchy, taken from radical feminism, have been welded together with these more orthodox Marxist concerns. Socialist feminists' attention has been primarily focused on women's work, both productive and reproductive. This has led particularly to concern with social welfare issues relating to income security and poverty, the relationship of women to the state and issues related to family and caring (Wilson, 1977; Barrett, 1980; Lewis, 1983; Baldock and Cass, 1983; Holter, 1984; Fraser, 1987). The issue of race has been recognised as a major concern recently by both socialist and radical feminism and will be discussed as a separate perspective.

Radical feminism has been a highly salient strand of feminist theory, positioned to the far left of the political scale, that is, to the left of socialist feminism and forms of Marxism (Oakley, 1981, pp. 336–7). It has been the voice of the most mobilised form of contemporary feminism, the Women's Liberation Movement. While radical feminisms cover a wide range of different approaches, the common thread is the identification of men and women as belonging to different classes. At the very least these classes are seen as having different interests and, at most, these interests are seen as totally antagonistic. There is also the recognition of the universality of women's oppression. Radical feminism has been concerned with patriarchal forms of oppression and has particularly focused on responses to physical aspects of sexual oppression. There has been major concern, among other issues, with reproduction (Firestone, 1979), rape (Browmiller, 1976), domestic violence (Scutt, 1983), pornography (Dworkin, 1983) and women's health (Boston Women's Health Collective, 1985). Within the social welfare area, radical feminists have been active in promoting special services for women, such as women's refuges, rape crisis centres, abortion clinics, and women's health collectives.

(v) Anti-racist perspectives

The fact that there has been so little attention paid to anti-racist critique of the welfare state and its oppression of people of colour is its own comment on race oppression. That Williams, the only analyst of social policy perspectives who explicitly acknowledges this critique, sees this approach as emergent rather than established (1989, chapter 4), attests to the greater relative power of women (and more specifically white women) as a group than of people of colour. Feminist views may not receive the degree of attention they merit but they have gradually gained recognition and a certain grudging legitimacy.

Anti-racist critique has been aimed at two levels, the international and historical and the intra-national and more local. Critiques point to the international issue of imperialism and the continued exploitation of the least developed countries by the more developed countries. In effect imperialism continues. In her treatise on Third World debt, Susan George suggests that debtor and creditor nations are more accurately described as dominating and dominated (1989, p. xiii). The First World is dependent for its affluence on this domination (Bello, Kinley and Elinson, 1982) and in particular on the exploited labour of the least developed countries (Elston and Pearson, 1981). This form of international racism can readily be ignored when analyses concentrate exclusively on what is happening in the First World. But this exploitation lies just behind the Western welfare state.

Within these liberal democratic states, an increase in relative power of non-dominant races during the postwar period must be seen as one element in the lead up to the resurgence of the extreme right. Intra-national struggles for sovereignty, land-rights and a better deal for indigenous peoples, such as Native Americans, Australian Aborigines, Maoris in New Zealand, the Inuit in Canada and the Sami people of Norway, Sweden and Finland reached a crescendo in the late sixties and the seventies. Equal rights struggles by Blacks in countries with multi-racial populations reached a new intensity. These struggles have developed their own, as yet inadequately recognised, theorising.

Black feminism has been the strongest source of an anti-racist critique of the welfare state, particularly in Britain and the USA. International Women's Year and the Decade of Women nurtured the women's movement in both non-western and Western societies and international issues of development have become a central concern of feminisms (Hendessi, 1986; Thiam, 1978; Baldock and Goodrick, 1983). The hegemony of white middle-class feminist perspectives has been exposed. Since the issue of cultural domination was brought to the fore, feminism has been trying to come to terms not only with the obviously different experiences and interests of women of colour but also the painful issue of white feminists' own racism (Barrett and McIntosh, 1985; Bhavnani and Coulson, 1986).

Black feminist writers, particularly in the USA and the UK, have developed a critique of the welfare state, exposing the manner in which racism renders Black women's lives very different from those of white women. Black women experience oppression through race, sex, and class simultaneously and this combination transforms the experience. Within a socialist feminist framework, for example, the force to be addressed is identified as 'a racially structured, patriarchal capitalism' (Bhavnani and Coulson, 1986, p. 88).

Key issues which Black feminists in the United Kingdom have identified as central relate to immigration, policing, welfare, and women's right to control their bodies. An area in which experiences can differ markedly is in relation to abortion. Whereas for white women the issue of the right to choose abortion is central, for many Black women the issue is one of the right to choose to have children and to avoid abortion, sterilisation and unwanted and possibly dangerous contraception. Nonetheless, the issue of women's right to control their bodies remains a universal one for women. Control currently resides with white patriarchs (Hooks, 1986, 132).

Another, linked example of the different position of Black women is in relation to motherhood. As will be discussed more fully in Chapter 6, for women of dominant groups, motherhood is a problematic status involving oppressive elements. However, it does also have its positive, glorified dimension. For Black women, their motherhood is more likely to be cast by dominant groups in a negative light, as dangerous and linked with notions of promiscuity and welfare-scrounging. Nonetheless, the notion of the family as the site of oppression of women is criticised by Black feminists because the family has often been the site for struggle, as it was within slavery, and it has been and remains a crucial site of support in a hostile world.

The issue of patriarchy and capital is also different for Black women. Black men may oppress Black women but they do not share power with white male capitalists. Joseph points out that 'there is more solidarity between white males and females than between white males and Black males' (Joseph, 1981, p. 101). This makes it incumbent on white feminists to

(1) recognise their implication in the partnership, as benefactor

and tools; (2) address the unique problems of Black women in
the labour force; (3) distinguish between the role of white men
and Black men in the partnership of capital and patriarchy.
(Joseph, 1981, p. 102)

Black feminism and more general anti-racist critiques (Sivanandan,
1982; Hall, 1980; Hall *et al.*, 1978) provide the basis for this recognition of racism as a fundamental axis of oppression which an
analysis of the welfare state cannot ignore.

Limits of the perspectives

The very broad theoretical perspective that I am adopting has a
decisive effect on the nature of the subsequent discourse. It determines what will be the focus of intellectual and social concern,
what evidence will be recognised, and how analysis will be
approached. For example, feminists observe and consider analytically important, inequalities which those who do not espouse a
feminist perspective will ignore or consider unimportant. A striking illustration of this exclusion can be found in the approach of
two Australians in a book on social policy published as recently
as 1989. The authors proclaim that

> inequalities and social division in Australia may be found in
> three interacting areas: an age dimension; ethnic and cultural
> dimensions; and socio-economic or class dimensions. (Graycar
> and Jamrozik, 1989, p. 10).

The authors might be commended for their concern with age, a
dimension of inequality that is often overlooked. However, in the
process, they ignore not only gender inequalities but also race.
Closer inspection of the book reveals this is not just an isolated,
unguarded statement. Australian Aborigines hardly rate a mention
at all and women are assigned a few pages, but only in relation to
employment and ageing.

All perspectives display the tendency to adopt a narrow focus.
Within an individualist discourse this is to be expected. An underlying tenet is that the market should be afforded the maximum
role and government involvement the minimum. One might
expect that a *laissez-faire* political philosophy would engender a

laissez-faire analysis. The problem is more surprising with the other perspectives. Despite the apparent scope of the social reformist, political economic and liberal and socialist feminist perspectives, they too finish up directing attention largely to the classic forms of 'social welfare', though feminists usually do extend their analysis to include reproduction and family as important sites for the exercise of power (Wilson, 1977; Dale and Foster, 1986). The anti-racist critique has the broadest scope as it encompasses broad international exploitation as well as more local race oppression.

The focus of analysis about who benefits from the welfare state is rarely on the 'welfare' received by the wealthy, despite Titmuss's early lead in relation to occupational and fiscal welfare. There is no shortage of pious statements about the need to adopt a broad perspective. The importance of Titmuss's framework is acknowledged with monotonous regularity (Sinfield, 1978; Rose, 1981; Jamrozik, 1983; Mishra, 1984; Grichting, 1984; Jordan, 1987). What we do not find, however is a follow-through. This holds for theory, research and policy analysis. Grichting, in what acts merely as a ritual statement of absolution, has described this omission as 'unfortunate and totally unacceptable'. He maintains that

> it deprives the study of social policy of a broader context of social justice and social interaction. By restricting social policy to welfare administration one perpetuates the practice of excluding subsidies to the middle class and the rich from discussions of the social welfare system. (Grichting, 1984, pp. 4–5)

Walker provides another link in the long chain of writing which makes the ritualistic case for a broad, structurally-based approach. He maintains that it is not useful to separate economic and social policy because adequate analysis of social policy requires concern with

> the production *and* distribution of a wide range of *social resources*, including income, assets, property, health, education, environment, status and power. (1981, p. 239)

The motivation for the generally narrow focus directed largely to the needy may be well-intentioned but it can hardly be excused in sociologists and other social analysts. Certainly it is the 'needy' who are economically and socially disadvantaged, it is they who suffer injustice and oppression and are excluded from full citizenship. However, to focus exclusively on the oppressed diverts attention from the oppressors and also from the interconnections between oppressor and oppressed. Sociological theory directs our attention to power relations, particularly to class relations. Poverty and oppression cannot be divorced from the workings of the economy and other broad facets of the exercise of power, including patriarchal and racial dominance. As discussed earlier, welfare measures are never straightforward and simple in their effects; they involve benefits and disbenefits. Other interests are inevitably served, a point that Gans (1972) brought home when, in the early seventies, he outlined the functions that poverty performs for the non-poor in US society.

The effect of a discourse exclusively focused on needs and the needy, is to strengthen that lineage which connects welfare to its historical roots in charity and the Poor Laws (see Chapter 3). The focus readily moves to individual deservingness and compassion. Such an approach implies not rights and equality but recipient and benefactor: not problems of a societal nature but individual responsibility. To imply individual causation of social problems results in 'blaming the victim', to use Ryan's expressive phrase (1971). Not only does such a discourse stigmatise the recipients of welfare, but in a time of economic downturn, it allows the scope of welfare to be cast as an optional, rather than an essential, aspect of citizenship. This means that there will be less chance that the newer claims of politically less powerful groups, such as women and people of non-dominant races and ethnic groups, will be listened to.

The problems of a narrow discourse are particularly obvious at present. Under the onslaught of individualist New Right economics, even the relatively modest claims of the social reformers are under pressure. New Right individualists maintain that extensive government intervention cannot be afforded. Furthermore, they claim that welfare cannot be effective in a complex modern industrial society, because it results in too many unintended effects. Mishra marshals a number of telling anti-welfare views from the US literature. They point to the wrongheadedness of government intervention to create a more just society, reaffirming individualistic values. Aaron, for example, pointed approvingly to the 'collapse of that bubble of faith that government action is a force for good', while Gilder's comments take us right back to the days of the Poor Laws. He maintained that welfare has created 'increasing reluctance of the American poor to perform low-wage labour' and went on to recommend that, 'in order to succeed the poor most of all need the spur of their poverty' (Mishra, 1984, pp. 32–3).

Revisiting basic issues

Clearly such views call into question the basic tenets of the welfare state, tenets which for a certain period appeared to have been beyond question. Given that these basic tenets are back on the agenda, albeit to a greater or lesser extent in various countries, it is important to scrutinise just what is at stake. To do this it is useful to consider four dichotomies which were the subject of spirited debate in the past. This process will help to crystallise the key issues in today's political tussle over the welfare state.

These dichotomies are: residual versus institutional welfare; absolute versus relative poverty; selective versus universal provisions; and horizontal versus vertical equity. An individualist position is located at or near the pole associated with residual welfare, concerned with absolute poverty, and using selective provisions to achieve only some horizontal equity. A social reform position would be located at the other pole supporting institutional welfare, concerned to deal with relative poverty through universal provisions to achieve vertical as well as horizontal equity. Those taking positions to the left of the social reformist position would also be likely to find themselves at this pole when it comes to day-to-day social policy options. It is not that they would not prefer to promote more radical alternatives, but these generally fall beyond the political limits of current democratic societies and their welfare states.

(i) Residual versus institutional welfare

In the fifties and sixties, as many of the world's welfare states took their mature form, there was an extensive debate about the desirability of an 'institutional' rather than a 'residual' model of social welfare. As a normative position, a residual or marginal view of the role of welfare holds that state provisions should come into play only when there is a breakdown in the 'natural' mechanisms for the support of individuals – the family, the market and voluntary charities. The state is the 'lender of last resort' (Olsson, 1989, p. 265). Minford's safety-net, based on the proposition that people should be prevented from falling 'below a certain minimum living standard due to personal misfortune' (1987, p. 70), represents residualism. Misfortune rather than the inevitable characteristics of the labour market, is seen as the major determinant of the need for collective solutions. Need rather than right is the basis of public provisions and these are to be kept to a minimum. Where a residual approach to welfare is adopted, eligibility is targeted only to the most disadvantaged. No merit is seen in provisions that maintain people at more than subsistence level.

An institutional view, on the other hand sees welfare provisions as 'normal, "first line" functions of modern industrial society' and 'implies no stigma, no emergency, no "abnormalcy"' (Wilensky and Lebeaux, 1965, pp. 138–9). Esping-Andersen and Korpi (1987, p. 40), add that the institutional model 'does not recognise any fixed boundaries for public welfare commitments'. Thus hypothetically an ever-increasing amount of social life becomes the legitimate concern of the collective. The institutional welfare state aims to ensure a decent standard of living for its citizens, and guarantees 'full citizenship rights . . . unconditionally' (Esping-Andersen and Korpi, 1987, p. 40).

That Minford himself claims to prefer the safety-net position, however restricted, and does not propose a 'no public welfare' stance, illustrates the generality of the view that some measure of 'welfare' provision should be an essential ingredient of a modern capitalist society. Galper has commented on this in relation to the USA, suggesting that by 1971 there was little difference between conservatives and liberals in respect of a general acceptance of, and interest in, social policy (Galper, 1975, p. 10). Wilensky and Lebeaux date the change to the Great Depression of the twenties and thirties when unemployment was so widespread that it could not be attributed to the personal failings of individual workers (Wilensky and Lebeaux, 1965, p. 139). Nonetheless this may still, and often does, mean a minimalist and merely formalised residualist view of welfare.

Some countries such as the USA, Canada and Australia, can still be described as having residual provisions, a point returned to in Chapter 3. During the post-Second World War boom, however, support did weaken for the argument that provisions were too generous and that government involvement was too extensive. There even developed a broad consensus among most conservatives, as well as non-conservatives that, over time, benefit levels would increase and the role of government expand. The political debate focused largely on priorities and time frames: more on the question of when rather than whether. There were admittedly some dissonant voices, such as Hayek (1949, 1960) and the London-based Institute of Public Affairs, established in 1957, and their counterparts in other countries. But this discourse was far from dominant even among conservatives, as the historical picture of the Australian conservative party platform presented earlier demonstrates.

Events of the past two decades have changed this. There is no longer general agreement on an inexorable move from a residual to an institutional welfare state. In 1980, Friedman could jubilantly proclaim that the tide was turning on three-quarters of a century of Fabian socialism in Britain and half a century of New Deal liberalism in the USA (Friedman and Friedman, 1980, p. 284). A vocal body of opinion is today calling for a re-emphasis on the market, with correspondingly less emphasis on government provisions. This trend is occurring in virtually all OECD countries, though it is particularly strong in Britain (Harris and Seldon, 1987; Lawson, 1988; Papadakis and Taylor-Gooby, 1987; Le Grand and Robinson, 1984), Australia and New Zealand (Sawer, 1982; James, 1989), and the USA (Friedman and Friedman, 1980; Steinfels, 1982; Eisenstein, Z., 1984; Levitas, 1986). The legitimacy of institutional welfare has been challenged and blamed for problems in the economy. Residual welfare is undoubtedly on the political agenda.

(ii) Absolute versus relative poverty

The issue of residual versus institutional welfare is linked logically to approaches to poverty through the classic distinction between absolute poverty and relative poverty. People in absolute poverty suffer from a lack of sufficient resources to provide for their daily requirements; that is, they have insufficient food, health care, clothing and/or shelter. This form of poverty was traditionally approached through residual remedies. Poor Laws were early legislative attempts to make some general minimum provision to deal with absolute poverty. As welfare states developed and standards of living improved for citizens of industrialising societies, there was a diminution of absolute poverty. However, this remains a fundamental issue for certain groups within capitalist societies, especially minority racial groups such as Australian Aborigines, Native Americans and Black Americans, and for those nations, which are now referred to as the 'least developed nations' of Africa, Asia, South America and Oceania.

Poverty was officially rediscovered in a number of the advanced capitalist societies in the sixties and seventies. These were, not surprisingly, mainly countries which had not developed highly-institutionalised welfare states. As part of President Lyndon Johnson's 'Great Society' programme, the USA launched its 'War on Poverty' in the sixties. Australia followed suit with a government Commission of Inquiry into Poverty, which was set up in 1971 and reported in 1975. In the United Kingdom, in 1979 Townsend's massive study of poverty was published, the culmination of decades of concern by social scientists with defining and researching poverty. By 1983, with the ascendance of economic individualism, the Prime Minister, Margaret Thatcher, could still state with conviction in the House of Commons that 'the fact remains that people who are living in need are fully and properly provided for' (quoted in Mack and Lansley, 1985: epigraph).

One of the strands of the debate about poverty has involved the deliberate attempt to move the discourse away from the restrictions of an absolute definition. This was effectively achieved and definitions were infused with a relative quality. Poverty was redefined as a form of inequality of power and status, as well as resources. A certain minimum standard of living was still central to the definition but not determined by standards relating only to what is necessary for keeping people alive. An acceptable relative standard takes into account the standard of living enjoyed by the non-poor and encompasses the right to be a fully participating member of the society. Townsend defined relative deprivation or relative poverty as

> the lack of resources necessary to permit participation in the activities, customs and diets commonly approved by society. (1979, p. 47)

Such a relative definition is implied in any institutional model of welfare. Relative definitions can also encompass the provision of additional resources to those who have suffered deprivation, a process that in the sixties came to be known as 'positive discrimination'. Nonetheless relative definitions involve the potential implication that poverty in the poorest countries is of less importance, or even that there is less of it, than in the developed countries (George, 1980, p. 3). In many ways the distinction between the notions of absolute and relative poverty is a false one. Ringen has suggested that it is not really clear whether any definition has ever been other than relative. All do, in fact, take account of the context in which people live (Ringen, 1988). What the debate is really about is the level of generosity (George, 1988). Those who insist that concern should be with relative poverty are in fact claiming that support should be at a decent level, a level that offers a standard of living that is indistinguishable from other citizens. Those concerned with absolute poverty are concerned only with maintaining a minimum standard. Poverty when extended to take in contextual attributes merges into the issue of equality and inequality. In fact it is usefully seen merely as referring to the extreme end of an inequality continuum, 'the tail end of inequality' (George, 1980, p. 3).

(iii) Selective versus universal provision

Whether services should be provided on a selective or universal basis has been a fundamental debate in discourses on social policy. Selective services are targeted only to those who meet specified criteria of need. Universal services are exactly that – available to everyone, regardless of their personal circumstances. The mechanism most commonly associated with selective services is the means test, which is used to screen out people on the basis of income or assets or both. The implication underlying a means test is that self-support is primarily the duty of the individual. State involvement is a last resort. The pragmatic reason for applying a means test is that governments are unable or unprepared to fund universal provisions.

The debate about the merits and costs of providing universal or selective services has itself been a selective debate. Fiscal and occupational welfare, as well as other forms of government assistance, have not routinely been encompassed within the discourse, because they have not been identified as welfare. Social welfare alone is the subject of this debate (Jamrozik, 1983).

The debate is complicated by the fact that all provisions and services are offered in terms of some criteria, be it membership of an age category (a child who is too young is not admitted to a universal education system) or having children (for receipt of children's allowance), or, as with certain fiscal benefits, whether one has a business of a certain type (for an export subsidy). The real essence of the universalism/selectivity debate is the criteria on which selection will be made. Selective services take into account the particular circumstances of the individual. Universal services take account of individual circumstances only to ascertain that the person is a member of the broad 'universal' category for whom the service is intended (Parker, 1975, p. 149).

In addition to the straightforward economic advantages of cost-saving and rationing services, an argument for selective or targeted services relates to control. A persistent line of reasoning has been that if benefits are not carefully hedged around with restrictions, people would be encouraged to rely on welfare, thus destroying work incentives and independence. So, while only those with the most extreme views would reject the idea that compassion must be shown in some circumstances, many favour tight controls. Those who advocate a residual approach to welfare are inevitably in favour of selectivity. The conservative British organisation, the Institute of Economic Affairs, has been campaigning for greater selectivity since its inception (Harris and Seldon, 1971, 1978, 1987). A perennial cry of such campaigners is that people abuse the system. A favourite argument, for example, is to suggest that a benefit which goes to single mothers encourages women to get pregnant so that they can live in comfort at the public's expense (Swan and Bernstam, 1989).

For those who support universal services, a fundamental objection to selectivity is that by associating a provision with only the poorest, traditional notions of charity are invoked. The provision then tends to become stigmatised, and devalued. The fact that only the poorest make use of a service also implies that the causes of social disadvantage lie within individuals, not within the social structure (Townsend, 1975, p. 126). Even in Sweden, where universalism is a basic plank of the welfare state, the one form of selective, means-tested social assistance remains associated with 'a

negative attitude towards both recipient and the assistance itself'
(Bergmark, 1990, p. 4). Old attitudes about the undeserving poor
die hard.

The more widely available a provision, the more likely it will
be seen as a right. Selective provisions result in 'a nation divided'
to use Townsend's phrase (1975, p. 121), with first and second
(and sometimes third) class citizens. Titmuss pointed to targeting
as one of the reasons for the failure of the US 'War on Poverty'.
Because programmes were highly targeted, they required people
to identify themselves as poor. This resulted in stigmatisation. To
avoid this, he argued, what was required, was an 'infrastructure
of social welfare utilised and approved by the non-poor as well as
the poor' (1968, p. 113), a point which is taken up in relation to
the USA in Chapter 3.

Universalism has been an issue of historical importance in
debates about 'prevention'. Early in the twentieth century, the
Webbs and other supporters of universal principles pressed the
idea of breaking 'the vicious descending spiral of poverty, disease,
neglect, illiteracy and destitution' (Titmuss, 1968, p. 129). This
they saw as dependent on easy access to services. However, Titmuss recognised that motives for promoting universalism were
varied – a 'mixture of humanitarianism, egalitarianism,
productivity . . . , and old fashioned imperialism'. The latter, he
suggested in the sixties, was no longer operative, with 'the God-
dess of Growth having replaced the God of National Fitness' (1968,
p. 130).

This principle of universality encompasses the notion of equality
of opportunity but does not guarantee equality of outcome. The
case of universal education proves this with great clarity. Education
has been universally available in many societies for over a century,
yet traditionally privileged groups, particularly higher-class males,
have benefited most (Jencks, 1972; Deleeck, 1985). Some form of
positive discrimination seems necessary to overcome initial disadvantages. Titmuss was also concerned with this issue of more equal
outcomes in the sixties (1968, p. 135). He asked the question:

What particular infrastructure of universalist service is needed in
order to provide a framework of values and opportunity bases
within and around which can be developed socially acceptable
selective services aiming to discriminate positively, with mini-

mum risk of stigma in favour of those whose needs are greatest? (1968, p. 135).

Positive discrimination and affirmative action, harnessed to promote equal opportunity, have gained in popularity since the sixties when the concepts were developed in the USA in relation to racial discrimination. In countries such as the USA, the United Kingdom and Australia, race has remained a driving force in these policies, though they have generally been extended to encompass the discrimination suffered by women and some other groups such as people with disabilities. In the Nordic countries a coherent network of policies directed towards women has been developed. This constellation of policies has been usefully referred to as 'equality policies'.

There are important differences between the bases of positive discrimination and selectivity. As already discussed, selectivity is about rationing; positive discrimination is about taking action to ensure that people can make use of their rights to universal, or for that matter, selective services and entitlements. The onus is not only on individuals to claim their entitlements. Public authorities accept the obligation to seek and encourage those at a disadvantage, and provide compensatory programmes so that they are able to make effective use of equality of opportunity (Parker, 1975, p. 152).

The selective principle is associated with a number of practical disadvantages. Because a selective system is almost inevitably complex, there is a high likelihood of people not being aware of their entitlements. Regulations specifying who is eligible for what are usually spelled out in minute detail. The quicker regulations change, the less people will be able to keep informed of their rights, and the most needy are likely to be poorly informed. For maximum usage, an entitlement would be universal, simple and well-publicised. With elaborate targeting, based on means-testing, there is also increased risk of creating poverty traps. These arise because people on the upper margin of eligibility may face penalties for increasing their income by even small amounts. If they take employment, the income they earn may then make them ineligible for all or part of the assistance. Or they may face higher tax rates, so that overall they are worse-off than if they had not tried to increase their income.

There is also a problem in maintaining the value and conditions of any benefit which is restricted to a narrowly-targeted and powerless group. It is all too easy for governments to allow rates and quality of service to decline. When the very poor finish up being the only ones who receive a particular benefit, it is unlikely that they will have the organisational structure or the political clout to prevent the erosion of their entitlements (Castles, 1989, p. 30). European countries which have best maintained their welfare systems through the current phase of New Right economic individualism are those such as Sweden and Norway, which have a wide spectrum of welfare-state coverage and the support of the middle classes (Esping-Andersen and Korpi, 1987, p. 54). Where services are selective or of poor quality, there will be few who will feel moved to defend the welfare state.

Advocacy of selective income support mechanisms and services implies that poverty is an absolute condition rather than a relative one. It implies that the diversion of appropriate, and almost always modest, resources to specific groups will allow them to overcome their disadvantage (Townsend, 1975, p. 126). Its philosophical base is in individualism (Room, 1979, pp. 201–4). Universalism, on the other hand, is based on collectivist principles relating to citizenship rights. Once again to quote Richard Titmuss, one of the most adamant supporters of the social reformist position, universalism is 'preeminently about equality, freedom and social integration' (1968, p. 116), though he ignored the inequality inherent in the nature of the capitalist economic system.

(iv) Horizontal versus vertical equity

Social policy may impinge on horizontal or vertical equity. These are concepts that are most often discussed in relation to income, taxation and social security. Concern for horizontal equity is expressed in connection with attempts to spread the burdens of social support over a broader range of social groups. The most common form of compensation is in respect of the cost of raising children. Forms of allowance in respect of children have the effect of lightening the cost to individual parents. They spread some of these costs horizontally to other citizens who are not raising children. This spreads a measure of general social responsibility for a nation's children.

Vertical equity is about making the society-wide distribution of resources more equal through reducing the spread of the income-and-wealth ladder. One of the commonest mechanisms used specifically to promote this is progressive income tax; another is tax on capital gains. Achieving greater vertical equity is, ostensibly at least, a principle which also underpins the concept of the social wage. There has been a strong tradition, particularly in Britain, of investigating the effect of social welfare provisions on vertical equity. As will be discussed more fully in Chapter 4, the studies have persistently shown that only direct income transfer payments and some forms of public housing provisions, contribute to greater vertical equity. Apart from these social expenditures, the better-off tend to benefit more than the poor. This applies particularly to such services as education, health and expenditure on cultural activities and recreation (Jencks, 1972; Townsend, 1979; Townsend and Davidson, 1982; Goodin, Le Grand *et al.*, 1987; Harding, 1984; Deleeck, 1985). The trend is exacerbated if occupational and fiscal welfare are assessed as well. These forms of welfare benefit men more than women, as well as favouring those on high incomes more than those on low (Keens and Cass, 1982).

The principle of achieving greater vertical equity is certainly not one that is favoured by economic individualists. As we shall see (Chapter 4), many countries, including the United Kingdom and Australia, have recently reduced the progressivity of their taxation systems. Indeed the emphasis on the market and wealth expansion promotes greater rather than less vertical inequity. It is significant that recent official policy documents in Australia consistently fudged the issue of vertical equity, not a popular concept with the Hawke Labor government. Instead of emphasising the fact that the concept implies bringing the top down as well as the bottom up, official documents only mentioned bringing the bottom up. For example, one of the documents in the Australian Government's extensive review of social security carried out in the late eighties defined vertical equity merely as providing 'adequate support to low income families' (Cass, 1986, p. 5).

Vertical equity has always proved more problematic than hor-izonal equity. Those who are better-off are not keen to have their advantages reduced. As Gough (1979) pointed out, the working class has largely financed its own welfare state provisions, thus promoting horizontal equity but not vertical. Additionally, where needs are covered through social insurance, the state merely super-vises thrift and saving among workers, rather than promoting equality through collective measures. After a study of social welfare in a number of European countries, Deleeck came to a similar conclusion.

> The result of numerous research is that the system of social services and benefits programs indeed implies a horizontal redistribution . . . but not a thorough change in vertical income structure. (Deleeck, 1985, p. 51)

Welfare and citizenship

The expansive side of the four dichotomies – institutional welfare, relative poverty, universal services and vertical equity – provides the basis for a discourse on citizenship (a liberal discourse, to use the term liberal in its popular form). Here the language is not of the poor and needy being treated with compassion, but about citizenship and rights. Feminists in particular have been concerned with the debate over citizenship over recent years (Mitchell, 1987; Pateman, 1987; Fraser, 1987; Hernes, 1987b, 1988) because it allows a focus on fundamental, albeit classic political liberal, issues in the debate about equality.

The legitimacy of the liberal democratic state is tied to principles of equal treatment and universal principles. Hence, demonstrable failure to deliver on these principles provides a lever for pressure groups. Anti-racist and liberal feminist projects aimed at promoting equal opportunity are able to make use of this lever. The outcome of such political action does, of course, ultimately depend on broader issues of power. Not only how much pressure can be exerted, but how much resistance this meets is relevant.

A discourse on citizenship encourages questions about what it is that prevents equality and provides a means of escape from at least some of the restrictions of traditional definitions. It can incorporate both reproduction and production (Dale and Foster, 1986, p. 135). In the Nordic countries, where well-developed welfare state mechanisms ensure women a higher standard of living than in other countries, feminist writers have focused on the issue of citizenship rights, since, despite women's high standard of living, 'welfare is not synonymous with power' (Hernes, 1987b, p. 31).

Bryan Turner in his book *Equality* uses a tripartite definition of citizenship, seeing it as comprised of civil, political and social citizenship. Scandinavian women are currently most concerned with civil and political citizenship while all three forms remain unachieved for many groups in most other societies. While civil and political citizenship are by no means unrelated to 'welfare', particularly when it is broadly defined, I want at the moment to focus on social citizenship, which Turner defines as 'the institutional apparatus of the welfare state as the guarantor of rights of economic and social well-being'. Turner concludes that

> the principle of equality is simply another dimension of citizenship where citizenship rights imply that persons should be treated equally, irrespective of their particular attributes. (1986, p. 21)

The achievement of equality is complicated by the fact that capitalist countries maintain a two-part system of citizenship. Following T. H. Marshall, Turner calls this a 'hyphenated system' because at the same time there is continuity of 'de facto inequalities in terms of class, status and power' (1986, p. 119). For economic individualists, *de facto* inequalities are actually defended in terms of the principle of freedom, which in its turn is fundamental to civil and political citizenship.

Much discourse on welfare is concerned with class as a sub-text, Turner's hyphenated element of citizenship. If we are concerned to analyse the basis of the inequality, we must ensure that we approach our analysis through a framework that takes into account this subterranean dimension of citizenship. This is why I am so concerned with a broad approach. We must ensure that our theory does not avoid addressing the dimensions of inequalities based on class, status and power. Turner himself gives scant attention to gender or race as dimensions of *de facto* inequality, though presumably he subsumes these as dimensions of status inequality.

Conclusion

The welfare state has been the subject of much political debate and scholarly analysis. The field of scholarship has its own jargon, its own concepts and its own philosophical conflicts. The concepts and political positions discussed here provide valuable conceptual tools with which to proceed to a more explicit analysis of the contribution of the welfare state to equality of citizenship. What this survey of conventional discourses has also aimed to do is to uncover the major recurring limitations of these discourses.

We have seen that analyses which focus directly on welfare often exclude from view much that is fundamental to issues of equality. This is partly because certain groups, such as women and non-dominant racial groups, have been ignored, but also because the focus has largely been on the powerless rather than the powerful. Class analysis has made very clear that such discourses almost inevitably serve dominant interests.

This protection of dominant interests means that the information that we need adequately to assess who benefits is difficult to get hold of. Because there are important areas which researchers and analysts have largely avoided, there is a dearth, not only of information, but even of analytic frameworks for making sense of the information that is available. We have public and readily available international figures, for example on most countries' gross domestic product, per capita income and the like. We do not have figures which tell us the contribution of women's labour, or allow us to assess outcomes rather than throughputs. Social and environmental well-being are inadequately assessed. Nor do we know how much one country contributes to another's wealth, through, for example, the provision of the cheap labour for international companies or the interest paid on the national debt. Our current frameworks imply that countries are individually responsible for their wealth or poverty.

The situation has similar dimensions within a nation. The contribution of the poorer members to the richer is hard to track down. Thus it is difficult to carry out a complete analysis of who benefits from the welfare state. Nonetheless we must keep the broad questions to the fore. The aim is to assess the total distribution of benefits, or at least to contribute to the ongoing task of doing this.

We turn now to some history of the development of social

welfare and a consideration of its trajectory in a number of countries. The historical picture does not give us 'the truth'. What can be pieced together is inevitably constrained by the available evidence, and by the discursive form in which the available data were recorded and interpreted. We are unlikely to find feminist and anti-racist interpretations of events. However, if we are to gain a sociological understanding of the current state of affairs, it is important that we are aware of its antecedents. Also it is possible to look back on at least some part of this history through a lens of our choosing and, therefore, to reinterpret some of the evidence that is available.

3 Cross-national Trends in Welfare State Development

Chapter 2 was concerned with various ways of conceptualising the welfare state and with assessing the potential of the various frameworks for shedding light on the question 'Who benefits?' That focus is continued in this chapter through a consideration of the historical development of the welfare state. The emphasis will again be on those elements that have particular significance for current discourses. Essentially the discussion will be concerned with how, at various stages of history, social welfare provisions have measured up in terms of the broad interests already discussed, particularly in relation to class, sex and race. We will, in effect, be considering the movement towards an institutional welfare state and considering the development of concern for relative rather than absolute poverty. Issues of whether horizontal or vertical equity is promoted are central, as is the issue of the universality of provisions. However, these questions will not necessarily be addressed in an explicit and formal manner, as that would be tedious. They should rather be seen as providing an implicit framework for the discussion.

This chapter focuses on social welfare, with special emphasis on social security. Social security is the lynch-pin of social welfare systems since it is concerned with basic income support. Not only is social welfare a central issue but the discursive frameworks within which the history of welfare has generally been written do not actually embrace, in any systematic manner, other forms of welfare. We only find sporadic mention of fiscal and occupational welfare, for example.

As we turn to the practical provision of public welfare we will consider a range of historical questions, all germane to the questions of 'Who benefits?' These include: Why is it that welfare systems have developed? What are some of the variations between capitalist countries? What are the similarities? How do we account for these? What are the patterns which seem to be specifically determined by the requirements of the capitalist economic system? Are the major beneficiaries the same in each society? Given the political pressures from the New Right, will the welfare state survive? If so in what way or form?

What follows in this chapter is divided into two parts. In the first a brief tour of the international scene is undertaken to make a broad assessment of national commitments to the welfare state and current international trends. The second part is devoted to a consideration of the historical development of a number of welfare states. This is done in some, though clearly not exhaustive, detail. The countries to be dealt with are Britain, Australia, the USA, Japan and the Nordic countries with the major emphasis on Sweden.

Broad national approaches to welfare

When we take a comparative look at welfare systems in a range of capitalist societies, a certain pattern is evident in the way they have developed and the interests that have been served. This is certainly so at the macro-level: the broad parameters show considerable similarity. At the micro-level, however, the level of practical provisions and detailed history, there is a wide degree of variation between nations. Accounts which proclaim the welfare state as an essential part of capitalism (Wilensky and Lebeaux, 1965; Gough, 1979; Offe, 1984), tell an important part of the story, but only part. Differences in detail must be linked to historical and cultural circumstances.

Theorists have generally identified three broad social systems which deal with the tasks that support day to day living in capitalist societies. These are the household system, the economic or market system, and the public welfare system. Some writers prefer the term family or 'socialisation' system rather than household system (Rose, 1986). 'Household', however, is to be preferred because it does not privilege that particular form of primary association based on kinship. Many households are not family-based. Also, for those that are, the type of family varies greatly. Despite this variation, welfare provisions are usually predicated on a traditional family unit, a point that feminists and particularly Black feminists have emphasised. The implications of this will be dealt with in more detail when we consider women's welfare state in Chapter 6.

Historically, the household system has been the most basic for the provision of support. Indeed, until relatively recently it provided virtually the only source of social support for individuals. It has also been the major unit for the distribution of goods and services on a day-to-day basis. With industrialisation and the development of capitalism, the role of the market expanded. The exchange of labour for wages became the most fundamental way of distributing resources, with a 'family' wage then exchanged on the market for goods and services needed by the breadwinner's household. But the labour market fails to accommodate those who cannot sell their labour. That is, those who are ill, very old, very young, or just not required at the time, notably the unemployed. These people originally were forced to rely on others, usually family members, who were in paid employment. This presented problems because the logic of capital implies that wage levels will be kept low by employers who want to ensure the profitability of their enterprises. Wages are not therefore likely to be high enough to support additional family or household members.

Government organised welfare must be seen essentially as an outcome of this contradiction between the survival needs of workers and their household and family members, and the drive for profitability inherent in the structure of capitalism. Social welfare originally developed to supplement the household's role of social support where the market failed to provide. However in many countries, as the distinction between institutional and residual welfare systems indicates, collective provisions have developed well beyond minimal forms of social support. While all of the advanced capitalist societies have some welfare provisions, their generosity and degree of institutionalisation varies greatly.

Countries that can be said to have 'institutional' welfare state structures, all share relatively high material wealth. This applies very clearly to the 'model' welfare states of the Nordic nations and the Netherlands. However, some countries with high material wealth do not have unequivocally institutional forms of welfare. Japan provides the most clear-cut case here, while the USA also has high material wealth but remains a reluctant provider of welfare. There is certainly no inevitable evolutionary process which parallels economic growth. Also, as the earlier consideration of the New Right makes clear, enthusiasm for collective provisions is likely to vary over time.

Any attempt to make international comparisons of complex phenomena is fraught with difficulties, and welfare is no exception. Government expenditure on social welfare is one traditional basis on which comparisons are made, yet this is problematic for a number of reasons which have already been broadly canvassed. First, expenditure on social welfare ignores the distributional effects of other government interventions. Second, the manner in which statistics are kept varies greatly. When comparing economic trends and state provisions across national boundaries it is difficult to know when one is comparing like with like. Most countries keep fairly extensive records on the characteristics of recipients of provisions, recording take up rates, outlays and the like. Countries also generally keep figures on national and individual incomes, taxation rates and revenue. But the modes of record-keeping are diverse and often not immediately comparable. A third set of problems resides in the various levels of government which may be involved in delivering social welfare. There will be differences in the number of relevant levels of government, and statistics may not relate to equivalent administrative levels.

The complexity of international comparisons is readily recognised in a recent United Nations attempt to rank nations in relation to development. Two methods were adopted. The classic ranking by per capita gross national product, and ranking through the use of an index which takes into account some indices of quality of life. This index covered life expectancy at birth and adult literacy and clearly represents an attempt to measure outcomes rather than merely throughputs. For many countries, their rank position varied radically, depending on the index. Out of 130 countries, for example, the United Arab Emirates ranks near the top (at position 127) only behind Switzerland, the USA and Norway, in terms of per capita gross national product. In terms of the human development index its position drops to 77. Cuba, on the other hand, improves its position from 66 on the income scale to 92 on the human development index (*The Economist*, 26 May 1990, p. 81).

The OECD countries occupy much more consistent positions

in respect of both indices, though there is still some degree of variation. The USA, for example, while second only to Switzerland in terms of the income measure, drops to 112 in terms of the human development index. Major improvers, when human development is compared with per capita income are Spain (from 105 to 115), New Zealand (from 109 to 118), Britain (from 113 to 121), Australia (from 114 to 124) and Holland (from 117 to 127). Switzerland, the Nordic countries, Japan and Canada remain highly ranked on both scales (*The Economist*, 26 May 1990, p. 81).

These United Nations rankings are claimed, of course, to be indicative rather than exact. They do, however, broadly conform to other international data. If the general picture which they paint does show considerable consistency over time this may be partly because the methods of producing international statistics is becoming more uniform. This greater uniformity must be seen as largely due to the role that organisations such as the United Nations and the OECD play as shapers of international discourses. The constant compilation of statistics and the determination of what is deemed relevant is, however, a contadictory process. It has the potential to act as part of the process of construction and reconstruction of hegemonic discourses with certain interests inadequately recognised or totally ignored. As mentioned earlier, Waring has specifically pointed to the absence from these indices of issues relating to the environment and women's interests (Waring, 1988).

These measures illustrate clearly some of the problems embedded in international statistics. However, they are not specifically the social welfare measures with which I am concerned here, though they do traverse similar territory. When we consider information focusing more specifically on conventional welfare state statistics and restricted to OECD countries, a somewhat different, though still incomplete, picture emerges.

Table 3.1 compares countries which are members of the OECD in terms of government receipts relative to gross domestic product during the mid-eighties. This offers a reflection of national commitment to collective solutions and a broad indication of the extent of the institutionalisation of a country's welfare measures. The broad picture with respect to commitment to welfare state expenditure is one which is confirmed by a great deal of other data (Einhorn, 1987; OECD, 1988).

The table reflects the generally recognised leadership of the

Table 3.1   *Government receipts as a percentage of Gross Domestic Product –*
1984 or 1985

Sweden	59.8
Denmark	57.0
Norway	56.1
Netherlands	54.3
France	48.5
Austria	47.0
Belgium	46.5
Germany	45.4
Italy	44.1
Ireland	43.6
United Kingdom	42.8
Finland	40.6
Canada	39.9
Iceland	34.8
Greece	34.6
Switzerland	34.4
Australia	34.1
Portugal	33.2
Spain	31.2
United States	31.1
Japan	30.3

Source: OECD, *OECD Economic Surveys 1986/1987: Australia* (Paris,
OECD, March 1987).

Nordic countries in terms of welfare state development. On almost
any of the conventional measures, Sweden, Norway and Denmark
come out at or near the top, with the Netherlands rarely far behind.
At the other end of the spectrum we persistently find the USA and
Japan. Between the extremes there is some variation, depending on
the focus of the analysis and the form of measurement on which
the comparison is based. Nonetheless, the Second World War
tendency to assume continuing gradual development of the welfare
state has, as already indicated, come to an end. There has been an
international reversal of the policy direction of the earlier period
though the pace of change varies considerably from country to
country. The literature on the 'crisis' of the welfare state and the
rise of the New Right demonstrate an unstable situation but the
general direction of change is clear. A crucial element of these
changes is a move to reduce the public sector because it is seen as
being in competition with the development of the private sector.

From the end of the seventies, similar policies were pursued in a wide range of countries, including the United Kingdom, the USA, Australia, Spain, Sweden, France and New Zealand and the policy direction has been independent of whether or not the government was officially conservative (Henderson, 1989, p. 33). The policies have not developed independently and in isolation; each country is plugged into an international economic discourse through organisations such as the OECD, the International Monetary Fund and GATT (the General Agreement on Tariffs and Trade). Each is attuned to the developments of other countries, through regular analysis and advice. Capitalism is clearly international and becoming more so. Nonetheless each country remains affected by its own history and current circumstances.

In the late 1980s David Henderson, head of the economics and statistics department at the OECD recognised member countries as moving to 'economic liberalism' and proceeding in a 'market oriented direction'. The term 'structural adjustment' (1989, p. 32) was, however, often preferred by international officials because of its less obvious political overtones. Henderson, identified four major common elements in this move in a market-orientated direction: changes in taxation, and the loosening of capital markets, labour markets and product markets (1989, pp. 32–43). He summarised the following changes:

– taxation – almost every member country has introduced measures of reform, chiefly with a view to (a) broadening the basis of taxation, for example by reducing special exemptions and concessions; (b) bringing down high marginal rates of personal income tax; and (c) putting greater emphasis on broadly based consumption taxes.

– financial markets – a principal area of liberalisation has been the freeing of international capital flows . . . domestic markets have been opened up by such measures as the abolition of credit controls and interest rate ceilings, the removal of restrictions on the sphere of operation of banks and other businesses, and allowing greater participation by foreign enterprises.

– product markets – a wide range of actions . . . but most striking developments have concerned deregulation – especially in transport and communications – and the privatisation of public enterprises.

– labour markets – changes are notably through deregulation and by promoting more decentralised forms of collective bargaining, and to ensure that social security systems do not unduly weaken the incentives to work, to save and to change jobs. (Henderson, 1989, p. 34.)

These international macroeconomic trends are of central concern to any consideration of the question of who is benefiting from state developments. The changes impinge on social welfare policies most directly through cuts to government expenditure, or at least consistent attempts to achieve such cuts. Economic rationalism has had the effect of reshaping welfare provisions to a greater or lesser extent in all OECD countries. These effects will be dealt with progressively as each country is considered and as other aspects of social policy are discussed.

As this overview of OECD countries demonstrates, the countries chosen for discussion roughly illustrate top, middle and bottom positions on a hypothetical ladder of world welfare states. The Nordic states, particularly Sweden, will be dealt with as examples of top-rung, highly-articulated, or 'model' welfare states. Britain in the early nineties represents a middle position but is considered first as an early developer. The USA, Japan and Australia provide examples on the bottom rung but with interestingly different characteristics. The US was a late starter and has been resistant to collective solutions to welfare problems. Japan is an even later comer and today still relies heavily on families to deliver what in other countries would be provided by government or market services. Australia provides an illustration of a welfare state laggard which took a rather different route to collective provision through its 'wage earners' welfare state' (Castles, 1985). Of particular concern in dealing with each country will be what has happened over recent years. This allows us to assess the generality of the move to the political right and provides the ground for later discussions of the implications of this for our task of understanding whose interests are being served.

The British welfare state – fr**ó**m P**o**or Laws to the New Right

During the eighteenth and nineteenth centuries, processes of industrialisation and agricultural modernisation produced in England many landless poor. This occurred at an earlier stage than in other countries and led early to attempts to deal with a relatively large unemployed and ultimately unemployable sector of the population. England was therefore the first of the industrialising countries to develop a centrally organised, relatively comprehensive system of residual assistance for the destitute poor (Thane, 1982, p. 101). The often brutal process of forcing the rural poor off the land in order to consolidate properties for farming and other purposes (Thompson, 1968, chapter 7), contrasts with the tide of events in Sweden where the state in the nineteenth and twentieth centuries was involved, not in evicting peasants from the land, but transferring land to 'peasant proprietorship' (Allardt, 1986, p. 110). Of the process of agricultural enclosure, Thompson has said it was 'a plain enough case of class robbery, played according to fair rules of property and law laid down by a parliament of property owners and lawyers' (1968, p. 239). These historical differences between the two countries remain fundamental to understanding the more positive attitudes of Swedish people to government and the welfare state even today.

Conventionally the origin of the modern British welfare state is traced back to 1834 and the enactment of the New Poor Laws, which established a centrally regulated, uniform system of poor relief (Evans, 1978, p. 62). The official rationale for this legislation resonates with sentiments recognisable as antecedents of those offered by the New Right as a basis for restructuring welfare today. In the 1830s the old Poor Law was under review because of concern about the cost of welfare and, more particularly, concern with the possibility that people would prefer welfare to employment. With relief payments adjusted to family size and wage levels very low, the Royal Commission on the Poor Laws, was worried about the undermining effect on the work ethic. The Commission saw its role as

> to cut the costs of welfare through conditional, deterrent relief
> and thus to relieve the tax-payers' burdens, restore work incen-

tives, and reimpose a proper subordination upon the labour classes. (Digby, 1989, p. 31)

Similar intentions to control the poor are detectable in Britain at least as early as the fourteenth century. The Statutes of Labourers of 1349–57 were decreed in the wake of the Black Death, a plague which had left a severe labour shortage. Similar action was taken by the rulers of many of the continental European countries which had been similarly affected.

The Poor Law Amendment Act of 1834 was significant for the manner in which it enshrined the concept of 'less eligibility'. In doing this it established not merely an administrative principle but also a moral code. The intention was to ensure that a person in receipt of welfare would experience a lower standard of living than an employed person. The 1834 Poor Law Report (Vol. xvii) expressed it thus:

> The first and most essential of all conditions . . . is that his [the pauper's] situation on the whole shall not be made really or apparently so eligible as the situation of the independent labourer of the lowest class. (Evans, 1978, p. 62)

The fear of undermining people's preparedness to labour has left the 'less eligibility' doctrine enshrined in British welfare administration to become ever since, as George put it, a 'ghost haunting many a well-intentioned piece of social reform' (1973, p. 12).

Traditional patriarchal responsibility for and power over children were also of concern. Responsibility was to be restored to parents. The 1834 Act decreed that 'all relief afforded in respect of children under the age of sixteen shall be considered to be afforded to their parents' (Evans, 1978, p. 62). This is another element of the 1834 Act which echoes into the late twentieth century. In Britain, in 1986, the age at which unemployment benefits could be claimed was raised from 16 to 18 (Dominelli, 1988, p. 51) with the clear intention to return responsibility to parents. In Australia the same principle was reasserted in 1987 (Carson and Kerr, 1988, pp. 75–6).

Over the decades following the institution of the new Poor Law regulations, distinctions were gradually made in the treatment afforded to various groups of paupers. During this period, Golding and Middleton suggest, notions of deserving and undeserving were indelibly stamped on the culture. Not that the distinctions were new. As early as the sixteenth century, a legislative distinction had been made between the 'impotent' poor, war-casualties, and the 'thriftless'. The latter category in turn became linked to criminality and the idea of a culture of poverty was born. The blurring of the distinction between criminality and destitution generated 'a murky area of inexact morality that remained prey to centuries of special pleading' (1982, p. 10). The remnants of this confusion are still obvious in the strength of feeling expended against those accused (usually inaccurately) of being welfare cheats.

Golding and Middleton point to the significance, during the nineteenth century, of the steady expansion in the number of newspapers for the dissemination of discourses about poverty. The number in Britain rose from 267 in 1821 to 563 in 1852, and over 2000 by the turn of the century (1982, pp. 19–21), providing

> house room to the slogans, mythologies, passion and debate surrounding society's continuing bewilderment about what to do with the poor. (Golding and Middleton, 1982, p. 19)

The central position assigned to the labour force role, particularly for adult males, has been a recurrent theme in the development of social policy in Britain and all other countries. However, approaches to employment have changed from time to time. The term unemployment itself only came into general English usage around the mid-1890s, coinciding with the recognition of unemployment as a social problem and not merely an individual one (Garraty, 1978, p. 4). Nonetheless, the connection between employment and first-class citizenship status has persistently acted to reinforce the inferiority of non-employed statuses.

Improved conditions of employment, and welfare provisions, were gradually exended as they were fought for, partly by workers, and often by political liberals, often in turn in coalition with a variety of conservatives (Marshall, 1965; Gough, 1979). Concern about the fitness of working-class men for military service and for the workforce has been a recurrent theme in the history of social policy. Over more recent years concern with the education and training of the workforce has moved to the fore. It was in the aftermath of Britain's disastrous involvement in the Boer War between 1899 and 1902 that, on the recommendation of an Interdepartmental Committee on Physical Deterioration, school meals and school health checks were introduced (Digby, 1989, p. 44).

Attention to the demands of labour also represented a bid to ensure the legitimacy of capitalism and head off the threat of socialism. Britain had been sensitised to revolutionary potentialities by oveseas experiences, particularly the French Revolution, but also by its own history of activism, for example by the Chartists. At times 'radical action stemmed from a conservative rationale' (Digby, 1989, p. 45). This is nowhere more graphically expressed than in the oft-quoted statement made by Conservative Member of Parliament Arthur Balfour, who was later to become Prime Minister. In 1895 he distanced himself from left politics by claiming that

> social legislation, as I conceive it, is not merely to be distinguished from socialist legislation, but it is its direct opposite and its most effective antidote. (Digby, 1989, p. 45)

Similar sentiments had underpinned the introduction by Bismarck of the world's first state social insurance scheme in Germany in 1883. Social policies to deal with workers' demands were seen as complementing laws repressing socialist political activity. In a speech to the Reichstag in 1879 in which social insurance provisions were first mooted, the Kaiser indicated that unity among the people of Germany was not merely being promoted 'through the repression of socialist excesses, but also through positive furthering of the welfare of the workers' (quoted in Levine, 1988, p. 54).

In Britain as in other Western European countries, many British reforms were targeted at the male workforce. Health and unemployment insurance was established for miners, and their hours were made shorter in 1908. Employment exchanges were established in 1909. Unemployment benefits were dependent on a test of willingness to work and were clearly aimed at enhancing labour's efficiency and mobility (Digby, 1989, pp. 45–6). This motivation to strengthen capitalist control did not go unnoticed by labour at the time. As one critic expressed it,

> Wrapped in the cloven hoof of state paternalism could be clearly seen the insidious attempt of organised capital to tighten further the shackles of slavery around its exploited wage-slaves. (Wills, 1913, p. 5)

Developments must also be understood partly as a response to the expansion of the male franchise, which increased male working-class power. This took on a very tangible dimension in 1906 when 30 Labour parliamentarians were elected to the House of Commons (Digby, 1989, p. 45). Workers were, however, ambivalent about seeking assistance from the state, because of their extremely negative attitudes to the workhouse system. Self-help organised by the labour movement was preferred. Nonetheless attitudes gradually changed as more labour representatives moved into Parliament.

In 1908, during the Edwardian period, old-age pensions were introduced. This was considerably later than in a number of other countries. They were added into the German social insurance provisions in 1889, available at the age of 70 (Levine, 1988, p. 60). The Danes introduced a non-contributory age pension, available at the age of 60, in 1891 (Levine, 1988; 1891). The British system had an age limit of 70 but in structure was more like the Danish system. Both incorporated the Poor Law element of worthiness. The British old-age pension was non-contributory and available to those with very low incomes who met criteria of 'deservingness' similar to those of the 1834 Poor Laws. The pension did not provide a subsistence income; it was identified as a supplement. As a Member of Parliament at the time pointed out, it was for 'the very poor, the very respectable and the very old'. When the first pensions were taken up in 1909 the majority went to women (Thane, 1982, pp. 83–4), reflecting a numerical sex imbalance among the aged which continues today.

The next significant piece of British welfare legislation, The National Insurance Act of 1911, established a contributory scheme covering medical treatment, a sickness benefit and unemployment benefits for workers in specific industries – shipbuilding, engineering and building and construction. Most of the workers eligible for the unemployment benefit were skilled and very few women were covered. The scheme was administered by the existing and very popular Friendly Societies and other insurance organisations (Thane, 1982, p. 86).

The Pensions Act of 1908 and the National Insurance Act of 1911 provided, in very embryonic form, the income security mechanisms of the modern British welfare state; that is, a combination of non-contributory and insurance-based benefits. By the outbreak of the First World War, a range of state interventions in other areas had also effectively charted much ground which would be covered by later provisions. The regulation of working conditions and wages, workers' compensation, job creation, town planning, public housing, child health and protection were among the many areas which received the attention of an increasingly interventionist state (Thane, 1982). It is salutary to consider the wide range of issues that were addressed and to recognise a continuity between these issues and those of today.

In Britian the interwar years were not noted for changes to welfare provisions, in contrast to the USA where the New Deal of the 1930s laid the foundations of today's welfare state. However, these years in Britain were not just a time of chaotic attempts to deal with the high levels of unemployment of the 1920s and 1930s. The central government assumed responsibilty for public housing in 1919, though by 1921 Lloyd George's promise to servicemen returning from the First World War that they would be provided with 'homes fit for heroes', foundered on the rocks of economic contraction. The Poor Laws were finally dismantled. Free elementary education was established in 1918 and the school leaving age was raised from 12 to 14 years. Health and unemployment insurance was extended to include half rather than only one-quarter of the population. Altogether the proportion of gross national product devoted to the social services doubled from 4 per cent to 8 per cent (Digby, 1989, pp. 49–50). However, the change was largely without a central direction.

It was not until after the Second World War that the British welfare state took its mature form. In a climate of relief after the war, a climate diffused with an idealism for a new, more just society, welfare legislation had bipartisan support. There was a clear sense of rebuilding a better Britain. Goodin and Dryzek suggest that deep and widespread uncertainty expanded people's 'moral horizons' and this propelled the development of the welfare state after the Second World War. They tested this hypothesis for 23 countries and found that those whose civilian populations suffered most 'wartime uncertainty and risk sharing' demonstrated the greatest welfare state growth (1987 pp. 66–7).

While this political consensus was hailed as the coming of a new era, from the vantage-point of history we should recognise it as conditional and temporary. The importance of the war context is highlighted by the fact that in Britain the term welfare state itself seems to have been first used in 1941, by Archbishop Temple, to distinguish Britain's 'welfare state' from the German Nazi 'power and warfare state' (Flora and Heidenheimer, 1984, p. 19).

Beveridge provided a blueprint for the modern British welfare state in his 1942 report *Social Insurance and Allied Services*. Though his recommendations were not enacted *in toto*, his broad framework became government policy, resulting in a form of coverage for all. In 1945 family allowances were instituted, providing support in respect of children at the rate of eight shillings for the first child and five shillings for subsequent children (Thane, 1982, p. 243). This embodied the principle of horizontal equity by spreading the costs of supporting children more evenly across the population. The National Insurance Act of 1946 provided pensions and sickness and unemployment benefits for all insured people. The wives of insured men were covered, but as dependents and not in their own right. Employed married women were allowed to choose to opt out of all insurance payments except for the part covering injury at work (Cole, 1986, p. 53). Sole female parents, other than widows, were not covered, nor were the long-term unemployed as, after one year, eligibility for benefit ceased.

The National Health Service was established in 1948, and to mop up those not covered by the Insurance Scheme, the National Assistance Act of 1948 consolidated coverage for non-contributors under the National Assistance Board (Thane, 1982, p. 154). This involved means-tested assistance which has remained stigmatised despite the attempt of the Labour Government of 1966 to revamp it by incorporating its administration into a new Ministry of Social Security, which, as the name suggests, also encompassed social insurance. At that time the entitlement was renamed Supplementary Benefit and in 1988 this was changed to Income Support. Despite these classic bureaucratic strategies of altered names and administrative arrangements, the provision has remained residual, highly selective and stigmatising.

The National Insurance Scheme provided for flat-rate contributions and flat-rate benefits. Beveridge believed that the benefit rate should be set at subsistence level, no more and no less. No more because this would interfere with individual responsibilities, no less because people deserved an adequate standard of living (Rees, 1985, p. 84). In the event, the rate was somewhat below subsistence. A major modification to Beveridge's principles was introduced by the Labour Government in 1975 when it introduced the State Earnings Related Pension Scheme (SERPS). This provides an earnings-related pension in addition to the basic pension. This jettisoned the former principle of equality embodied in the flat-rate benefit.

Apart from linking retirement income to earlier earnings and thus perpetuating income differentials, SERPS did make benefits similar to those of private insurance schemes more available to a range of workers. The scheme was targeted for dismantling by the Thatcher government, and though this was not achieved because of resistance, 'drastic modifications' were made in the 1986 Social Security Act (Papadakis and Taylor-Gooby, 1987, p. 110) which offered very positive support for private personal pensions. This encouragement was effective and by 1989 pensioners were drawing only about half of their total income directly from the state pension system. The rest was coming from savings and private pension schemes (Willetts, 1989, p. 267).

Over recent years there has been a dramatic move away from the postwar compromise between capital and labour which resulted in the establishment of the modern British welfare state. The move is away from the principle of social security provided on a universal collective basis towards 'individual provisions purchased in the market' (Dominelli, 1988, p. 46). It must be remembered, though, that the debate about whether services should be bought, at least by those who could pay, did begin soon after the establishment of the Beveridge scheme (Rees, 1985, pp. 94–5), though it was muted first by the aftermath of the wartime effort, then by macro-economic prosperity which rendered less pressing the issue of competition over scarce resources.

The policy directions taken by the British welfare state, starting during the seventies under Labour, show all the characteristics of a move to economic liberalism, referred to earlier in the chapter. Under Thatcher these policies took on a uniquely strident tone. The principle of enforcing labour discipline, always an element of state welfare, even at its most liberal and gentle, took on particularly punitive overtones in the eighties, as exemplified in the breaking of the miners' strike.

The crusading commitment of influential members of the Thatcher Conservative Government to individualist principles was perhaps seen with greatest clarity in the promotion of the community charge, or as it became popularly know, the poll tax. Introduced in 1989, it involved the abolition of council rating systems based on property values. Traditionally those with properties of higher value paid higher rates to local councils. While the motivation behind the introduction of the poll tax was essentially party-political, in that it was aimed at breaking the power of Labour-controlled local governments, it was also quintessentially individualistic (Oppenheim, 1987). Each person over 18 became equal before the taxer. The claim was made that this was a benefit tax; the charge was a flat rate because all people benefit from a similar range of services.

A recent study confirmed, however, that, as for so many national services, wealthier residents actually do benefit more from local services. Bramley, Le Grand and Low, after a study in the County of Cheshire, found that the better-off used services costing from 40 to 70 per cent more than those who were least well-off (1989, p. 28).

Black families were especially hard-hit by the community charge, for three major reasons. First, because they live in areas in which a relatively large number of services are required to support dense and poor local populations, the individual rate was high. Second, since Black families are generally larger, a greater amount was required from each household and, third, because incomes were low, the relative proportion paid was greater (Oppenheim, 1987, p. 40).

The poll tax not only aroused opposition from Labour Party supporters and the left, it threatened to split the Conservative Party. The community charge abandoned any commitment to the principles of social equity or *noblesse oblige*. But many significant nobles did feel obliged. The Queen, the Duke of Westminster and Lord Bath, three leading members of the British aristocracy, indicated that they would pay the tax for workers on their estates (Coultan, 1990, p. 23). The issue finally became a factor in the removal of Margaret Thatcher from the leadership of the Conservative government in November 1990, as demonstrated by a subsequent modification of the tax.

When the New Right refocuses the discourse on welfare on to individual rather than collective responsibility, 'individual' encompasses 'individual' patriarchal responsibility for family members. For many purposes, though not the poll tax, the family is treated as a unit, thus diluting gains towards independence made earlier by women and young people. For example, parents became liable to pay compensation in respect of offences committed by their children (Willetts, 1989, p. 267).

The reassertion of class and patriarchal principles was also evident in the abolition of unemployment benefits for those under 18, the reduction of benefits for those between 18 and 25, and the introduction of a number of schemes which pressure claimants to work for their benefits. Young people under 18, who are ineligible for benefit, are offered training in the Youth Training Scheme, which explicitly aims to train them in good work habits. As Minford expressed it in 1988 on radio, the scheme also aims to 'drive wages down to create jobs' (quoted by Dominelli, 1988, p. 52). The withholding of benefit for up to six months for those who voluntarily leave their jobs was another measure to promote labour discipline (Dominelli, 1988, p. 51). Similar restrictions were introduced in Australia by the Hawke Labor government though unemployment benefit can be withheld only for a maximum of three months.

Discrimination on the basis of race also has been increasing in the British social security system since the seventies. Child benefit has been denied to parents if their child lives overseas; benefits require a continuous qualifying period of residence – the 'presence' clause, which affects those immigrants who return frequently to their original country; and sponsors of immigrants must take financial responsibility and sign a declaration excluding the immigrant from 'recourse to public funds'. Failure of a sponsor to provide support has become a criminal offence. Cross-checking computerised mechanisms between police and social security information systems effectively render social security a system of internal immigration control (Dominelli, 1988, p. 58).

Nationalised industries have also been the target of those radical right policies which aim to re-establish the supremacy of the market. In a speech delivered in July 1988, Nigel Lawson, then Chancellor of the Exchequer, rejected the Keynesian economic period of 'post-war consensus' as not only failing 'to deliver economic success' but also causing 'grave damage to the economy' (1988, p. 8). Nationalisation of industries, such as railways, coal and electricity, by the postwar Labour government, was part of a deliberate attempt to redistribute benefits within the society. The welfare of workers and citizens loomed large and it was intended that the benefits from key industries should shift from owners to workers (both largely male) and to the public. It is noteworthy that there was not a great deal of opposition from Conservatives. As Harold Macmillan said in his memoirs, 'we could never return to the classical laissez-faire' (1969, p. 81). He tellingly adds, however, that Labour did not show signs of wanting to nationalise any profitable industries (1969, p. 82). This not only indicates the limits to Conservative acceptance of redistribution, but also foreshadows the relatively narrow parameters of the political settlement between left and right in respect of the welfare state.

The Conservative government has also been reversing national ownership through processes of deregulation and privatisation. In 1988, the Chancellor was able to claim that the government had returned 17 major businesses, involving 650 000 employees, to private hands. These included British Aerospace, British Shipbuilders, Jaguar Cars, British Gas and British Airways. The transfer of local water services to private shareholdings followed in 1989. However, the pace then slowed because the most attractive enterprise bargains had been snapped up.

British economic policy was in line with, and even leading, the market-orientated direction of OECD countries. Incentive was offered by government to investment through the reduction in the 1988 budget of the top taxation rate from 60 to 40 per cent (Dominelli, 1988, p. 60) and an extensive programme of deregulation, particularly in the telecommunications and finance sectors. Housing finance was also deregulated and, according to Lawson, 'transformed into a highly competitive and innovative market-place' (1988, p. 10). A deregulated finance industry had by 1988 provided the finance for the private sale of over one million public houses and flats. Shareholding became more widespread with the number of shareholders trebling between 1979 and 1988 (Lawson, 1988, p. 9). However, this certainly did not make it an activity of those in the lower reaches of the income range.

This brief historical examination of the development of the British welfare state demonstrates very clearly that it is first and foremost a capitalist welfare state and strongly patriarchal. There are also strongly racist elements which are only now being recognised. Male employment has remained a pivotal issue with an ever-present nervousness about the possibility of destroying people's preparedness to work.

The postwar consensus which the welfare state reflected can be viewed on three levels. First, it represented a change in the balance of national politics, with the Labour government decisively shattering the Conservative Party's hold. A system of two parties of almost equivalent support emerged. Second, there was a significant shift in policy with new citizenship rights established. Third, it represented a shift in the balance of power between capital and labour, with the labour unions taking on a new importance. While the settlement was forged in the unique environment of the war, it was maintained by the leadership of the Conservative Government during the 1950s as an 'acceptable compromise', about which 'few partisans on either side enthused, but it proved durable' (Gamble, 1987, pp. 189–90).

Until 1976 flat-rate pensions embodied a strong egalitarian principle and contributed to greater vertical equity, even though the better-off continued to supplement their entitlements through private pensions. The SERPS Act institutionalised the differential rewards of the occupational system into a lifetime reality. When this change is considered together with other Labour Government policies, such as attempts to cut government programmes, it becomes clear that the dilution of the British welfare state's capacity to deliver greater equality started before the election of the Thatcher Conservative government. Nonetheless, overall there was some general shift towards greater equality of income under the Labour Government in the 1970s. This was reversed during the 1980s, with the gap increasing between higher and lower incomes and the proportion in poverty growing (Willetts, 1989, p. 268).

The attack on the social welfare state was certainly pursued with great enthusiasm by the Thatcher Conservative government. Welfare became less institutional and increasingly residual, with a heavy market reliance. Gough has suggested that the Conservative Government made a determined effort to eradicate collectivism from British life (1990, p. 46). Certainly the settlement on which the welfare state was based was rejected. He summarises the effects of government policies between 1979 and 1987 as follows:

– falling relative levels of benefits and services coupled with absolute declines in housing and probably health
– greater opportunity for 'exit' from state welfare programs
– some expansion of occupational and private provision of social services and benefits
– greater centralisation of the control and administration of welfare services
– the emergence of mass unemployment and a class of very long-term unemployed
– redistribution towards the rich and, to a much lesser extent, the middle-income groups, coupled with rising relative poverty. (1990, p. 45)

This is the end of an era for the British welfare state. The postwar settlement has not stood the test of time and both Conservatives and Labour are intent on re-emphasising the market. Britain stands on the brink of this new phase of its development at the same time as it faces integration into Europe. This will inevitably bring significant changes. If the breaking-down of trade barriers is uncontrolled, this would provide a competitive advantage to countries with the weakest welfare states (Marquand, 1989, p. 216), something of which the Community is very well aware. On the other hand, the European Community may act to further the interests of those who are disadvantaged. British law has in the past taken a less liberatory stance on many matters than that embodied in the Treaty of Rome (Atkins, 1986, p. 58) and already the European Court has been appealed to on some issues of sexual discrimination, and its judgements have supported greater equality. The next phase of the British welfare state will certainly be a more international one.

The Australian experience – a wage earners' welfare state

The Australian welfare state has developed by a rather different path from the British and from that taken by the other nations of northern Europe. Around the turn of the twentieth century Australia, together with New Zealand, took something of a lead in terms of progressive social policies. The initial promise did not continue, though, and Australia must now be counted among the world's welfare laggards. On top of this, the effects of recent New Right policies have jeopardised even the modest level of provisions that had been achieved.

In 1901, at the time of the federation of the Australian colonies, 'universal suffrage' for those over the age of 21 was enacted, though this universality excluded Australian Aborigines and Torres Strait Islanders who were not routinely included as voters until the 1960s. All white adults could both vote and stand for national office. This was the first time that women in any country had the right to do both, though there were a number of earlier instances of women having the vote (Sawer and Simms, 1984). Australia also had a particularly strong labour movement. Almost from its inception, the Labor Party had considerable electoral success. In a state election in New South Wales in 1891, for example, Labor won more than 30 per cent of the vote. This translated into 35 of the parliament's 141 seats and gave considerable scope to offer minority party support in return for concessions. In 1899 the world's first Labor government was elected in the state of Queensland (Castles, 1985, pp. 18–19).

Parliamentary politics were thus of key importance to the labour movement from the late nineteenth century. The national Labor Party was formed in the 1890s in the wake of the defeat of a major shearers' strike. The Party had members elected to the federal parliament from that parliament's inception in 1901. In the 1904 election, a total of 15 members were elected. Soon after there were two brief periods of Labor Party minority government, and, between 1910–13 and 1914–16 Labor majority governments. Similar electoral success was not to be achieved by a labour party in any other country until 1932 when the Social Democratic Party won power in Sweden (Castles, 1985, p. 18).

The force of the labour movement had a direct effect on a range of policies. Age pensions were legislated at the national level in 1908, though they had been in existence in some states from the turn of the century (Kewley, 1977, chapter 3). In the case of pensions there was support from all parties. It must be noted, however, that these pensions were largely for the deserving white poor who had resided in the country for more than 25 years. The vast majority of Australian Aborigines, all people of Asian origin (unless born in the country) and ex-prisoners were excluded.

Recipients had to be 'of good character' (Kewley, 1977, pp. 75–6). Similar racist exclusions were made in relation to the Maternity Allowance which was established in 1912 and provided five pounds on the birth of a live, white child.

The strength of the union movement and the Australian Labor Party have left a distinctive and indelible stamp on Australia's welfare state. Social democratic efforts which elsewhere were devoted primarily to the development of the social wage were directed in Australia more at securing acceptable conditions of work and wage levels, though effectively only for male workers. A great deal was actually achieved, hence Castles' aphorism 'wage earners' welfare state'. Labour or social democratic politics are traditionally associated with a strong state and it was no different in Australia. Government action was employed to redress inequality. At its most optimistic, labour politics, in Australia as elsewhere, interpreted these state processes as leading down a parliamentary road to socialism. As John Curtin, Prime Minister of Australia during the Second World War, expressed it, 'I believe predominantly that government should be the agency whereby the masses should be lifted up' (Wilenski, 1986, p. 20). Despite this tradition, the policies of the Labor government of the 1980s clearly showed the hallmarks of economic liberalism, with its negative view of government intervention, its concentration on the private sector, privatisation at the expense of the public, and deregulation of the labour market.

A key early development in Australia and New Zealand was the establishment of a centralised system of industrial conciliation and arbitration. This was concerned with wage fixing, ruling on claims about other conditions of work and with disputes. As Castles points out, the establishment of this system effectively meant that wages were no longer determined in terms of market forces, as is decreed by the pure logic of capitalism. The idea that the worker's freedom was merely confined to the freedom to enter into a contract or not, was rejected. The capacity of industry to pay was also ruled out as a basis for determining wage rates in 1909 (Castles, 1985, p. 14). Human need was injected into the system as a relevant consideration.

A landmark decision was made in the Harvester case of 1907. Here the President of the Commonwealth Court of Conciliation and Arbitration, who had been Attorney General in a federal Labor minority government, pronounced that wages for unskilled male workers should be paid at a level

> appropriate to the normal needs of the average employee regarded as a human being living in a civilised community (Macarthy, 1976, p. 41).

Importantly, the 'basic' wage was to cover the needs of not only the worker but also a wife and three children, and allow them to live 'in frugal comfort'. As will be discussed more fully in Chapters 5 and 6, this has had important ramifications for the relationship of women's wages to men's, since women's needs were assumed to be covered by the male rate. Women's minimum rate was for many years set at only half, and later three-quarters that of men. Equal pay was formally granted only in 1972.

A number of other policies successfully promoted by male workers also had the effect of excluding the competition of cheaper labour. The most notorious measure was the strict control of immigration through a White Australia Policy, which prohibited all immigrants of colour. This infamous policy was built firmly on the racist sentiments of workers but it did have the effect of preventing employers undermining the white male wage-earners' welfare state through the employment of labourers from the South Pacific or Asia. While self-interest expressed through racism prompted unionists to support the White Australia Policy, unadulterated racism allowed Australia's indigenous people to have their labour exploited in a manner close to slavery. Australian Aborigines on pastoral properties worked in homesteads and with livestock without proper wages and often for meagre rations only. The union movement turned a blind eye to this until the 1960s (Sanders, 1985).

This early strategy of the political left of pursuing white males' interests largely through improved conditions of employment has left its stamp on the Australian welfare state. It has meant that the classic social welfare provisions remain underdeveloped. Even in the 1990s Australian income security arrangements take a residualist and highly selective form. The only general provision based on insurance has been in the area of workers' compensation, where employers pay the total contribution.

Only two provisions have been claimed to be universal, and both relate to children. Their relative generosity must be interpreted at least partly in terms of a racist obsession in Australia with an expansion of the white colonising population. The first was the maternity allowance which has already been mentioned. After the removal of the racist element this finished its life as a genuinely universal benefit, but was abolished in 1976 when it was deemed to be absorbed into the family allowance. The second is the allowance in respect of children, initially called child endowment and more recently the family allowance. At its inception this excluded Asian and Aboriginal women and women from Papua or the islands of the Pacific (Kewley, 1977, p. 104). While this benefit has since become racially universal, it has been restricted according to income, as part of the Hawke Labor government's drive to cut government spending. In 1987 a means test for family allowance was instituted and, where family income reached $A50 000 per annum, the allowance became subject to a steep rate of taper and quickly cuts out altogether.

All pensions and benefits are flat-rate and means-tested both in relation to assets and income, though this does not, of course, apply to private pension schemes which the government supports through fiscal welfare (see Chapter 4). The only time Australia has had a non-means-tested form of social security was during the seventies. The Whitlam Labor administration (1972–75) made pensions available without restriction to all those over the age of 72. This decision was, however, reversed by the subsequent Fraser conservative government (1975–83) and more stringent means-testing was gradually introduced. From the outset, income security has always been paid from federal consolidated revenue and there is no national insurance scheme. Indeed, since the 1930s, there has been no noticeable lobby supporting such a scheme. The means of financing the universal health scheme has been through a 1.5 per cent levy on income, supplemented from consolidated revenue.

Private insurance to cover a range of contingencies has been, and remains, widespread among the better-off. As in Britain, one strand of this practice had its origins in working-class mutual help. Private insurance is most often subscribed to in respect of costs of health care in private facilities and for retirement benefits. Superannuation has traditionally been contributed to by employers for those in higher-paying occupations. Payments by employees and the self-employed have also attracted taxation concessions, rendering the area a strong source of both occupational and fiscal welfare.

As part of its macro-economic policy of increasing national savings, the Hawke Government's policy was to make superannuation more widely available. The ultimate effect will be to widen the gap between those well provided-for in their old age through superannuation and those who rely on a government age pension, paid at the same (low) rate as for the unemployed, widows, invalids and supporting parents. Especially vulnerable are women, many immigrants of non-English speaking backgrounds and particularly Australian Aborigines, because they have high rates of unemployment.

Until the mid-seventies health care was covered only by private insurance, together with a system of free medical treatment for the poor located mainly in public hospitals. A national health scheme was established by the reforming Whitlam Labor Government in 1975. It was then partially dismantled by the subsequent Conservative Government, and then restored in somewhat different form by the Hawke Labor Government in 1983. This form of toing-and-froing has led Castles to conclude that Australia has the world's 'most reversible' welfare state (1989, p. 30). Øyen has also remarked on the vulnerability of the Australian social security system, suggesting that protection of social welfare provisions actually arises from their reflection of established inequalities. If the better-off get more, as they are accustomed to in other arenas, they are likely to provide political support (Øyen, 1986, p. 278). Levels of inequality can then be reduced, at least to a degree. While flat-rate and means-tested provisions do more effectively reduce inequality, in the process they produce dilemmas, because support from the middle classes remains tenuous for provisions from which they benefit little.

The reversibility of social welfare in part reflects the relative strength of the parties of the right (currently Liberal and National) in Australia. They have held power more often than has Labor, and they have tended to modify or reverse policies enacted by Labor governments. From the mid-eighties, though, the Labor Government undertook its own process of dismantling. Although there was debate about its extent and comment on its artificial, politically manipulated quality, a tax revolt was widely deemed to have occurred among the Australian middle classes during the seventies. Reductions of tax rates were pursued under the claim that they were demanded by the electorate. A similar trend occurred somewhat earlier in Denmark and a number of other countries, including the USA (Einhorn, 1987, p. 17).

For funding government programmes both Denmark and Australia have relied heavily on taxing employees' wages and salaries. This is a highly visible form of taxation, because employees' contributions are deducted from weekly earnings on a 'pay as you earn basis' (PAYE). In Australia, despite levels which were low by international standards, taxes were publicly decried as too high and reductions have been a policy issue for both political parties. While governments justified the reductions in terms of a tax revolt, the policy is more accurately seen as part of the broad economic liberalisation programme. The intention has been both to cut government income, and hence spending, and to offer workers some compensation for the cuts to wages levels that they had suffered. Recent research by Papadakis has in fact confirmed that there is continuing 'strong' support for public welfare and a tendency to exaggerate the extent of welfare backlash (1990, p. 126).

There have never been extensive public housing programmes in Australia. The issue of housing was dealt with mainly through private ownership involving a range of tax incentives and other programmes; 'large sums have been scattered in many complex and confusing programs to a wide range of income groups' (Jones, 1990, p. 177). Only the poorest have ever been able to qualify for the small pool of publicly-provided houses or flats. Despite some persistent attempts over recent decades to address the problem, Australian Aborigines, who make up about two per cent of the population, remain the worst-off in housing, as they do in respect of so many indices of well-being. Many Aboriginal people have no housing or remain housed in the sort of shelters associated with the worst shanties on the outskirts of the poorest Third World cities. Direct government expenditure on Aboriginal Housing programmes for 1986/87 represented 3.5 per cent of direct outlays on housing (Jones, 1990, p. 197). Also, Aboriginal families are likely to be over-represented in public housing, again reflecting their generally impoverished circumstances. They have a rate of home ownership at about one-third of that of the population generally (Choo, 1990, p. 42). The issue remains one of the country's most intractable social problems.

The labour movement's strategy of establishing a living wage, together with various government schemes to assist home purchase, have been relatively effective in promoting a high rate of private home-ownership for non-Aboriginal people. In its turn this had something of a levelling effect on wealth distribution. The rate of home-ownership peaked in the 1960s at just on 72 per cent (Milligan, 1983, p. 119). However, despite various incentives, including the introduction of a First Home Owners' Scheme, which accounted for 6 per cent of direct Commonwealth outlays on housing in the 1986/87 financial year (Jones, 1990, p. 195), the rate of home-ownership has fallen over recent decades. In the mid-1980s it was 69 per cent, due partly to a drop in disposable income coupled with rising house prices. However, the drop is partly a statistical effect caused by a widening of the base number of households. From the seventies on, young people started moving out of the family home at a much earlier age to establish their own households. The dwellings were almost always rented and this has altered the balance between rented and owned accommodation. When the data are analysed in detail they show an increase in home-ownership at each age level (Ironmonger, 1989, p. 9).

Australia has never followed the practice of allowing tax concessions in respect of mortgage repayments on the residential home, something which almost certainly advantages the better-off. However, they benefit in other ways. For example, there is no capital gains tax on the sale of the house of residence, no imputed rent on the family home and its value is not counted as an asset for means test purposes. Also, some of the allowances in respect of purchasing rental property can be manipulated to great advantage by those who have sufficient funds to purchase more than one home. Those who rent have always been and remain a particularly disadvantaged group.

Throughout the century, despite a great deal of self-congratulation about the progressiveness of the Australian state, the amount of national revenue devoted to the social wage has been very low. Expenditure on welfare in Australia in the mid-eighties compared with Switzerland (OECD, 1987), at the bottom of the OECD countries (see Table 3.1). The residual character of the Australian provisions, with their heavy dependence on means-testing, has led also to something of an obsession with poverty lines and their measurement. If there are means tests, then cutoff points must be established. These points are obvious spots for dispute over the distribution of benefits. The centrality of issues about means-testing has persistently directed debate towards issues of poverty, rather than to issues of principle relating to equality and citizenship. Much of the discourse has also been focused on technical issues relating to processes of measurement (Cox, 1981), diverting the discourse away from fundamental problems which are embedded in the residual nature of welfare.

It was only in the late 1980s that the monetary value of the basic pension entitlement reached the Australian Labor Party's modest target of 25 per cent of average weekly earnings, though it also came close to this target during the term of the Whitlam Government. Ironically this target was reached because of reductions in wages in real terms rather than through significant increases in pension rates. Nonetheless, for the poorest, some significant improvement in standard of living was achieved. Late in the decade, the Hawke Government launched a campaign 'to overcome child poverty by 1990'.

A significant family income supplement was made available on a means-tested basis in respect of children and rent. This, together with a concerted effort to encourage sole parents (largely female) into the labour force, led to an increase of 12 per cent in the income of single-parent families (who have persistently been the poorest), between 1982 and 1990. This compares with an increase of only 3.3 per cent for two parent non-farm families (Bradbury, Doyle and Whiteford, 1990, p. 3). These supplementary benefits were indexed to the cost of living, but remain problematic nonetheless. A mode of tackling the problem which directs benefits to highly-targeted groups is likely to be vulnerable to erosion when political will wanes (Castles, 1989; Øyen, 1986).

The labour movement has traditionally been more concerned with employment conditions than the social wage. While this, as Castles concluded (1985, p. 76), has proved a viable strategy for the movement, it has had problems especially in relation to those groups whose attachment to the labour market is tenuous. The strategy has to an extent altered 'the reward structures of capitalism' in a direction more favourable to working-class interests. A measure of its success showed up in a relatively narrow range of wealth and income distribution. This was typical of Australia until the past two decades. Because this relative equality of income and wealth has not lasted (Castles, 1991), this tends to negate a key advantage of approaching issues of equality through the employ-

ment system to the neglect of the social wage. What is left are the
many disbenefits of a poorly developed social welfare system and
employment structures which disadvantage many groups. There
is a lack of broad support for the highly selective welfare measures
that exist, particularly benefits for single parents and the unemployed, because the better-off have less need to use them. All
round, the result has been a precarious social welfare system.

After the Hawke Government came to power, a social contract
with the union movement, was signed. This was known as the
Prices and Income Accord, or more commonly just the Accord.
The union movement formally took a more central role in government (Stilwell, 1986) in a manner reminiscent of the British situation under the Wilson Labour Government in the seventies. A
significant difference, however was that the Australian unions were
docile. The unions were implicated in the restructuring of the
economy, with one of the major goals being the reduction in real
wages. This was achieved through a series of agreements to reduce
significantly the conditions ensuring regular review and adjust-
ments of wage rates. Between 1986 and mid-1987 alone, a 3.75
per cent cut in real average earnings was achieved (OECD, 1987,
p. 16), through the unions agreeing to discount the normal cost-
of-living increase and to delay the payment of this reduced rate of
increase.

Although one of the original elements of the Accord was that
prices should be controlled as well as the cost of labour, this was
effectively done for only a few months. After that, price control
mechanisms fell into disrepair. Not all employees lost out, though.
At higher levels, incomes increased significantly. Income inequality
increased by over 20 per cent between 1982 and 1989 (Lombard,
1991, p. 12), a familiar pattern internationally (Lekachman, 1982,
p. ix).

Wage rates were not the only domain in which the union movement was party to accepting reductions. Other conditions of
employment, hard-won through union activity, were lost or came
under consideration. The centralised power of the union movement itself was weakened as enteprise-level bargaining gained
acceptance. This trend, one which Australia shares with other
OECD countries, is one which in multiple ways threatens the
whole fabric of Australia's wage earners' welfare state.

The involvement of the union movement in (junior) partnership with government did demonstrate a continuity with the history of the welfare state in Australia. Once again, despite some lip-service, the social wage received little attention. Union effort was directed towards broad industrial issues, such as restructuring union organisation itself and restructuring industry awards and the mechanisms of industrial regulation. While the major focus remained on relatively traditional areas of industrial policy, those who historically have been disadvantaged remained so. The issue of 'Who benefits?' was hardly raised, let alone effectively answered. It was falsely assumed that an improved industrial climate would automatically benefit all.

The USA – the traditional laggard

The United States, together with Canada, has lagged in respect of welfare provision (Rose and Shiratori, 1986, p. 3), though Canadian provisions are rather more developed and started somewhat earlier. There has been a stronger emphasis in the political discourses of these countries on individualism, the family and market systems. Considerable faith is evident in the capacity of the market to deal with citizens fairly and efficiently. Alongside the market and closely linked with it has been greater development than in other countries of private forms of charity. The most readily recognised are the Ford and Rockefeller Foundations. At the local level, a range of smaller organisations and the 'community chest' have been a major feature, with the United Way of America providing a central, highly institutionalised form of coordination. During the 1970s the income of the 596 largest tax-exempt foundations was more than 'twice the net earnings of the nation's largest commercial banks' (Horowitz and Kolodney, 1974, p. 43). These charitable organisations not only exemplify the individualist philosophy of the USA but wield very considerable power and influence in the society generally.

During the debates about how to deal with the devastation caused by the 1930s depression, the roles of charity and government were explicitly debated. Republican John Tilson graphically expressed, in 1930, the widely-held belief that private charity was the way to deal with the depression. He envisaged a road 'lined on both sides with ten thousand charitable agencies maintained by generous givers to minister to those in need' (Levine, 1988, p. 234). This point of view was gradually swayed towards more collective solutions by the magnitude of the problems to be faced. By 1932, under Roosevelt, the position, originally expressed by Democrat Edward Elsik that 'it is the duty of government to take care of its people and see that they do not starve or freeze', became national policy (Levine, 1988, pp. 234–40). This New Deal marked a turning point, though the individualist philosophy which had prevented earlier welfare state developments has remained a stronger force in the USA than in other Western welfare states.

The USA is still without some of the basics of a mature welfare state. For example, there is no universal health scheme. Looking at figures for 1969, Kaim-Caudle compared 10 countries on the generosity and coverage of their social security mechanisms. The USA appeared at the bottom of the assessment (1973, p. 301). As the discussion of Table 3.1 indicated, this position has not altered appreciably and, as for so many countries, the rightward swing has made coverage in many areas even more problematic.

While Australia has a social security system which has been generally rather mean, the US has a bifurcated system, one which is 'highly lop-sided in favour of middle class interests' (Hanson, 1987, p. 170). Hanson suggests that this 'strongly bifurcated organisation' may be the most distinctive feature of the US welfare state (1987, p. 169). One arm of the welfare state consists of social insurance schemes, administered at the national level. The key programmes are Old Age, Survivors, Disability and Health Insurance (OASDHI) and Medicare, the health insurance programme for the aged. Social insurance schemes also cover workers' compensation, railroad employee retirement, public employee retirement and unemployment insurance.

In terms of this insurance coverage, the US welfare state measures up quite well to the criteria of institutional welfare. Also, these programmes have proved 'politically sacrosanct' and Congresses resisted President Reagan's attempts to trim their costs (Hanson, 1987, p. 168). They provide non-means-tested benefits, to a broad constituency, including all classes, though, with a bias towards those who are better-off. Predictably, because of the link with employment, there has been a race bias because people of colour have always been the poorest group, with inferior employment opportunities. For similar reasons women have generally been disadvantaged as well, although, because of the demographic characteristics of the population, women do predominate as recipients of age-related benefits. However, this is more often in their status as wives rather than in their own right (Fraser, 1987, p. 94).

The other arm of the US welfare state consists of public assistance, which is non-contributory. The major programmes here include Aid to Families with Dependent Children (AFDC), Old Age Assistance, Aid to the Blind, Aid to the Partially and Totally Disabled (now collectively Supplemental Security Income), Medicaid, Health Care for the Indigent, and General Assistance (Hanson, 1987, p. 195). Eligibility is selective and targeted to the poorest. These programmes have all the hallmarks of residual welfare with notions of deservingness very much part of the continuing public debate that surrounds them. The target unit is the family, whereas for social insurance it is largely the individual. Funding is jointly provided by national, state and local governments. This is an unstable alliance which leaves the programmes vulnerable. Over the years they have experienced variable fortunes, though during the sixties funding was improved. These programmes were most affected by the onslaught of Reaganomics, the 'tax revolts' and associated moves to cut spending at both state and local government levels.

When we compare social insurance with public assistance, we find trends in the opposite direction. For OASDHI, with only the odd hiccup, benefits have continually increased since 1950. The 1984 monthly rate represented $US140, compared with $US60 in 1950 at 1967 dollar values. If we then look at benefits from AFDC we find that these rose slightly over the two decades from 1950, but that since 1976 they have decreased. At 1967 values the benefit level was $US28 per month in 1950. Between 1967 and 1976 it hovered a little above $US40. By 1984 it had fallen to around $US38 (Hanson, 1987, p. 178).

Women-headed families are very much over-represented in the residual programmes. This mirrors the 'feminisation of poverty' syndrome which the US shares with other countries, including Britain, Australia and rather more surprisingly Sweden (Gunnarrson, 1990). During the 1980s more than 80 per cent of families encompassed by the AFDC programme, over 60 per cent of families receiving food stamps or Medicaid and over 70 per cent of families in subsidised or public housing, are mother-headed

(Fraser, 1987, p. 91). This compares with, for example, unemployment insurance benefits, where women made up only 38 per cent of beneficiaries (Fraser, 1987, p. 94).

It is this area of public assistance which accounts for the US welfare state still being described as underdeveloped. This raises two questions. Why this bifurcation? Why are public assistance programmes so vulnerable? On the issues of underdevelopment, many writers have pointed to the attitude of 'unbounded confidence in the efficacy of individual effort' (Kaim-Caudle, 1973, p. 184). Wilensky argued that in the USA there are tax revolts at far lower levels than in Europe (Wilensky, 1979). Glazer (1986) makes a similar point. He claims that there is a quite fundamental lack of support for social policy, though he does concede that social security, in the form of social insurance, with its main emphasis on age pensions and support for the better-off (that is 'the deserving'), has received unconditional support from both major political parties. He suggests that this is not only due to the fact that the old are growing in number and therefore their support is politically essential, but also because 'pensions do not lead to antisocial behaviour in the aged'. He develops the thesis that the lack of support for social programmes is partly based on the fact that the USA has many and obvious social problems and, far from arguing that more state intervention will fix these, people are inclined to argue the reverse. Along with almost all the 'malestream' analysts, he fails to raise the issue emphasised by feminists that the clientele of public assistance is largely made up of women, and often women of colour, who are some of the least powerful in every society.

Only in two periods of US history has there been any general enthusiasm for social welfare programmes. At these times, in the 1930s and the 1960s, the response was triggered by an 'elite sense of political crisis', itself created by 'the protests of excluded groups' (Jenkins and Brents, 1989, p. 891). Piven and Cloward have pointed to the general docility of the poor in most countries, but particularly in the USA with its very strong rhetoric of individualism. Most of the time the poor 'are led to believe that their destitution is deserved and that the riches and power that others command are also deserved' (1977, p. 6). However they point to times when they have been 'able, if only briefly, to overcome the shame bred by a culture which blames them for their plight' (Piven and Cloward, 1977, p. 7). Such uprisings occur infrequently and only in extreme circumstances. On one of these occasions the New Deal was forged; on the second, 'War on Poverty' was declared.

During the thirties, spurred by the miseries of the great depression, the people's reaction to it, and the rise of Keynesian economic theory, President Roosevelt gained support for his New Deal project and social security was introduced. Beween 1932 and 1943, public assistance reached its highest level ever (Hanson, 1987, p. 171). In the second period, the early sixties, influenced by the 'civil rights revolution', the 'Great Society' project was created. War on Poverty (some say 'skirmish') was declared by President Kennedy, and subsequently pursued by President Johnson (Glazer, 1986) until protesters were mollified, and this unaccustomed interest in poverty was overtaken by the pressing issue of the shooting war in Vietnam.

It is largely the achievement of the New Deal period which has allowed commentators, such as Wilensky and Lebeaux (1965) and Galper (1975) to point to an acceptance of social policy as an integral part of the modern US capitalist state. However, the limits to this were made very clear in relation to the Great Society project. When results were not forthcoming within a very short time, about five years, anti-interventionists had a field day (Kristol, 1974). Much of the debate about what was hailed as the failure of government intervention must be seen as the beginning of the current phase of New Right discourse. There is, of course, historical continuity as well. The links with discourses about the Poor Laws and the supposed problems of dampening people's enthusiasm for employment were predictably in evidence. This debate has continued.

Glazer designates the two arms of welfare in the US, as Welfare I and Welfare II. While he sees Welfare I, the contributory social security programme and education, as 'almost sacrosanct', he sees Welfare II, which covers the residual programmes as 'in increasing disrepute' (1986, p. 42). In the aftermath of the Great Society project, Glazer suggests resistance to Welfare II programmes increased, not so much because the programmes did not deliver to the poor, but because they failed to affect positively the 'ambience of life of the great majority of Americans'. They had expected 'less juvenile delinquency, less crime, lower taxes, fewer slums and less illegitimacy' (1986, p. 42). Nor does Glazer hold out much hope of a change to the attitudes which lie behind this reluctance for state intervention. He attributes his pessimism to five features of US society, all of which promote diversity rather than the universalism that would be necessary to underpin an articulated welfare system. These five features are: the strength of the states in a federal system; the ethnic and religious diversity of the population; the complexities of a dual population of Black and white Americans; a strong ideology of individualism and a preference for having problems dealt with by non-state organisations (1986, pp. 50–62). It is noteworthy that he fails to raise the importance of traditional gender attitudes as a restricting factor.

Glazer believes that it is this combination of features, rather than their individual uniqueness, that accounts for the US situation. Certainly, cultural uniformity and the fact of having only one significant level of government have been posited as reasons for the success of the Swedish welfare state. In addition, however, the political success of a social democratic party was crucial. In the USA the lack of a strong labour movement within official politics must be seen as of key significance. Also, private interests have played a key role. The commercial insurance industry, which in all countries has been against government insurance schemes, was a source of resistance to the 1930s reforms (Kaim-Caudle, 1973, p. 184). It was only the scale of the calamity that was the Great Depression that overcame this resistance. The importance of commercial lobby groups has had an added significance in the US where the variety of services delivered on a profit basis has been greater than in Europe or Australia.

The downturn in support for expenditure on public assistance which started in 1970 (Coser and Howe, 1977) has continued, finding enthusiastic support in the rhetoric of President Reagan during the 1980s. However, because of the successful mobilisation of political support, reductions were not achieved to the social insurance programme, though Reagan was keen to do this. The resistance came not only from beneficiaries but also from non-government organisations that administer nationally-funded programmes and from federal and state employees. Predictably, the residual assistance for poor families was not so effectively defended. Benefits were not, however, reduced by the amount that Reagan would have liked. Congress intervened to reduce the size of the cuts and a few states reversed the effects through state legislation (Hanson, 1987, p. 187). Programmes also became generally more restrictive and punitive, with the intention of reducing the number on welfare. Workfare policies were adopted in many states. These in effect force recipients to work off the cash benefits they receive (Fraser, 1987, p. 96).

The trend in relation to residual welfare benefits supports the thesis of Piven and Cloward, based on a study of US history, that relief arrangements are only expanded in response to civil disorders. They observed that when stability is restored, welfare is cut back, partly by making it so punitive that people in need of assistance are discouraged from applying. The humiliation of those out of work has the effect of coercing the poorly-paid to stay in their jobs through ' the spectacle of degraded paupers'. The role of the discourse about the ineffectiveness of welfare state provisions also forms part of this 'work-maintaining function' (1971, p. 345).

O'Connor identifies two major strands of discourse which challenge New Deal and Great Society economic policies. The first he calls neo-liberal. This reacts against too much government intervention in the economy, asserting the primacy of capital accumulation and the need to promote 'individual incentives, savings and work discipline' (1984, p. 233). The second strand, which O'Connor labels neo-conservative, focuses on proper individual–state relations and the basis of social integration. Within this view the current crisis is judged a moral crisis caused by excessive government intervention in society. The remedy proposed is to depoliticize social issues by 'cutting back welfare, reviving familist, patriotic, and other older social motivations, and repersonalising dependency via charity'. Reagan recited both arguments and utilised the term deregulation as 'the code word for depoliticising the economy and society' (O'Connor, 1984, p. 234). (In its turn 'depoliticising' is here used as a code word for conservatising.)

Deregulation in the US involved a shift of power away from government bodies towards 'large-scale capital and the sun-belt accumulation centres, and to the patriarchal family and Church'. This shift of power away from national government bodies was particularly significant, as their policies often represented the outcome of earlier political struggles and in turn these policies promoted the 'development of economic and social movements'. The effects of earlier expansion of the national government showed, once again, that this is a process which can generally favour the interests of non-dominant groups. Predictably, conservative groups have tried to reverse this trend through calls for less welfare and for small government. Ironically, federal intervention has at times actually been encouraged by the New Right as a method of reversing earlier gains made by groups such as women, Black Americans and gays (O'Connor, 1984, pp. 234–6).

Contemporary neo-liberal and neo-conservative discourses have found fertile soil in the USA, with its strong history of individualism. The New Right has been particularly noisy in this country which probably remains the most ambivalent of all the modern capitalist states about collective welfare provisions. The lack of a strong socialist tradition has meant that earlier *laissez-faire* philosophies, which were well and truly tempered in most other capitalist societies, have been subject to less challenge from more collectivist positions. Non-government organisations, both for profit and not for profit, still operate in many areas (including child care and health) which in European countries, and even Australia, would be seen to be primarily the responsibility of government. Given the current political situation, it seems likely that this reliance on the market will continue. It is unlikely there will be much, if any, development of the US welfare state in the foreseeable future.

Japan – welfare state or welfare society?

Japan was an even later starter in the welfare state stakes than the USA, and still has to catch the rear of the field. Rose and Shiratori see these two laggards, despite their cultural differences, as sharing a number of characteristics. At the most general level, they are alike in commanding large-scale economies of great international 'displacement' capacity. Also they are 'alike in *not* accepting the premises of socialism or social democracy that are pervasive throughout European mixed-economy welfare states' (1986, p. 6). They suggest that a Japanese politician would be 'ideologically more at home in Texas than Sweden . . . and a Texas politician more at home in Kobe than in Copenhagen' (1986, p. 7). Even though it is debatable whether Japan can be said to be a welfare state at all, it must be acknowledged that on a number of indicators of general well-being, Japanese society compares very favourably. Life expectancy is among the highest in the world, infant mortality among the lowest, and levels of education and health are very high. In fact, on the United Nations Index of Human Development, Japan was the highest-ranking country (*The Economist*, 26 May 1990, p. 81).

Japan had no comprehensive social security provisions until the 1960s. Therefore family and occupational welfare have been relied on more heavily than in other countries. The history of pensions and health insurance for public servants and some other elite employees does, however, date back to the period prior to the Second World War (Watanuki, 1986, p. 259). As is the case with occupational welfare everywhere, this favoured men, rather than women and men in high-status jobs most of all (Rose and Shiratori, 1986, p. 6). Prior to the development of this occupational welfare, any social policies that were enacted in Japan were aimed at producing and reproducing 'a sufficient quantity and quality of labour force' and at producing and reproducing 'the health and physical strength of a military force' (Maruo, 1986, p. 65). This is a theme reminiscent of the early history of the British welfare state. The links with economic development are very clear in relation to education, which became a priority after 1868 when a policy of economic modernisation was adopted (Thane, 1982, pp. 103–4).

By the early 1970s the basics of a national social security system were in place. A children's allowance scheme was introduced in 1971, though it applies only from the third child and is means-tested. Free medical care for the aged was instituted in 1972 and the coverage of the age pension system was extended in 1973. A total of eight different pension schemes, all related to occupation, cover the population. In all but one of the schemes, the treatment of a spouse (the wife) is as a dependant. Only in the People's Pension scheme, which covers self-employed people, is a wife treated as an independent contributor (Noguchi, 1986, p. 175). Coverage also remains unequal because of 'the dualistic structure of the public and private sectors, and the separation of big business, small business and the self-employed' (Maruo, 1986, p. 68). The cost of these provisions has taken social security payments as a ratio of national income from 5 per cent in 1960 to 14.5 per cent in 1983 (Watanuki, 1986, p. 262). Despite the significant increase, this still does not match the level of northern European countries in 1955.

A high standard of living, dependent on the economic wage, is still predominantly looked to by the Japanese government as the key to the nation's well-being. The social wage is of far less concern. The extent of welfare provided through the family system has frequently also been used to justify low spending on social welfare. The caring family is still claimed as part of the welfare apparatus by some commentators (Maruo, 1986). This tends to be done without due (or any) recognition of the fact that it is women and not men who provide most of the caring labour.

If we trace the official discourse about the welfare state over recent years, a familiar pattern of waning enthusiasm emerges. In official policy statements there was a brief period, from the sixties to the early seventies, when politicians talked quite straight-forwardly about developing social security, with an eye to achieving a Japanese welfare state (Watanuki, 1986). This was during a phase when economic growth was high. The next phase in the discourse is evident after the oil crisis of 1973, when economic growth fell to a lower level. At this stage the phrase 'Japanese-type of welfare society' became popular. This was identified as involving 'the minimum security by the government plus the spirit of self-help' (Watanuki, 1986, p. 264), policy parameters similar to those of economic liberals the world over.

The role of the family and the development of community have also been stressed, two familiar themes of conservative welfare discourses. Watanuki points out that it is nowhere made clear how community and neighbourhood effort could be kindled when they have never been features of urban life in Japan (1986, p. 266). With family and community support being evoked as cheap options for the provision of care, it became clear that the epithet 'welfare society' was a code flagging that government spending for social security was unlikely to reach the level implied by the term welfare state. Greater emphasis was also placed on private companies' role in securing this welfare society. In a ruling Liberal Democratic Party document released in 1979, this concept was expanded beyond the provision by private companies of traditional forms of occupational welfare. It was envisaged that the firms would also play a role in providing a range of 'kinds of security as commodities, starting with life insurance and various kinds of personal social services' (Watanuki, 1986, p. 265).

Policymakers in Japan have recently been confronted with a problem which other countries faced much earlier: the ageing of the population. Care of the elderly has remained almost entirely a family matter in Japan, though this is changing as more women join the labour force. Still, only 9.3 per cent of aged people were living alone in 1985 (Watanuki, 1986, p. 264), compared with 41 per cent for both the United States and the United Kingdom and 30 per cent for France in 1981 (Maruo, 1986, p. 68). Reciprocally, the proportion of old people living with their children is much higher, though it is dropping. The figure has fallen from 87.3 per cent in 1950 to 64.6 per cent in 1985. The change has occurred at the rate of about 1 per cent per year, a rate that has alarmed those concerned with social welfare. Nonetheless, families in Japan still clearly dispense more 'welfare' than families in European countries, the United States or Australia (Maruo, 1986; Watanuki, 1986; Noguchi, 1986).

As is typical of so many countries, there is relatively little acknowledgement of the role women play in caring, though there is some recognition of the associated stress. Watanuki (1986, p. 266) points to high suicide rates among carers and exhausted daughters, both natural and in-law, suggesting reliance on British-style community care as the only feasible alternative for providing relief for family members. The cost of Swedish-style services would be 'astronomical'. Maruo estimated that were the Japanese government to provide social services for the aged at the rate they are available in Sweden then the number of home-helpers would need to be increased by about fifty times and the number of homes for the aged by twenty to thirty times (Maruo, 1986, p. 70).

The Japanese welfare state, if indeed that title is appropriate, has been arrested in an embryonic form by neo-conservative economic policies which favour restricting government expenditure and reliance on private, including family, measures. Significant state development seems unlikely in the foreseeable future. This also means that welfare servicing will remain highly patriarchal, as the family is once again emphasised as a site for the provision of care, particularly for the elderly, at cheap rates or no cost to government. The occupational system rather than government is also being looked to, another development that is likely to magnify the disadvantages of women and male workers in less-favoured industries. However, an emerging factor in Japanese politics is an increasing women's voice. This will have to be reckoned with in the future, which may mean that projections based on past trends will prove inaccurate.

The Nordic countries – model welfare states

Since the 1960s, the Scandinavian countries have had a world reputation for their 'model' welfare states. Pilgrimages are made by political activists, policymakers and social scientists to learn from their experiences (Sweden, Norway and Denmark were among the countries visited during the research for this book). Many social policies are versions of Scandinavian programmes, though inevitably adapted to the social circumstances of the country in which they are implemented. In their turn, the Scandinavian countries have been influenced by others but in particular by developments in Britain. The work of Titmuss has been particularly influential.

Until after the Second World War, trends in social policy in the Nordic countries were not exceptional. Since then, a comprehensive and generous system has developed. The strength of the Nordic welfare state lies in the combination of programmes and entitlements rather than in particular features. There are, of course, differences between the Scandinavian countries; where these differences are of particular interest I will comment on them. However, to make the discussion manageable, Sweden will be the main focus.

The early history of welfare in the Scandinavian countries has key elements in common with Britain and other European countries. Sweden has a history of Poor Laws, which during the nineteenth century were enacted, and later amended to have a tougher effect on the 'undeserving' poor (Esping-Andersen and Korpi, 1987, p. 43). As we have seen, the notion of deservingness, with its negative consequences for those to whom it is directed, still plays a part, though a small part, in Swedish society. In looking to features that might explain the more distinctive features of the Swedish state, Allardt locates the origin of today's provisions historically in Sweden's lack of rigid social divisions. The peasantry were not excluded from political activity. In fact they formed one of the four estates of the constituency of parliament, as this form of constitutional government gradually evolved during the sixteenth and seventeenth centuries. Peasants also shared defence, with a 'universal' (male) system of conscription created at the end of the seventeenth century (Allardt, 1986, p. 110).

When agricultural reform occurred during the eighteenth and nineteenth centuries, it was directly mediated by the state. Privatisation occurred, as it did in Britain, but the transfer of land-ownership was to peasant proprietorship. While this created distinctions between the landed and landless populations, it left the people with a positive attitude to government. As Allardt puts it

> The land reforms established a positive tie between the rural population and the state at the time preceding industrialisation and the great migration to the cities . . . the state in the Scandinavian countries has not traditionally been conceived as an oppressive monolith, as in many continental countries (Allardt, 1986, p. 110).

When this history is compared with the brutality of the enclosure movement in England and the intervention of the state, on behalf of large landowners, to evict peasant farmers from the land (Thompson, 1968, chapter 7), it highlights the basis of the positive image that the Swedish state has carried as 'benefactor of the common people'. The strength of the land-holding peasantry has also had a political effect that has proved important in Swedish politics. It has been a moderate force and has counterbalanced the political right and prevented it from developing into a strong political force (Allardt, 1986, p. 110). In Castles' view it was this absence of strongly organised opposition from the right, together with a strong labour movement, that allowed the development of the Swedish welfare state (Castles, 1985). This relative political homogeneity is in keeping with a high level of homogeneity of religious, ethnic and racial background. This is in contrast to the situation in, for example Britain, the USA, Canada and Australia. But Swedish homogeneity should not be overstated. The Sami people and guest immigrants are two groups recognised as suffering disadvantages, in much the same manner as do equivalent groups in other countries.

This positive attitude to the state contrasts with, for example, the USA and Britain. That suspicion of government has not been an important element of Swedish society is intriguingly shown by official data-collection traditions in Sweden. These have been well-developed from a very early stage. Sweden and Finland have been collecting statistical records of their populations longer than any other country. Until recently the government collected and published extensive records on individual citizens, without obvious signs of protest (Allardt, 1986, p. 111).

Sweden introduced factory inspection in 1889, subsidised voluntary sickness benefit societies in 1891 and made employers liable for compensating workers for industrial accidents in 1901. A concern about labour market policies became evident early in the century. In 1908 the government provided subsidies to municipal employment offices. Sweden did not have a phase of non-contributory age pensions, but in 1913 universal and compulsory old-age and invalidity insurance was established, followed in 1916 by compulsory occupational injury insurance. In 1914, the foundation of a non-contributory social assistance scheme was laid when a State Board was established to administer relief work and cash support for the unemployed (Olsson, 1989, p. 268).

Although there were these early social welfare provisions, the modern Swedish welfare state, as with the British and Australian, is really a post-Second World War construction. In 1946 a universal pension for citizens at 67, with no eligibility requirements, was established. Other Scandinavian countries followed in the 1950s. In Sweden in 1959, after a strongly-fought battle of principles, an earnings-related contributory scheme (ATP) was introduced. While this cut across the principle of equality, the Social Democrats believed that this scheme was necessary to head-off the propensity of people on higher incomes to take out private insurance. These private schemes, *inter alia*, allowed the private funds to accumulate massive capital sums, which in turn made them a force which the government needed to reckon with (Allardt, 1986, p. 112).

The ATP scheme clearly did exacerbate income inequality and there is an observable distinction between this scheme and the residual and selective provisions which meet the need of those not covered by the ATP scheme. A study carried out in the late 1980s, of people receiving social assistance, which accounts for about 6 per cent of those in receipt of some form of welfare state support, showed that recipients did feel stigmatised. Relief was expressed by some respondents when they were able to transfer to a pension to which they felt entitled. Further, they appreciated that their pension cheque came regularly through the mail and they no longer had their finances 'scrutinised' each month by welfare workers (Gunnarsson, 1990, p. 12).

Added to this, the middle classes, as elsewhere, make more use of available services, such as health and education. However, the Social Democrats opted for less concern about issues of redistribution in the short run, giving more weight to the principles of universality and solidarity. The Swedes have largely left the issue of redistribution to the progressive taxation system and collective bargaining (Allardt, 1986, p. 113; Esping-Andersen and Korpi, 1987, p. 70). However, the effects of taxation 'do not fulfil redistributional ambitions' (Calmförs *et al.*, 1986, p. 28). Though there is an institutional welfare state which provides far better for the requirements of individuals than in most countries, Sweden's tax system, as is the case for virtually all other countries, favours the better-off. The 'well informed and financially strong individuals and firms' are able to 'lower their taxes through tax avoidance and tax evasion' (Calmförs *et al.*, 1986, p. 25). Also, under the influence of economic liberalism, the system seems destined to be made less progressive in the 1990s (Vandenberg, 1990, p. 34).

In ideological terms the Swedish welfare state, as with all the Nordic states, represents the outcome of a series of political compromises made by Social Democrats. Longue suggests that 'a sense of optimism about historical development' and a sense of political inevitability, allowed them, throughout, to preserve a belief in socialism as the final goal (Longue, 1987, p. 132). Importantly, though, even the compromises have largely been made possible, as with most other welfare states, by economic growth. This has allowed governments to appropriate some of the growth for redistribution through the public sector. The better-off have not been required to bear the burden. 'As the poor got richer, so did the rich' (Longue, 1987, p. 136).

With the exception of Norway, nationally-owned industry has played little part in social policy in the Nordic countries. Sweden, though, has pursued a weaker policy, which is referred to as 'socialisation'. This has been a consistent theme of Social Democratic politics. Socialisation stops short of collective ownership. It implies 'a more diffuse process of societal control and allows a wider range of forms of ownership' (Tilton, 1987, p. 143). It is a policy which represents a compromise that avoids directly challenging private ownership. The first real challenge in Sweden to private ownership can be seen to be the widely-known Meidner Plan put forward in the mid-1970s (Tilton, 1987, p. 151). This plan proposed the gradual transfer of ownership and power over enterprises to local unions and to the national union federation, LO. It was not a process of nationalisation or state control. Its original aim, over time to transfer majority ownership of enterprises to workers, caused so much political dissension that it was watered down. The limits to consensus became evident. Now the Plan merely represents a series of regional public pension funds dealing in stocks and investments. 'The funds promote public capital formation but do not seriously challenge private ownership of the means of production' (Tilton, 1987, p. 164).

The limits of Swedish consensus became very clear in 1982 in relation to this issue of worker-participation in capital accumulation. When the severely watered-down Act, which was subsequently passed, was before parliament, one of the largest protests Stockholm had ever seen was staged. About 100 000 people marched through the streets of Stockholm to express their disapproval of this policy. This was not the usual march of leftist protesters that has become so familiar the world over, however. The gathering consisted of leaders of the largest national industries, small business owners, some white-collar workers and even school children from 'fashionable suburbia'. It has been observed that they probably 'represented a collective manifestation of the propertied class unequalled in any country' (von Otter, 1985, p. 1). Nonetheless, similar *angst* has been evident in many countries which have attempted to collectivise ownership, as this is clearly recognised as heralding changes in the nature of power and control. Denmark, West Germany and Holland are among the nations in which discussions of proposals to establish collective ownership have also foundered in recent years (von Otter, 1985, p. 16).

Labour market policies have been a particularly celebrated aspect of the Swedish welfare state. Full employment has been the goal, and corporatist arrangements have been explicitly concerned with the economic productivity of public spending. Much attention is devoted to fitting people into the labour force, a concern of all the Nordic states. In Norway the importance of this commitment was symbolically demonstrated when, in 1954, the constitution was amended to include the following commitment:

it shall be the duty of the state authorities to create conditions which ensure that every able-bodied person can earn a living by his labour (Esping-Andersen and Korpi, 1987, p. 58).

Esping-Andersen and Korpi identify three features as distinctive of the Scandinavian welfare state model. The first is that social policy is comprehensive, both in covering a broad range of 'social needs' and in providing an integrated system of 'social protection'. Second, entitlements are constituted as a democratic right to an 'adequate level of living' and are highly institutionalised. The third distinctive feature is the 'solidaristic and universalist nature of social legislation' (1987, p. 42). Provisions still do, however, more effectively support those who are better-off than those who are not so well-placed, most obviously through income-related benefits. Disadvantages fall particularly on migrant workers (Knocke, 1988), the Sami people and women. Though women's material circumstances are probably closer to equal than in other advanced capitalist societies, they remain at a disadvantage. This is evident in terms of material equality but most evident in relation to issues of power (Hernes, 1987b), as will be discussed in detail in subsequent chapters.

The Swedish welfare system is made up of two parts. First there is a national social insurance scheme, the contributions to which are entirely paid by employers. In 1988 these payments were at the rate of 34.5 per cent of an employer's wages costs (Swedish National Board of Health and Welfare, 1988, p. 15). Central government revenue, raised through a range of taxes, supports other provisions, with, all told, one quarter of its budget spent on social welfare. This is supplemented by funds from municipal and county councils. This money provides an extensive and intricate range of social services, for example school meals, pre-school child care and care for the elderly, to name only three areas. Social insurance covers a wide range of benefits and services, including: health, dental, occupational injuries and pregnancy services; parental leave, children's allowances and family supplement; pensions and benefits in respect of unemployment, retirement, disability and for survivors. All social benefits are available to all residents, whether or not they are Swedish citizens.

Despite the strength of its social democratic traditions, Sweden has experienced the worldwide swing to the right. This involved an increase in the inequalities that the architects of the Scandinavian 'model' had been wrestling with. Issues of privatisation, cuts to government spending, and the promotion of decentralisation (with a potential to fragment collective provisions) entered the political agenda in the mid-seventies (Olsson, 1988). The political tensions over welfare provisions were clear enough in Sweden, though generally weaker than in the more reluctant welfare states. The change of political climate was dramatically embodied in the failure in 1976 of the Social Democratic Labour Party to be re-elected to government for the first time since 1932. The centre–right coalition parties governed for six years but in 1982 the Social Democratic Labour party was once again returned to office. The traditional conflicts of capitalism remained apparent though, and the Employers Confederation conducted a 'major ideological onslaught on the principles behind the welfare state', from outside parliament. Economic policies, clearly recognisable as inspired by economic liberalism and which weaken the welfare state, were pursued (Olsson, 1988, p. 71).

Some privatisation occurred. This was most noticeable in housing a susceptible area as the Thatcher Government's policies in Britain demonstrated. In Denmark there were also moves towards privatisation of pensions. However, in none of the Nordic countries is there a move towards private health or private education. This can be partly explained in terms of the effort that has been expended in ensuring that services are of high quality. Esping-Andersen and Korpi (1987) indicate that it is clearly recognised that support for state provisions by the better-off is dependent on high standards of service. If hospitals and schools are not of high quality, those who can afford to do so would turn to private alternatives.

While privatisation of housing occurred over recent decades in each of the Scandinavian countries, its pursuit was uneven. In the postwar period, policies were similar, with the exception of Finland, where housing remained a marginal government activity. In the other countries, low-interest loans stimulated housing construction, and the goal was to achieve maximum volume. This was in fact achieved and Esping-Andersen and Korpi judge that in Sweden, Norway and Denmark, housing policy moved from 'residualism to institutional overnight' (1987, p. 64). However, at the end of the 1950s Denmark changed direction. Since then housing production, including financing, has been largely market-dominated, with 82 per cent of construction totally private by the end of the 1970s. Tax deductions were provided in respect of interest payments. The rate was at first generous but was later reduced. To at least partly balance the advantage this provided to the better off, rent assistance to pensioners on an income-tested basis was established, and this was gradually increased. However, the 'negative distributional effect' remained (Esping-Andersen and Korpi, 1987, pp. 66–7).

In Sweden during the decade from the mid-1950s, an ambitious promise to construct a million dwellings in a decade was achieved. However, after this impressive collective achievement, Sweden too moved in the direction of Denmark, though much later, from the mid-1970s. Generous tax deductions favoured private home-ownership, especially because marginal tax rates were high and inflation could be hedged through the value of the home. Home-owner tax deduction rose from 12 per cent of expenditure on public housing in 1965 to 77 per cent in 1975, though this was still only about half the proportion in Denmark (159 per cent). Norway's housing policy was the most successful in terms of average cost per household, and distributionally the most egalitarian. Very little public expenditure has ever supported tax deductions for home-owners. Only 11 per cent of expenditure on housing took this form in 1975 (Esping-Andersen and Korpi, 1987, p. 67).

The Swedish model of the welfare state has been based on notions of solidarity, of locking all into support for the system. To achieve this locking-in of the better-off has meant a system that is not immediately redistributive. The reasoning behind this approach is the avoidance of a middle-class backlash or tax revolt, such as was experienced in Denmark in the seventies. There, more taxation revenue has been raised from wages and salaries than in Sweden and Norway.

In Sweden there was a marked trend to increase the contributions that employers made, through pay-roll tax, to social spending. The level was increased from 3 per cent in 1954 to 48 per cent in 1981. Contributions by employees, on the other hand were reduced from 10 per cent to 1 per cent (Allardt, 1986, p. 118). This apparently had political advantages as 'pay-roll taxes are nearly invisible' and employers form a small voting block. Ultimately, too, such costs are handed on (Einhorn, 1987, p. 216). It is doubtful whether employers would be so politically tractable in other countries. The history of the USA is certainly one in which business lobby groups have played a key and noisy role. Pay-roll tax has been politically unpopular in Australia too, where it has been commonly claimed by employers that it reduces employment opportunities.

Despite a flexible and compromising approach, tensions about government spending in Sweden increased. In an analysis made in 1988, Olsson came to the conclusion that while privatisation had been much discussed, and while there were embryonic signs of privatisation in areas of retirement pensions, day care for children and medical insurance, these did not threaten the basic collective structure. Olsson was less sanguine about moves towards decentralisation. These, he predicted, would provide local bodies with greater flexibility which, under economic pressures, might lead to significant dilution of current provisions. Once again, as was suggested by Fraser (1987) for the US, the principle seems to emerge that larger administrative units, and particularly a sympathetic government at the national level, are most likely to promote the interests of less-powerful groups. Improvements to Sweden's economic state were achieved through concentrating on business profitability, encouraging higher rates of employment and reducing government spending, though not in the area of income security. Nonetheless the Swedish welfare state has clearly been tossed by 'thunderstorms which do not stop at national borders' (Olsson, 1988, p. 89), as well as being subject to internal conflicts.

As the 1989/90 Swedish Budget Papers put it, the intention from 1982 was 'that Sweden should work and save its way out of the crisis'. A 'third way policy' was initiated which emphasised 'greater competitiveness and the curbing of government spending' (Ministry of Finance, 1989, p. 7). The pattern is a familiar one in OECD countries. Over the decade of the 1980s, with inflation the major concern, the currency was devalued, regulation of capital flows in and out of Sweden liberalised and government spending curbed. Tight budget controls meant that by the 1989/1990 budget it was in balance, for the first time since 1962 (Ministry of Finance, 1989, p. 28). By 1988 the unemployment rate had been reduced to 1.6 per cent and the level of economic activity was considered 'good' (Ministry of Finance, 1989, p. 16).

By the beginning of 1990, more drastic economic measures were being proposed in what is well-recognisable internationally as a tussle between economic liberalism and social democracy. The Swedish Treasurer, in a proposal intended to 'cool down an over-heated economy' pushed forward with a package which included 'freezes on increases in prices, rents, share dividends payments and wages, plus a ban on strikes' and a radical change in the country's generous sick-leave policy (Vandenberg, 1990, p. 33). The government fell over the proposals, but returned after 22 days of 'high political drama', minus the Finance Minister who, in the interim, retired. He was replaced by a treasurer who, it was believed, would be seen as more concerned with 'traditional social democratic eoc-nomic policies' (Vandenberg, 1990, p. 34). While the Swedish welfare state has undoubtedly been under less pressure than has been the case for most OECD countries, it has not escaped inter-national trends to restructure capital. The game of compromise and the maintenance of the flexibility of the Swedish welfare state will no doubt continue.

Conclusion

This discussion of the disparate histories of social welfare in Brit-ain, Australia, the USA, Japan and Sweden, demonstrates some-thing of the complexities and variety of national policies and poli-tics. It shows us a range of social forces that are relevant to the development of the welfare state. The picture is necessarily very partial to this point. The following three chapters add other dimen-sions of government interventions, including occupational and fiscal welfare, and gender dimensions.

However, some of the common threads that have emerged to date are worth contemplation. The first, very obvious, one is the manner in which, despite the success of the welfare state in provid-ing support for those who are unable to support themselves, it is those who have traditionally held power who are best positioned to maintain their advantage. This may not always hold in the short term but does seem to be so in the longer term.

Another general principle is that colonised racial groups and women the world over, remain low in the hierarchy of power and wealth, despite programmes which may have improved their condition. While important gains are made, these are usually partial and remain contested. It is clear that government intervention is necessary to create any shift of power and/or resources to the less-powerful. Yet an inescapable conclusion to be drawn from this survey is a residual commitment to *laissez-faire*, individualist economic doctrines. While the strength of such philosophical commitment varies considerably, there is in the ascendancy a determination to prune government spending and this counters moves towards greater equality. Economic liberalism seems everywhere destined to exacerbate inequalities.

4 The Distribution of State Welfare

This chapter continues the process of challenging myths about the welfare state and broadening our approach to conceptualising issues relating to welfare and equality. As has already been discussed, inequality is partially sustained by the manner in which popular discourses about welfare concentrate only, or mainly, on the poor and only, or mainly, on social welfare. In the previous chapter I have built up a picture of the characteristics of social welfare in a number of Western capitalist countries. The relevant literature on this topic is vast. We even have a discipline, social administration, that was developed expressly to study social welfare. When we come to consider inequality and the distribution of a much wider range of state interventions, however, there is relative silence. In particular, there is a dearth of research about the wealthy (Spånt, 1979/80). No country that I investigated, including Sweden, with its well-developed culture of research and planning, collects and maintains comprehensive wealth statistics. The tendency has certainly been to study down, rather than to study up: that is, to study the powerful rather than the powerless.

Titmuss's conception of fiscal and occupational welfare opened up a limited discourse, and some research has been undertaken within this framework. But such studies are few and they are far from comprehensive. They usually concentrate on benefits at middle or lower income levels, rather than the highest. Also, despite the potential of these concepts, both fiscal and occupational welfare tend to be defined narrowly. Thus the statistical information base from which this chapter must draw is limited. A broad qualitative picture of who benefits and how much, when all state interventions (and potential interventions) are accounted for, is just not available. Therefore it is not possible to provide the detailed overview that it is possible to provide in respect of social welfare. Rather, this chapter can only attempt to highlight the importance of these other forms of state activity and indicate something of their influence on equality and inequality. Examples are chosen for their illustrative effect; they clearly do not constitute an exhaustive picture.

When we look at the distribution of all state benevolence, it becomes clear that an ideology of *inequality* is integral to the contemporary welfare state. As Le Grand has observed, inequality is implicitly accepted even by those writers such as Tawney, Crosland, Titmuss and Marshall whose names are so regularly associated with attempts to promote equality (1982, p. 151). This is because, not only did they fail to challenge the capitalist basis of the economic system, but they also largely ignored other entrenched power relations, such as those based on sex and race. The identification of this acceptance of an ideology of inequality helps account for the manner in which the relative advantage of those who are better-off is maintained. We have the paradox that the better-off continue, virtually unchallenged, to benefit more than the poor from state-mediated interventions at the same time as the welfare state is hailed as a mechanism for promoting social justice.

There has been one reasonably consistent strand of research which does comment on the relative advantages of the better-off. This is research which asks the question: 'Who actually does benefit from social welfare provisions?' A recurrent rediscovery that major benefits accrue to the better-off seems, however, to be routinely and repeatedly greeted with surprise. The message does not, in any consistent manner, make its way into either the conventional wisdom or even the knowledge-base of experts in the welfare field. The information is at times, however, used as the basis for criticism of the welfare state for the purposes of advocating cuts to the social wage. If it can be claimed that it is mostly the middle classes that benefit, then cuts can be justified as merely reducing benefits to the better-off. This in turn means that the ideology that the welfare state aims to benefit the poor can be maintained in the teeth of cutbacks. This was well illustrated in Australia in 1987 when the universal child payment became means-tested and no longer available to those with a family income above $A50 000. The Labor government pointed out that this was a high family income, average individual annual earnings being around $A20 000 at the time. Therefore the more affluent families were seen not to need the money. More fundamental issues of to whom the savings would be directed and the problems raised by infusing a universal benefit with a residual element were hardly even rehearsed at the time.

If we have information about who *really* does benefit from the range of state activities, this should go some way to exposing the ideology of inequality, because that ideology is partially maintained by misinformation, in the form of a belief that the better-off pay for welfare through their taxes but reap little benefit. Some of this misinformation is quantitative and concerns how social welfare resources are actually divided. A significant part, however, relates to ways of conceptualising and the tendency to keep separate, discourses relating to richer members of society from those relating to poorer. Prest and Barr, experts in the area of public finance, suggest that when it comes to a consideration of effects of the distribution of benefits by the state, there is no valid basis for making a distinction between an old age pension and disbursements to farmers (1985, p. 15). Yet such a distinction persists in public conceptions and in scholarly discourses. Conventionally, discourses about welfare and discourses about 'economics' are kept separate. The division means that people can, with equanimity, see the welfare state as having created a fair and equal society, by merely leaving out of the discussion the issue of disbursements to the better-off, including to such groups as farmers. Even more significantly, they can see groups such as farmers as hard done-by in relation to, and in effect as paying for, those in receipt of 'social welfare'.

This chapter aims to challenge the division between welfare and economic discourses. This is done first by considering the quantitative issue, that is, who actually does benefit from traditional welfare provisions. The second part of the chapter will be devoted to widening the conceptual frame by considering non-traditional forms of welfare, mainly occupational and fiscal. An attempt will also be made to extend the analysis even further to other, less well-recognised, but real and important benefits mediated by the state. At this stage there is no well-developed discourse about many of the benefits that the state mediates and they are therefore difficult to categorise and even more difficult to measure. Nonetheless it is imperative that an appropriate discourse on the real distributional role of the state is developed if the conceptual misinformation which forms the very fabric of the ideology of inequality is to be exposed.

I. Who benefits from social welfare?

Social security

When we consider who benefits from social welfare we find, not surprisingly, that the form that is most redistributive is the direct transfer of income. This holds true regardless of a nation's degree of commitment to the welfare state. This has been demonstrated, for example, for Britain (Heidenheimer *et al.*, 1990, p. 249), the Nordic states (Persson, 1986), Australia (ABS, 1987; Harding, 1984), Japan (Watanuki, 1986), the USA (Hanson, 1987), Belgium and the Netherlands (Deleeck, 1985). The general picture is that income from social security is the most important form of assistance for redistributing income towards the bottom levels of the income ladder. It is abundantly clear that the poor would be very much worse off without these provisions. However, the critical question is, how much do the poor get in comparison with others?

Flat-rate pensions redistribute more towards those on lower incomes than do benefits related to previous income. Indeed, of Swedish age pensions, Stahlberg has pointed out that 'the progressivity of the national basic pension system is cancelled out by the regressivity of the national supplementary pension system', which is earnings-related. Some other Swedish pensions do redistribute. In the case of the disability pension, for example, redistribution is claimed to be from white- to blue-collar workers because blue-collar workers are more likely to sustain injuries (1988, p. 28). It does, however, seem questionable whether the redistribution is actually sufficient to compensate for the suffering incurred. In the US regressivity also occurs as a result of the dual system of income security. Those in receipt of benefits via social insurance do vastly better than those receiving other forms of income transfers. The latter are poorer to start with, yet in 1985, those in receipt of the Old Age, Survivors, Disability and Health Insurance (OASDHI) had levels of benefits at about four times the level received via Aid to Families with Dependent Children (AFDC) (Hanson, 1987, p.

178). This difference involves gender and race dimensions, as those in the AFDC programme are predominantly woman-headed families and Black mothers are over-represented. Even so, the level of income of these families is substantially increased by the transfers. They would certainly be worse off without social welfare provision.

Because Australia has flat-rate pensions and stringent means-testing, there is a significant amount of redistribution through social security transfers. The bottom fifth of income-earners receive just under five times the amount received by the top fifth (ABS, 1987, p. 22). However, as is the case for virtually all comparable research, these figures overstate the general advantage to low income earners because they do not show the whole picture. They ignore government contribution to the retirement of the non-poor, through tax relief on contributions to private occupational insurance schemes. Also they ignore the fact that, when assessing the distributional effect of state interventions, a range of what are normally considered 'economic' measures should also be taken into account. These measures are addressed later in the chapter.

Health and other services

When we come to consider who benefits from other social welfare services, the lack of vertical redistribution is immediately obvious. In 1958 the British sociologist, Abel-Smith published an article addressing the question 'Whose Welfare State?', and came to the conclusion that the middle classes were the major beneficiaries. Summarising findings of numerous European research projects in the mid-1980s, Deleeck likewise concluded that the social services imply horizontal redistribution but not a real change in the vertical income structure (Deleeck, 1985, p. 51).

After analysing data relating to transport, health care, housing and education Le Grand came to the conclusion that 'almost all public expenditure on the social services in Britain benefits the better off to a greater extent than the poor' (1982, p. 3). His study drew on data from the seventies, but work in the eighties has confirmed the pattern. Indeed under the Thatcher Government the trend was exacerbated (Le Grand and Winter, 1987; Papadakis and Taylor-Gooby, 1987). Some of the results of an earlier study 'astonished' Le Grand. For example, despite the popular wisdom that the wealthy use private means of transport, it was found that, in 1978, the richest fifth of the population undertook ten times more rail travel than the poorest fifth. Bus services were much more equally used. Here usage was in fact least among the top fifth of income earners. Any advantage the lower socio-economic groups gained from bus travel was more than counter-balanced by the effects on equity of expenditure on roads because car-owner-ship is heavily skewed towards higher income earners. Higher income earners are also likely to have their car usage subsidised by their employers, or by the taxation system in the case of the self-employed, and thus receive occupational or fiscal transport benefits as well (Le Grand, 1982, pp. 108–15).

Benefits from health and related services, too, are unevenly spread. The Black Report, published in 1980, demonstrated that inequalities in British health care, which have been regularly docu-mented, had not diminished. This conclusion was confirmed by a study of health status in the north of England by Townsend, Phillimore and Beattie (1988). Conclusions that Deleeck came to for Belgium and the Netherlands apply to virtually all countries for which data are available. What he found was that, on average, persons with high incomes, higher schooling level and higher professional status, 'consume (not so much) more in quantitative terms, but they also (and especially) consume qualitatively better care' and at the same time demonstrate lower mortality and mor-bidity levels (Deleeck, 1985, p. 48). For a very wide variety of other social services which, for Belgium, include public play-grounds, vacation colonies and youth hostels; public libraries, public record libraries; sports amenities and swimming pools; museums, theatres, concerts, ballets, opera, cultural performances and art exhibitions, the evidence shows a distribution of benefits similar to that for health services. Usage increases with occupa-tional status, income and years of schooling and when the costs of usage is imputed, the higher socio-economic groups benefit most (Deleeck, 1985, p. 49).

Housing

Public expenditure on housing, like income security, has often been seen as providing direct benefits to lower income groups. This is usually through rent subsidies or the direct government provision of rental accommodation at cheaper than market prices. In Australia, for example, government funds directly devoted to public housing do advantage the poorest since access to public housing, like pensions, is stringently means-tested. The largest proportion of public revenue devoted directly to housing is actually spent on public housing and rental assistance, rather than assistance for private purchase (ABS, 1987, p. 55; Harding, 1984, p. 76), largely because there is no tax relief in respect of mortgage payments. However, if we look to indirect spending, we find that it is home-owners who are significantly advantaged because the family home is privileged by being exempt from capital gains tax. Not only this; if the capital were to be invested elsewhere, the income accruing would be taxable. Yet the taxation system ignores imputed rent; this is not treated as income from capital for taxation purposes. Estimates are not even available of what this privileging of capital invested in family homes costs the government in forgone revenue, let alone any detailed statistics on how the benefits from this policy are distributed. Nonetheless, very clearly the benefits increase with the value of the home that is owned. Also, there is a home-buyer's grant available in respect of a person's first home purchase. This tends to be less regressive than the absence of a capital gains tax, but the poorest are excluded because of an inability to raise the requisite bank loan and for want of an initial lump sum in savings, both of which are required for eligibility. It quickly becomes apparent that were the full picture to be taken into account in Australia, it would transpire that it is not the poor who benefit most from government housing policy, and the situation in Australia is similar in many respects to other countries (Kemeny, 1983, p. 106).

In Britain, as in Australia, the USA and many OECD countries, direct government expenditure on public housing does benefit directly those on low incomes, as does rental assistance. However, there remain the fiscal benefits of tax relief in respect of mortgage payments (Le Grand, 1987, p. 102) and a failure to tax capital gains from housing sales. In an attempt to upgrade housing stock, grants have also been made available for the renovation of older homes. The main recipients of these grants have been young households with above-average incomes (Papadakis and Taylor-Gooby, 1987, p. 149). When the total picture is considered, therefore, we find 'owner-occupiers receiving more than private or public tenants and the better off receiving more than the less well off' (Le Grand, 1982, p. 100).

The considerable tax advantages made available to home owners tend to reverse the principle of progressivity, though this is more ambiguous in the case of the sale of council houses to their tenants by the Thatcher Government. As tenants, these purchasers were receiving some government subsidy already. Nonetheless, the principle that the relatively better-off gain most applies here as well. It was largely skilled workers who took up the offer to purchase their houses at discounted prices (Papadakis and Taylor-Gooby, 1987, p. 161). The effect of this initiative showed up in the significant increase in owner-occupation in Britain which rose from 55 per cent in 1979 to 64 per cent in 1986 (Papadakis and Taylor-Gooby, 1987, p. 152).

As was discussed in Chapter 2, in the Nordic countries too, housing policy does not necessarily act as an equaliser, though there is considerable variation. Denmark's housing policy over-whelmingly favours private buyers and for Sweden too this is the case, though the benefits are somewhat less. The Norwegian poli-cies have however, proved the most egalitarian and probably are unmatched in this respect in any other OECD country (Esping-Anderson and Korpi, 1987, pp. 67–9).

Education

Another virtually universal finding is that education is the public provision whose benefits are most systematically related to income. The higher the family's socio-economic position, the more benefits are received from government expenditure on education (Le Grand, 1982; ABS, 1987; Deleeck, 1985; Olsson, 1989, p. 303). Figures for Britain for 1978 show that the wealthiest one-fifth of the population received about three times the amount of public expenditure received by the poorest fifth (Le Grand, 1982: p. 57). In Australia the benefits of the top fifth are almost five times those of the bottom fifth (ABS, 1987, p. 22). For both Britain and Australia these statistics, however, cover all households and because the aged are both likely to be relatively poor and not make use of education facilities, the figures can exaggerate the trend somewhat. However, if we just take all households with children, the data demonstrate clearly that the rich really do reap far more benefits from the education system than the poor, though less than the all-inclusive comparison indicates. For many other countries, including Sweden (Olsson, 1989, p. 303), Belgium and the Netherlands, education is recognised as a sphere in which there is particularly unequal distribution of benefits (Deleeck, 1985, p. 43). In the face of the ubiquity of inequality within education, a number of prominent researchers have rejected the possibility of achieving that popularly acclaimed goal for education: equal opportunity (Jencks, 1972; Le Grand, 1982).

The better-off and social welfare: universal versus selective provisions

While it may come as little surprise to find inequality well entrenched within education, and the lion's share of benefits going to the better-off, the effects can be similar even in programmes directly targeted at the poorest. In the USA, criticism from the New Right of the effects of the Great Society programme led Haveman (1987) to apportion its estimated economic costs and benefits. As he sums it up, 'the War on Poverty–Great Society initiative does not appear to have imposed large net losses on the non-poor, on whose political support such efforts rely' (1987, p. 86). Indeed he found that it is conceivable that some advantage went to the non-poor. In order to maintain legitimacy, he sees it as necessary for there to be advantages for the non-poor, a recognition of the power and generality of the ideology of inequality. In much the same way as the Swedes argue the case for locking the middle class into support for the welfare state, he suggests the way forward is to deliberately extend the benefits received by the non-poor. He believes that

> with some reorientation to improve their integration, administration, incentives and efficiency, existing social policy could be made to yield net gains to both the poor and the non-poor. (1987, p. 87)

This takes us back to the issue of selectivity versus universalism (see Chapter 1). In an abstract logical sense, it seems incontrovertible that selective, targeted services and benefits would be more effective in directing resources to the poor. However, the political reality is much more complicated. Such an approach can raise issues of legitimacy, as the US Great Society project exposed, not to mention the problem of stigma. It is also likely that stringently-targeted services will not be of high quality because of the lack of power of the client group to insist on this. It has been increasingly argued by economic liberals with an eye to cost-cutting and avoiding increases in taxes, that the more selectivity there is, the more the poor will benefit (Beltram, 1984, p. 190). However, the case for greater selectivity is also argued by political liberals in many countries including Sweden (Esping-Andersen and Korpi, 1987, p. 70) because they accept as an inevitability, the electorate's reluctance to support any expansion in government spending. Thus they suggest that what funds are available should be spent on those in greatest need.

In Australia, recent reforms of the social security system by the Labor government resulted in more generous benefits for the poor but more highly-targeted provisions. This was presented as a better way of deploying scarce resources. It certainly lifted the income of the poorest by a significant amount (Farrar, 1989). However, it is problematic whether continued support for such provisions will be forthcoming from an electorate in which only a powerless minority, and with increasing targeting an ever-diminishing minority, are able to claim these benefits. This strategy has already also produced the side-effect of increasing poverty among those not directly targeted. While the government had its eyes firmly fixed on families with dependent children and feminised poverty, the aged increasingly slipped below the poverty line (Farrar, 1989).

Selective benefits and services claim support from the public on the abstract grounds of social justice and equality. These are fragile forms of appeal and where they are relied on, as they largely have been in Australia, the generosity of benefits and the quality of services tend to be low, and support tenuous. In Sweden on the other hand, most benefits are explicitly universal and services are of high quality in an attempt to maintain user support, particularly from those who could afford to pay market prices for services (Esping-Andersen and Korpi, 1987, p. 70). The net result of these different policies (given their unique political contexts) is Australia's reversible welfare state compared with Sweden's more durable institutional form.

Nonetheless the evidence shows that for societies with either universal or selective approaches, inequality is maintained. This is clearly a bottom line. Benefits from social welfare provisions do deliver assistance, and life is more secure for the needy when such benefits are available. But, it is also clear that benefits do not redress inequality. The social wage, whatever its positive features, rarely alters the relative position of people in the social hierarchy, even though it may be claimed that its aim is to create greater equality.

This is the outcome because groups who are better-off are able to monopolise the political process and ensure that their interests are met (Deleeck, 1985). Mishra has in fact noted that it is the very absence of fundamental redistribution which is one of the political conditions for the development of a broad network of social amenities (1977, p. 111). If the economic cake is increasing, some benefits may be transferred to disadvantaged groups without much opposition. In times of economic cutbacks, issues of distribution are much more strongly contested. Powerful groups are better able to press energetically their claims in the battle over resources. The recent success of more powerful interests is illustrated by research into government expenditures in Britain by Le Grand and Winter (1987). This showed that, during the early years of the Thatcher Government, services that were extensively used by the middle classes were favoured by government policies, even though there was an avowed intention to cut virtually all government outlays. A similar effect has been noted in other countries, including the USA under Reagan (Jordan, 1987, p. 6).

II. Who benefits from occupational welfare?

Occupational welfare and the political context

Occupation is a crucial determinant of well-being in all advanced industrial societies. This is straightforwardly so in the sense that it provides the primary source of income for most people. Except in New Zealand and Australia with their flat-rate pension schemes, occupation is also a key determinant of the level of benefit available from the social welfare system. On top of this there is occupational welfare itself.

Occupational welfare includes those benefits that accrue to wage and salary earners over and above their pay, including those referred to as fringe benefits. Titmuss, in an essay written in 1958, illustrated this occupational division of welfare with the following examples:

> pensions for employees, wives and dependants; child allowances; death duties; health and welfare services; personal expenses for travel, entertainment, dress and equipment; meal vouchers; motor cars and season tickets; residential accommodation; holiday expenses; children's school fees; sickness benefits; medical expenses; education and training grants; cheap meals; unemployment benefit; and an incalculable variety of benefits in kind ranging from obvious forms of realisable goods to the most intangible forms of amenity. (1974, p. 51)

The receipt of shares in a company is one of many common benefits which even Titmuss's long list omits, and one which often has very clear tax advantages. Titmuss did recognise that a key feature of occupational welfare is its link with the taxation system – the 'ultimate cost falls in large measure on the Exchequer' (1974, p. 50). The value of occupational welfare is magnified by the fact that it generally avoids the level of taxation that is levied on ordinary earnings. It would therefore frequently make sense to treat much occupational welfare as fiscal welfare. The reason for not doing this is because people are only able to gain the benefits through their occupational position. Nonetheless, it is important to remember that the advantage to the individual would be vastly less were all benefits merely treated as the deferred earnings that they really represent and they were thus subject to normal income taxation (Tachibanaki, 1987, p. 3).

As was indicated in Chapter 2, most writers on the welfare state are silent on occupational welfare. Gough (1979) is one theorist who actually raises the issue, but he explicitly excludes occupational welfare from his analysis of the welfare state, seeing it as a private transaction. In the early eighties, Hilary Rose 'reread' Titmuss from a gender perspective. She pointed to the considerable capacity of the Titmuss paradigm to illuminate class, gender and race inequalities. However, neglect of occupational welfare has seriously reduced this potential. This omission of occupational welfare must be recognised to serve certain 'social and political functions', since it sanitises and depoliticises the study of inequality and avoids any threat to the advantages of those who are already well-off. Those prepared to narrow their gaze, and avert it from the larger picture in this manner, are rendered acceptable to the state bureaucracy as researchers and policy workers (Rose, 1981, p. 493). Rose's criticism is an incisive one, and one which can be applied more generally when we find the narrowness of conventional approaches are not challenged. In Australia, the same charge of political expediency can be laid against those prepared to redefine, for policy purposes, 'vertical redistribution' as merely offering assistance to the poor (see Chapter 2), rather than also alluding to the implications for reducing the relative advantage of the wealthy.

The extent of occupational welfare

The benefits of occupational welfare are considerable. However, the statistics are notoriously poor, even in Scandinavian countries, which are acclaimed for the comprehensiveness of their approach to such matters (Esping-Andersen and Korpi, 1987, p. 74). That the statistics are poor must at least in part be attributed to the processes Rose alluded to, those of sanitising and depoliticising (1981). In the absence of detailed data, the benefits of the wealthy are sheltered from public scrutiny.

An international comparison of non-wage labour costs carried out by the Swedish Employers Confederation found that for the year 1978, for nine OECD countries, non-wage labour costs supporting private occupational welfare ranged from 3.6 per cent to 11.4 per cent of total wages and salaries (Table 4.1). These figures must, however, be recognised as serious under-estimations because the definition used was far more restricted than that offered by Titmuss. The costs which are mainly accounted for here are those which most closely resemble social welfare, and include 'insurance taken by the firm or branch; supplementary retirement insurance; contractual or voluntary guaranteed sickness or accident pay; supplementary unemployment insurance; contractual additional family allowance; life insurance; other' (Tachibanaki, 1987, p. 3). As Table 4.1 shows, costs were highest in Italy, though only in the USA and in the UK did they represent a higher proportion of total wage costs than employer contributions to public welfare schemes. The low proportion in Sweden is explained in terms of the high proportion of statutory non-wage payments and the high standard of statutory services. The question of the relative effects on efficiency and strengthening the national economy of statutory versus private

Table 4.1   *Non-wage labour costs as a percentage of wages and salaries, 1978*

	Contribution to public welfare schemes	Contribution to private occupational welfare
Canada	4.4	4.0
France	29.3	7.2
FR Germany	16.2	6.2
Italy	23.9	11.4
Japan	7.8	4.5
Netherlands	20.0	8.6
Sweden	36.2	3.6
United Kingdom	7.0	7.1
United States	8.5	9.4

Source: Tachibanaki, 1987, p. 52.

occupational welfare is not a question which has yet been directly answered (Tachibanaki, 1987, p. 22).

Occupation and social security

Apart from Australia and New Zealand, with their flat rate basic social security pensions, paid from consolidated revenue, occupational status is the major factor determining a person's level of income support. In virtually all other countries today, pensions are in some way linked to earnings. In this manner those with highest earnings during their years in the labour force will be advantaged throughout their years of retirement. Earnings-related benefits produce what Deleeck has called the Matthew Effect, from the biblical reference to the Gospel of Matthew (Deleeck, 1985, p. 50). The principle embodied is that

> For whosoever hath, to him shall be given, and he shall have more abundance: but whosoever hath not, from him shall be taken away even that he hath. (Matthew 13:12)

Nowhere does the Matthew Principle work more clearly than in this area of óccupationally linked social welfare. Because women are likely to earn less than men, and have non-continuous employment histories, this determinant role of occupation is seriously disadvantaging. Because of their disadvantages within the employment system, the effects are similar for oppressed racial groups and people with disabilities.

Private occupational pension schemes magnify these effects. The conditions of these schemes vary widely and are often very complex. They are, however, similar in one essential feature: greater benefits accrue, both directly from employers, and indirectly from the state by way of taxation concessions, to those on higher wages or salaries (Reddin, 1982).

When we look to the British social insurance scheme, we find that payment of the basic pension is dependent on contribution status. Employees must pay contributions in nine out of every ten years of their working lives to qualify for the basic flat rate pension. To qualify for the maximum rate of the SERPS pension, the earnings related segment which was added in 1978, twenty years of contribution are necessary. The first maximum pension will not be available until 1998. Those who do not meet the basic contributory criteria must rely on the means tested and much more stigmatised form of social welfare, Income Support. In 1988, 20 per cent of National Insurance Pensioners were dependent on this fund for additional support apart from those who did not qualify for a National Insurance pension at all (Fuery *et al.*, 1988, pp. 52–4).

The Swedish pension system differs from other social insurance schemes in that employees are not called on to contribute directly at all. Contributions in their entirety are made by employers through a pay-roll tax. The form of coverage is similar to the UK, with a base rate and an earnings related element with maximum benefit accruing after thirty years of contribution. The pension rate is calculated on the basis of the best fifteen years of earnings. More than 90 per cent of employees are covered (Fuery *et al.*, 1988, p. 5). The only country with a higher coverage is Switzerland, which has had a compulsory scheme since 1985 (Fuery *et al.*, 1988, p. 83).

Occupation and private pensions

Private retirement pensions have been a major conduit for occupational welfare. In Britain, for example, private pensions or superannuation have a long history, though mainly for male workers in more privileged occupations. There is evidence of a pension scheme for male civil servants as early as 1834. Banks, railway companies and some other large enterprises provided retirement allowances before the First World War, but largely as employer benevolence. After the Second World War such benefits were deliberately used to attract staff (Papadakis and Taylor-Gooby, 1987, p. 106). By 1958 superannuation accounted for more than half of total expenditure outlaid by large firms on fringe benefits. While the precise eligibility details have varied, the principle of providing tax relief for contributions was established almost two centuries ago. As early as 1799, at the same time as income tax was introduced, tax relief was made available for life insurance contributions. In 1921 contributions of both employer and employee as well as the investment income from superannuation funds were exempted from tax liability (Papadakis and Taylor-Gooby, 1987, p. 107).

If we take together the additional remuneration represented by contributions the employer makes to an employee's private pension and the value of tax exemptions, it is clear that private occupational pensions provide a very valuable source of welfare. However, access has always been problematic. Workers in the public sector, large firms and highly unionised sectors have been the most likely to benefit. Women have had low rates of involvement, though this has improved over recent years for full-time workers. In Britain, between 1972 and 1982, the proportion of full-time male workers with private coverage rose from 55 per cent to 69 per cent. For women the equivalent rise was greater, from 34 per cent to 57 per cent. Though this still leaves full-time women workers at a disadvantage in relation to men, it is part-time workers who are very badly catered for and women make up over 80 per cent of part-time workers. In 1981 only 7 per cent of part-time workers were in a private pension scheme (Papadakis and Taylor-Gooby, 1987, p. 121). As part of a package put together in 1986 by the Thatcher government to encourage private pensions, a subsidy of 2 per cent of earnings was made available for a period of five years for those switching to private insurance. Those who could afford it were able to develop a particularly favourable retirement deal with this additional subsidy. Despite the Thatcher rhetoric, this scheme is unlikely to prove a fund-saver for government.

Although the Thatcher Government encouraged membership of private pension schemes, the British public remains devoted to state pensions. In a recent survey Papadakis and Taylor-Gooby found that 91 per cent of their respondents saw state pensions as very important, with a further 7 per cent finding them fairly important. The commitment was much stronger than that to occupational pensions, where 57 per cent claimed they were very important and 32 per cent saw them as fairly important (Papadakis and Taylor-Gooby, 1987, p. 130). Nonetheless, over time, there is every possibility that commitment to the public scheme will be weakened. Those 'outside the charmed circle' of well provided-for occupations will be 'left to look after themselves, the weak guardians of a residual social security system' (Reddin, 1982, p. 147).

This would clearly exacerbate the tendencies towards a dual system of reward. Some will retire in considerable comfort while others will have to depend on modest public provisions (Papadakis and Taylor-Gooby, 1987, p. 130). Any redistributive effects of social insurance are thus weakened by state support for private provisions. This highlights a key equity issue, that private occupational pensions, as with occupational welfare generally, show great variability. Pension coverage varies, not only by occupation but also by industry, and what is offered varies between schemes (Papadakis and Taylor-Gooby, 1987, p. 122).

Private pensions have been important in many countries, including the USA, Canada, Austria, Belgium and Switzerland. They have been less important in, for example, the Nordic countries, Germany, the Netherlands and Australia. Given the international nature of economic individualism, it is not surprising to find that an increasing privatisation of pensions, as has been happening in Britain, is a widespread phenomenon. Denmark had moved to a point in the early 1980s where expenditure on private pensions equalled around 40 per cent of total public pensions expenditure. Denmark has moved the furthest of the Nordic states from the 'Scandinavian model', as at the time comparable figures for Sweden, Finland and Norway were about 12, 10 and 7 per cent respectively (Esping-Andersen and Korpi, 1987, p. 74).

In the USA, the Old Age, Survivors, Disability and Health Insurance (OASDHI) scheme covers nearly 95 per cent of the population. On top of this, about 70 per cent of people are covered by private-sector retirement schemes (Fuery *et al.*, 1988, p. 48). In Belgium, insurance can also be voluntarily subscribed to to supplement unemployment benefits, pensions and health coverage, with regressive redistribution the inevitable result (Deleeck, 1985, pp. 49–50).

In Australia, alongside its equalising flat-rate pension scheme, there is increasing government encouragement of private superannuation, with schemes often under government supervision. Contributions attract very generous taxation concessions, and employers often pay contributions at twice the rate of employees. Because age pensions are means-tested, private superannuation often nullifies that entitlement but the rate of private pension is likely to be far higher anyway. Because women live longer they do receive more in public pensions but are less likely to have superannuation and, if they do, it is likely to be of a modest kind. As in other countries, fewer Australian women than men are in private pension schemes. For male workers in 1987 the proportion covered was 50 per cent, for women it was only 26 per cent. While overall 48 per cent of full-time workers were covered, only 8 per cent of part-time workers were in a superannuation scheme. This is a benefit very much for those who are better-off. The proportion covered increases steadily with income, from 3 per cent in the lowest income category to 72 per cent in the highest (Gunasekera and Powlay, 1987, pp. 15–20).

As in many other countries, part of the economic logic of encouraging private pensions in Australia was to promote savings for its potential to encourage investment and reduce inflation. The official rhetoric also suggested that private pensions would save the government money on age pensions, especially as the population ages during the coming decades. However, it is not really the case that the government will save money, especially not where higher-income earners are concerned. The subsidy to the private pension contributor through various taxation concessions is significant, often more than would be paid out to them through the social security system. This is partly accounted by the fact that the rate of the basic pension remains low, at only 25 per cent of average weekly earnings in 1989, compared, for example, to the USA social insurance pension (OASDHI), where the figure for those who were previously on average weekly earnings was 41 per cent.

In Australia, revenue lost through tax expenditures during the late eighties was about 40 per cent of the amount that was paid in direct outlays on age pensions and allowances for the aged. Yet private pensions only affected about 20 per cent of the aged population. On average the government paid out $A5775 for each pensioner and $A8190 for each superannuant (*The Australian*, 2 October 1990, p. 2). Tax expenditures on private occupational pensions in Australia thus make a dramatic contribution to inequality. This represents a higher rate of tax expenditures than in Britain, for example, though the principles of tax concessions are similar (Krever, 1989). In both cases, however, the official figures are likely to underestimate the actual revenue forgone as they do not take into account the fact that, without the various concessions, the taxable income of some taxpayers would be in a higher marginal tax rate bracket (EPAC, 1987, p. 9).

Other forms of occupational welfare

Australian private pension schemes provide a stark example of the manner in which government and employer policies can magnify inequality through the medium of the occupational system. A similar principle applies across many forms of occupational welfare, though the degree of benefit varies. Nonetheless, benefits are almost always directly linked to occupational status and inversely linked to economic need. They are, at best, tenuously related to the principles of merit or efficiency. Such policies plainly embody the ideology of inequality but the precise advantages that accrue to workers are generally hard to pin down. Thus the area remains analytically murky, with little systematic effort to unpack its distributional dimensions. The reasons for this are multiple but it is often strategic, for taxation and public relations reasons, to keep such benefits shaded from publicity. This is facilitated by the fact that, because these advantages go to the better-off anyway, they can often be well-hidden in the complex accounting systems used by those earning larger incomes. The process of exploiting taxation benefits is made easier when taxpayers are in command of the book-keeping systems of private businesses. The art of 'creative' accounting was not, after all, developed to serve the interests of poorer people or even the interests of the general public.

To take a comprehensive view would be to apprehend all benefits that are associated with occupation, but the evidence is not available to do this. In the absence of a capacity to deal comprehensively with occupational welfare, however, I will finish this section with a discussion which sketches some of the broad parameters. This section is included primarily for its alerting effect.

We need to define benefit broadly and incude a range of intangible qualities, including such slippery elements as the contribution to general enjoyment and personal development. For example, the amenity of spending one's day-to-day working life in the comfort and protective environment of an oak-panelled office, rather than in the dangerous environment of the foundry, is an obvious, and potentially multi-faceted benefit. Earlier, in the discussion of the redistributive effects of welfare payments in Sweden, it was noted that it was claimed that disability pensions 'redistribute towards blue collar workers' (Stahlberg, 1988, p. 28). A rather more accurate way of looking at this would be to consider this as some small compensation for occupational disbenefits.

Making available shares at favourable prices to employees is a time-honoured form of occupational welfare. The manner in which this is done varies greatly from firm to firm and from country to country. To illustrate the practice I have chosen a Swedish example. In Sweden the practice of issuing a kind of debenture referred to as 'convertibles' has grown in popularity since 1983. In 1988 there were over 200 companies and 200 000 employees involved in such schemes. Convertibles are loans to the company which can be taken up, after a specified period of time, as shares. The main motivation for companies to issue convertibles is to increase 'employee involvement, for personnel policy reasons' (Sköldebrand, 1989, p. 2). The take-up rate among eligible employees is about 42 per cent (Sköldebrand, 1989, p. 5). However, the scheme has the same problems for equality as other forms of occupational welfare. That is, it advantages a selected group of higher-status workers and those in large firms. They are also workers in private companies, and men are more likely to be employed there, while women are far more strongly concentrated in the public sector. At the same time, it should be noted that the public sector in Sweden, as in most countries, dispenses considerable occupational welfare to its employees. It was intended that the convertibles scheme would take the edge off demands for higher wages. For those not in a financial position to take up the offer of convertibles, higher wages would clearly be more beneficial. Also, government funds would be swelled by increased taxation revenue from higher wages. The debenture funds are usually lent to banks at lower than market rates, and bank profits are taxed at lower levels than wages. Overall the 'government income is weakened and banks profit from this movement of money' from the convertibles schemes (Sköldebrand, 1989, p. 9).

Japan has a world reputation for the occupational benefits which its companies provide to their workers and the way they lock them into lifetime employment with the same firm. Benefits do vary greatly, however, with only an elite corps of workers benefiting from the 'privileges of life-long employment, seniority wage system and large lump sum retirement allowances' (Watanuki, 1986, p. 266). These benefits vary significantly with size of firm. Companies employing more than 5000 staff spend more than twice as much on non-obligatory welfare, as a percentage of labour costs, as do firms employing less than 100 (Tachibanaki, 1987, p. 56). Such privileges are mainly extended to 'regular' full-time employees. They are denied to 'part-time, temporary, subcontract and other categories' of workers. In addition, they only last while the enterprise is profitable, and receipt of the benefits is dependent on performance that conforms to management expectations. 'Failure to progress satisfactorily leads to intense pressure to resign, from management and from other workers' (Moore, 1987, p. 142). Female workers are subject to particularly explicit exploitation and exclusion from occupational benefits. Most of the many women in part-time work remain entirely without benefits (Kalleberg and Hanisch, 1986; Mackie, 1989). As late as 1982, an article in *Japanese Quarterly* explicitly outlined the advantages of the part-time employment of married women, to include that 'they are patient because they are accustomed to domestic chores', and there is no 'need to pay them high wages', nor 'health insurance, pension or retirement allowances or other welfare benefits' (Hiroshi, 1982, p. 322). However, there are some signs of change. An Equal Employment Opportunity Act was passed in 1986 and the service and retail industries have established the same entitlements for part-timers as for full-timers (Hiroshi, 1982, p. 322).

While this discussion has largely concentrated on pensions as a key form of occupational welfare, the effects of other forms are very much in line. Research carried out in Australia illustrates the point, though it must be noted that it approached the issue of occupational benefit in a fairly standard and therefore limited way. The study presents information on 14 categories of payment outside wages or salary. These were: holiday costs, low interest finance, goods and services, housing, electricity, telephone, transport, medical expenses, union dues, club fees, entertainment allowances, shares, study leave, and superannuation. The study found that those in the top earning category received 3.8 times the benefits of those in the lowest. For those in top and middle management the benefits received were estimated to add 35 to 40 per cent to the value of their basic earnings. For low-income earners the estimated increase was less than 10 per cent (Jamrozik *et al.*, 1981, p. 97). Benefits received by these low-income earners typically consisted of being able to purchase goods and services from their employer organisation at cost or discount prices (Jamrozik *et al.*, 1981, p. 17). Industries with a high concentration of women offered fewer benefits and full-time workers did much better than part-time (Jamrozik *et al.*, 1981, p. 97).

We are back once again to the general Matthew Principle of occupational welfare, that those who are already better-off, benefit most. It certainly is, as Titmuss suggested, a 'concealed multiplier of occupational success' (1974, p. 52). Its cost is borne by the whole community in the first instance through higher prices, or in the case of government employment, costs of services. However, for my purposes, a less obvious but crucial effect is that there is a reduction in government revenue. This is because there are many ways in which the tax which would be automatically paid on direct income is avoided altogether, or at least minimised when income is received as occupational welfare. Were a government to receive this forgone revenue, it would in its turn be available for collective purposes. Another crucial feature is that this is largely concealed welfare. Indeed, this is not recognised as an area of government intervention at all. Those who benefit are not identified and do not identify themselves as the recipients of welfare. Thus this vast area escapes attention when analyses of equality and the effects of government intervention are undertaken.

III. Who benefits from fiscal welfare?

Defining fiscal welfare

Even though fiscal welfare has received more official attention than occupational welfare, it is still common to regard the taxation system almost entirely in economic terms, except for allowances which deal directly with states of dependency. These allowances are routinely treated as categories of welfare. As has already been documented in respect of occupational welfare, this way of conceptualising policies in itself works to the advantage of the privileged. Thus governments have welfare policies for the poor, and economic policies for everyone else. As Keens and Cass expressed it,

> fiscal welfare differs from social welfare not only in terms of the group for whom it provides but also in terms of generosity, stigma, and the extent to which expenditure is made public (1982, p. 33).

Fiscal affairs have two distinct dimensions – one is spending, the other is revenue-raising, which provides the funds to spend. So far, in discussing social welfare I have been dealing with spending. I will now consider more closely the equity effects of raising the money which pays for these and other state activities. Governments utilise a range of techniques for revenue-raising, including taxation on sales, services or products, resource rent, royalties and bonds – to specify only a few examples of what, in advanced capitalist societies, is a complex operation. Because of the daunting size of tackling the task in a comprehensive manner, the discussion here will focus mainly on taxation. Ideally other forms of revenue-raising should be subject to detailed analysis as well.

Levying taxation

The taxation systems of advanced industrial societies have gradually developed to provide support for governance. As the state became more interventionist, governments required increasing funds to support their programmes. Income tax, today a major tax, started as a tax on the richer members of society. However, as more services were provided, income tax was gradually extended to all citizens. Even before universal income tax, though, the costs of welfare services were often distributed in a regressive manner. In Britain, as early as 1912, a family earning 18s per week was paying 10.25 per cent of its income in indirect taxes and contributions to National Health and Unemployment Insurance. For families with a weekly income of 35s, the proportion of income paid was only 5.27 per cent (Thane, 1982, p. 100).

Taxation not only provides governments with money as a raw material. The process of taxation in itself offers the single most extensive tool for socio-political engineering available to the state. Taxation must be considered 'an instrument of social policy rather than merely as a source of finance' (Pond, 1980, p. 47). Taxation can be used to redistribute money and other resources and for the encouragement, or discouragement, of various activities and practices. Taxation relief may be given for investments in certain industries, farming being a time-honoured one. But there is a limitless range of possibilities. For example, in South Africa, diamond-mining was encouraged in this manner and, in Australia, gold-mining, the film industry, and reafforestation, to mention but a few examples. Attempts may be made to discourage certain behaviour patterns too. For example, taxes in many countries are high on tobacco and alcoholic beverages, not only to raise revenue, but at least partly in order to discourage the use of unhealthy products and cut the longer-term costs of their usage. While the capacity of the taxation system to redistribute costs and benefits is extensive, the possible political consequences tend to act as a brake to rapid radical change. The community unrest caused by Thatcher's poll tax, which significantly redistributed costs, illustrates the political resistance which may be engendered by radical change.

While a valid question to ask of a taxation policy is, is it effective in achieving whatever goals are officially claimed for it (for example, encouraging mining, or discouraging smoking), here we are concerned with its distributional effects only. The issue of fairness is generally accepted as central to modern taxation systems, though what is defined as fair is contested. The principles of equity and redistribution were clearly enunciated in a British Budget announcing the capital transfer tax in 1974. The Chancellor of the Exchequer of the Labour government, Mr Healy, announced this measure as part of a 'determined attack on the maldistribution of wealth in Britain'. In the same budget he announced his intention to introduce a wealth tax and for the same reason (Stephenson,

1980, p. 4). The recent negative reactions to the poll tax were largely on the ground that it violated principles of fairness, that is, it did not distinguish between people on the grounds of capacity to pay or, for that matter, in terms of the benefits they received.

Progressivity in the tax system

Ostensibly, fairness is built into a taxation system through the administrative device of progressivity. A tax system is progressive if, as income rises, the amount extracted as a tax liability rises as a proportion of the income (Prest and Barr, 1985, p. 293).

Progressivity of taxation can be supported on grounds other than fairness. The argument that users should pay can also be invoked because, on the whole, those who are better-off actually receive more benefits from the public coffers than do the less well-off, as we have seen in relation to much social welfare. They are also likely to have more to lose and therefore benefit more from defence, the legal system, policing and the general social infrastructure. Owners and shareholders of businesses are likely to reap most advantage from infrastructural services such as communications and financial systems. Also, the better-off are likely not only to reap the most direct benefits from the education system by becoming qualified themselves, but they also make more use of other highly-qualified practitioners such as lawyers, architects, accountants, artists and the like. One could go on and on listing areas of greater benefit; a major problem, of course, is how to actually value such benefits. There seems to be no easy way of converting these advantages into money terms at this stage (Cope, 1987, p. 42). Nonetheless, we need to be aware that such advantages should be taken into account.

The issue of what is a fair rate of progressivity with respect to income tax rates is contentious and clearly political. With the rise of the New Right, even the relatively ineffectual levels of redistribution that were being pursued have been reduced in many countries. For example, the top marginal tax rate in the UK was 98 per cent in 1978, but by the mid 1980s it had been dropped to 60 per cent. At the other end of the scale, taxation burdens were extended. The tax threshold – that is, the level below which no income tax is payable – was at 80 per cent of the average industrial wage in 1983. By the late 1980s the level had been reduced to 25 per cent of the average industrial wage (Cope, 1987, p. 42). These changes have directed the tax burden away from wealthier taxpayers.

This redistribution, as has already been discussed, is rationalised as due to a tax revolt by the middle classes. It is also suggested that high marginal tax rates act as a disincentive to work and to enterprise generally. Yet, contrary to much popular opinion, high marginal tax rates have not been shown by research to act as a disincentive to work. The exception is that higher effective tax rates have been observed to act as a disincentive for 'secondary' workers such as married women, teenagers and people past retirement age (Prest and Barr, 1985, p. 302). Yet an argument frequently used against high marginal rates is that they act as a disincentive to those in the primary labour market as well as acting as a counter to the energetic development of capitalist enterprise more generally.

A progressive taxation system does not end with rates of income tax. There are other forms of tax such as capital gains and consumption (value added) taxes, as well as local council rates and charges. With respect to fairness, we have to ask what is being taxed and what is being exempted. Finally, we cannot divorce taxation systems from the expenditure to which the collected taxation is put. As Prest and Barr quip, 'if income tax were highly progressive but the revenue used mainly to subsidise the production of Rolls Royces or the import of mink coats, the overall effect could be regressive' (1985, p. 293).

Tax exemptions/expenditure

A key problem with discourses about taxation is that they generally focus on taxation as a source of revenue only, and rarely ask what is exempted. Tax exemptions are largely ignored because they are identified as social, rather than fiscal policy. However, while 'tax allowances may be a form of public welfare, they are also a form of public expenditure' (Pond, 1980, p. 31). Many governments, including the Australian and British, do not give a great deal of prominence to tax exemptions as public expenditure and in some calculations they ignore them altogether. Pioneering work to bring about a redefinition was undertaken in the USA by Surrey, who pointed out that exemptions affect the private economy in the same

ways as expenditures. He estimated that in 1973 these exemptions,
expenditures represented about one-quarter of the US federal
budget. Yet, at that time, they fell outside the normal processes
of scrutiny. His work led to the development of a Tax Expenditure
Budget which provides estimates of the costs of the major exemptions. Canada too developed a 'Tax Expenditure Account' in order
to allow the scrutiny of these costs (Pond, 1980, p. 31).

In Britain, official recognition was afforded the argument that
tax allowances are, in effect, expenditures in the 1979 Public
Expenditure White Paper (Cmnd 7439). However, the way in
which the altered accounting procedure has been adopted militates
against its effectiveness for assessing the contribution of allowances
to equity. This shows up clearly in budget documents. For example, in *The Government's Expenditure Plans 1990–91* (Cm 288-1),
the last three pages before the final 'Notes and Glossary', were
devoted to 'Direct Tax Allowances and Relief'. No account of this
information was taken in the earlier parts of the document. In
the various analyses of public expenditure the classic headings of
defence, health and personal services, social security, education
and science, Scottish and Welsh Offices and Northern Ireland, and
'Other' are persistently used. On the government's own figures,
however, taxation exemptions and allowances outstripped any of
these. Nonetheless, the fact that the information is provided, even
if at the back of the Budget Papers, is an advance on the earlier
procedures.

In the USA and Canada, where govenment accounting does take
note of tax allowances as expenditure, this certainly unmasks some
of the relativities of government intervention. For example, it can
readily be seen that in 1986 the outlay to homeowners in the US
was more than four times the amount spent on public housing
assistance, at $US68.8 billion compared with $15.4 billion
(Hanson, 1987, p. 195). Over recent years the momentum to
recognise and reduce the effects of tax allowances and exemptions
has increased. The OECD reports among its members a widespread trend to reduce tax exemptions and privileges as well as to
phase out industrial subsidies (Henderson, 1989). These efforts
would increase tax equity, provided they were not counter-balanced by other measures which favour the better-off. Such reforms
are not necessarily easy to achieve, however, and success depends
on the political strength of the defending group. For example,

reform of concessions to farmers within Europe has proved politically volatile. At the end of 1990, the four years of international
negotiations between those nations party to the General Agreement
on Tariffs and Trade (GATT) failed to reach agreement about the
reductions to subsidies to European farmers. The political strength
of the rural lobby, particularly in France and Germany, where
angry demonstrations were staged, rendered farm interests successful in fending off efforts to change the system (Hadler, 1990, p.
3).

Defining income for taxation purposes

Probably the most basic issue about fiscal welfare is how the
revenue is collected in the first place and, most importantly, what
is exempted from the tax-net. Definitions of what is to be counted
as income are complex and far from neutral in their effects. In the
1930s Henry Simons, building on work carried out in the 1920s by
Haig, proposed two ways in which income may be conceptualised,
using a 'flow' and 'accretion' definition. The flow approach is the
more usual and refers to 'the net value of payments received by
an individual over some period of time'. This is the common basis
for assessing income tax. Income is basically defined as earned and
unearned receipts over a period, usually one year. In the accretion
definition 'income is the sum of consumption and changes in net
wealth over some period of time' (Wagner, 1973, p. 141). The
flow approach caters well to administrative convenience and, is, it
is often claimed, in general usage for this reason. As many analysts
point out, however, the accretion approach is conceptually superior
because it allows for increases in capital even when the capital item
is not cashed in. The approach also takes account of all advantages,
be they in cash or kind (Wagner, 1973; Pond, 1980; Cope, 1987).
However, the accretion approach would expose to taxation much
more of the wealth and income of those who are better-off.

 The Haig–Simons approach was discussed in the British context
by Hicks in 1942. He paraphrased the point of view as follows:
'Income is what a man can spend and still expect to be as well off
at the end of the accounting period as he was at the beginning'
(quoted by Cope, 1987, p. 79). Benefit remains, of course, even
wider than this and includes the value of the amenity enjoyed
along the way. This accretion notion has been explored in the

concept of a comprehensive income tax (CIT), which was taken up by a Royal Commission in Canada in 1966. The concept involves the principle that tax is 'levied annually on all accretions to economic power', with all accretions to be taxed at the same rate (Cope, 1987, p. 78).

The British Royal Commission on the Taxation of Profits and Income, in 1955, came very close to recommending an accretion form of definition. The Commission maintained that

> no concept of income can be really equitable that stops short of the comprehensive definition which embraces all receipts which increase an individual's command over the use of the society's scarce resources (Cmnd 9474, quoted in Pond, 1980, p. 52).

There are problems about what to include even with a comprehensive definition: what about increase in pension rights, the value of an increase in skill, profits retained by companies, increased value of furniture or paintings not intended for sale? Then there are questions such as how to cope with inflation? Fluctuations would often be wide and such a scheme could be difficult to administer, though the more computerised transactions become, the more feasible such a scheme becomes.

Whatever the practical difficulties, and however unlikely it is that a CIT will be introduced, it is important to explore the concept of a more comprehensive notion of income. What the exercise does is highlight limitations of present arrangements (Cope, 1987, p. 78), alerting us to the extensive range of income that is currently exempted from income tax merely by being ignored. It also underlines the fact that a narrow definition of income best serves the interests of the better-off.

Opportunities for tax exemptions

Not only is the basic definition of what is income problematic, but this is compounded by the issue of what are allowable deductions and the effect of these. Deleeck has noted that, for Belgium, 'the redistributional aspect of the progressive tax system is counteracted by tax deductions' (1985, p. 45) – a common problem. Taking education allowances alone, he found that after accounting for education expenditure, the overall income distribution became more unequal (1985, p. 46).

Although there is a move in OECD countries to cut down on tax exemptions and privileges, this is still an important area of advantage for many. What is tax-exempt or subject to lower rates varies considerably from country to country, though the broad principles are not so different. Expenditures which can be construed as necessary to produce taxable income are the most common official deductions, and these are not normally even classed as tax expenditures. Because taxation systems are almost all complex, and because they are legalistic, their rules can often, with some application, be skirted. There are loopholes which can be exploited. Yet an equitable tax system must be premised on the fact that people actually pay what, technically, they are obliged to, otherwise the notion of progressivity of the structure becomes irrelevant. It is clear that the poorer members of many societies are not exempted from the burden of tax to any great degree except for transactions within the informal economy, and these are often of a minor nature (Gershuny, 1983). In Britain, while higher rates of tax are at least nominally required of people at higher income levels, the proportion actually contributed to total taxation revenue by each income quintile of the population in the early eighties was roughly the same (Prest and Barr, 1985, p. 301), though this is likely to have altered even more in favour of the better-off in the light of changes made by the Thatcher government. The situation is similar in Australia. 'Effective tax rates are high for those with relatively little wealth. For the rest, tax rates are low' (Dilnot, 1990, p. 16).

The opportunities for claiming deductions, and for avoiding or evading tax, are not evenly spread. The opportunities for tax minimisation are much greater for people such as the self-employed and owners of businesses, because of the complexity of their transactions. Minimisation is much more difficult for those wage and salary earners who are subject to deductions of their taxation contributions at the source by their employer (Heidenheimer *et al.*, 1990, p. 203). On the other hand, business affairs can be arranged so that certain forms of expenses such as private entertainment, holiday expenses, and even the purchase of some items for the home can, legitimately, be claimed as tax-exempt or taxable at a lower rate. As we have seen, occupational welfare is largely the preserve of the better-off and it is coextensive with fiscal welfare.

The amount of income, both legally and illegally obtained, that goes unreported has been estimated, in a range of countries, to represent at a minimum around 6 per cent of Gross National Product and at a maximum about one third (Heidenheimer *et al.*, 1990, p. 204). While this area is inevitably a hazy one, there are almost certainly wide cross-national variations. It appears that the Scandinavian countries, despite their high tax rates, have a smaller unreported sector than some other countries, such as Italy and the USA, which have lower tax rates (Heidenheimer *et al.*, 1990, p. 205). Hence the chestnut that the practice of tax minimisation is due to high marginal tax rates can be put to rest. Attitudes to taxation morality and the structure of the labour market seem to be a more fruitful source of explanation (Heidenheimer *et al.*, p. 205).

Housing and taxation

In most countries, owner-occupation of housing is afforded special treatment with respect to taxation. There are tax allowances made to offset housing purchase and these disproportionately benefit higher-income groups, because they are the ones who have the income threshold necessary to gain a housing loan and make the necessary repayments (Deleeck, 1985, p. 47). In many countries, including Britain, the USA, Sweden and Denmark, tax relief is available on the interest on the mortgage borrowed to purchase the principal home. In some countries the rationale for this policy can be located in housing policy aimed at encouraging the private meeting of housing needs. The original rationale in Britain for this tax relief was, however, quite different and represented a similar form of tax treatment to other investment. House-purchase was treated as money expended in order to gain an income. Where the house was not rented and was lived in by the owner, tax was levied on an 'imputed rent'. Income was imputed as that which the occupier could have obtained in cash if the dwelling were let, with costs of maintenance offset. This was the system until 1963. The last valuations underpinning this imputed rent were made in 1936 so that by 1963, when it was abolished, the tax was not worth much. Today, for owner-occupied homes, the interest paid on a mortgage is tax-deductible but the investment is not taxed by way of imputed rent or capital gain. In the debate over the abolition of the practice of imputing rent as income, it was argued that no income was imputed from the use of other assets, such as cars and works of art (Whitehead, 1980, pp. 90–5).

As has already been discussed, provision of privatised assistance to home purchasers in Sweden and Denmark has increased the degree of inequality. In Australia, interest on mortgage payments is not tax-deductible, but the main home is exempt from capital gains tax and there is no system for taxing imputed rent, even though the 1990–91 government tax expenditure analysis did acknowledge that this left a gap in the total accounted for as tax expenditures. Taxation policies connected with owner-occupied housing clearly advantage those who are better-off. The higher the value of the home the greater the tax advantage, a clear reversal of the principle of progressive taxation.

Tax allowances for dependants

One of the more traditional tax concessions is in respect of dependants, most often children and wives. Some form of financial assistance to defray the expense of raising children is provided in most OECD countries. This acts as a method of promoting horizontal equity between those with dependent children and those without. In some countries this is paid through the social security system by way of a weekly allowance, and is thus counted as social welfare. When this is the case, the effect is usually progressive, as the amount paid is likely to be tied only to the age of the children and not to income. Where an allowance is made via a taxation concession, the effect may be regressive, as the wealthier are likely to receive a rebate in respect of a higher tax rate.

A dependent spouse still attracts tax relief in some countries, though the numbers are dwindling. In Britain this was called the 'married man's allowance' and paid on the assumption that the husband was the family breadwinner until its abolition in 1990 (Naffine, 1990, p. 9). In Australia, in an attempt to render at least the language, if not the concept, gender-neutral, this tax concession was changed to the 'dependent spouse rebate' rather than dependent wife rebate. However, it remains effectively a dependent wife rebate. In the vast majority of cases it is paid to the male partner in respect of a dependent wife. In around only 2 per cent of cases does the allowance go to a female taxpayer in respect of a dependent male partner (Keens and Cass, 1982, p. 24). Despite strong pressure from the women's movement during the 1980s to abolish this taxation rebate and the Hawke government's general enthusiasm for reducing such concessions, the strength of its conservative support has ensured that it has remained.

In Britain the recently-abolished married man's allowance provided the eligible tax payer with an additional rebate of £1250 in 1985/86. As Kay and King's much-used textbook on the British tax system puts it, 'any income of the wife is aggregated with his, and in recognition of these obligations he is given an addition . . . to his personal allowance' (1986, p. 26). This income, which was exempt from taxation, was in addition to the personal 'tax-free' allowance (then £2000). A working wife does receive the same tax-free allowance as her husband. However, in its structure the taxation system is only just moving away from the principle that a wife is dependent on her husband and that he is responsible for their joint taxation.

Deductibility of gifts to charitable organisations

There is one form of deduction found in many countries, including Britain, Australia and the USA, that warrants separate mention. This is tax deductibility in respect of gifts to approved public institutions. Such a provision has the obvious intention of facilitating the donation of money for charitable purposes, to educational and cultural institutions as well as for welfare purposes. With such impeccable moral credentials, its distributive effects are rarely questioned. Yet they are problematic and underline the need to be ever-questioning in the consideration of 'Who benefits?'

Only the better-off have substantial amounts of money to spare for donations to charitable institutions. Thus it is not likely that the poor will benefit from the tax savings. If the poor do give money to charitable causes, it is likely to be small amounts which will not therefore attract significant savings, especially where the tax rate being paid is low. Or they are likely to provide 'donations' to needy relatives (Finch, 1989, chapter 1). This means that we have a situation in which if the rich help the poor (via a charity) they recoup some of the gift as a tax concession. If the poor help each other directly, they do not qualify for such tax relief. The questions of who benefits from various charities is also an important and relevant question. Many of the benefits certainly go to the better-off. This is very clearly seen in the case of private schools in countries such as Britain, Australia and the USA, but also applies widely in relation to universities, hospitals, heritage and high cultural areas and a range of charities which cater largely for the middle and upper classes. Through tax-deductability, governments subsidise these facilities, though they may be entirely privately-run and privately accountable. Much of the donated money also supports middle-class interests through the provision of salaries and opportunities for professional workers.

IV. Who benefits from government intervention?

Investigation of the intricacies of taxation systems largely confirms that fiscal welfare, like occupational welfare and most social welfare, conforms to the Matthew Principle. Essentially all three welfare systems entrench the current social hierarchy, though there is variation from country to country and from time to time. The picture of inequality would be exacerbated were we to employ a comprehensive definition of income and if we took account of the benefits that flow from all government mediation. To gain a complete picture we would need to consider the whole range of activities covering – to take just a few examples – finance, banking and commerce, communications, transportation, defence, law, policing, religion, sport, recreation and cultural pursuits, and not only deal with the conventional welfare areas. Ideally a comprehensive picture would also assess benefits and disbenefits from governments' failure to take certain action. A striking example of such failure to act was seen in Sweden in relation to the Meidner Plan. This would have gradually transferred ownership and control of capitalist firms to employees. However, mobilisation of opposition prevented workers benefiting to any extent.

Over recent years there has been a reassertion of the ideology of inequality as those in traditionally privileged positions claw back the gains made by less-privileged groups during the sixties and seventies. Goldthorpe has pointed to research which underlines the difficulties faced by a 'legislative and administrative . . . piecemeal' approach to equality, suggesting that this 'strategy grossly misjudges . . . the flexibility and effectiveness with which the more powerful and advantaged groupings in society can use the resources at their disposal to preserve their privileged position' (1980, p. 252).

This tendency has been increasingly evident over recent years. The official doctrine of progressivity within taxation systems is still in place but it has been weakened, by lowering of the top tax rates in this era of economic rationalism and 'tax revolts'. Moves to privatisation and to cut government expenditure, as well as other policies favouring the market, magnify the tendency of occupational and fiscal welfare and other government activity to benefit the already blessed. The rest of this chapter will be devoted to issues beyond social, occupational and fiscal welfare which are germane to this overall consideration of the issues 'Who benefits?' The discussion cannot provide a systematic coverage because we are moving into an area that is poorly charted. What will be attempted is the raising of a number of issues; the intention, once again, is to alert. This discussion is intended to further illustrate how the debate must be extended if we are to deal adequately with the manner in which capitalist states mediate the welfare of people, both within their national borders and outside.

The issue of wealth is clearly central, yet statistics on wealth are everywhere problematic. This can hardly be accidental, when most countries have organisations devoted to the collection of information to underpin government activity, not to mention the international bodies such as the OECD. Studies routinely decry the lack of available information and the lack of international comparability. In Australia the sensitivity of the issue was vividly demonstrated during the eighties. In opposition, the Labor Party repeatedly promised a comprehensive wealth survey. After its election in 1983 it failed to deliver on this promise and indeed showed great reluctance even to discuss the issue.

The lack of comprehensive data applies even to Sweden, with its highly-developed statistical procedures and a long record of research and rational planning. After compiling a report for the Swedish Commission on Wage-earners and Capital Growth at the end of the 1970s, Spånt concluded that 'the regular official statistics on wealth in Sweden are completely unreliable as a source for wealth studies' (1979/80, p. 141). Despite this inadequacy, a number of independent studies of wealth distribution allowed him to draw something of the picture. His data spanned 1920–75 at between five- and ten-year intervals, though it must be noted that the data are very much framed within the conventional discourses about wealth and are likely to understate the extent of inequality.

The most significant change in Sweden over the twentieth century is the increase in the importance of home-ownership. In 1920 this represented 17 per cent of wealth. By 1975 home-ownership represented 45 per cent. This picture is fairly typical of Western Europe generally. In the USA and UK company shareholding has been more important (Spånt, 1979/80, p. 144). In the UK under the Thatcher government's policy to encourage company shareholding this difference was somewhat magnified.

The relative success of the Swedish welfare state is reflected in the finding that at each period studied, the wealth distribution became more equal. The share of wealth of the richest 2 per cent of the population fell from about 60 per cent in 1920 to 28 per cent in 1975. The bottom 95 per cent increased their share of 'registered net wealth' from 23 per cent in 1920 to 56 per cent in 1975 (Spånt, 1979/80, p. 145). Spånt suggests that were claims on private and public pension funds to be included in these calculations then the equalising effect would have been even greater.

Nonetheless, there remain significant discrepancies in the distribution of wealth. A micro-analysis showed that 800 households owned about 3 per cent of Swedish wealth, and this represented about 150 times what would be their share were the distribution 'completely uniform' (Spånt, 1979/80, p. 145). As in most countries, income was more equitably distributed than wealth. While the top decile of wealth holders held 55 per cent of wealth, they received only 20 per cent of total household disposable income (Spånt, 1979/80, p. 145).

While wealth distribution in most welfare states remains very unequal, the degree of inequality does vary from society to society. Predictably, Sweden has a less unequal distribution than most countries. Norway, the Netherlands, Austria and Israel are also accepted as nations with 'relatively uniform wealth distribution' (Spånt, 1979/80, p. 137). Australia, with its workers' welfare state, had a history of relative egalitarianism, though this characteristic was gradually eroded over recent years (Gruen, 1989). All the statistics must be treated with caution, however, because they are rarely, if ever, kept in an optimal manner. Equally, or more important, is the lack of comprehensiveness of what is included in the figures. Similar arguments to those made earlier in this chapter

in respect of what is covered by the concept i
in respect of wealth. Those with private busine
greater access to assets than those that show
property. The houses, cars, yachts, paintings
events and so on, may officially belong to an ii
entity.

Wealth distribution became more unequal di
most countries. In the USA, during the presidency of Ronald
Reagan, while, despite the rhetoric, little overall reduction in
government spending was achieved, a significant redirection of
funds occurred away from the poorer members of the society.
This has resulted in 'a dualised society'. There is a primary labour
market consisting of workers with high qualifications and members of strong unions and a 'casualised and fragmented work force'
which is made up largely of women, Blacks and recent immigrants
and which works for very low pay, often part-time and with
poor employment conditions (George, 1988, p. 131). This is not a
section of the workforce that receives occupational welfare, and
social welfare provisions have become harsher, along with industrial employment conditions. Welfare often involves 'workfare', in
which income support is conditional on undertaking compulsory
employment (Jordan, 1987, p. 6). There has also been a dramatic
increase in homelessness with estimates running as high as three
million homeless as well as up to 20 million going hungry (George,
1988, p. 132). Similar trends in homelessness are evident in other
countries, including Australia (Burdekin *et al.*, 1989) and Britain
(Murie, 1989, p. 225).

In Britain there has also been a significant trend to greater
inequality. While the rhetoric of the Thatcher government was
about pruning the state, and in particular cutting welfare, a more
correct understanding is that restructuring, rather than pruning,
was occurring. This restructuring very systematically moved benefits to those who were better-off. Some regions fell behind economically and those that improved their economic performance
were largely ones which were relatively privileged from the outset.
This dualisation in Britain is referred to in geographical terms
as the north/south issue. Since the advent of the Conservative
government in 1979, the Gross Domestic Product per head
increased, for example, in East Anglia by 7 per cent while in the
West Midlands it fell by 4 per cent (Rose, 1989, p. 252).

The process occurring in Britain mirrors the international North/South situation, with rich countries becoming richer, and many poorer countries becoming poorer. As was discussed in Chapter 2, poor countries in fact provide a source of wealth for Western capitalist societies. While the discussion here has concentrated on the internal affairs of the OECD countries, a more complete ledger of inequality could not be accurately drawn up unless we considered the manner in which the economies of the richer countries often gain their sustenance at the expense of the less-developed countries of the world.

5 Men's Welfare State

The more the details of state intervention are examined, the clearer it becomes that the welfare state is essentially different for different people. Women experience the welfare state differently from men. So too do the various classes and people of differing racial and ethnic backgrounds (Williams, 1989). We could also consider welfare from the point of view of the old, the young, people with disabilities, people from different regions (for example, the North/South divide in Britain), and so on. However, I am not going to deal with all these perspectives; my concern is mainly with the gender dimension. In this chapter I am specifically concerned with men's welfare state and in the next, women's.

In some ways it may not seem necessary to write a chapter on men and the welfare state. The conventional literature has been malestream and the provisions of the welfare state which I have dealt with in earlier chapters were developed by men from within the dominant male perspective, to solve problems as men perceived them. The significant point is that this is rarely acknowledged. Even when this point is dealt with, as it is by feminist writers, rarely is men's position explicitly considered. Feminist writers, not unreasonably, have been mainly concerned with effects for women. Conventional writers (largely but not exclusively male) on the other hand, sometimes throw in a section on women but without acknowledging that the rest of the time, while claiming generality, they are actually focusing on men, and almost invariably men from dominant groups (Edwards, 1989). It is, however, important to consider the position of men quite directly if we are to be able to understand the welfare state in terms of gender politics. It is also useful to do this before we turn in the

next chapter to women's welfare, because this reveals the framework into which women have been fitted.

If one takes the position, as I have, that *all* state intervention
should be considered for its effect on people's welfare, it is overwhelmingly obvious that men's interests are better catered for by
the state than are women's. As will be discussed in more detail in
the next chapter, this does not mean that men are more likely to
be recipients of social welfare, particularly those forms of support
which are most socially stigmatised. Indeed, in most countries
men are under-represented both as social welfare recipients and as
welfare service delivery workers. This can be accounted for by a
complex of factors. First, women's longevity ensures that they
will predominate among the aged and therefore among pensioners
and as recipients of forms of caring services. Second, the state
more readily provides support for mothers in their parental role
than it does fathers and, therefore, sole parents supported by the
state are far more likely to be female than male. Third, it tends to
be women who fill the caring roles associated with the social
welfare system, though it tends to be men who fill its managerial
positions. At the same time, men occupy superior positions within
the market economy and this provides greater rewards which, in
turn, provide more effective inoculation against the need for social
welfare.

Commenting on this gendered dualism for the USA, Fraser
notes that the social-welfare system

> is officially gender neutral. Yet the system as a whole is a dual
> or two-tiered one; and it has an unmistakable gender sub-text.
> There are programs oriented primarily to individuals tied to
> participation in the paid workforce . . . [and] a second set of
> programs oriented to households . . . designed to compensate
> for what are considered family failures, generally in the absence
> of a male breadwinner. (1987, p. 93)

Historically, the less clearly recognised beneficiaries of the welfare
state have been, and remain, those capitalists who profit from
access to a regulated, tolerably healthy and educated labour force,
motivated to seek paid employment in order to avoid becoming a
social welfare recipient with its associated privation and social
opprobrium. Because the families of these capitalists share the
profits, some women are beneficiaries too. However they rarely

share equally, especially in respect of power and control, which remains overwhelmingly in the hands of men.

When considering the benefits conferred by the welfare state, some form of accounting is necessary to apportion the benefits, not only according to class, but also according to gender, race and other potential bases for differential distribution such as age and disability. Such an accounting would also recognise that over the past 200 years, through the politics of industrial development, a rise in the standard of living of the working class, including that of women, has been achieved in the advanced capitalist societies. There has also been a gradual expansion of social and political rights. What has not been significantly altered, though, is the hierarchical ordering of the broad categories of beneficiaries of these improvements. In the absence of a mechanism for doing social accounting in some precise manner, we can only constantly direct our analysis towards the differential effects of state interventions and focus on the persistence of the socially patterned chances of winning and losing.

The superior economic position of men from dominant groups derives from their favoured position in the occupational structure, both as employer and employee. This, in turn, is linked to their superior position in the power structures of all societies. Men have had control over the development of the modern state, through the domination of its major political structures. Thus it is not surprising that they have been able to monopolise its advantages. In the discussion that follows, I will consider those features of the contemporary state that play a crucial part in the maintenance of the position of men of dominant groups.

Liberal theory and the patriarchal welfare state

Legislators and administrators, until very recently, have almost all been male and of higher social class. It was assumed that these men should make decisions for women as well as the 'lower orders' of men. With the gradual development of labour politics, working men's interests achieved a voice, though an unequal one. Nonetheless, the supply of labour has proved a bargaining chip, one which men have monopolised. In fact the development of the welfare state can be seen largely as an expression of male class politics. It is not necessarily the case that women, in particular, and a range of 'muted groups', have been inactive in promoting their own interests. However, they have been hampered by a lack of direct representation in the formal political arena and other corridors of power.

Gender inequality is firmly embedded in the political philosophy which underpins the bourgeois, liberal, democratic state (as it is in other forms of state). This liberal philosophy, which developed during the eighteenth and nineteenth centuries, has as its fundamental claim, a doctrine focused on individuals and based on principles of universalism and egalitarianism. Yet women were largely ignored and the family was not expected to function in accord with these principles. Kinship positions are ascribed, not achieved in open equal competition. The roles of husband as breadwinner and wife as homemaker were taken as given. John Rawls in his influential work, *A Theory of Justice*, first published in the 1970s, recognised this when he pointed out that 'the principle of fair opportunity can be only imperfectly carried out, at least as long as the institution of the family exists' (1985, p. 74). As with most other philosophers, however, he ignored the family and the private domain, leaving traditional patriarchal dominance unchallenged (Kearns, 1984).

Pateman points to the 'profound ambiguity' that resides in liberal conceptions of public and private. Women are traditionally located within the private sphere, men in both. By accepting the division between the public and private spheres and excluding the private from scrutiny, liberal theorists, right up to and including Rawls in the 1970s, 'have excluded women from the scope of their apparently universal arguments' (Pateman, 1987, p. 105). While patriarchy cannot logically be reconciled with liberalism's egalitarianism, a reconciliation can be achieved by default if the marital relationship, with women's role as subordinate domestic labourer, is excluded from philosophical purview.

It has been left to feminists, from suffragist to radical feminist, to expose the implications of the public/private dichotomy both for liberal theory and for gender politics and practice. The effects are very much in evidence in the dualised character of welfare systems that is evident in so many countries. Women are still often treated on the basis of their links with the private sphere, despite the increasing inapplicability of the division. Fraser suggests we can

> summarise the separate and unequal character of the two-tiered, gender-linked, race- and culture-biased US social-welfare system in the following formulae: Participants in the 'masculine' sub-system are positioned as rights bearing beneficiaries and purchasing consumers of services. Participants in the 'feminine' sub-system, on the other hand, are positioned as dependent clients. (1987, p. 97)

This gendered fudge in liberal thinking, together with the greater power of working-class men than working-class women, everywhere resulted in men achieving the vote earlier than women. On top of this, in many instances when the vote was granted to women, the right to stand for parliament initially was withheld. In Britain, male suffrage was achieved in 1910, whereas full female suffrage was not achieved until 1928. In Sweden, men gained the vote in 1909, women in 1921. In Australia, white male suffrage was in place from the 1850s, over forty years before women had similar rights. Australian Aborigines did not achieve equal voting status until the 1960s (Hanks, 1984, p. 23).

Four states in the USA (Utah and Wyoming being the first in 1870), the Isle of Man, New Zealand, and the Australian colonies of South and Western Australia, granted women the vote before the turn of the twentieth century (Sawer and Simms, 1984, chapter 1). However, it was not until this century that any nation granted women the same rights as men to both vote and stand for political office. In 1901, on the occasion of the federation of the Australian states, this right was enshrined in the Constitution of Australia. Although some few women did run for office over the next 40 years, the federal parliament remained an all-male affair until 1943 when the first woman was elected (Sawer and Simms, 1984, p. 5). Even in 1990, men make up 88 per cent of that legislature, and this is the average for all other legislatures in Australia as well (Sawer, 1990, p. 64). Women in Japan received the right to vote as late as 1947 (Takayama, 1990. p. 75). Today women remain seriously under-represented in parliaments around the world. Only in the Nordic countries has an appreciable dent been made in the male monopoly. In these countries men now make up only about 65–70 per cent of elected national representatives, with women's representation at between 30 and 35 per cent (Hernes, 1987a, p. 22).

While the debate that raged in each country about women's right to vote certainly encompassed issues of equality of citizenship, this issue was not necessarily decisive. In Britain, the influence of John Stuart Mill, who argued in terms of universal principles, was strong, and the debate in Australia and New Zealand was also affected by Mill. A number of strategically-placed Australian colonists actually corresponded with him through contact with his brother-in-law (Arthur Hardy) who settled in Adelaide and promoted women's suffrage in South Australia.

Nonetheless, other factors were important and possibly decisive in a number of the countries in which female suffrage was achieved relatively early. For example, in the colonial situations of the USA, Australia and New Zealand, women tended to form a minority of the settler population and therefore posed less of a threat than in countries such as Britian where they formed a majority (Sawer and Simms, 1984, p. 3). Also, there was a discernible spirit of innovation in these newly-colonised societies and less rigid social divisions (Wertheimer, 1977, pp. 259–61). Nonetheless, while women's contribution was recognised as essential for the founding of a colonial society, it was not seen as the equivalent of men's. Women were still cast as the moral guardian of the home and 'colonial helpmeet', a conception of womanhood that was endorsed as well by most feminists of the time (Dalziel, 1977; Summers, 1975).

Men and social welfare

Social welfare for men has essentially revolved around the role of worker and the status of family breadwinner. A crucial interest for employers and workers alike has been the maintenance of at least a minimum level of health, as this not only ensured that the wheels of industry would keep turning, but also allowed the private support of women and children. The earliest health coverage in Britain was provided by friendly societies which developed from the 1830s. By 1904 friendly societies had six million members, at a time when trade union membership was around 1.3 million (Thane, 1982, p. 29). Some of the friendly societies were organised by trade unions, some by the clergy, some by philanthropists. Insurance was also provided by trade unions and by some commercial insurance companies. The subscribers were essentially male workes in secure employment. Few admitted women to membership, indeed few women actually earned enough to pay their contributions. The National Insurance Act of 1911 which established both health and unemployment insurance continued to benefit most the 'better-paid male workers', but it did benefit some women as well. In fact there was an unexpectedly high usage by women, an outcome which prompted an inquiry that reported in 1914. The resultant report indicated that women had high levels of previously untreated illness (Thane, 1982, p. 87).

When it comes to retirement provisions, men in some respects are disadvantaged by those provisions which are based on traditional roles. Men are assumed to be breadwinners and likely to marry younger women. As a consequence even today, in many countries, including Britain, the USA, and Australia, women receive retirement pensions at an earlier age than men. In these countries, the official retirement age for men is 65 years and for women 60 years. This higher retirement age for men can be seen as involving a cash transfer from men to women, the effects of which are amplified by women's longer life-expectancy. Under current British pension arrangements, for example, if a man and woman work all their lives and both retire at 65 the woman receives a national insurance retirement pension 37.5 per cent higher because she is deemed to have deferred her retirement for five years (Prest and Barr, 1985, p. 369). A man would have to postpone his retirement to the age of 70 to gain a similar rate. Nonetheless, the likelihood of a woman gaining this rate is not great because women rarely work continuously throughout their lifetimes and, with lower rates of pay, their pension contributions are likely to be lower. Thus, in practice, men usually enjoy far higher retirement pensions and many women receive their retirement benefits as dependants of their husbands.

While an analysis of men's social welfare will inevitably vary from country to country, particularly in the light of the degree of institutionalisation of the welfare system, there are general trends which have already become clear throughout earlier chapters. Men are far more likely than women to be dealt with within the social welfare system as individual workers, and women on the basis of their family role, either as dependent spouse or as mother. For the USA, Fraser demonstrates that men predominate as claimants of unemployment insurance while women are significantly over-represented in programmes that are family orientated (see Chapter 3). She points out that 'men's programs' tend to be labour market-orientated; to have explicit criteria of eligibility; offer cash benefits and be federally organised. Programmes in which women predominate, on the other hand, are likely to have a welfare orientation; to allow more administrative discretion in the assessment of entitlement; often provide at least some assistance in kind rather than cash and are usually funded at a number of different levels of government and through charities (Fraser, 1987, pp. 93–7).

This broad US pattern mirrors patterns in many other countries, though there are clear differences too. For example, the social security system in Australia, with its absence of contributions and with virtually all benefits flat-rate and means-tested, finishes up with benefits for the unemployed being stigmatised in a similar manner to those that are available for sole mothers. Nonetheless, what does hold good for Australia, as for the USA, is the treatment of men in relation to their occupational status and women as family members (Shaver, 1987, p. 107). Even in Sweden, with its institutional welfare state, this general pattern is still observable. The relatively small amount of social welfare that is provided on a needs, rather than a contributory rights, basis goes largely to women. As has already been discussed (see Chapter 3), this has the effect of positioning the recipients as 'dependent clients', which in turn opens them to the attention of the therapeutic arm of the 'juridical–administrative–therapeutic state apparatus' which Fraser has so emphatically identified as gendered in its focus (1987, p. 98).

In most countries, including Australia and the USA, involvement in war left in its wake a series of welfare provisions which are very much male benefits. They illustrate the significance of the male monopoly over violence and coercion and, hence, the right and duty to bear arms, to which feminists have drawn attention. In Australia, after the First World War a 'segregated and comprehensive welfare system' was established, which included not only disability coverage and compensation for loss of breadwinner, but also the provision of housing and a range of resettlement assistance (Wheeler, 1989). Benefits were almost entirely provided to white men and their dependants, though some few women nurses were covered as well. Aboriginal war veterans were excluded from the benefits which their non-Aboriginal ex-comrades received (Hewitt, 1990, p. 5). Indeed, returning Aboriginal servicemen suffered a return to systematic discrimination. As one ex-soldier expressed it, they were 'treated like dogs with collars on', compared with their 'equal' treatment in the armed forces (Rintoul, 1990, p. 3).

Not only has the Australian repatriation system been more generous than any that has been available to the civilian population, it has not been stigmatised in the same way as social welfare. Indeed, it is not referred to as welfare at all. Repatriation benefits are administered by a separate, dedicated government department. So well quarantined from a definition of welfare have these provisions been that, until the last decade or so, textbooks on welfare in Australia tended to omit all reference to this system of benefits. These repatriation benefits are also unusual in that the client group, since their inception, has had representation as a key partner in a corporate form of decision-making in respect of the development and control of the benefits system. However, the system is still typical of social welfare generally in so far as women's rights depend on those of their husbands. Women, as widows of servicemen, received support more than twenty years before there was any corresponding provision for civilian widows, and they have persistently enjoyed more favourable treatment than civilian widows (Wheeler, 1989).

The family wage

Men's superior role in the public sphere has been associated with financial responsibility for the family. Social welfare intervention was provided for those falling outside the 'normal' pattern, which assumes that non-working people would be 'sustained and protected by the family where the individual male wage-earner is the patron in charge' (Olsson, 1989, p. 265). The role of the husband as provider was subscribed to by Beveridge, as was the notion of self-help.

The state in organising security should not stifle incentive,

opportunity or responsibility; in establishing a national minimum it should leave room and encouragement for voluntary
action by each individual to provide more than that minimum
for himself and his family (1942 Beveridge Report quoted by
Rose, 1986, p. 81).

Nonetheless, Beveridge showed some tact. In recommending pensions for couples, he had wanted husbands and wives to receive a
'joint benefit' because he recognised that it was insulting to treat
wives as dependants. However this recommendation was ignored
(Rees, 1985, p. 81). The notion of the male breadwinner with
dependant wife permeated the postwar social welfare legislation.

The concept of male as breadwinner is most explicitly represented in the concept of the family wage, a concept that remains
important in a number of countries. Because of its centralised
wage-fixing mechanisms, the history of the family wage in Australia provides a particularly clear example for our purposes here
and is thus worth considering in some detail.

In an historic decision in 1907, the High Court of Australia
established a federal 'family wage' which was intended to provide
for a man, his wife and two or three children 'in frugal comfort'.
A female minimum wage was formally set in 1919, at 54 per cent
of the male 'family' rate. This was intended to cover single women,
since by definition a married woman was covered by the 'family'
element of her husband's wage. Women breadwinners were
ignored, but men received the family wage whether or not they
supported a family. It was not until 1974, two years after the
granting of equal pay to women, that the 'family' element of the
minimum wage was abolished on the grounds that an industrial
tribunal was 'not a social welfare agency' and that 'the care of
family needs is principally a task for governments' (Ryan and
Conlon, 1988, p. xv). That the family element was jettisoned after
the equal pay case, rather than then being applied to both men and
women indicates, as Ryan and Conlon suggest, 'that the family
wage had been no more and no less than a ploy to discriminate in
favour of males' (Ryan and Conlon, 1988, p. xvi).

The family wage was also a theme in Britain from the nineteenth
century, until the introduction of equal pay legislation in the 1970s.
As in Australia, the issue was used by unions as one basis for their
bid to increase wages. This meant that it was an ambiguous mea-

sure as far as women were concerned. When Eleanor Rathbone established the Family Endowment Society in Britain in 1917, she saw defeat of the notion of the family wage as central to women's fight for equal pay. The family allowance was a way to undermine the claim by men that a family wage was needed (Dale and Foster, 1986, p. 12). Over the years many women did, however, support a family wage as a means of increasing family income. The vestige of the concept was found in Britain in the married man's allowance until its abolition in 1990 (Naffine, 1990, p. 9). In Australia the dependent spouse taxation rebate represents an echo of the family wage.

Pressures to break down the gendered dichotomy of breadwinner and homemaker developed on a number of fronts. The institution of maternity leave in many countries recognises women as both mothers and workers. Paternity leave provisions, which are less widespread, are perhaps the more revolutionary, because they recognise that men have family responsibilities beyond financial support. Sweden led the world in making benefits in relation to child-rearing available to fathers as well as mothers (Swedish Institute, 1989, p. 4). These arrangements have provided a model for other countries as the case is argued for greater recognition of the role of fathers. A total of 15 months' leave is available to Swedish parents in respect of child care. This can be taken up to the child's eighth birthday. The leave can be split between parents, though the maximum that one parent can take is one year, leaving three months for the other. It is, however, possible for the second parent to formally relinquish entitlement, to the benefit of the other. Combinations of part-time work and leave allow the leave to be taken over an extended period. Payments for parental leave is part of the general social insurance entitlement, and is paid at similar rates to sickness benefit.

In addition, all fathers are entitled to 10 days' paternity leave when their child is born. While these provisions are an obvious sign of recognition of the role of fathers, and an attempt to relieve women of the sole responsibility for child care, they have not resulted in a parity of responsibility. One father in five takes some leave during the first year of the child's life. However, this is likely to be for a much shorter time than the one year that is available. On average 41 days are taken. However, 72 per cent avail themselves of the short paternity leave of up to 10 days immediately after the birth of a child. Also men take between 6 and 7 days per year in sick leave in respect of a child's illness. This latter rate is only slightly lower than for mothers.

In 1990, Australia introduced unpaid paternity leave for fathers. In effect this made the year that was formerly available to mothers, available to mothers or fathers. While it is too soon to assess the usage, because the leave is unpaid, and women generally have lower earnings, it is almost certain that the male rate of take-up will be low.

Male workers and the usurpation of advantage

A family wage for men, with reciprocally lower wages for women, can be seen as a response to the threat from women's cheaper labour. In fact, the origins of the gender segregation which is so typical of workforces today is at least partially due to the deliberate action of male workers to exclude female competition and thus to ensure their own welfare. The capitalist state colluded by meeting some of the demands of male workers, as in the Australian case of the family wage.

British history provides us with valuable insights into the processes through which male workers secured their employment, though there are parallels in the history of most countries. While the 1834 British Poor Laws can be seen as largely the outcome of class politics, the Factory Acts more specifically reflect gender politics. The Poor Laws were essentially concerned with male workers as the labouring class, and with ensuring that state assistance remained less attractive than employment (see Chapter 2). The Factory Acts, on the other hand, focused extensively on women and children and had the effect of excluding them from competition with men. The Factory Acts of 1833, 1844 and 1847 progressively reduced the hours children under 13 were allowed to work in factories to six-and-a-half per day. The 1844 Act restricted the time that women, as well as those under the age of 18, could work, to 12 hours, and this was reduced to ten in 1847 (Evans, 1978, p. 43). 'Tory philanthropists and paternalists' were the activists in these reforms. As Walby demonstrates, whether it was their intention or not, they colluded with male workers in a patriarchal alliance. Walby challenges earlier interpretations of the 'protective' legislation, enacted as nine Factory Acts between 1844 and 1901, which so many commentators have claimed as a victory for progress and enlightenment. Even Marx hailed them as a victory for workers. Walby points out, however, that where they reinforced gender inequality through their impact on women's paid work, the legislation should be described as 'patriarchal rather than as reformist'. She does, however, exclude from this judgement those parts of the Acts that dealt with children and young people and where women and men were dealt with equally (1986, p. 101).

A reading of two of the clauses of the 1847 Factory Act, 'An Act to limit the Hours of Labour of young Persons and Females in Factories', graphically demonstrates the patriarchal basis of the protection of women and highlights the junior citizenship status conferred upon them. Clause 2 of the Act states,

Be it enacted, That . . . no Person under the Age of Eighteen Years shall be employed in any such Mill or Factory . . . for more than Ten Hours in any One Day, nor more than Fifty-eight hours in any One Week . . .

and Clause 3,

And be it enacted, That the Restrictions respectively by this Act imposed as regards the working of Persons under the Age of Eighteen Years shall extend to Females above the Age of Eighteen Years (Evans, 1978, p. 54).

In addition to this state intervention, exclusionary tactics were pursued by male workers in many different occupational areas (Walby, 1986). This reaction has been recorded by feminist researchers in many countries; including for Britain in respect of printers and spinners (Cockburn, 1983, Walby, 1986) and for Sweden in respect of industrial work and government employment (Dahlberg, 1982, p. 151). For Australia, Ryan and Conlon (1988) produce an impressive array of historical evidence from Arbitration Reports of very direct discrimination practised to keep women from competing in the labour market. For example, during the period 1909 to 1912 in New South Wales, women were prohibited from taking apprenticeships in more than 20 trades, including those of baker, butcher, pastrycook and bootmaker. Some bans were industry-wide, for example in the iron trade (Ryan and Conlon,

1988, p. 63). In many awards women were only permitted in the lowest classifications. In the Aerated Waters Award of 1912, five grades of work were identified, with women allowed to be employed only in the lowest grade.

'Protective' restrictions were enacted in virtually all capitalist societies and, in the light of a detailed reading of the evidence, 'protective' takes on a new meaning. It is not coincident that repressive policies towards the Australian Aborigines and other colonised people were also described as protective. In Australia, certain administrators were designated as 'protectors', and these were often the police.

In 1909 in Sweden, a prohibition against industrial night-work for women was enacted. Dahlberg observes that no similar move was made in regard to employment where women did not compete with men. Women were not afforded the same 'protection' in the low-paid women's sectors of the labour market nor, in that notoriously exploitative form of employment, home-work (1982, p. 152). In the clothing industry, in many countries, home-work remains to this day a common form of production, and it is still ineffectively regulated and the workers are still overwhelmingly female.

In Australia, with its strong union movement and its male 'wage earners' welfare state', many restrictions were enforced to maintain men's monopoly, and some still apply today. These included restrictions on night work, on the weight women could lift and a widespread bar to the employment of married women (Bryson, 1989, p. 94). In a strongly unionised mining town, Broken Hill, the unions imposed a general ban on the employment of married women. The last Australian state to remove its marriage bar from permanent public service employment did so as recently as 1973. Even though there were many restrictions, as in Sweden, these were selectively imposed. For example, in nursing and child care, where lifting can be a serious problem, there were no weight limits (O'Donnell and Hall, 1988, p. 119). The lack of appropriate protective legislation in female-dominated occupations renders highly suspicious the explanation of protection as emanating from concern for women's well-being.

Because of the oppressive conditions in factories, and women's simultaneous responsibilities for family care, it can certainly be suggested that reforms restricting women's involvement in the workforce did improve women's welfare. Also, it was not in women's interests to have their low pay affecting male workers' pay, and a family wage was tantamount to a family pay rise. However, the promulgation of equal pay would have obviated the negative competitive effect. Indeed, a few Australian unions took this tack in arguing their wage cases, even if most did not. For example, in 1912 it was argued in the Fruit-Pickers Case that where women and men did the same work they should be paid the same wage (O'Donnell and Hall, 1988, p. 48). While the judgement confirmed the same rate of pay for the same work, it also confirmed that when women do 'women's work they should be paid less than men' (O'Donnell and Hall, 1988, p. 48). Few women, however, received the same pay rates, because it was easy to define similar work as different and because, by and large, men and women performed different work in different industries. Jobs defined as women's, such as nursing and, later, typing, received only a fraction of the male rate, although the fraction has very gradually increased.

The issue of women's protection was contested, particularly by the workers who would be affected, but the protective legislation was inevitably passed by male parliaments. Within the women's movement, opinions were sharply, and often bitterly, divided over the issue (Banks, 1981, Chapter 7; Dahlberg, 1982; Walby, 1986). However, the welfare approach, which had the effect of protecting men's jobs, won through in the end. In most countries such protective measures have only recently been rescinded, largely in response to pressures for equal opportunity.

Restricting the training available to women was another strategy used to achieve a male monopoly (Dahlberg, 1982: 152; Walby, 1986; O'Donnell and Hall, 1988, chapter 6). Restrictions ranged across a wide range of education and training. For example, in Britain in 1829 at a conference of spinners, the meeting resolved to teach spinning only to certain male kin (Walby, 1986, p. 98). Women were also excluded from many professions. These exclusions from training in the higher-paying and higher-status occupations effectively consigned women to the less desirable jobs, which is where they remain today. Women in Sweden during the second half of the nineteenth century did start to move into the public service. However, even this amount of opportunity was for reasons of economy, as their wages were lower, and they filled only the lowest positions (Dahlberg, 1982, p. 152). In Australia, in the New South Wales Public Service, there was a brief time at the end of the nineteenth century, when opportunities for women were widened, though this was essentially for single women. However, resistance by male public servants eventually succeeded, and the upper echelons reverted to being an all-male preserve (Deacon, 1989). Today, men still fill 90 per cent of senior public service management positions throughout Australia (Sawer, 1990, p. 104).

Men's earnings, in all countries, are significantly higher than women's. A study of ten OECD countries revealed that men's hourly rates of pay ranged from 40 per cent higher than women's in the USA, to 10 per cent higher in Sweden which had the smallest gap (Hobson, 1990). The gap between men's and women's economic position is, not surprisingly, at its greatest in those family situations in which the wife is not in paid employment. To have a husband/partner dependent on his wife/partner remains very unusual. As Table 5.1 shows, in Sweden, total husband-dependency occurred among 1.3 per cent of cases and in the USA in 2.5 per cent. On the other hand, total wife-dependency occurred in 11.2 per cent of couples surveyed in Sweden in 1979 and 35.5 per cent surveyed in the USA in 1981. Hobson found that in an additional 5.8 per cent of families surveyed in Sweden in 1979, the husband was partly dependent on his wife. That is, she contributed more to the family income than did he. The equivalent figure for the USA was 5.2 per cent. However, in by far the greatest proportion of families, wives were wholly or partially dependent on

Table 5.1 *Women's economic dependency in Sweden and the USA*

Degree of dependency	Sweden	United States
Husband totally dependent	1.3	2.5
Husband highly dependent (50–99)	1.2	1.6
Husband dependent (10–50)	4.6	3.6
No dependency	11.6	6.7
Wife dependent (10–50)	44.8	22.4
Wife highly dependent (50–99)	25.3	27.8
Wife totally dependent	11.2	35.5
N	3390	98418

Note: The Swedish survey year is 1981 and the United States survey year is 1979.
Source: Hobson (1990).

the income of their husbands. This applied in 81.4 per cent of cases in Sweden and 85.7 per cent in the USA (Hobson, 1990).

Thus we see that men still retain much of the advantage laid down in earlier years. This is generally maintained through the continued segregation of women in the lower-paid segments of the workforce to which they were originally confined, very largely by the protective and exclusionary moves made by male workers. While these arrangements are progressively being challenged as rates of female employment increase, and through some direct policies which attempt to redress women's disadvantage (see next chapter), men still fill both the higher-paying occupations and the higher positions within each occupation. This means, too, that they fill the key positions of power and authority.

Men and state power

William Goode, in the 1960s, when writing on the family, pointed to the manner in which, in every society, in every age, the positions that men fill have been officially valued as the most honorific and the most powerful. This is abundantly clear in contemporary societies, even though the most recent feminist challenges have been more successful than ever before. Men still exercise power in the key arenas: in commerce and industry, in government, in the media and education (especially tertiary education), in the trade unions, in the professions, the church, the law, and significantly, the police and the military. Importantly for theoretical purposes, we must recognise that those holding power are in a strategic position, over time, to define and redefine the structures of power. This makes it possible, if there is too much competition in one arena, to redefine this as less powerful. As has already been argued, we must be alert to the possibility of this form of fight-back as we analyse the incursions into traditional power arrangements which have been made by women and other groups, as they challenged traditional patriarchal arrangements. This process of redefinition has been commented on for the professions, where occupations (primary-school teaching is a good example) lose prestige as they become more widely accessible. There is no compelling theoretical reason why this process should be confined only to the occupational arena.

Men hold most of the major positions of power in modern societies and men's influence becomes increasingly monopolistic, the higher the level of power. Kanter devised a classification of organisations according to how well they reflected the distribution of the gender characteristics of the population they serve. She designates as 'skewed', groups in which the non–dominant members represent 15 per cent or less. Where they represent between 16 and 39 per cent she calls them 'tilted'. 'Balanced' groups are those which range between 60/40 and 50/50 representation (Kanter, 1977). When it comes to high power-wielding groups, the groups are likely to be 'skewed' and at best 'tilted'.

Connell has suggested a very useful conceptualisation of state organisation along two axes, from central to peripheral and from more masculinised to less masculinised (see Figure 5.1). The degree of masculinisation refers to both staff-composition and the ethos of the organisation. He points out that the more central the state apparatus, the more masculinised (skewed) and the corollary, the more peripheral the less masculinised (tilted). Connell avoids using the term feminised because this would be likely to overstate the case of even the most peripheral of state organisations. Of all state

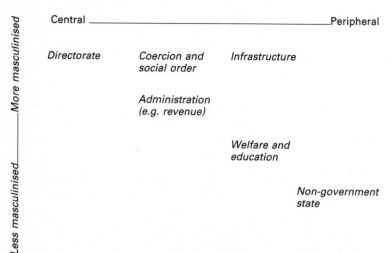

Figure 5.1   Gender-structuring of state apparatus

Source: Connell (1990).

apparatuses, he suggests that those concerned with structure, that is, those organisations which maintain the form of the state, are the most masculinised. These include the departments of the head of state, the structures of coercion and social order, and those maintaining the state infrastructure, such as departments of trade, industry and finance. Sections of the state apparatus with a more social focus, such as welfare and education, are less masculinised, while the 'non-government state', as Shaver has termed it (1982), or what has more traditionally been referred to as the voluntary or non-government sector, he specifies as the least masculinised. This latter part of the model, however, is very much a mixed bag, with much activity still within a male-dominated framework. Nonetheless, it is in this area that women play a large role both as volunteers and low paid workers (Vellekoop-Baldock, 1990). Importantly, this area has provided the space within which, mostly with government support, specifically feminist programmes have been developed. These include women's health services, refuges, rape crisis centres, child sexual assault services and a range of neighbourhood and community services (Connell, 1990).

The more feminised areas of the state apparatus will be dealt with more extensively in the next chapter. Here, as part of men's welfare state, we are concerned mainly with the masculinised poles of the axes. Because of their political importance I will concentrate on the central, rather than the peripheral, structures. However, it is instructive first to look briefly at men's role within the less masculinised areas; that is, those typically connected with social welfare.

Men and caring

The distinction which feminists have made between 'caring about' and 'caring for', between the notion of concern versus the actual labour of caring, is crucial for understanding gender positions within the welfare state (Graham, 1983). Men are expected to care about others, particularly their family and friends. Those in organisational positions are likely to be charged with the task of overseeing the task of caring, again the 'caring about'. They are, however, far less likely than women to be involved in 'caring for' others; the daily, undervalued routine of providing care, in hospitals, nursing homes, child care centres and the like (Rose, 1983a; Finch and Groves, 1983). In the highly-masculinised state apparatus focused on coercion, though, men are likely to carry out daily people-maintenance tasks because there is routine gender segregation in gaols and the armed services. While the state sometimes describes roles within these institutions in caring terms (prisoners are 'looked after'), they are mostly better understood in punitive or custodial terms.

The development of the welfare state can be seen to have involved a shift of some of the responsibility for financial provision from male kin to the state. It has also involved a shift of some of the responsibility for caring labour from women within the private domestic sphere and through voluntary work, to more bureaucratised state-supported structures. Men take a much more explicit role in these formal structures and occupy virtually all positions of management. For nations pursuing welfare state development, there has been a confidence in administrative solutions to social problems, solutions which are developed and applied by expert bureaucrats and professionals. This faith in administrative solutions comes through very clearly in the work of Titmuss. His work also strongly implies that these experts are men, though the universal principles which underpin his argument have the potential to support equality (Rose, 1981).

As has already been discussed, the development of state mechanisms for dealing with what were previously private issues has benefited women and non-dominant groups. During the eighties, however, the view that social problems can progressively be solved by the application of rationally-devised state-implemented social policies, foundered on the rocks of the economic rationalist view that such a course is no longer affordable (and is not efficacious anyhow). This view underpins a trend towards moving services out of the public arena, to be provided privately or through non-government agencies. This trend, expressed in a range of policies, including the promotion of community care in Britain and Australia, must be investigated for ways in which, once again, care will be allocated to women as a private activity, unpaid and unrecognised (Croft, 1986; Bryson and Mowbray, 1986). All cutbacks to the public welfare sector are likely to affect women more than men. There is research evidence from Denmark and the United Kingdom which suggests that voluntary services, which in themselves require unpaid labour power, do substitute for government-provided services. A recent study showed the amount of voluntary effort to be higher in the UK, something which the researchers linked to a smaller proportion of government funds spent on public welfare. Also, more of the volunteers' time in the UK was spent on fund-raising than in Denmark (Boolsen and Holt, 1988). In fact, in the Scandinavian countries there is virtually no volunteer effort in the welfare field, something which is its own comment on the degree of institutionalisation of the welfare state (Vellekoop-Baldock, 1990, p. 139).

As Hernes has pointed out, 'men's status, income and influence are to a large extent determined by the market' (1987b, p. 78). What rationalist economic policies essentially aim to do is to reinvigorate the market sector, which advantages men's interests, at the expense of the public sector. The legitimation of this task is pursued through identifying the market as the key contributor to the national product, while denying the contribution of the public sector. In fact the latter is seen as a cost, partly through not counting unpaid domestic and caring labour in the national product (Waring, 1988). The effect is to imply that 'men dominate on the income side and women on the expense side' (Hernes, 1987b, p. 79). This position is based on an unsupportable economic theory which largely ignores the public sector's 'large investment in the private sector and strongly over-estimates the private and industrial sectors' relative contribution to the public good' (Hernes, 1987b, p. 79).

Within the European Community, this point of view clearly dominated in a conference organised by the Trans-European Policy Studies Association, in conjunction with the Commission of European Communities, in the mid-eighties. The meeting concluded that there must be a broadening of the concept of social policy beyond the 'protective and redistributive role' and recognised a need to free up the effects of calls on the state. It called for 'a decrease in the demands made on the state' and the creation of 'alternative dimensions to satisfy needs' (Vandamme, 1985, p. 193).

Arguments today about the burden of the welfare state have been neatly coupled to negative views about large government bureaucracies as cumbersome and uncaring, which no doubt they often have been. This connection provides an appealing political strategy because this draws on community scepticism about bureaucracy and, at the same time, privileges private bureaucracies. Private organisations are not subject to the same criticisms, despite the research evidence which shows that large organisations, public and private, are likely to have similar limitations and face similar problems (Evatt Research Centre, 1988). Thus the conclusion is drawn that economic and social problems will be solved by reducing government activity and increasing private. A view critical of this position points out that it is those in superior economic positions (that is, males from dominant groups) who will be likely to have their interests best served by the extension of the market.

Corporatism and citizenship

We turn now to the central, rather than the more peripheral state apparatuses, particularly those concerned with maintaining the economic structures. We find that, for some countries, these central structures are conveniently approached through the concept of corporatism. Not that this concept is universally applicable, at least in its tripartite form, which refers to an alliance of business, government and labour. Nonetheless, even in nations such as the USA and Britain, which are not obviously corporatist in the tripartite sense, alliances are formed by powerful interests. Therefore, the processes of corporatism are still relevant especially to gender and race politics, since women and non-dominant groups are inevitably excluded from such alliances. Because of the importance of corporatism as a form of interest representation, the phenomenon merits close consideration.

When certain interest groups are privileged in a formal and routine way within the structure and processes of government, this is referred to as corporatism (Jessop, 1982). In its most discussed form, corporatism involves a three-way alliance, consisting of government, capital and organised labour. While many theorists restrict their use of the term corporatism to this tripartite form (Offe, 1984, pp. 149–50), this does not exhaust the possibilities. Cawson emphasises the manner in which corporatism disperses power to 'groups whose contribution to the economic and social product is indispensable to society, or at least is recognised as such in bargaining' (Cawson, 1982, p. 41). Thus groups outside capital and labour can officially share power with governments. For example, in Australia, after the First World War, the body representative of returned servicemen achieved a key role in policymaking and implementation in respect of repatriation issues (Wheeler, 1989) and has maintained its capacity powerfully to promote the interests of this particular group of men. Established churches, and some professional groups, may be similarly privileged with respect to certain issues.

When corporatist arrangements exist, the critical question for equal citizenship is: whose interests are not represented? The very nature of corporatism is that power is dispersed to groups outside the traditional parliamentary system of government and outside the market system, which involves the logic (though not necessarily the reality) of open competition. Offe (1984) and Cawson (1982) recognise in corporatism some potential for breaking through some of the restrictions of more traditional forms of state power, while Mishra has hailed corporatism as providing the means for salvaging the welfare state. Whatever these possibilities may be, this dispersal of state power clearly has to be reckoned with. Offe declares that not to come to grips with new forms of the state is both 'unrealistic and anachronistic' (1984, p. 250).

As Offe makes clear, corporate structures are still very much class-based. That is because 'not only do the representatives of capital participate on [at least] equal terms, but also their private power goes unchallenged' (1984, p. 248, my parenthesis). This leaves capital in a position to 'determine the limits of the negotiability' because, for capital, the possibility of withdrawing investment, on which the national economy relies, remains an ever-present and powerful threat. Labour, on the other hand, finds itself hedged around with 'legal and factual restrictions' as part of its price for entry into the power game (Offe, 1984, pp. 149–50). In Britain and Australia, where labour is included by left governments and excluded when the right is in power, history clearly demonstrates the contingent basis of even male working-class power. Left governments are under far greater (virtually irresistible) compulsion to cut capitalists into the power game than are right-wing governments to offer participation to labour.

Australia under the Hawke Government provided something of an object lesson on the importance of both class and gender. There was a systematic development of corporatist arrangements after the Labour government's election in 1983. An explicit programme for the representation of employers and trade unions on a range of advisory and administrative bodies was pursued, and tripartite policy conferences were arranged. These arrangements continued to favour male representation because, at senior levels, all three structures are highly masculine. The relationship between the trade union movement and government was formalised in a Prices and Incomes Accord. An elaborate system of controls of wages, including a ceiling on the annual maximum face-value 'increase' that the unions could request, was effected. The union movement accepted this wage restraint in exchange for promises of an improvement in the economy, and some concessions such as a new taxation policy. In real terms, wages were reduced by more than 10 per cent over a period of seven years. Wage restraint, which the unions agreed to, together with unemployment and cuts to government expenditure, subsidised efforts to produce an 'economic recovery'. The commitment to control prices, which was the employers' side of the Accord, was pursued in only the most desultory manner.

Early in the Labor government's term of office, a much publicised Economic Summit was held and later a Tax Summit. Both were arranged to discuss major government policy directions. Women were almost entirely excluded from these meetings. Predictably, the lone woman delegate represented the non-government welfare sector, the non-government state (Shaver, 1982). Welfare issues were largely incorporated into the general industrial arena in the guise of the social wage, albeit as a minor consideration. The official definition of the social wage adopted in the Accord was 'expenditure by governments that affects the living standards of the people by direct income transfers or provisions of services' (Sharp and Broomhill, 1988, p. 75). Had this part of the Accord been given prominence, the interests of women and other muted groups would have been far better served.

As with other forms of power distribution, we must ask who gets represented when the boundaries between state and civil society are blurred in this manner. Where trade unions and representatives of employers deal with governments in tripartite arrangements, many groups are conspicuous by their absence – women, racial and ethnic minorities, young people, old people, the unemployed, to name only a few. As Hernes, speaking of the Scandinavian countries' experience with corporatism, puts it:

Corporatism as a mode of interest intermediation, redistribution and policy formation is a male world of civil servants, organisational leaders and technical professional experts which defines an ever-increasing part of the public interest. It is also an institutionalised form of group access rather than individual access to politics. As a matter of fact these 'groups', i.e. organisations and professions with political clout, have very clear gender profiles. (1987b, p. 75)

Tripartite corporatist arrangements do offer a form of representation to (male) workers. It is indicative of the nature of gender relations that working-class men have, through the concerted action of trade unions and through labour parties, achieved a certain measure of power in formal politics. Trade unions are integral players in the corporate power-game but they still represent male interests more effectively than female. Women may be trade-union members, but they are poorly represented on governing bodies. With a history of treating women's employment as competition, it is unlikely that union leaders could readily recognise and support women's interests. Willetts has hypothesised for Britain that a Labour government in the eighties might have propped up traditional manufacturing and, through close links to male-dominated trade unions, 'might well have presided over a much smaller increase in female participation in the labour force' than has the Conservative government (Willetts, 1989, p. 272).

Mishra in his book *The Welfare State in Crisis* (1984) looks to corporatism as a way through the economic 'crisis' of the eighties. He singled out Sweden and Austria as having the most developed forms of corporatism and proposed the term, the 'integrated welfare state' (1984, p. 103) for their governmental systems. He outlined the distinction between the new form and the old 'differentiated welfare state', thus:

the differentiated welfare state refers to the notion of a set of institutions and policies added on to the economy and the polity, but seen as a relatively self-contained, delimited area set apart from them. The integrated welfare state suggests that social welfare programs and policies are seen in relation to the economy and the polity and an attempt made to integrate social welfare into the larger society. (1984, p. 103)

While recognising that the integrated welfare state cannot over-come the basic inequality on which the capitalist system is based, Mishra does see this emerging state form as offering the most attractive possibilities for dealing with some equity issues and for negotiating the fiscal problems which capitalist societies are facing. A major problem with Mishra's analysis is that he ignores all groups whose interests are excluded by corporatism. Indeed he does not notice the gendered nature of both forms of state. He also underplays the importance of the historical context. As we saw earlier, Sweden has a history of more consensual politics, as well as a greater trust in government action than is the case in many other countries. It is not, therefore, clear how far Sweden's corporate system is generalisable. Jordan is another analyst who points to the way a few countries, notably Sweden, Austria and Norway have, through a corporate method of economic manage-ment, kept down unemployment and sustained their public ser-vices. He suggests that what they have in common is that they are 'small, homogeneous and rich, with efficient industrial sectors, and a strong continuity of (mainly social democratic) governments' (1987, p. 5). Their success nonetheless inspires social democrats and trade unionists in other countries, even where critical con-ditions differ. The Australian union movement, after visits of rep-resentatives to Sweden, Norway, Austria and West Germany, drew up a plan for the economic and social transformation of the nation, entitled *Australia Reconstructed* (Australia Parliament, 1987). This leaned heavily on the Swedish model.

Whatever the outcome for a particular country, it is important to recognise that new power alliances have been forged and new social forces activated through corporatist arrangements. Labour politics, in many countries, have eschewed traditional confron-tational approaches in favour of tripartite cooperation. In the United Kingdom, tripartite corporatism has not been pursued recently because the Conservative governments have not been pre-pared to enter into such arrangements with the union movement. There remains some legacy of the uneasy social contract established by the Wilson Labour Government in the seventies. Indeed the Labour Party, at its October 1989 Conference, declared a move away from traditional confrontationist politics.

The implications of corporatism are inevitably fundamental for issues relating to the distribution of power. If alliances between the government, business and unions are formed we need to be clear exactly who is benefiting and who is paying. Corporatism, at least so far, has not changed the gender or the race balance of power because the parties to the alliance directly represent the traditional patriarchal pattern. It is possible that this arrangement in the longer run could, however, work directly against women. Women have put considerable effort into gaining access to the parliamentary arena and gains have been made, particularly in the Scandinavian countries. If parliamentary power is diminished, much of the effort that has been put into women taking their place in government may turn out to have been misdirected.

Welfare and the role of the state

Having discussed corporatism as a specific form of state organisation in relation to the question of whose interests are represented, a consideration of the role of the state more generally is called for. The debate about the nature of the state has been an intensive one over the last two decades, so my treatment of it cannot be exhaustive.

During the sixties and seventies 'the state' was rediscovered by Marxists, and theorists entered into a spirited debate on how it should be conceptualised. Miliband (1969, 1973) and Poulantzas (1973a and b) are generally located as key stimulators of this debate.

Inter alia, their interchange focused attention on the issue of the extent to which the state should be seen as the means through which, to use Marx's and Engels's phrase, the 'ruling class assert their common interests' (1976, p. 99). They put it more bluntly in the *Manifesto of the Communist Party*, suggesting that 'the executive of the modern State is but a committee for managing the common affairs of the whole bourgeoisie' (Marx and Engels, 1968, p. 46). While there was much divergence and disagreement about theoretical details, there developed fairly general agreement that the proposition that the state merely furthers the interests of capital is too simplistic. The broad conclusion was reached that, though the state is not neutral, within it there is a degree of institutional autonomy and groups can and do have a measure of 'relative autonomy' in pursuing other interests (Poulantzas, 1973a). This, together with the significant expansion of the modern state, led to the linked descriptor that the state is 'interventionist' (Poulantzas, 1973a; Holloway and Piccioto, 1977).

There was widespread agreement that the modern state in advanced capitalist societies is very active and that it can, and does, act in interests other than those of capital. However, as theorists such as Gough (1979) and O'Connor (1973) were careful to emphasise, the state still plays a central role in the maintenance of the capitalist system. Despite the fact that much of this debate has emanated from the United Kingdom and the USA, race and gender issues have been largely absent. There has, however, been a separate debate among feminist theorists though this also, until recently, ignored race (see Chapters 2 and 6).

These Marxist theoretical formulations were developed at a time of intense political activity, in which a range of groups with varied interests competed and often cooperated. This was the time of student activism, anti-Vietnam War protests, anti-nuclear marches, urban social protests, Black, feminist, gay and other demands. Challenging discourses within the social sciences were in the ascendency, and the social sciences were enormously popular. Space was available for the development of competing discourses – feminisms, national liberation, land rights, Black power, gay liberation, civil liberties, environmental and peace issues. Part of the response to this social ferment was the development of theories about the power and importance of social movements (Castells, 1983; Touraine, 1981).

Issues of 'relative autonomy' and the state as interventionist, together with theories of social movements, have particular importance for theories relating to the politics of 'muted groups'. Yet the mainstream of the literature has remained largely focused on dominant male interests, if we add in the working class, as traditionally defined, as a dominant group. Despite the non-conservative politics behind much of the theorising, it has been left largely to feminists and some theorists of social movements to explore more explicitly the scope and limitations of the liberal principles of equality and universalism underpinning the bourgeois, liberal, democratic and male state (Pateman, 1987; Franzway, Court and Connell, 1989; Watson, 1990). It is surprising that more attention was not paid directly to this issue by male Marxist theorists. After all, it is a topic that is fundamental to the complex debate about the problematic legitimacy of the state, which has received so much attention (O'Connor, 1973; Habermas, 1975; Offe, 1984).

It is understandable that, in the context of the sixties and seventies, through a dialectic process between theory and political activity, a simple unidimensional view of state power was rejected. This simplistic view was superseded by a position that allowed more scope to non-capitalist interests (including those of women), though Marxists certainly stopped short of a pluralist view of the state as a neutral umpire. During those decades, many interest groups did achieve some recognition, sparked initially by their own struggle but later translated into the development of state programmes. These programmes included the US Great Society Programme and a wide range of anti-discrimination, equal employment opportunity and affirmative action programmes aimed at minority race and ethnic groups, women, gays, people with disabilities and other groups. Previously-ignored interests gained some advantages through the state, though these stopped far short of conferring equality. The state still remained essentially patriarchal, racist and capitalist, though less determinedly so.

Much has been written on how and why there was a swing in the sixties to a rights discourse and the development of a 'new left'. Much has also been written about the recent so-called crisis of the state and the inability of the capitalist economy to bear the weight of the increasing demands made on the more liberal welfare state (O'Connor, 1973, 1984; Mishra, 1984; Offe, 1984). It has been this complex set of factors that has led to moves to restructure the capitalist economy. Part of that process has been the recapturing of the dominant discourse by conservative economists. As I pointed out earlier, they offered solutions which promised to restore advantages to those who had traditionally been powerful. This discourse largely excludes women's interests. The women's movement has represented a challenge to traditional male power. Left critics have not been successful in producing a competing discourse, though some attempts at 'alternative economic strategies' have been made (Rose, 1983b) – for example, as previously mentioned in this chapter, the Australian Council of Trade Unions' *Australia Reconstructed* and the attempt by the British journal *Marxism Today* to arouse interest in a competing discourse around the concept 'New Times' (Hall and Jacques, 1989). Feminist and other liberatory enterprises also continue, but their messages are increasingly falling on deaf official ears.

The swing to the right and the new enthusiasm for economic liberalism involves the promotion of an environment favourable to capital development. It incorporates a move away from government spending on social welfare. Indeed, a crucial element of these changes is the reduction of the 'sphere of administrative action by public bodies' in favour of the 'sphere of individual decisions and action', that is, the market (Henderson, 1989, p. 33). This policy direction represents a move away from support for the interests of non-dominant groups, towards greater support for the interests of higher-class men. Corporatist processes which ensure this in many countries were well illustrated by a policy in Australia which saw the government provide extra support for superannuation, instead of supporting a wage rise. This scheme, however, was not a universal one and required labour unions to negotiate individually. It will thus benefit most the strongest unions (Castles, 1989, p. 29).

Conclusion

Men's welfare state still largely pivots on the role of breadwinner even though women are being more and more drawn into the role of worker. Occupation remains the crucial basis for the distribution of all three forms of welfare – social, occupational and fiscal. Historically, major welfare gains have come through the actions of male-dominated trade unions and, in many countries, corporatism has strengthened this role. Decision-making of trade unions has rarely deviated far from a traditional approach and has 'shared society's assumption that people should adjust their lives to the job and not the other way round' (Sassoon, 1987b, p. 176). There is currently great divergence between countries with respect to the power of unions. The most dramatic decrease in power was seen in Britain in the aftermath of the 1984 miners' strike. However, as discussed in Chapter 3, OECD analyses suggest that left political power of unions has been eroded in most member countries.

The state, whether corporatist or not, remains both capitalist and patriarchal (as well as racist, ageist, etc). In the light of the shift to economic liberalism, the state can be seen to be acting more like 'a committee for managing the common affairs of the whole bourgeoisie' (Marx and Engels, 1968, p. 46) than was the case during the sixties and seventies. This simultaneously reinforces its sexist nature. Not that this support of capitalist and patriarchal interests is achieved to the total exclusion of other interests, because this would create severe legitimacy problems. However, although oppositional groups are still struggling to be heard, their voices are muted once again. The gains of these groups are very much dependent on state intervention, and expenditure cuts have potentially severe effects. Where the groups have already achieved a degree of organisation, though, pressures can be maintained. For women, for example, this is being done through women in parliament, in government bureaucracies and through women's groups. Crucial policies are also on the books and though these can be dismantled, this is not necessarily an easy or quick procedure. Also, oppositional groups have gained experience in making use of the mechanisms of the state to further their interests. Men's welfare state remains distinguishable from women's, though it is less different in terms of power than it was in its pre-1960s form. The following discussion of women's welfare state provides the reciprocal part of this picture.

6 Women's Welfare State

Elizabeth Wilson, in the first feminist analysis of the modern welfare state, recognised the distinctive experiences of women:

> Only an analysis of the welfare state that bases itself on a correct understanding of the position of women in modern society can reveal the full meaning of modern welfarism (1977, p. 59).

That a different welfare state is experienced by men and women is highlighted by the legislation which has been enacted in many countries to address women's multiple disadvantages, particularly in relation to employment. The Scandinavian collective term 'equality policies' neatly encapsulates the focus of a cluster of policies which are referred to elsewhere by a variety of terms including anti-discrimination, equal employment opportunity and affirmative action. Similar policies are also employed in some countries to deal with other forms of discrimination based, for example on race, ethnicity, disability and sexual preference (Ronalds, 1987). Indeed, as will be discussed later in this chapter, this type of policy had its origin in the USA in the 1940s, as a response to the anti-racist demands of Black Americans.

As became clear when discussing men's welfare state, women's social position remains constrained by its historic association with the role of wife and unpaid domestic labourer, dependent on a male breadwinner and subject to the authority of the husband as head of the family. The effects of patriarchy are still strong, despite the reality that rates of employment among married women are high, and despite the number of women who are without a male partner. The shadow of this traditional relationship to a patriarchal husband is still a presence affecting women's involvement, not only in the home, but also in the economic sphere and their relationship to the state as citizen, client and employee, to use Hernes' tripartite categorisation (1987b).

Feminist analysis has revolutionised our understanding of the state, especially through its focus on the public/private dichotomy. We are now able more clearly to see the links between different aspects of women's situations. Feminists have cogently argued that women's oppression can be fundamentally understood in terms of the very nature of the division between public and private (Pateman, 1987). Women remain essentially associated with the private sphere, notably the home. Because the domains are treated as separate, and the public domain takes precedence, the husband/father who straddles both dominates in both spheres. Women are therefore second-class citizens in both.

State relations are ambiguous for women nonetheless, as they are for the working-class and muted groups generally. The liberal state represents hegemonic dominance at the same time as it allows the possibility of gains, based on principles of universal rights and the equal treatment of citizens. While liberal principles stop short of providing the scope for radical reform of the social structure and the achievement of equal outcomes, they have provided, and continue to provide a basis for a considerable range of political action. The language of rights 'remains one of the key practical tools of the politics of social justice' (Franzway, Court and Connell, 1989, p. 17). Indeed, over the last two centuries much has been achieved by, and on behalf of women, even though those exercising state power have remained overwhelmingly male. Gains include: married women's property rights; women's right to custody of their children; the vote and right to stand for parliament; the right to education at all levels; increased rights over and improved control of fertility; the formal right to, if not the actuality of, equal pay and the equality policies just mentioned. In this chapter I want to consider the state of women's rights and interests within the welfare state of the early 1990s, looking first to the key area of women's economic position, then to women's traditional caring role, and finally to a consideration of policies aimed at redressing inequality.

Women's economic position

Given that women were historically denied property rights and systematically excluded from the better jobs in the paid workforce, it is only to be expected that women will be poorer than men. Over recent years this fact has been publicly 'discovered' and hailed as a new phenomenon: the feminisation of poverty (Pearce, 1979). The term has been taken up with considerable enthusiasm, presumably because of its evocation of an undeniable situation (Scott, 1984). While to talk of the feminisation of poverty does direct attention to women's situation, to the extent that this implies that this is a new phenomenon, it almost certainly is inaccurate. Even though, in the past, we have mostly lacked the 'herstory' to demonstrate it (Gittens, 1983), it seems clear that women have, throughout history, borne the major 'burden of poverty, the exhausting labour of the micro-administration of insufficient resources for their families and themselves' (Rose, 1983b, p. 1).

Women's relative economic position is masked in two-parent households by the tendency of statistics not to deal with access to the family income, but to assume equality of access. Research on the topic of family finances has, however, demonstrated that in general women do not have equal access to, nor control over, family finances (Edwards, 1982; Pahl, 1989). Research has also repeatedly shown that some women who move out of a marital relationship, even though their apparent access to family income diminishes and they are close to, or below, the poverty-line as sole parents, report an improvement of their economic, as well as their social circumstances (Thorogood, 1987; Graham, 1987). Graham, in reviewing successive studies over the past twenty or so years in Britain, found that the proportion indicating an improvement in their economic situation ranges from one fifth to two thirds (Graham, 1987, p. 59). On this basis, it is clear that many women experience poverty within marriage.

However, it is only when women move out of a couple-relationship, to head their own family, that their poverty gains recognition. The female-headed sole parent family, particularly where the mother is dependent on social welfare benefits, shows up in national statistics in most countries as the most disadvantaged household type (Kamerman, 1984). With the numbers of such families generally increasing, this has aroused concern often in the form of anxiety about the 'breakdown of the family'. Given the evidence about women's financial status within marriage, this new-found concern for women's poverty smacks of what Barrett and McIntosh (1982) identify as 'familism'. Familism accepts the 'naturalness' of the traditional bourgeois family, with its male breadwinner, and implies that this form best secures the protection of women and children.

While rates of sole-parent families remain low in some countries – such as Israel, with only about 4 per cent (mostly widows), and Japan – the trend in most industrialised countries is for an increasing proportion (Kamerman, 1984). The proportion of single-parent households has virtually doubled in the USA, Sweden, Australia, France and West Germany, for example, over the last two decades. The rate of increase in Britain has been somewhat slower. Sweden, with around 30 per cent of families headed by a sole parent (in 1985), has the highest proportion. Next comes the USA with 22 per cent. Australia has a rate of 14.4 per cent, which is similar to a number of countries including Canada and France, while the British rate at 13 per cent is slightly lower (Burns, 1987; Graham, 1987, p. 58). The US figure masks significant differences between Black and non-Black families. For the non-Black population the rate of one-parent families is 14 per cent. For Black families the figures reach 65 per cent. This must be linked with the low, marginal and economically insecure position of Black men, at the same time as the welfare state makes available a form (however inadequate) of financial support for mothers and their children. Research suggests that the economic effects of race are broadly similar to this for Afro-Caribbean families in Britain and for Aboriginal women in Australia (Thorogood, 1987; Hunter, 1990).

Sole parents are much more likely to be mothers than fathers. Over 80 per cent of one-parent families are headed by mothers in virtually all countries. In France and West Germany the figure reaches more than 90 per cent (Burns, 1987; Kamerman, 1984, p. 259). It is these female-headed families which are likely to be the poorest families (Kamerman, 1984). Of the nine countries which Kamerman studied, only in Sweden, and to a lesser extent France, with their well-developed family support policies, did unemployed single mothers come close to receiving the average weekly earnings of a production workers. Nonetheless, even in Sweden, as we have already seen in Chapter 3, to the extent that poverty is identified, it falls disproportionately on women, particularly female sole parents (Gunnarrson, 1990).

In the USA in 1987 female heads of households had an annual income of $US13 660 compared with $US24 556 for male heads of households (*Sydney Morning Herald*, 14 August 1987). They made up about half of all families with children in poverty, despite the fact that they represented only one-fifth of such families (Kamerman, 1984: 250). Also, two-thirds of all adults in the USA who lived below the official poverty-line were women (Fraser, 1987, p. 91). In Britain, although sole-parent families make up only 13 per cent of all households with dependent children, as in the USA, they make up about half of all families in poverty (Graham, 1987, p. 58).

Unlike Sweden, where almost 90 per cent of female sole parents are in the labour force, in Australia almost the same proportion (89 per cent) were in receipt of social security benefits in 1985 (Raymond, 1987, p. 40). At the same time, about 43 per cent of all sole parents fell below the officially-recognised poverty line. However, this situation of sole parents improved somewhat in response to a three-pronged government policy instituted in 1987. There was a concerted attempt to get sole parents into the labour force; an additional benefit in respect of children was made available to families with low incomes; and a national child support scheme made compulsory a contribution towards child maintenance from non-custodial parents. These policies, over a two-year period, significantly improved the financial circumstances of female-headed families (Farrar, 1989). Though these particular policies did have many negative elements, including strict targeting of assistance and the failure to alter macro-economic circumstances which affect women, the speed with which an impression made on the problem of sole-parent poverty illustrates the effective role that governments can quite readily play in redressing aspects of inequality.

While the evidence is overwhelming that women as sole parents are poor, the broader dimensions of women's inferior economic position are established by also considering women within couple-households. Hobson investigated this recently, drawing on information from the Luxembourg Income Study. Her study included nine OECD countries and compared husbands' and wives' income to assess the dependency level, which is essentially the 'gap between the wife's and husband's proportion of family income' (Hobson, 1990, Hobson, 1990). The extent of wives' dependency varied, with Holland and Switzerland having the highest levels of total financial dependence, with 68.2 and 52.9 per cent respectively. However, even for Sweden, the country with the lowest levels of total dependence, wives' economic situations were significantly worse than their husbands' (see Table 6.1). In only 11.6 per cent of families was the wife's contribution to the family income equivalent to the husbands' (or greater) and in a similar proportion of families, the wife was totally dependent.

Table 6.1 *Women's economic dependency in several Western societies (percentages)*

Country	Dependency level	Dependent working women	Total dependency	No dependency
Sweden (1981)	40.6	33.4	11.2	11.6
USA (1979)	58.8	36.6	35.5	6.7
USA (1986)	49.8	29.3	29.4	9.6
Holland (1984)	74.7	20.3	68.2	3.4
UK (1979)	60.8	42.0	32.6	5.7
Canada (1981)	59.0	36.3	35.9	7.5
Australia (1981)	60.7	27.4	46.0	7.2
Australia (1985)	59.3	32.6	39.6	7.8
Germany (1984)	62.9	27.0	49.2	6.2
Norway (1979)	55.7	41.5	NA	NA
Switzerland 1982)	77.0	51.4	52.9	2.6

Note: The results in Table 6.1 are based upon data from the Luxembourg Income Study. 'No dependency' represents those couples in economically egalitarian marriages, where the dependency range is between −9 and 9 and 'Total dependency' refers to couples where the wife has no contribution.
Source: Hobson, 1990.

Even where wives were employed, their contribution to the family income was much lower than their husbands'. In Switzerland employed married women's contribution to the family income was only about half that of their husbands. An anomalous finding was that in Holland, with the largest proportion of totally dependent wives, where wives were actually in paid employment, their incomes came closer to their husbands' than for any country – that is, within 20 per cent (see Table 6.1). A rough summary for all nine countries suggests that for women in paid employment, less than 10 per cent earn the equivalent of their husbands and on average they contribute one-third less to the family income, leaving a large dependency-gap. It is in the context of this weak economic bargaining situation that we must view the research that has shown that women do not usually have equal control of family finances. However, we must also recognise that even this degree of relative independence is recent. We now turn to some of the details of the herstory of this move towards greater equality.

Women's role – from legitimate dependence to proletarianisation?

Since the time of industrialisation, poor women have not had much option but to stay in the labour force despite restricted work opportunities and low rates of pay. However, in the light of restricted employment opportunities for women, and with the model of the bourgeois family, with its full-time mother as home-maker in the ascendance (Poster, 1978), most married women became financially dependent on their husbands. For these married women the pattern of their lives can be seen as more appropriate for a rural or peasant society than an industrialised one: family and home were central and they were marginal to the mainstream production processes. As we have just established, even during the eighties, the proportion of women who were totally dependent on their husbands ranged from 11.2 per cent in Sweden to 68.2 per cent in Holland (see Table 6.1). In all countries, the vast majority were at least partially dependent. Women can, therefore, be seen to be 'incompletely proletarianised' (Curthoys, 1986, p. 337). Their relationship to the economy is still, at least to some extent, mediated through kinship, or in the absence of a spouse, the state, via the welfare system. In a capitalist society where the key sources of power are tied to the economic system, women's association with the private realm is a major impediment to equality.

Women's association with the public realm has, however, been changing as women have increasingly joined the labour force. State policies are moving in tandem with this trend, hastening it in some instances, through special labour market programmes to assist with training and job-placement. In other instances, often only after pressure from the women's movement, policies are only gradually recognising the trends. In the late twentieth century women's lives are being modernised, as they are drawn into the economic system. However, they are being drawn essentially into a secondary, rather than a primary, labour market (Fraser, 1987, p. 94). Thus women have achieved a greater degree of economic independence and, at the same time, have become more firmly embedded in class relations, which are themselves male-dominated. This tendency represents one aspect of the effect which many feminist writers point to as a move from private patriarchy to public patriarchy (Hernes, 1987b).

The gradual absorption of women into the class structure as paid workers, rather than as kin of male workers, has been a process to which a number of strands of social policy have contributed. Social security provisions are moving away from treating women as mothers and wives, towards treating them as workers. For example, in the USA, having toyed around with notions of work-fare since the sixties, the federal Omnibus and Budget Reconciliation Act of 1981 finally required all able-bodied applicants for the major welfare programme, AFDC (Aid to Families with Dependent Children) to register for employment or job training, except mothers with children under six years (Digby, 1989, p. 18). This new direction will affect women predominantly, as they head more than 81 per cent of the families receiving AFDC (Fraser, 1987, p. 91). Exemption was given to even fewer mothers in a recent programme in New Jersey, which required mothers to take paid employment unless they have a child under two years of age (Digby, 1989, p. 20). Such programmes have a potential for promoting independence if they can result in employment with adequate pay and conditions, and if good child care is available. However, the problem has been that it is difficult to provide training that fits the trainee for the open market and in many cases the training has taken the form of make-work. Also trainees have suffered financially. While the programmes appear to provide generous benefits, with up to two years of subsidised training, education, transportation and child care, the returns, even with the addition of some reduced welfare payments, may be only slightly higher than the full welfare benefit. Given that costs of working are likely to be quite high, the training period may represent a

reduction in an already marginal standard of living with no job at
the end (Digby, 1989, p. 20).

Similar directions have been pursued in Australia. Until the first
half of the 1980s, women were eligible for support from the state,
in a situation of 'legitimate dependency' (Bryson, 1983). If they
had no man around to support them, they were eligible for a
supporting parent benefit or a widow's pension. The widow's
pension is an entitlement for which there has never been a male
equivalent. This approach to policy has its roots in the pension
system established in the first decade of the century and the repatriation welfare system emanating from the First World War when
widows of servicemen gained entitlement to state support as part of
their deceased husband's rewards for service to country (Wheeler,
1989). Given a demand for women's labour and with fiscal restraint
a government priority, from the mid-eighties a change in government policy became evident. Efforts were being made to direct
into the labour force sole-parent pensioners and beneficiaries and
older widows with no dependent children, no longer eligible for
support in respect of their widowed status. The latter were eligible
for support, but only by way of their employment status, that
is, if no work was available, unemployment benefit could be
claimed.

The 1988 Australian federal budget announced a new employment training scheme for sole parents, the JET scheme (Jobs,
Education and Training). The prelude to this resembles events in
the USA. First, there was a reduction in the time for which the
state provides support on the basis of parental status. This had
gradually been extended over earlier years to the point where
eligibility could be maintained while the sole parent had the care
of at least one child, under the age of 25, if the 'child' was in full-
time education. This age limit was reduced to age 16 in 1987.
After this time the parent must join the labour force. The JET
scheme is a follow-up which aims, through retraining, to assist
beneficiaries to obtain employment.

The move by the state to translate women's dependent domestic
status into independent worker status, was made quite explicit.
As the Minister for Employment, Education and Training's press
release put it,

JET will offer concerted, practical support and direction to

use for arguments
for one parent families.

improve sole parents' job skills and help them into the labour market . . . JET will build on previous Government moves to encourage sole parents out of dependence on the social security system and into economic independence (Canberra, 23 August 1988).

The Australian policy suffers from similar problems to the US scheme, in that it does not guarantee employment at the end and women are likely to be financially worse off during training. Policies to facilitate the employment of women, rather than encourage welfare dependence, have been the basis of state labour market policies in Sweden for many years; in fact the Australian government's recent changes of direction explicitly looked to the Swedish experience for guidance. As with Swedish welfare state policies more generally, they have been in place for much longer, are more generous and are integrated with a comprehensive family package which leaves workers with far fewer associated disadvantages. While the Swedish policies do deal with women as workers, the parenting role is catered for in a range of work-related provisions as we have seen, such as paid maternity and paternity leave, leave to cover sickness of children and the possibility of shorter hours.

Recent government policies which facilitate the proletarianis-ation of women are part of an international trend, recognisable among OECD countries, to deregulate the labour market. Part of this trend involves removing the 'disincentive effect of the social security system' (Henderson, 1989). As can be seen very clearly in the US and Australian cases, for women this means restricting the circumstances under which the status of mother provides eligibility for state support. For younger single women, and young men, this general policy direction is clearly seen in a rise in the age at which unemployment benefit is available, something which has occurred in both Britain and Australia. This involves a focus on education and training, and a reduction of government costs by passing the economic responsibility back to parents. Workfare schemes developed for young people fit with this reassertion of control of young people by parents and the state. Fitting the popu-lation for labour force participation remains a dominant theme.

Education and training

As education policy has been closely linked to work force participation within industrialised societies, it would be expected that, if
women are becoming more completely proletarianised, there
would be a concomitant increase in level of education. This certainly is borne out by the data. In most countries, school retention-
rates for girls have reached the same levels as for boys or are higher
(ABS, 1987, p. 113; Pascall, 1986; Swedish Institute, 1989), though
the figures hide complexities and can be misleading. For example,
Australia excludes from its education figures apprenticeship training where it is carried out mainly in the workplace. The skilled
trades requiring such apprenticeships offer access to elite blue-
collar jobs with good rewards in respect of both pay and conditions. About 90 per cent of these apprenticeships are undertaken
by males (O'Donnell and Hall, 1988, p. 97).

The figures can also be misleading because females are not evenly
spread within education. They are under-represented virtually
everywhere in education and training connected with science, technology and engineering, and in the highest levels of tertiary education. They are concentrated in the lower levels of educational
attainment, and where they achieve qualifications, these are likely
to be in areas with already high female concentration, and therefore
lower status and conditions (Skrede, 1984b).

Rates for women in tertiary education have risen dramatically
over recent decades and the enrolments of women at colleges
and universities together now outnumber those of men in many
countries, including Sweden and Australia (Swedish Institute,
1989; Milne, 1989, p. 8). Nonetheless, the pattern of distribution
mirrors the segregation of the workforce. Sweden closely
resembles the broad pattern for other countries. Women make up
only 22 per cent in technical studies but 86 per cent in nursing.
Women students are still significantly under-represented among
post-graduate students, and this inevitably leaves women poorly
represented in higher academic posts. In Sweden women constitute
just over 25 per cent of all university teaching staff, but only about
5 per cent of these have full professorial posts (Swedish Institute,
1989). Even this low rate is higher than in many other countries,
with the overall figure for women staff in Australia at 19 per cent
but only 2 per cent at professorial level (Grimes, 1987, p. 74).

Women and employment

With women becoming increasingly dependent on paid employment, an understanding of women's welfare state must focus on women's working conditions. Predictably, the most compelling feature is the manner in which women's life outside the home is constrained by traditional notions of life within.

The work that a majority of women do is still in the service sector (cleaning, cooking, nursing, typing) and these jobs are 'treated as natural extensions of their domestic roles and consequently devalued' (Wajcman and Rosewarne, 1986, p. 16). Male definitions of skill prevail, with their emphasis on technology and management. Through recent downturns in the economy, women's employment has continued to rise at a rate faster than men's, but the conditions of that work have deteriorated. Much is part-time, intermittent or performed on a contract basis. These inferior conditions apply more and more to jobs for men as well, a general process which has been tellingly referred to as a 'feminisation of work' (Wajcman and Rosewarne, 1986, p. 15).

The significant increase in the number of women in paid employment over recent years in all the advanced capitalist societies has been accounted for almost entirely by married women, particularly those with young children. By 1983 women made up 41 per cent of the British labour force (Jordan and Waine, 1986/87, p. 64) and by 1988 a similar proportion of the Australian and the Japanese workforce (Takayama, 1990, p. 74). Sweden has the highest proportion of women in employment of all the advanced capitalist countries, with 82 per cent of all women employed (compared with 90 per cent of men), and making up 48 per cent of the workforce in 1987 (Swedish Institute, 1989, p. 2). The rates for the USA and Canada fall below that of Sweden but above those of the UK, Australia and Japan. Some of the industrialised non-capitalist nations have higher rates of employment of women. In the Soviet Union, for example, women make up 51 per cent of the workforce and about 90 per cent of women are in employment (Zacharova and Posadskaya, 1989). In former East Germany, 91 per cent of women were in the workforce (Kerschgens, 1990, p. 19). For many countries the trend for the male workforce is in the opposite direction, with the proportion dropping over recent

202 Welfare and the State

decades (Vogel *et al.*, 1988, p. 71; Jamrozik and Hoey, 1981), a trend which amplifies the concentration of women workers.

In many countries, including Britain, the employment participation rates for non-married and married women are similar, if all work is taken into account (Martin and Roberts, 1984, pp. 9–10). In 1985 the proportion of married women in employment was 52 per cent, a dramatic change from the 1931 figure of 10 per cent (Close, 1989, p. 8). In Australia today, married women are also as likely to be employed as single women, whereas in 1966 only 27 per cent of married women were in the labour force, when the overall rate for women was 35 per cent. In Sweden there has also been a dramatic increase in the number of women with family responsibilities who are employed. In 1967, only 37.6 per cent of women with a child under 7 years were in paid employment. By 1987 this figure had not only reached 85 per cent, but was higher than the overall rate (NLMB, 1989, p. 11).

This trend is not, however, apparent in the Netherlands or Switzerland, as we have seen and overall the rate of entry of women into the workforce has varied enormously from country to country. For example, Norwegian women were slower to enter the labour force than their Swedish sisters, and continue to have higher rates of part-time work. Leira attributes this to 'different images of the mother – child relationship', different requirements of the labour market and different ways of integrating family and economic policy. In the absence of strong demand for women's labour, child-care policy in Norway emphasised the educational role of day-care rather than its role in facilitating women's employment. Therefore, Norway did not achieve the near-universal provision that it did in both Sweden and Denmark (Leira, 1989, p. 196).

While the proportions of married and non-married women in employment are now likely to be similar, married women's working patterns, particularly where there are dependent children, vary in significant respects from those of non-married women and from men. They are much more likely to be in part-time rather than full-time work and their work histories are likely to be broken. The increase in women's part-time employment is usually taken to stem from the desire of mothers to combine child care and paid employment. While this explanation tells part of the story, it is too simplistic.

Both state policy and wider economic forces must be taken into account if a satisfactory understanding is to be arrived at. There is evidence, for example, that in many countries some mothers would prefer to work longer hours if child care which they consider appropriate was available (Ministry of Labour, 1988; Leira, 1989; Women's Bureau, 1990). Here we need to look to child-care policy, as is illustrated by the situation in Norway, to explain women's employment patterns. Because the feminisation of work applies also to jobs traditionally done by males and not only to parents, the changes at least partly represent a restructuring of the labour market to allow employers greater flexibility in their industrial practices. As Smith suggests for the USA, the trend towards part-time work must be seen 'as part of a larger puzzle in which employers are striving for a cheap exploitable labour force' (1987, p. 75). Married women have become a pawn in this game.

Overall, women's weekly working hours in Australia in 1986 averaged 29.5 compared with 39.8 for men (O'Donnell and Hall, 1988, p. 20). This difference in hours worked is made up partly by the higher amounts of overtime worked by men. However, it is mainly accounted for by women's high rate of part-time employment. In 1990, 83.7 per cent of all part-time employment was undertaken by women, mostly by married women. Whereas 92 per cent of employed men were in full-time employment, only 62.5 per cent of women were, leaving 37.5 per cent of women in part-time work (Women's Bureau, 1990). Despite Sweden's higher rate of female employment, a similar pattern of part-time work is evident there, particularly during the child-rearing years. Indeed the part-time pattern is even more marked in Sweden than Australia (Lever-Tracy, 1988, p. 219), largely because conditions of part-time work for parents are superior to those in Australia. This facilitates the combination of paid employment and responsibility for child care with minimum loss of economic benefit. In Sweden in 1985, 44 per cent of employed women worked part-time, compared with only 6 per cent of men (Swedish Institute, 1989, p. 2). Australia has been moving towards the Swedish situation over recent years and part-time work can now be undertaken, at least in the public sector, with occupational benefits and conditions proportionate to those for full-time work. Maternity leave is now covered in wage awards for virtually all workers, but, with the exception of some public service occupations such as teaching, it is unpaid. This explains why the number taking up the right to maternity leave is not high (Glezer, 1988, pp. 3–4). Australia moved closer to the Swedish model in July 1990 when paternity leave (unpaid) became a right.

In Japan, there has been a significant rise in the proportion of part-time work that is done by women, as their proportion in the workforce rose to 41 per cent. In 1960, women undertook only 43 per cent of the part-time work. By 1988 this figure had risen to 72 per cent (Ryan, 1990, p. 10). The penalties attached to part-time work in Japan are particularly severe for women, because the rate paid is only 75 per cent of that for full-time work. Given that women's wages are only just over half those of men's anyway, this represents an extremely exploitative example of the 'feminisation of work' (Ryan, 1990, p. 11).

(i) Unemployment

Unemployment rates confirm both women's inferior position in the workforce as well as their commitment to employment. In the vast majority of OECD countries, over recent decades women have suffered consistently higher primary rates of unemployment than men. In 1990, registered unemployment rates in Australia were 7.1 per cent for women and 6.4 per cent for men (Women's Bureau, 1990, p. 12). In Denmark, with an even higher overall rate of unemployment, in 1987, the unemployment rate for women was 10 per cent compared with 7 for men (Danish Statistics, 1988, p. 124). In West Germany, Sweden and the USA the respective rates in 1981 were 4.5, 2.4 and 2.6, for men and 6.9, 6.6 and 7.4 for women (Björklund, 1984, p. 38). By 1985 the picture had changed for Sweden. Under the impact of a labour shortage men's and women's rates were both down to 1.9 per cent (Swedish Institute, 1989, p. 2). However this efect does not necessarily suggest that women's rate will stay the same as men's under conditions of higher unemployment. Indeed, as late as 1987, the women's rate was 4.1 per cent compared with 1.9 for men (NLMB, 1989, p. 17).

The figures for unemployment among women in Britain stand out as different, with women actually having lower rates than men. But this is largely an artefact of the conditions for registration as unemployed (Björklund, 1984, p. 38). However, we need to recognise that virtually everywhere, with the possible exception of times of severe labour shortage, the official unemployment rates, for both men and women, are under-estimates. For women the likely under-estimation is greater, compounded by the fact that women have higher rates of hidden unemployment and more part-time workers who would prefer to work longer hours (Björklund, 1984, pp. 23–4). In Sweden, for example, even when there is a low rate of unemployment, many workers would prefer to work longer hours (Ministry of Labour, 1988, p. 33). In Australia, women make up three quarters of the 'hidden unemployed', a category which accounts for more people than those officially unemployed (Women's Bureau, 1990). This statistic covers people who would prefer employment but who are not actively seeking work, because of illness, or experience of discrimination on the grounds of, for example, age or race or for reasons of discouragement about its availability.

(ii) Relative economic disadvantages of women's employment

For a web of reasons, everywhere in advanced capitalist societies, men earn more than women. This has already been discussed under the heading of women's dependency levels, which are based on the gap between husbands' and wives' earnings. When we look at the same picture from the point of view of payment for the job, we find a similar diversity between countries in respect of the gap between men's and women's average rates of pay. Of ten countries studied by Hobson (1990), the USA had the lowest average hourly rate for women. This was only around 60 per cent of the rate for men in 1986, while rates in the United Kingdom, West Germany, Canada, the Netherlands and France ranged between 70 and 80 per cent. The highest rates were found in Australia with about 86 per cent of the male hourly rate in 1985, and Sweden, with 90 per cent in 1981 (Hobson, 1990). The Japanese rate of about 52 per cent is exceptionally low (Ryan, 1990, p. 11).

The issue of pay rates is complex, and different indices give slightly different pictures, though the depressed state of women's income remains the same. To illustrate this we can look in more detail at Australia, with its comparatively high hourly rate and its highly-centralised industrial system. Despite the fact that, legally, equal pay was achieved in Australia in 1972, by 1989, women on average were still only earning 83 per cent of the full-time weekly rate of men. Since women have fewer opportunities for overtime, when total earnings for full-time workers were compared, the women's rate dropped from 83 per cent to 78 per cent. Because of women's high rates of part-time work, if we compare all workers, women's average weekly earnings fall to only 65 per cent of men's (Women's Bureau, 1990). At 78 per cent for full-time employment this rate is much the same as for Sweden in 1985, where women also rarely worked overtime. In that year, women in industrial production jobs, however, came close to equal pay, with earnings on average at 90 per cent of the male rate (Acker, 1989, p. 2).

Women's average earning rates in both Australia and Sweden are higher than for virtually all other countries. This can be explained in terms of the relative effectiveness of strongly central-ised mechanisms for wage-bargaining. Relatively uniform wage rates apply and these are centrally set through a corporate process involving employers, unions and government. The relatively favourable outcome for women must be seen as more a product of class power than gender power, however. In Australia, as in Sweden, the discourse on equality between the sexes has largely been separate from, and treated as incidental to, the questions afforded most importance, those concerned with 'production, class and societal power' (Acker, 1989, p. 2). In both countries central-ised wage determination, which has delivered gains to women, is being weakened under the pressure of economic liberalism and so women's position must be recognised as insecure (Acker, 1989, p. 2; O'Connor, 1990, p. 3). There is evidence in both countries that the wage-gap between higher-paid and lower-paid workers is widening for both men and women. The trend among OECD countries to reduce the centralised power of unions (Henderson, 1989) bodes badly for women and other groups who have habitu-ally fared badly in the employment market.

Women's vulnerability to poverty is very clearly over-deter-mined. Research suggests that full-year, full-time work is the best defence against poverty (Cass, 1985) and demonstrates that women are vulnerable in terms of both criteria. The effects of part-time work and low rates of pay are compounded by the intermittent nature of women's working life. Most women have broken work-histories. A recent Australian study of divorced parents, which included 456 women, found that while all but 3 per cent had been in paid employment at some time during their marriage, only 2 per cent had a continuous employment-history compared with 80 per cent of their ex-husbands. For two-thirds of the women the reason for their interrupted work-history was marriage or children. For only 9 per cent of the few men who actually had a broken work-history, was this for family reasons (Funder, 1986, p. 77).

Estimates of loss of income to women from child-bearing show quite startling results. A UK study using 1980 data estimated a lifetime loss for a woman bearing and raising two children of £122 000 (Beggs and Chapman, 1988, p. 41). This is equivalent to $A370 000 and is very similar to one of the estimates ($A384 000) from an Australian study which computed different amounts according to education-level and number of children. What is perhaps most significant is that the major loss is associated with the birth of the first child. This accounts for almost half of a women's potential lifetime earnings. Subsequent children account for only between 5 and 10 per cent of additional loss. The loss is somewhat higher for women with higher education, because of their capacity to command a higher level of income when they are employed (see Table 6.2). There is a great deal of variation in the proportion lost according to education-level (Beggs and Chapman, 1988, p. 39). Beggs and Chapman also report research from the USA which has estimated far lower rates of loss, around $US43 000 ($A75 000) in 1981. This difference is partly accounted for by assuming higher future working-rates for today's younger mothers. While Beggs and Chapman acknowledge this as a possibility, they point out that they themselves actually underestimated income losses for older women by assuming employment at current rates (Beggs and Chapman, 1988, p. 41). Although there can be much debate about the precise assumptions underlying such projections it certainly cannot be disputed that having children seriously reduces women's lifetime earning capacity.

Child care

This loss of income makes the significance of women's caring role very clear. Because it remains women who take prime responsibility for caring within the society (Finch and Groves, 1983; Bryson and Mowbray, 1986; Dalley, 1988), it is not possible to consider

Table 6.2 *Forgone total earnings at age 60 from different education and child-bearing scenarios ($000)*

	Investment Rate of Interest		
	0%	5%	7%
Number of children		*High education*	
0	0	0	0
1	439	1316	2100
2	537	1576	2499
3	615	1776	2762
		Average education	
0	0	0	0
1	336	929	1455
2	384	1059	1656
3	419	1145	1782
		Low education	
0	0	0	0
1	282	738	1141
2	310	817	1264
3	330	868	1340

Source: Beggs and Chapman, 1988, p. 40.

women's welfare state without taking into account the availability of forms of care for family members, and child care is obviously central.

Daytime care of children of school age is effectively provided for under the guise of compulsory education, though even this leaves the time between the start and finish of school and the normal hours of paid employment to be catered for. At school, supervision is inevitably, though incidentally, provided as students are educated to take up their roles as workers and citizens. Governments in capitalist countries have, however, been more reluctant providers of care for children of pre-school age, something which cannot be divorced from a noted historical reluctance to facilitate women's employment. With the exception of the period of the Second World War, when in Britain, the USA, Australia and Sweden (Ruggie, 1984, p. 255), for example, governments provided for the care of children of women workers who were required to fill the labour shortage, child care has not, until very recently been a priority service in the advanced capitalist nations. There remains great variation in the degree of particular governments' commitment even today.

In many countries, day care for children is still not a priority of government. In Britain, problematic attitudes have a long history, reflecting not only reluctance on the part of the authorities but also on the part of mothers. The first nursery was opened by a voluntary organisation in Marylebone in 1850. This was inspired by the French example, where between 1840 and 1867 over 400 crèches were established throughout the country (Wilson, 1977, p. 44). Despite initial support by influential charity workers, early British nurseries were not very successful. Nor were they popular with poor mothers who preferred to maintain informal arrangements. Sweden opened its first crèche in 1854, to cater for the children of poor mothers (Ruggie, 1984, p. 254). The Swedish authorities were not keen on crèches, seeing them as only appropriate in cases of dire necessity, though nursery schools were greeted with enthusiasm (Ruggie, 1984, p. 254).

Concern with high infant mortality-rates led to other attempts by the British state to intervene in child care. In 1891, a regulation was enacted making it illegal for a woman to return to work within four weeks of childbirth. The onus was, however, on employers to enforce the regulations, which meant that the law was more honoured in the breach than the observance. It was criticised by some feminists at the time as another example of the attempts of male trade unionists to eject women from the workforce. A more realistic solution emerged in 1911, with the introduction of the National Insurance scheme which allowed workers to insure for maternity leave (Wilson, 1977, p. 47).

Underlying much of the British debate on child care and infant mortality last century was the liberal view of the home as a private haven which should not be invaded by government. In 1874, a speaker to the National Association for the Promotion of Social Science claimed to be prepared to 'see even a higher rate of infant mortality' rather than see intrusion 'one iota further on the sanctity of the domestic hearth and the decent seclusion of private life' (Hewitt, 1975, p. 180). This liberal philosophy still affected government attitudes in Britain in the eighties, casting child care as largely a private, domestic responsibility (Ruggie, 1984, p. 183). Where public day care has been provided, it has been mainly of a custodial kind, provided largely for the poor to alleviate problem circumstances. The interests of 'non-welfare working mothers' were excluded (Ruggie, 1984, p. 148). Day care that is utilised by working parents has been largely sought through informal, kin or friendship networks or on a private commercial basis. While commercial care facilities are, in theory, subject to regulation by local authorities, the policing of the regulations is haphazard (Ruggie, 1984, Chapter 5). Educational programmes are available for children of pre-school age, but the hours that these are available are unlikely to be suited to the hours a mother works.

Child care is not extensively provided on a collective basis in the USA either and must largely be purchased on the commercial market. Vicki Smith contends that child care in the USA remains 'one of the most formidable issues influencing women's labour market status'. She suggests that it needs to be given priority as an issue by trade unions and working women's organisations (1987, p. 250). In Japan most child care is provided by relatives, though private centres are springing up to meet the new demand as more and more mothers join the labour market (Takayama, 1990, p. 75).

In Denmark, Norway and Sweden, child care has been afforded much more central importance. In Sweden and Denmark it is provided as a universal service, aimed both at serving the needs of working parents and the educational needs of children (Ruggie, 1984, p. 292). Denmark was the first of the Scandinavian countries to provide extensive day care on a 'mass consumption' basis, as the rate of dual-income families rose (Leira, 1987, p. 11). Norway has not provided the same volume of day care as Sweden and Denmark, but the amount still outstrips that which is commonly found in Western Europe. The Scandinavian countries do not have services provided on a commercial basis; they are supported by central and municipal governments. Consumer contributions to costs vary, with rates around 22 per cent for Denmark, 21 per cent in Norway and 10 per cent in Sweden in 1984 (Leira, 1987, p. 7). From the mid-eighties, services in Denmark were under some financial pressure, along with state social expenditure generally, and some cost-saving measures were instituted (Leira, 1987, p. 47). The Swedish government, on the other hand, has been extending services, having committed itself, through legislation in 1985, to the provision of municipal day-care for all children aged 18 months to 6 years by 1991 (Swedish Institute, 1989, p. 4).

Australian policies in the late eighties fell somewhere between Britain and Sweden, though the number of places falls far short

of the Scandinavian countries. In Australia up to 1972, the very
small amount of care that was available was provided by local
government and charitable organisations and, as in Britain, this
was largely reserved for families where there were severe social
problems. Non-welfare working mothers, also as in Britain, relied
on informal arrangements or commercial centres, something which
many still do. However, since 1972, there has been a gradual but
significant increase in available services, under pressure partly from
the women's movement but, probably more decisively, under
pressure of the demands of the labour market for women workers.
The federal government funds non-profit organisations to provide
services, and subsidises the fees of parents on a means-tested basis.
Despite this commitment, in 1988 the care funded by government
was only sufficient to cater for 9.5 per cent of pre-school children,
though this represents a marked increase from the 1982 figure of
5.8 per cent (O'Donnell and Hall, 1988, p. 65). The vast difference
in national provision is illustrated by the fact that the Swedish
commitment to provide full coverage of day care was triggered
by dissatisfaction with a coverage of 42 per cent of all pre-school
children, when the full demand in 1984 was estimated to be 64 per
cent (Swedish Institute, 1987, p. 2).

Women and caring

The concept of social welfare involves not only financial support,
but also the provision of care for those in need and in states of
dependence, that is, children, the sick, the elderly and those with
disabilities. Caring is pivotal to the welfare state and it is a gendered
activity. It is women who do the caring, and women (particularly
older women) who receive a great deal of the care. Thus women's
welfare state is very much concerned with this issue, though it is
only recently, through the writing of feminists, that caring has
begun to be discussed at all in a systematic and critical manner.
Fraser has pointed to this phenomenon, suggesting that

> As clients, paid human service workers and unpaid caregivers,
> then, women are the principal subjects of the social welfare
> system. It is as if this branch of the state were in effect a 'Bureau
> of Women's Affairs' (Fraser, 1987, p. 92).

Neglect of the issue of caring, and its gender component, must be understood as part of the general acceptance of the naturalness of the traditional sexual division of labour. This is compounded by the low status afforded much caring work, which renders it invisible to those who frame dominant discourses. Second-wave feminism has, however, positioned caring labour as part of the debate about the nature of women's subordination. Caring also becomes a fundamental concern in the determination of the sort of society that feminists strive to attain.

As has already been raised in relation to men and caring, feminist theories have made the vital point that caring is a bifurcated concept and activity. It essentially consists of 'caring about' and 'caring for' (Graham, 1983). 'Caring about' connotes feeling for other people and is most often associated with love and concern between family members. 'Caring for' is the practical side of these feelings, the day-to-day tending work. 'Caring for' involves actually providing the physical protection and assistance that dependent people need. The dual elements are epitomised in the role of mother. Here the two aspects of caring are firmly fused. Mothers are expected to care about and for their offspring. More than this, they are considered unnatural if they fail to do so. Fathers are expected to care about their children and this involves taking appropriate responsibility for them. However, fathers are entitled to merely oversee the process, to ensure that 'caring for' is carried out rather than having to do it themselves (Dalley, 1988, p. 8). For a minority of wealthy women this has also been the case, but it is far from the norm. Even in these families, the mother's caring role is very much more strongly sanctioned than the father's.

The association of these dual elements of the caring role with gender is generalised across a wide and significant range of social interaction. Women's welfare state very clearly involves both sides of the caring equation. It is the coupling of the two elements of caring which in large measure accounts for women's economic and social subordination. Responsibility for informal caring is at the base of women's lower employment rates, the intermittent nature of their employment and partly accounts for the extent to which women take part-time paid work. When women are in paid employment they are likely to be in jobs which mirror the caring role within the family. Women are the carers of the society, both inside and outside the home.

This applies in three locations – within the private sphere of the home, in the public sphere of the welfare state and within that less masculinised sphere, identified in the last chapter as the 'non-government state', traditionally called the voluntary sector. This latter sector has often been treated as an extension of the domestic, yet in certain areas the relationship with the state has a long history. Today, with very general interest in cost-cutting, we find a renewed interest in voluntary services. This is evident not only in countries such as Britain (UK Parliament, 1989, p. 5) and Australia (Vellekoop-Baldock, 1990, p. 111) where the welfare state is in fairly poor condition, but also in countries such as Norway (Waerness, 1984, p. 80) which have managed to maintain an institutional orientation. There is an increasing emphasis on community care, with its reliance on networks of, largely female, carers, both paid and unpaid and an associated system of state-regulated voluntary organisations. In the circumstances, this area is becoming even more appropriately referred to as the 'non-government' state (Shaver, 1982).

In virtually all countries, service work, both paid and unpaid is dominated by women. Women are nurses, infant teachers, child-care workers. They also perform roles which service the needs of men, not only as wife, but also as secretary, 'girl Friday' and hostess. A study of 17 countries, covering Europe, the USA, Canada and Britain, found that in the early 1980s by far the highest proportion of women workers were in service occupations and in seven of the countries, these occupations accounted for over 80 per cent of employed women. The countries with the highest concentrations were the Netherlands, Sweden and Canada (Skrede, 1984a, pp. 12–13). Although not included in Skrede's study, Australia too has particularly high levels of occupational segregation.

While over recent decades, under pressure from the women's movement, some greater recognition has been afforded to women's caring labour, there is also evidence everywhere that as governments seek fiscal economies, more responsibility falls back on women both within the family and in the wider community. As we saw in Chapter 3, Japan provides us with a striking example of the way women's caring activities are relied on at the same time as they go unrecognised. Although the circumstances are more extreme in Japan, because of the relative lack of welfare state development, the social processes are not different in kind from elsewhere. It is therefore worthwhile considering the situation there in some detail.

Most writers about welfare in Japan fail to acknowledge the gendered nature of caring at all. For example, Maruo emphasises the importance of the provision of welfare by the family in Japan without ever mentioning that care may be differentially provided by women and men. She provides convincing figures that a great deal of care for the elderly is provided within the home and that this practice has wide social acceptance (1986, p. 69). The picture is very different from Western societies. In Japan, 55 per cent of aged people express the desire to live with their family while the comparable figure for the United Kingdom is 9 per cent, the USA 6 per cent and Canada 5 per cent. In 1983, fewer than one aged person in 33 was living with her or his family in the USA or the UK. In Japan the comparable figure was more than half. The Japanese government now provides some socialised services for the aged, but these are minimal and availability varies greatly from district to district. As far as workers are concerned, the services rely heavily on part-time workers, and presumably, as in other countries, these are women, though Maruo, significantly, does not say so. However, whereas in Sweden there is nearly one home helper in the local area for every 25 elderly people, and in Britain about 1 to 100 in the London boroughs studied, in Japanese cities the ratio is 1 to 300 (Maruo, 1986, pp. 68–70).

The process of rendering women's caring labour invisible and the failure to separate the concept 'caring about' from 'caring for' is complete in Maruo's paper. She suggests that:

> The absence of public provision of welfare services for the elderly in Japan does not mean that they receive no care. Traditional Japanese values lead most adult children to care for their elderly parents within the same household. The persistence of community values is also reflected in the institution of district welfare commissioners. The minister of health and welfare appoints 160,000 commissioners to work on a voluntary basis to mobilise semi-voluntary home helpers to provide a variety of personal social services for the elderly within their local community. The elderly in Japan now rely on the state for pensions and for most health care, but they still look to informal com-

munity and family arrangement for much personal care (Maruo, 1986, p. 71).

The tendency to ignore women is not, of course, restricted to Japan. In the same collection, Richard Rose (1986), in looking at family as a source of the provision of services in the UK, does not mention women either. He merely suggests that 'meals are a joint product of the market and the household' (1986, p. 84). He even quantifies the output, estimating that 'more than four-fifths of meals are produced at home by unpaid household labour' (1986, p. 85). He estimates household health care to equal around 37 per cent of the total cost of health in 1981 (1986, p. 93). When it comes to care of the aged, he suggests the 'household has a virtual monopoly'. In only 8 per cent of cases were home-helpers used; in 6 per cent, health visitors, and meals on wheels or old persons' lunch clubs catered for only 5 per cent in 1982 (Rose, 1986, p. 91). Rose pronounces that 'Pluralism in health care still prevails; the household remains important' (1986, p. 93). The household (largely the women in the household) also remains important in Australia where it is estimated that the government provides around 7 per cent of the services used by the aged (Kendig, 1986).

Women and power in the welfare state

Virtually all official positions to do with policymaking, adminis-tration, and importantly, enforcement on behalf of the state, were in the past in the hands of men. This situation has been changing slowly over recent years, and at a different pace in different coun-tries. However, there is still nowhere where the unequal power of the sexes has been completely redressed. The general disadvantage of women has not been overcome even in Scandinavian countries, where women enjoy probably the most extensive citizenship and the highest standard of living. As Hernes puts it:

> Although the generally low level of social inequality, combined with a highly developed and universal social insurance network, assures Scandinavian women a comparatively high standard of living, this is not synonymous with power nor with the ability to shape and influence their own status, despite the fact that the ability to influence one's status is considered an integral part of

personal welfare in all Scandinavian welfare thinking. (1987b, p. 72).

In Chapter 5 the masculine bias of corporatism was discussed, including Hernes's point about the corporate nature of the state as an impediment to women's equal citizenship in the Nordic countries. Women have limited representation in these corporatist decision-making structures, yet these are now taken as given. They represent compromises between capital and workers, 'an institutionalisation and legitimation of class conflict at its most civilised and refined'. Women's claims challenge these intricate arrangements (Hernes, 1987b, pp. 81–2). In Australia, where there is a long history of tripartite corporatism, with government, unions and capital cooperating (and often conflicting) to regulate conditions of employment, women have also found themselves poorly represented. This continues to be the case, though with marginal improvement.

Even where corporate arrangements are not prominent, as in Britain today and in the USA, the decision-makers remain predominantly male. The virtual exclusion of women from the military, the state's major and highly symbolic coercive institution, is also of central importance. Women are generally forbidden to take part in combat roles and are very much under-represented in the armed services. Of the NATO forces in 1979–80, the US had the highest proportion of women, with eight per cent. The lowest proportion was West Germany's one-tenth of one per cent.

Women thus remain a 'protected' group rather than acting as 'protectors'. Contemplation of the military role is salutary, since it exposes the actual and symbolic power of physical force and throws into sharp relief the undervaluing of caring for people, a role in which women do predominate. Herein lies an unsolved dilemma for feminists. Should full equality be sought through having women fully accepted into the military, thus achieving parity within the coercive role of the state? Such a solution fits with a liberal 'equal opportunity' policy, though liberal feminists are not necessarily keen to push their argument this far. Radical feminist answers would point to the development of essentially women-focused activities such as caring and cooperation, rejecting patriarchal militaristic strategies. Socialist feminists would broadly see that if class oppression is overcome so would be capitalism and war.

Equality policies

Perhaps the most conspicuous difference between men's and women's welfare states today lies in the policies which have been developed in many countries explicitly to address women's relative disadvantage. The extent and nature of these policies varies greatly, with the Scandinavian countries generally leading the way in policies and, particularly, in results. Elsewhere we find far lower proportions of women occupying the parliamentary benches, and nowhere else do we find a systematic effort to encourage fathers to take a share of child-rearing. While feminists within these countries, and indeed the governments themselves, recognise the shortcomings of the 'equality policies', they do make a systematic attempt to address major issues. Here I shall consider in detail the US experience with anti-discrimination and affirmative action policies. Similar principles underpin the British and Australian programmes. These will then be contrasted with the broader Swedish approach.

The first national commitment to equal employment opportunity can probably be attributed to President Franklin D. Roosevelt, and this related to race rather than gender. In 1941, in response to pressure from Black protestors, he issued an Executive Order prohibiting discrimination by Federal contractors. With no associated penalties, it is not surprising that little came of this. However, the stage was set for later action. Requiring Federal contractors to meet certain employment standards became a key strategy of anti-discrimination programmes in the USA. In 1961, in response, once again, to civil action by Blacks, President Kennedy issued an Executive Order which required that Federal contractors take 'affirmative action' to ensure that employees and applicants for employment were treated 'without regard for their race, creed, colour or national origin' (Sawer, 1985, p. 2). This was the first time that the term affirmative action had been used officially. Until 1965, however, the aim was pursued on a voluntary basis, or rather more accurately, voluntarily ignored. In that year the order was strengthened through the establishment by the Office of Federal Contract Compliance (OFCC), of regulations which had the force of law. At the time it was estimated that approximately one-third of all employed people in the USA worked for employers who held government contracts, and the figure rose to over half if associated firms were counted. Thus the potential scope of the policy was extensive. But the government again chose voluntary compliance, eschewing the use of its coercive legal options. The ineffectiveness of sanctions has been a recurrent theme in relation to anti-discrimination and affirmative action in most countries. This is probably a predictable outcome, given that the lawmakers have to date been very much male, pale and hale.

By 1967, under pressure from the women's movement, sex became one of the proscribed grounds for discrimination. Contractors were also required to develop 'written affirmative action plans', in keeping with guidelines set by the OFCC (Sawer, 1985, p. 2). A troublesome debate about quotas and goals developed largely in relation to higher education which, in 1970, was forced into the centre of the affirmative action debate through a class action by more than 500 complainants against a range of universities, including Harvard, Columbia and the state Universities of California and New York (Sawer, 1985, p. 4). To this time all action had been precipitated under administrative law but, in 1972, legislative assent was achieved to the amendment of Title VII of the Civil Rights Act to cover all private employers of 15 or more people and all organisations with 15 or more members. Although no quotas were set by the Act, the courts have at times ruled that employers found guilty of discrimination should meet targets set by the court (Sawer, 1985, p. 6).

While the US legislation has arguably delivered gains for both Blacks and women, resulting in increased representation in a range of employment areas (Sawer, 1985, p. 14), any gains are problematic. Many cogent criticisms have been levelled at the programme. It has been suggested that women finish up competing against minority-group men; even where entry is made more accessible, pressures in the work-place result in many women moving out with their positions then taken by men; and that the problems of traditionally sex-segregated 'women's jobs' are ignored (Bacchi, 1990, p. 170). As well, with the ascendancy of the New Right and cuts to government expenditure, gains are threatened, especially because they were often made within government employment.

The most fundamental problems, however, reside in the nature of the action taken. The anti-discrimination laws and, to a somewhat lesser degree affirmative action, are based on the liberal, individualistic assumption that likes should be treated alike, what Westen has called the 'fallacy of equivalences' (Westen, 1982, pp. 582-3). Such an approach inevitably favours those who are most like the white, middle-class males who orchestrate and profit most from the current social system.

Even though the idea of indirect discrimination has been widely recognised, what is not adequately recognised is that women and men are not equal in the treatment they require. With different experiences and responsibilities, unlike treatment is likely to be more appropriate than like, if the intention really is 'to prevent people being treated in a fashion which is unfair and harms them' (Bacchi, 1990, p. 176). The problem for the USA, Britain and Australia is that the workplace has largely been dealt with independently of the home and it is clear, from the rest of our discussion, that the links between the two, and the differing roles played by men and women, cannot be ignored. This shows up particularly clearly in non-capitalist countries such as the Soviet Union. Here women are integrated into the workforce; indeed, they make up a higher proportion than men. With active women's movements only just emerging (Zacharova and Posadskaya, 1989), however, this involvement in the workforce has been developed alongside treatment of women in a highly traditional manner, and very much as mothers. Thus they undertake a second shift at home for the want of help from their male partners. They are, therefore, enormously overburdened and the official organisation for women, the Soviet Women's Committee, has operated 'according to the principle that women should be if possible, unseen as well as unheard' (Waters, 1990, p. 7).

In Chapter 5 we saw the way in which men's employment opportunities are based on minimal involvement in the home and we have seen the way family obligations impinge strongly on women's employment. Only the Nordic countries show signs of addressing the public and private domains simultaneously, though it would certainly be going too far to suggest that an acceptable balance between the two has been achieved even there. In Sweden, provisions for parental leave apply equally to men and women and there is official encouragement of shared parenting. The 1988 five-year plan, enacted as the government's Equality Policy to the mid-nineties, included the goal of having more men make use of parental benefits and increasing the proportion of men working in public child care (Swedish Institute, 1989, p. 4).

The British and Australian attempts to deal with discrimination owe much to the US experience, though they differ in detail and both lack the strength of sanction of the US system. Britain's Sex Discrimination Act was passed in 1975, and the Equal Opportunities Commission was established. In the same year the Equal Pay Act was passed and the Race Relations Act in the following year. Issues relating to retirement, social security and taxation were largely excluded from the Sex Discrimination Bill 'in order to escape the complicated parliamentary procedures and conditions attached to Bills with monetary implications' (Atkins, 1986, p. 58). The Equal Pay Act can easily be legally evaded by employers (Pascall, 1986, p. 32). The weakness of the Acts has been exposed by a number of cases dealt with by the European Court, which provided important support for claims that could not be redressed within the national legal system. While the European Court stressed the importance of the 'right to equal treatment', the enforcement of rights has been seen in Britain as secondary to the Act's educative function (Atkins, 1986, p. 58).

South Australia was the first of the Australian states officially to take up the issue of sex discrimination. As in Britain, a Sex Discrimination Act was passed in 1975 and a Racial Discrimination Act in the following year. Victoria and New South Wales followed suit in 1977. In 1980 the first affirmative action law was passed in New South Wales, using the term Equal Employment Opportunity. This applied to state government employment and higher education only, and required action plans which outline a strategy for redressing the discrimination suffered on the basis of sex, race and disability. Progress towards the goals set out in the plans is monitored annually. The only sanction provided, however, was and remains for the supervising agency to name the recalcitrant department in the State parliament. A number of other states have similar programmes and the federal government enacted an Affirmative Action Act in 1986. This applies to the tertiary education sector and all private sector employers with more than 100 employees. The federal public service is covered under a separate act which explicitly covers women, Aborigines and Torres Strait

Islanders, migrants whose first language is not English and people who are physically and mentally disabled (Ronalds, 1987, p. 87). Once again though, there are no effective penalties for non-compliance.

Despite reasonable similarity of the legislative approach to anti-discrimination, the Australian approach to women's issues has also differed in some interesting respects from that of other countries. As has been the case with the union movement's approach to class issues, there has been heavy reliance on the mechanisms of the state. Women's services, such as refuges, rape crisis centres and women's health services quickly, and to an extent successfully, lobbied the state for support. Also, an elaborate, though small, state apparatus was established to attempt to transform the state bureaucracy's dealings with women at both the state and federal levels. This was not, however, achieved through separate ministries or departments of women's affairs, but through establishing coordinating agencies in the centre of a network throughout the public service. The role of the network is to promote women's rights and to scrutinise the effects on women of all policies and their implementation. The preeminent federal unit is in the Prime Minister's department and at the equivalent level in most of the state governments. These central units have high-profile advisory councils, made up of prominent women from the community. In each government there was a women's unit, or at least a designated women's officer. Despite (or maybe because of) their apparently strategic watchdog position, the resources devoted to these units are minuscule. They account for less than 0.05 per cent of the staff resources of the federal bureaucracy, though even this has been put in jeopardy by the rise of economic rationalist policies (Sawer, 1990, p. xvii).

Apart from these networks' role in equal employment opportunity and affirmative action, they have succeeded in making it mandatory that all submissions to cabinet include an assessment of the proposal's implications for women. Another policy initiative has been the institution of women's budget statements. These are released annually, along with the official government budget. Essentially they represent an attempt to 'disaggregate the government's mainstream budget according to its impact on women' (Sharp and Broomhill, 1990, p. 2). The aim, like the policy in relation to Cabinet submissions, is to make more transparent the effect of policy on women and in this way to raise awareness and commitment to change. Each department must submit the relevant material for inclusion in the budget and this ensures that implications for women are at least given some consideration.

This bureaucratic development has led to the coining of the term 'femocrat' to refer to the bureaucrats whose role it is to work on women's issues (Franzway, Court and Connell, 1989, p. 133). The term originally carried a pejorative element, but this has since been deemphasised as the term has proved a useful descriptor. The movement of women into the bureaucracy and into the belly of the beast has been the focus of much debate and conflict within the women's movement. It has also been the subject of considerable academic analysis. Femocrats are readily seen by feminists as selling out the women's movement because of compromises they must make. Within the workplace they are under enormous pressure from traditional bureaucrats reluctant to take women's issues seriously. This led Yeatman to suggest that their position is sufficiently singular to warrant their recognition as a 'class of their own' within the bureaucracy (Yeatman, 1990, chapter 4).

The enactment of equality policies is one of the most distinctive legacies of the rights movements of the sixties and seventies. They have certainly provided a higher profile for issues of equality for women and for minority groups. They have also delivered some of the more tangible gains to particular groups of women, though these have often been delivered to those who were already privileged, those in senior government positions. However, as Pascall observes, these changes really make only a 'small ripple on a deep pool' (1986, p. 32), a pool of disadvantage that penetrates the very fabric of society.

Threats to recent gains

The gains of women and minority groups have been made through tenacious struggle. Nonetheless, it has been largely through the medium of state intervention, and not the market, that some steps towards greater equality have been made. Not that all government activities promote greater equality – far from it! Still, it is impossible to conceive of significant equity measures being taken in the absence of government activity (Wilenski, 1986, chapter 1). Cries for smaller government, then, represent thinly-disguised calls to return to a more inequitable distribution of power. They represent an attempt to remove from the agenda those issues of social justice which have been fought for so painstakingly over many decades.

The shift of the debate to one of economic rationalism is directly about citizenship rights. Calls for small government are often justified as a reaction or backlash against the restrictiveness of government activity and its wastefulness and unaffordability. It is true that the call for small government does represent a reaction and a backlash. But this backlash is more accurately seen as a form of resistance. As Laura Balbo put it,

> I would suggest that beyond other more specific goals, the cutting of public services, conservative abortion laws, and ideological support for the family all have this goal in common: to keep women over-burdened with the impossible tasks of satisfying needs, to deny them control over their time, energy, or choices, and to make any different pattern impossible to them. Women are indeed under attack. Should they succeed in modifying their position in the existing system the consequences might be devastating for the continuance of capitalism and patriarchy as we have known them historically. (1987, p. 67).

Conclusion

Women's welfare state in the past consisted largely of social welfare, which could be claimed via dependence on a husband or as a widow or a parent. Gradually, over this century, women have been drawn more and more into the labour force. This renders them in a situation more similar to that of men. With these changes in women's relationship to the welfare state, come opportunities to partake of occupational and fiscal welfare. However, because women have largely been absorbed into the secondary labour markets, their access to the benefits of employment are restricted.

A thin strand of liberal reform has gradually established greater equality for women. This has produced, with varying speed in the different countries, the universal franchise, rights to enter contracts and so on. Reformism, fired by demands from second-wave feminism, has also created an innovative set of policies aimed specifically at the promotion of gender equality, though these have been fairly disappointing in their outcomes. Not that anti-discrimination and affirmative action policies are not better than nothing, but everywhere they lack the power to overcome existing arrangements.

When the complex factors which have affected women's economic status are taken into account, the concept which best makes sense of what has happened is increasing proletarianisation. This process does indeed bring women's and men's welfare states more into line. Also, entry into the economic system mostly delivers greater benefits by way of money, power and social status than does the domestic arena and unpaid caring. In the absence of any indication that hegemonic values which maintain the economic as central, are changing, this process must be seen as a net gain for women.

At most though, we are contemplating changes of a liberal rather than a radical nature. There are clear disadvantages associated with this form of absorption into the capitalist labour market which must be recognised (Mitchell, 1986). These changes have moved women into class politics, an arena largely monopolised by men. Also, the changes have most benefited women who were relatively advantaged to start with. In addition, and quite fundamentally, while women continue to do the lion's share of domestic labour, paid employment means more money, but it also means a double burden of work.

Second-wave feminism was full of enthusiasm for achieving radical change. Women were seeking liberation as well as equality, but as the doctrine of economic rationalism has become more engulfing, women have trimmed their demands. Women's Liberation has become the women's movement. The early gains, in the form, for example, of women's refuges, rape crisis centres and women's health services, have become less popular with governments and funding has become less readily available. Because innovations of this type are no longer favourably received, they are in danger of falling off the agenda. Also, very little impression has been made on the organisation of work, despite the women's movement's early enthusiasm for more cooperative, less hierarchical structures and for more flexibility and less formality.

When we consider women's welfare state today, it becomes clear that while some significant gains have been achieved, these fall far short of the radical change which feminists have sought. The society, including the workplace into which so many women have moved, remains in the control of men and is competitive and hierarchical; caring is still undervalued, as is motherhood; peace is as distant a goal as ever and control of reproductive technology remains firmly in the hands of male medical personnel.

Class politics have been important in bringing about change as well as gender politics, though it is clear that without the power of the women's movement around the world, women would have achieved little. Nonetheless, the gains that have been made in the public arena are largely those that fit snugly with industrial development. Thus women's welfare state has most effectively delivered women into the proletariat and into the secondary labour market. Only some method which also alters the preeminence of the interests of capital can in the long run allow women to have the sort of caring welfare state of which feminists' dreams are made.

Conclusion: The Welfare State in the Twenty-first Century

This analysis has aimed to challenge conventional notions of welfare and conventional sociological and social discourses. It has been demonstrated that these avoid important questions by masking many of the effects of inequality, particularly those linked to class, gender and race. The conventional literature on the welfare state routinely approaches its topic from a point of view which privileges the interests of males of dominant groups. An analytic framework such as that developed here is thus more than an intellectual exercise. It aims to challenge this privileged position and is therefore also part, albeit a small part, of the political struggle over issues of equality. Foucault was right to remind us that the discourse is a 'power which is to be seized' (1984, p. 110), as was Marx when he indicated that the point is not merely to understand the world, but to change it.

The framework presented here is intended to help us more effectively answer the questions of who benefits from changes to the welfare state and how better to defend the interests of subordinate groups. What conclusions, then, does the foregoing analysis allow? What does it foreshadow for the future of social policy? What are the implications for a sociological enterprise focused on issues of power and inequality?

We have heard much over recent years about a crisis of the welfare state. We have been told of the impossibility of maintaining support for state measures to redress inequality. Margaret Thatcher and Ronald Reagan were the most prominent national leaders promoting this point of view. The weight of welfare measures has not only been claimed to be heavier than the 'productive' sector of the economy could bear, such measures have also been denounced for being bad for national vitality. Thatcher's oft-quoted aphorism referring to the 'nanny state' invokes images of dependent, pampered citizens.

The analysis undertaken in this book does indeed suggest that, given the momentum of current political economic orthodoxies, the limits of welfare state development have been reached, temporarily at least. However, the basis for this impasse does not lie in economic over-burdening, or in the flabbiness of the population as projected by Thatcherism, Reaganomics and the New Right. What is evident in virtually all countries, is resistance by those who have been the traditional beneficiaries of social arrangements, but whose relative position has been, at least marginally, worsened by more recent developments within the welfare state. The New Right is challenging the gains made by the New Left movements of the 1960s and 1970s.

The expression of this resistance, as well as the outcomes from it, vary greatly from country to country. They range from a significant attack on the benefits of subordinate groups in countries such as the United Kingdom, the USA and Australia, to a faltering and possibly a halt in what was believed by many to be the 'march along the parliamentary road to socialism' in Sweden. Japan appears to have changed its intention to emulate the Western welfare states. It has halted its journey, but not before a reasonable social welfare structure was put in place for the better-off. Nonetheless, all situations remain fluid. This seems particularly so for Japan, as it is difficult to predict policy directions under the influence of the newly-emerging political force that women represent. Overall, however, the differences between these advanced capitalist countries are becoming wider, rather than narrower. Sweden and Norway remain in their leadership positions but other countries exhibit considerable, though varying, degrees of backsliding.

Recent changes in policy directions and in the implementation of programmes are underpinned by a change in the leading political philosophy, from political liberalism to economic liberalism. I hesitate to use the term hegemonic to describe the emergent philosophy, because it is not clear how widely it is subscribed to and how resistant these doctrines will prove to further change. A range of surveys, in a number of countries, suggests that the public has not changed its views significantly over recent decades. It is clear, however, that economic liberalism has become hegemonic among key power-brokers. This is the dominant position, for example, of the international pacesetting organisation, the OECD. It is also clear that economic liberalism has had greater salience in some countries than others. The USA, the UK, New Zealand and Australia have shown very explicit enthusiasm for economic rationalist doctrines. The Nordic countries show somewhat less enthusiasm, but are by no means untouched by these doctrines. It remains to be seen how long this enthusiasm will last in countries such as the USA or Australia, in the light of their failure to swing their economies towards significant growth and lowered inflation.

Economic liberalism, at a minimum, purports to foster a competitive market and involves a simultaneous dampening of enthusiasm for state-organised, collective solutions. The settlement between conservatives and non-conservatives, which underpinned the development of the modern welfare state, was based on political liberalism. After the great depression of the 1920s and 1930s, the conservative elements of this coalition reluctantly endorsed collective action because this was seen to be the only way to ensure the key political values of liberty and freedom. As Beveridge put it, the state must also ensure freedom from want and squalor, as well as political freedom.

A great deal of commentary on the welfare state assumed this settlement was unassailable. The events of the 1970s and especially the 1980s, have shown this to be a falsely optimistic position. Clearly, the distribution of valued resources remains a contested issue. The rise of the New Right and the current 'welfare wars' represent just the latest battle in what has historically proved to be an ongoing contest of prodigious proportions.

The shift to the right, that is to economic rather than political liberalism, involves, as we have seen, a market orientation and a favouring of individual, rather than collective, activity. As we have seen, this has not always been successful. Indeed, in relation to certain interests such as law and order, some middle-class interests and especially the military, the trends may be in the opposite direction. Anti-collectivism is promoted, not only in relation to the state, but also in relation to that other traditional source of collective action, the trade unions. This fostering of individualism is expressed in attempts to weaken the centralised power of unions and to reduce the state, or at least stop the trend towards state expansion.

Attempts to weaken the power of trade unions and attempts to reduce the state apparatus, 'to roll back the state', are of crucial significance to subordinate groups. It has been through the collective interventions of trade unions that the working class has improved its conditions, though this applies most specifically to working-class males of dominant groups. Nonetheless, centralised trade union structures have proved of value to women as well. Their importance is demonstrated by the relatively high wage-rates of women, *vis-à-vis* men, in both Sweden and Australia. This must at least partly be attributed to highly-centralised and powerful trade union organisation.

Women, people of non-dominant racial and ethnic groups, as well as members of other subordinate groups, have made many of their gains towards greater equality through the direct intervention of the state, spurred to action by pressure from the groups themselves and their supporters. We have seen the results over recent decades, for example, in the extension of social welfare programmes, rights for indigenous peoples, in equal opportunity and anti-discrimination measures and through greater rights to participate more fully in their society. The state arena has been the one through which muted groups have been able to make themselves heard in order to stake their claim to greater equality. The achievements have been partial, but there have been achievements. Nonetheless, there are problems connected with making state interventions effective. This has been brought home dramatically by the plight of Eastern European national social systems. Many of these are not only in a state of near-collapse, but have maintained similar (or worse) gender, racial and ethnic inequalities to those of capitalist societies.

If we look more closely at the 'crisis of the welfare state', we find that it by no means affects all sections of the population equally. The benefits and advantages of the better-off have largely been maintained and even enhanced. Most of the belt-tightening has been done by those who are at the bottom of the social hierarchy. In fact there is a great deal of evidence that the better-off are doing better than ever. The gap between rich and poor is widening. In the USA, for example, social insurance has been able to withstand pressures towards cutback, through its strong middle-class support. It has been public assistance programmes that have been savaged. Similar effects can be identified in the UK, Australia and other countries. While there is considerable national variation and also variation between groups within nations, it does broadly hold that the middle classes, throughout this 'crisis', have been able to retain their relative advantages. Where benefits are genuinely universal, and they involve significant benefits to the middle classes, they are more effectively defended against pushes towards individualism. The most vulnerable welfare state provisions are those targeted to subordinate groups which do not have the weight of middle-class support behind them.

Trends around the world make it imperative that our sociological approach is tuned into these changes in relative power and affluence. This is why I have suggested that we must take the broadest of approaches. We need an international perspective because, if trends are world-wide, we need to look to different explanations from those that might apply to merely national trends. It has been common within Britain to blame Mrs Thatcher for the determined wheel to the right. In the USA many blamed the Reagan administration and in Australia the Hawke government. While it is clear that individual governments put their stamp on local policies and that local history plays an important part, when we find that similar pressures are showing up in Sweden and virtually all OECD countries, we have to recognise that global processes are at work. It is therefore clear that a global element is an imperative part of any sociological perspective. This need is underscored by the recent developments in Eastern European countries and in the Soviet Union, where we find oddly similar rhetoric about the need to strengthen the market, despite an enterprise of a fundamentally different nature and scale since it requires the abandonment of a total command economy.

The need for a global perspective is further reinforced by those world trends, most obviously exemplified in the formation of the European Community, which represent the development of essentially supra-national bodies. These trends presage the importance of new power-formations beyond the nation-state. The relationship between rich and poor nations, the North/South issue, is another compelling reason for opting for a global perspective.

We have seen, throughout the analysis, that states are both gendered and have a definite race and ethnic character. There are other recurrent axes of inequality too, such as age, disability, sexuality and region though, to make a large task more manageable, I have only paid passing attention to these. If we are to develop a framework for analysis that can encompass the range of axes of inequality, then we must adopt a more exhaustive definition of state interventions. As the social welfare field contracts, and as governments put their efforts into other state interventions, it becomes even more imperative that we keep our analytic sweep as wide as possible. Unless we do this we will not really be in a position to pose questions about who is benefiting from what state actions.

It could be suggested that we should abandon the notion of the welfare state altogether and contemplate a post-welfare state era. There are both theoretical and political advantages to seeing the state as 'interventionist' rather than as a 'welfare state'. These advantages lie in the greater scope offered for understanding who benefits from a wide range of state activities. This facilitates a meaningful assessment of the state's distributive and redistributive roles. It obviates the bias caused by only focusing on social welfare when analysing state-mediated transfers of benefits. If the scope of analysis was broadened in this way, it would be more difficult to ignore fiscal and occupational welfare and those other state activities which provide advantages to those who are better-off. This is important because the masking of other forms of transfers is not only detrimental to an accurate analysis of the nature of the state, but acts against the interests of those most disadvantaged. The meagre benefits that do go to the most needy as social welfare tend to be the ones that are most frequently scrutinised, even by sympathetic researchers and commentators. This makes them vulnerable to cuts and amplifies the state's capacity for social control.

The task of redefining all state interventions to make transparent who they advantage is a long-term goal. At this stage it is not entirely clear how best to do it. This does not mean that there are not some clear indications about how to approach the task. There clearly are. Those concerned with taxation have for many years debated how to develop a more comprehensive definition of income, one which does not so disadvantage wage and salary earners. Some useful work has been done here but it needs to be taken further. We need to consider whose interests are served by the range of other state interventions, such as law and order, the military, the telecommunications systems, finance systems and the like.

We also need to consider what is ignored. An example here is the manner in which tax expenditures in so many countries are not treated as outlays in the same manner as social welfare expenditures. Another key issue which has been neglected in sociological analysis is the role played by the market, and the contribution of this to equality and inequality. The market has been largely taken for granted in capitalist societies. The moves of former Eastern bloc countries to adopt a market problematises this in a new, and potentially valuable manner.

And then there is the matter of caring. Caring work, which is mostly undertaken by women, is ignored, undervalued or both. National and international accounting systems are blinkered in a manner that means they can recognise only the contribution traditionally made by men. They are not really concerned, in a rounded way, with the well-being of people and the environment. They are really concerned with issues of through-put. How much is manufactured, how much invested, how much spent on this and that. This is no substitute for a thorough consideration of the outcome of all this economic activity. Different cultural perspectives, similarly, are outside the scope of the dominant discourses.

Academic discourses must play a part and even take a lead in this process of redefinition. Throughout the discussion I have alluded to the work of Richard Titmuss and those influenced by his work. They, and others, raised the issue of broadening our basis for assessing 'Who benefits?' But analysts seem to be stuck in a groove. We utter the same nostrums, then fail to follow through. As sociologists we cannot but recognise that this process is not likely to be an accidental outcome. Hilary Rose put her finger on the explanation when she said that we make ourselves acceptable to those in positions of power in the current structure by not rocking the boat.

What we find happening to the welfare state, and within the sociological analyses of these processes, brings us face to face with a fundamental dilemma which underpins the welfare state. This is the tension between its capitalist substructure and its philosophical support for measures of equality, which inevitably must involve redistribution. Despite rhetoric which may be to the contrary, everywhere an ideology of inequality underpins the welfare state. This is so because of the class interests that are served.

It needs to be recognised that the gains that have been made, particularly for women, have been made largely in concert with the logic of capitalist development. Most changes do not challenge this logic. An expanding labour force allows an increase in consumption and a concomitant increase in profitability. The tendency to divorce, for example, not only feeds into the process of increasingly drawing women into the labour force, but it leads to more households and thus greater consumption. It can be added that there is no particular disadvantage, in terms of the logic of capital, in men taking more responsibility for caring labour (or even taking it over entirely). The logic does not intrinsically act as an impediment to women's equal treatment where the class structure is not challenged. The reality, nonetheless, is that in the day-to-day workings of the capitalist state and the economic system the tide of events is still largely determined by men.

The most fundamental issue, in class terms, relates to the fact that the economy is based on a market system – a capitalist market system. This means there is a limit to the pursuit of equality that is possible or, at least acceptable. Wilenski has termed this the 'dilemma for social democrats' explaining it as follows:

> Redistribution through the welfare state can . . . never totally offset [the] original transfer through profits to the owners of capital, since this would destroy the rationale of the capitalist system and halt investment. (1984, p. 14).

He expands on this by asserting that 'business in fact occupies a special position in relation to government' and its 'cooperation is vital to the maintenance of the activities of the state' (1984, p. 15). This cooperation has tended to be only forthcoming when business has believed that the government did not have the intention of seeking change of a genuinely radical kind. Capital has a potent weapon that can be used against governments that overstep the bounds of acceptable change. This is the withdrawal of capital, which needs only to be a significant amount, not a total withdrawal. Because capitalism is an international system, withdrawal to other countries is entirely feasible. Miliband, writing about the USA, alluded to this same process by suggesting that the operation of a capitalist economy has 'its own rationality to which any

government must sooner or later submit, and usually sooner'
(1977, p. 72).

These capitalist interests are not only class interests, but are also
male and represent a narrow range of racial and ethnic groups.
With this class, gender and race limitation always in the background, it should come as no surprise that moves towards greater
equality are not easily achieved. However, we can at least do more
to try to ensure that sociological discourses do not collude with
this form of domination by failing to address the very general
distribution of power and other resources to the privileged.

Recommended Further Reading

General: Rose and Shirataori 1986; Flora and Heidenheimer 1984; Goodin and Le Grand 1987; Gough 1979; George, 1988; Waring, 1988; Heidenheimer, Helco and Adams 1990; Le Grand and Robinson 1984; Mishra 1984; Offe 1984; Esping-Andersen, 1990.

For Britain: Cole 1986; Dale and Foster 1986; Digby 1989; George and Wilding 1984; Gough 1990; Jordan 1987; Papadakis and Taylor-Gooby 1987; Pascall 1986; Thane 1982; Turner 1986; Dominelli, 1988; 1988; Williams 1989.

For Australia: Castles 1985; Choo 1990; Edwards 1988; Franzway, Court and Connell 1989; Jones 1990; O'Donnell and Hall 1988.

For the USA: Abramovitz, 1988; Coser and Howe 1977; Fraser, 1987; Hanson, 1987; Joseph, 1981; Galper 1975; Wilenski 1975 and 1979.

For Japan: Watanuki 1986; Maruo 1986; Noguchi 1986; Mackie, 1989; Moore, 1987.

For Scandinavian countries: Esping-Andersen and Korpi 1987; Hernes 1987a; Einhorn, 1987; Longue, 1987: Olsson, 1988; Persson, 1986.

Men's Welfare State: Connell, 1990; Levitas 1986; Miliband 1969; O'Connor 1973, 1984; Ryan and Conlan 1988; Yeatman 1990.

Women's Welfare State: Bacchi 1990; Banks 1981; Barrett 1980; Barrett and McIntosh 1982; Dalley 1988; Finch and Groves 1983; Lewis 1983; Ruggie 1984; Sassoon 1987a.

References

B. Abel-Smith, 'Whose Welfare State', in N. Mackenzie (ed.), *Conviction* (London: MacGibbon and Kee, 1958).

M. Abramovitz, *Regulating the Lives of Women: Social Welfare Policy from Colonial Times to the Present*, (Boston: South End Press, 1988).

ABS (Australian Bureau of Statistics), *Effects of Government Benefits on Household Income: 1984 Household Expenditure Survey, Australia*, Catalogue No. 6537.0. (Canberra: ABS, 1987).

J. Acker, 'Welfare Policies are Made by Men for Men', *Worklife Research* (Stockholm: Swedish Centre for Working Life, 1989).

E. Allardt, 'The Civic Conception of the Welfare State in Scandinavia', in R. Rose and R. Shiratori (eds), 1986.

D. Altman, *The Homosexualization of America, the Americanization of the Homosexual* (New York: St Martin's Press, 1982).

V. Amos and P. Parmar, 'Challenging Imperial Feminism', *Feminist Review*, 17 (1984), pp. 3–20.

S. Ardener (ed.), *Perceiving Women* (London: Malaby Press, 1975).

S. Atkins, 'The Sex Discrimination Act 1975: The End of a Decade', *Feminist Review* 24 (1986), pp. 57–71.

Australia Parliament, *Australia Reconstructed*, A Report by the ACTU/ TDC Mission to Western Europe (Canberra: Australian Government Publishing Service, 1987).

C. Bacchi, *Same Difference: Feminism and Sexual Difference* (Sydney: Allen and Unwin, 1990).

L. Balbo, 'Crazy Quilts: Rethinking the Welfare State Debate from a Woman's Point of View', in A. S. Sassoon (ed.) 1987.

C. Baldock and B. Cass (eds), *Women, Social Welfare and the State in Australia* (Sydney: Allen and Unwin, 1983).

C. Baldock and D. Goodrick (eds), *Women's Participation on the Development Process*, Proceedings of the Women's Section of ANZAAS Congress, Perth (1983).

O. Banks, *Faces of Feminism* (Oxford: Martin Robertson, 1981).

M. Barrett, *Women's Oppression Today* (London: Verso, 1980).

M. Barrett and M. McIntosh, *The Anti-Social Family* (London: Verso, 1982).

M. Barrett and M. McIntosh, 'Ethnocentrism and Socialist – Feminist Theory', *Feminist Review*, 20 (1985), pp. 23–48.

J. Beggs and B. Chapman, 'The Forgone Earnings From Child-Rearing in Australia' (Canberra: Centre for Policy Research, Research School of Social Sciences, Australian National University, 1988) (mimeograph).

D. Bell, *The Coming of Post-Industrial Society* (London: Heinemann, 1974).

W. Bello, D. Kinley and E. Elinson, *Development Debacle: The World Bank in the Philippines* (San Francisco: Institute for Food and Development Policy, 1982).

G. Beltram, *Testing the Safety Net* (London: Bedford Square Press, 1984).

A. Bergmark, 'Social Assistance in Sweden – Means Tested Economic Support in a Modern Welfare State' (School of Social Work, University of Stockholm). Paper given at University of NSW, Australia, March 1990.

K. Bhavnani and M. Coulson, 'Transforming Socialist-Feminism: The Challenge of Racism', *Feminist Review*, 23 (1986), pp. 81–92.

A. Björklund, *A Look at the Male/Female Unemployment Differentials in the Federal Republic of Germany, Sweden, United Kingdom and the United States of America* (Swedish Institute for Social Research: Stockholm, 1984).

M. W. Boolsen and H. Holt, *Voluntary Action in Denmark and Britain* (Copenhagen: Danish National Institute of Social Research, 1988).

Boston Women's Health Collective, *The New Our Bodies Ourselves* (Ringwood: Penguin Books, 1985).

B. Bradbury, J. Doyle and P. Whiteford, *Trends in the Disposable Incomes of Australian Families, 1982–83 to 1989–90* (Sydney: Social Policy Research Centre, 1990).

G. Bramley, J. Le Grand and W. Low, *How Far is the Poll Tax a 'Community Charge'? The Implications of Service Usage Evidence*, Discussion Paper, 42, Suntory – Toyota International Centre for Economic and Related Disciplines (London: London School of Economics, 1989).

J. Brannen and G. Wilson, *Give and Take in Families: Studies in Resource Distribution* (London: Allen and Unwin, 1987).

S. Brownmiller, *Against Our Wills* (Ringwood: Penguin, 1976).

L. Bryson, 'Women as Welfare Recipients: Women, Poverty and the State', in C. Baldock and B. Cass (eds), 1983.

L. Bryson, 'The Proletarianisation of Women: Gender Justice in Australia', *Social Justice*, 16, 3 (1989), pp. 87–102.

L. Bryson and M. Mowbray, '"Community": The Spray-on Solution', *Australian Journal of Social Issues*, 16, 4 (1981), pp. 255–267.

L. Bryson and M. Mowbray, 'Who Cares? Social Security, Family Policy and Women', *International Social Security Review*, No. 2 (1986), pp. 183–200.

B. Burdekin, J. Carter and W. Dethlefs, *Report of the National Inquiry into Homeless Children and Young People* (Sydney: Human Rights and Equal Opportunity Commission, 1989).

A. Burns, 'Mother-headed Households: What is the Future?', Workshop/

Conference on the Future of the Household Economy and the Role of Women, University of Melbourne, 14–15 May 1987.

L. Calmförs, I. Hansson, L. Jonung, J. Myhrman and H. T. Sonderström, *Getting Sweden Back to Work* (Stockholm: Sns Förlag, 1986).

E. Carson and H. Kerr, 'Social Welfare Down Under', *Critical Social Policy*, 23 Autumn (1988), pp. 70–83.

B. Cass, 'The Changing Face of Poverty in Australia', *Australian Feminist Studies*, 1 Summer (1985), pp. 67–90.

B. Cass, *Income Support for Families with Children*. Issues Paper No. 1, Social Security Review (Canberra: Australian Government Publishing Service, 1986).

M. Castells, *The City and the Grassroots* (Berkeley and Los Angeles: University of California, 1983).

F. Castles, 'Is Australia the Poor Relation?', *Australian Society*, January/February (1991), pp. 47–8.

F. Castles, 'Australia's Reversible Citizenship', *Australian Society*, September (1989), pp. 29–30.

F. Castles, *The Working Class and Welfare: Reflections on the Political Development of the Welfare State in Australia and New Zealand, 1890–1980* (Wellington: Allen and Unwin, 1985).

A. Cawson, *Corporatism and Welfare* (London: Heinemann Educational, 1982).

C. Choo, *Aboriginal Child Poverty* (Melbourne: Brotherhood of St Laurence, 1990).

P. Close, 'Towards a Framework for the Analysis of Family Divisions and Inequalities in Modern Society', in P. Close (ed.), *Family Divisions and Inequalities in Modern Society* (London: Macmillan, 1989).

C. Cockburn, *Brothers: Male Dominance and Technological Change* (London: Pluto Press, 1983).

T. Cole, *Whose Welfare?* (London: Tavistock Publications, 1986).

R. W. Connell, 'The State, Gender and Sexual Politics', *Theory and Society* 19 (1990), pp. 507–44.

W. Connolly, *The Terms of Political Discourse*, 2nd edn (Princeton: Princeton University Press, 1983).

J. M. Cope, *Business Taxation: Policy and Practice* (Wokingham, Berkshire: Van Nostrand Reinhold, 1987).

L. A. Coser and I. Howe (eds), *The New Conservatives* (New York: Meridian, 1977).

M. Coultan, 'Tories Take a Hiding over Coming Poll Tax', *Sydney Morning Herald*, 10 March 1990, p. 23.

J. Cox, *Report on Poverty Measurement* (Canberra: Australian Government Publishing Service, 1981).

S. Croft, 'Women, Caring and the Recasting of Need – A Feminist Reappraisal', *Critical Social Policy* 16, Summer (1986).

A. Curthoys, 'The Sexual Division of Labor: Theoretical Arguments', in N. Grieve and A. Burns (eds), *Australian Women: New Feminist Perspectives* (Melbourne: Oxford University Press, 1986).

A. Dahlberg, 'The Equality Act' Working Papers (Stockholm: Swedish Centre for Working Life, 1982).

J. Dale and P. Foster, *Feminism and State Welfare* (London: Routledge and Kegan Paul, 1986).

G. Dalley, *Ideologies of Caring: Rethinking Community and Collectivism* (London: Macmillan, 1988).

R. Dalziel, 'The Colonial Helpmeet: Women's Role and the Vote in Nineteenth Century New Zealand', in *New Zealand Journal of History*, 11 (2) (1977), pp. 112–23.

Danish Statistics, *Living Conditions in Denmark: Compendium of Statistics 1988* (Copenhagen: Institute for Social Research, 1988).

D. Deacon, *Managing Gender* (South Melbourne: Oxford University Press, 1989).

H. Deleeck, 'Social Expenditure and the Efficiency of Social Policies in Europe', in J. Vandamme (ed.), 1985.

A. Digby, *British Welfare Policy: Workhouse to Workfare* (London: Faber and Faber, 1989).

A. Dilnot, 'Wealth: From Most to Least', *Australian Society*, July 1990, p. 17.

L. Dominelli, 'Thatcher's Attack on Social Security: Restructuring Social Control', *Critical Social Policy* 23 (1988), pp. 46–61.

V. Duke and S. Edgell, 'Attitudes to Privatisation: the Influence of Class, Sector and Partisanship', *The Quarterly Journal of Social Affairs* 3, 4 (1987), pp. 253–84.

A. Dworkin, *Pornography: Men Possessing Women* (London: Women's Press, 1983).

A. Edwards, *Regulation and Repression* (Sydney: Allen and Unwin, 1988).

A. Edwards, 'Feminism and Social Welfare: Alternative Representations of Women and Gender in Social Policy Literature' in A. Jamrozik (ed.), *Social Policy in Australia: What Future for the Welfare State?* (Sydney: Social Policy Research Centre, 1989).

M. Edwards, 'Financial Arrangements by Husbands and Wives', *Australian and New Zealand Journal of Sociology*, 18 (3) (1982), pp. 320–38.

E. Einhorn, 'Economic Policy and Social Needs: The Recent Scandinavian Experience', *Scandinavian Studies*, 59 (2) (1987), pp. 203–21.

H. Eisenstein, *Contemporary Feminist Thought* (Sydney: Allen and Unwin, 1984).

Z. Eisenstein, *Feminism and Sexual Equality: Crisis in Liberal America* (New York: Monthly Review Press, 1984).

Z. Eisenstein (ed.), *Capitalist Patriarchy and the Case for Socialist Feminism* (New York: Monthly Review Press, 1979).

D. Elston and R. Pearson, '"Nimble fingers Make Cheap Workers": An Analysis of Women's Employment in Third World Export Manufacturing', *Feminist Review*, 7 (1981), pp. 87–107.

EPAC, *Aspects of the Social Wage: A Review of Social Expenditures and Redistribution*, Council Paper No. 27 (Canberra: Canberra Publishing Co, 1987).

G. Esping-Andersen and W. Korpi, 'From Poor Relief to Institutional

Welfare States: The Development of Scandinavian Social Policy', in R. Erikson, E. J. Hansen, S. Ringer and H. Uusitalo, *The Scandinavian Model: Welfare States and Welfare Research* (New York: M. E. Sharpe, 1987).

G. Esping-Andersen, *The Three Worlds of Welfare Capitalism* (Cambridge: Polity Press, 1990).

E. Evans (ed.), *Social Policy 1830–1914: Individualism, Collectivism and the Origins of the Welfare State* (London: Routledge and Kegan Paul, 1978).

H. V. Evatt Research Centre, *The Capital Funding of Public Enterprise in Australia* (Sydney: H. V. Evatt Foundation, 1988).

A. Farrar, 'Deadline 1990', *Australian Left Review* 113 Nov./Dec. (1989), pp. 22–5.

J. Finch and D. Groves (eds) *A Labour of Love: Women, Work and Caring* (London: Routledge and kegan Paul, 1983).

J. Finch, *Family Obligations and Social Change* (Cambridge: Polity Press, 1989).

S. Firestone, *The Dialectic of Sex* (London: The Women's Press, 1979).

P. Flora and A. J. Heidenheimer, 'The Historical Core and Changing Boundaries of the Welfare State', in P. Flora and A. J. Heidenheimer (eds), 1984.

P. Flora and A. J. Heidenheimer (eds), *The Development of the Welfare State in Europe and America* (New Brunswick: Transaction Books, 1984).

M. Foucault, 'The Order of Discourse', in M. Shapiro (ed.), *Language and Politics* (New York: New York University Press, 1984).

S. Franzway, D. Court and R. W. Connell, *Staking a Claim: Feminism Bureaucracy and the State* (Sydney: Allen and Unwin, 1989).

N. Fraser, 'Women, Welfare and the Politics of Need Interpretation', *Thesis Eleven* 17 (1987), pp. 88–106.

M. Friedman and R. Friedman, *Free to Choose* (Melbourne: Macmillan, 1980).

M. Fuery, P. Huta, K. Gauntlett and A. Murray, *Occupational Arrangements in Overseas Countries*, Research Paper No. 42 Social Security Review (Canberra: Department of Social Security, 1988).

K. Funder, 'Work and the Marriage Partnership' in P. McDonald (ed.), *Settling Up* (Sydney: Prentice-Hall, 1986).

J. H. Galper, *The Politics of Social Services* (New Jersey: Prentice-Hall, 1975).

A. Gamble, 'The Weakening of Social Democracy' in M. Loney *et al.*, (eds), 1987.

H. Gans, 'The Positive Functions of Poverty', *American Journal of Sociology*, 78 (2), 1972.

J. Garraty, *Unemployment in History: Economic Thought and Public Policy* (New York: Harper and Row, 1978).

S. George, *A Fate Worse Than Debt* (London: Penguin, 1989).

V. George, *Social Security and Society* (London: Routledge and Kegan Paul, 1973).

V. George, 'Explanations of Poverty and Inequality' in V. George and R.

Lawson (eds), *Poverty and Inequality in Common Market Countries* (London: Routledge and Kegan Paul, 1980).

V. George, *Wealth, Poverty and Starvation: A World Perspective* (Hemel Hempstead: Wheatsheaf Books, 1988).

V. George and P. Wilding, *Ideology and Social Welfare* (London: Routledge and Kegan Paul, 1976).

V. George and P. Wilding, *The Impact of Social Policy* (London: Routledge and Kegan Paul, 1984).

J. Gershuny, *Social Innovation and the Division of Labour* (Oxford: Oxford University Press, 1983).

A. Giddens, *Central Problems in Social Theory* (London: Macmillan, 1979).

A. Giddens, *Sociology: A Brief But Critical Introduction* (London: Macmillan, 1986).

D. Gittens, 'Inside and Outside Marriage', *Feminist Review* 14 1983, pp. 22–34.

N. Glazer, 'Welfare and "Welfare" in America', in R. Rose and R. Shiratori (eds), 1986.

H. Glezer, *Maternity Leave in Australia: Employees' and Employers' Experiences* (Melbourne: Australian Institute of Family Studies, 1988).

P. Golding and S. Middleton, *Images of Welfare* (Oxford: Martin Robertson, 1982).

J. H. Goldthorpe, *Social Mobility and Class Structure in Modern Britain* (Oxford: Oxford University Press, 1980).

R. Goodin and J. Dryzek, 'Risk Sharing and Social Justice: the Motivational Foundations of the Post-War Welfare State', in R. Goodin, J. Le Grand *et al.*, 1987.

R. Goodin, J. Le Grand *et al.*, *Not Only the Poor: The Middle Classes and the Welfare State* (London: Allen and Unwin, 1987).

I. Gough, *The Political Economy of the Welfare State* (London: Macmillan, 1979).

I. Gough, *International Competitiveness and the Welfare State: A Case Study of the United Kingdom* (Sydney: Social Policy Research Centre, 1990).

H. Graham, 'Caring: A Labour of Love', in J. Finch and D. Groves (eds), 1983.

H. Graham, 'Being Poor: Perceptions and Coping Strategies of Lone Mothers', in J. Brannen and G. Wilson (eds), 1987.

A. Graycar (ed.), *Retreat from the Welfare State* (Sydney: Allen and Unwin, 1983).

A. Graycar and A. Jamrozik, *How Australians Live: Social Policy in Theory and Practice* (South Melbourne: Macmillan, 1989).

W. L. Grichting, *Security vs Liberty: Analysing Social Structure and Policy* (Lanham, MD: University Press of America, 1984).

S. Grimes, *Beyond Regulation? Women's Employment and Affirmative Action in Universities* (Sydney: Industrial Relations Research Centre, University of New South Wales, 1987).

F. Gruen, 'Australia's Welfare State: Rear-Guard or Avant Guard?', in P. Saunders and A. Jamrozik (eds), *Social Policy in Australia: What Future for the Welfare State?* (Sydney: Social Welfare Research Centre, 1989).

M. Gunasekera and J. Powlay, *Occupational Superannuation Arrangements in Australia*, Background/Discussion Paper No. 21, Social Security Review (Canberra: Department of Social Security, 1987).

E. Gunnarrson, 'Women, Poverty and Feminisation' (School of Social Work, University of Stockholm). Paper given at University of NSW, Australia, March 1990.

J. Habermas, *Legitimation Crisis* (Boston: Beacon Press, 1975).

R. Hadler, 'Europe Rejects "Neutral" Farm Deal', *The Australian*, 8–9 December 1990, p. 3.

S. Hall, 'Race, Articulation and Societies Structured in Dominance', in UNESCO, *Sociological Theories: Race and Colonisation* (Paris: UNESCO, 1980).

S. Hall, C. Critcher, T. Jefferson, J. Clarke and B. Roberts, *Policing the Crisis: Mugging, the State, Law and Order* (London: Macmillan, 1978).

S. Hall and M. Jacques (eds), *New Times* (London: Lawrence and Wishart, 1989).

P. Hanks, 'Aborigines and Government', in P. Hanks and B. Keon-Cohen (eds), *Aborigines and the Law* (Sydney: Allen and Unwin, 1984).

R. Hanson, 'The Expansion and Contraction of the American Welfare State', in R. Goodin and J. Le Grand *et al.*, 1987.

A. Harding, *Who Benefits? The Australian Welfare State & Redistribution* (Sydney: Social Welfare Research Centre, 1984).

R. Harris and A. Seldon, *Choice in Welfare 1970* (London: The Institute of Economic Affairs, 1971).

R. Harris and A. Seldon, *Over-Ruled on Welfare* (London: The Institute of Economic Affairs, 1978).

R. Harris and A. Seldon, *Welfare Without the State* (London: The Institute of Economic Affairs, 1987).

H. Hartmann, 'The Unhappy Marriage of Marxism and Feminism', *Capital and Class*, 8 (1979).

R. Haveman, 'US Anti-Poverty Policy and the Non-Poor: Some Estimates and their Implications', in R. Goodin and Le Grand *et al.*, 1987.

F. A. Hayek, *Individualism and the Economic Order* (London: Routledge and Kegan Paul, 1949).

F. A. Hayek, *The Constitution of Liberty* (London: Routledge and Kegan Paul, 1960).

A. Heidenheimer, H. Helco and C. Adams, *Comparative Public Policy*, 3rd edn (New York: St Martin's Press, 1990).

D. Henderson, 'Perestroika in the West', in J. Nieuwenhuysen (ed.) *Towards Freer Trade Between Nations* (Melbourne: Oxford University Press, 1989).

M. Hendessi, 'Fourteen Thousand Women Meet: Report from Nairobi', *Feminist Review*, 23 (1986), pp. 147–56.

H. M. Hernes, *Welfare State and Woman Power* (Oslo: Norwegian University Press, 1987a).

H. M. Hernes, 'Women and the Welfare State: the Transition from Private to Public Dependence', in A. S. Sassoon (ed.), 1987b.

H. M. Hernes, 'Scandinavian Citizenship', *Acta Sociologica* 31 (3) (1988), pp. 199–215.

T. Hewitt, 'The Diggers Who Lost Back Home', *The Sydney Morning Herald*, 25 April 1990, p. 5.

M. Hewitt, *Wives and Mothers in Victorian Industry* (Westport, Connecticut: Greenwood Publishers, 1975).

B. Hindess, *Freedom, Equality and the Market* (London: Tavistock, 1987).

T. Hiroshi, 'Working Women in Business Corporations – the Management Viewpoint', *Japan Quarterly*, 29 (3) (1982), pp. 319–23.

B. Hobson, 'No Exit, No Voice: Women's Economic Dependency and the Welfare State', *Acta Sociologica*, 33 (3) September 1990.

J. Holloway and S. Picciotto, 'Capital Crisis and the State', *Capital and Class* 2 (1977), pp. 79–94.

H. Holter, *Patriarchy in a Welfare Society* (Oslo: Universitetsforlaget, 1984).

B. Hooks, *Ain't I a Woman: Black Women and Feminism* (London: Pluto Press, 1982).

B. Hooks, 'Sisterhood: Solidarity Between Women', *Feminist Review*, 23 (1986), pp. 125–38.

D. Horowitz and D. Kolodney, 'The Foundations: Charity begins at Home', in P. Roby (ed.), *The Poverty Establishment* (Englewood Cliffs, New Jersey: Prentice-Hall, 1974).

E. Hunter, 'A Question of Power', *Australian Journal of Social Issues* 25 (4) (1990), pp. 261–78.

D. Ironmonger (ed.), *Households Work: Productive Activities, Women and Income in the Household Economy* (Sydney: Allen and Unwin, 1989).

M. James (ed.), *The Welfare State: Foundations and Alternatives* (St Leonards, Sydney: Centre for Policy Studies, 1989).

A. Jamrozik, 'Universality and Selectivity: Social Welfare in a Market Economy', in A. Graycar (ed.), 1983.

A. Jamrozik and M. Hoey, *Workforce in Transition* (Sydney: Social Welfare Research Centre, 1981).

A. Jamrozik, M. Hoey and M. Leeds, *Employment Benefits: Private or Public?* (Sydney: Social Welfare Research Centre, 1981).

A. Jamrozik, 'The Household Economy and Social Class', in D. Ironmonger (ed.), 1989.

C. Jencks, *Inequality: A Reassessment of the Effect of Family and Schooling in America* (New York: Basic Books, 1972).

J. C. Jenkins and B. G. Brents, 'Social Protest, Hegemonic Competition and Social Reform: A Political Struggle Interpretation of the Origins of the American Welfare State', *American Sociological Review*, 54, December (1989), pp. 891–909.

B. Jessop, *The Capitalist State: Marxist Theories and Methods* (Oxford: Martin Robertson, 1982).

M. A. Jones, *The Australian Welfare State*, 3rd edn (Sydney: Allen and Unwin, 1990).

B. Jordan, *Rethinking Welfare* (Oxford: Basil Blackwell, 1987).

L. Jordan and B. Waine, 'Women's Income in and out of Employment', *Critical Social Policy* 6 (3) Winter (1986/87), pp. 63–78.

G. Joseph, 'The Incompatible Ménage à trois: Marxism, Feminism and Racism', in L. Sargent (ed.), 1981.

A. Kahn and S. Kamerman, *Not for the Poor Alone* (New York: Harper and Row, 1975).

P. Kaim-Caudle, *Comparative Social Policy and Social Security: A Ten Country Study* (London: Martin Robertson, 1973).

A. Kalleberg and T. Hanisch, *Towards the Comparative Analysis of Labour Market Segmentation* (Oslo: Institute for Social Research, 1986).

S. Kamerman, 'Women, Children and Poverty: Public Policies and Female-headed Families in Industrialised Countries', *Signs*, 10 (2) (1984), pp. 249–71.

R. M. Kanter, 'Some Effects of Proportions on Group Life: Skewed Sex Ratios and Responses to Token Women', *American Journal of Sociology*, 82 (5) (1977), pp. 965–90.

D. Kavanagh and A. Seldon (eds), *The Thatcher Effect* (Oxford: Oxford University Press, 1989).

J. A. Kay and M. A. King, *The British Tax System* (Oxford: Oxford University Press, 1986).

D. Kearns, 'A *Theory of Justice* – and Love: Rawls on the Family' in M. Simms (ed.), *Australian Women and the Political System* (Melbourne: Longman Cheshire, 1984).

C. Keens and B. Cass, *Fiscal Welfare: Some Aspects of Australian Tax Policy, Class and Gender Considerations* (Sydney: Social Welfare Research Centre, 1982).

J. Kemeny, *The Great Australian Nightmare* (Melbourne: Georgian House, 1983).

H. Kendig (ed.), *Ageing and Families: A Social Perspective* (Sydney: Allen and Unwin, 1986).

H. Kerr, 'Labour's Social Policy 1974–79', *Critical Social Policy* 1 (1) (1981), pp. 5–17.

E. Kerschgens, 'When Jessica Meets Natasha: A Feminist View of German Reunification', *Australian Feminist Studies* 12, Summer (1990), pp. 15–28.

T. H. Kewley, *Social Security in Australia* (Sydney: Sydney University Press, 1977).

W. Knocke, 'Migrant Women at Work in Sweden – Structural Marginality and Mechanism of Marginalisation', in M. Pijl (ed.), *Marginalisation and Strategies Against Exclusion* (The Hague: ICSW Netherlands Committee, 1988).

R. Krever, 'The Plain Guide to the Super Saga', *Australian Society*, October (1989), pp. 36–7.

I. Kristol, 'Welfare: The Best of Intentions, the Worst of Results', in P. Weinberger (ed.), *Perspectives on Social Welfare* (New York: Macmillan, 1974).

N. Lawson, *The State of the Market* (London: Institute of Economic Affairs, 1988).

J. Le Grand, *The Strategy of Equality* (London: Allen and Unwin, 1982).

J. Le Grand, 'Measuring the Distributional Impact of the Welfare State: Methodological Issues', in R. Goodin and J. Le Grand *et al.*, 1987.

J. Le Grand and R. Robinson, *Privatisation and the Welfare State* (London: Allen and Unwin, 1984).

J. Le Grand and D. Winter, *The Middle Classes and the Welfare State*, Discussion Paper No. 14, Suntory-Toyota International Centre for Economic and Related Disciplines (London: London School of Economics, 1987).

R. Lekachman, *Greed Is Not Enough* (New York: Pantheon Books, 1982).

A. Leira, *Day Care for Children in Denmark, Norway and Sweden* (Oslo: Institute for Social Research, 1987).

A. Leira, *Models of Motherhood: Welfare State Policies and Everyday Practices: the Scandinavian Experience* (Oslo: Institute of Social Research, 1989).

C. Lever-Tracy, 'The Flexibility Debate: Part-time Work', *Labour and Industry*, 1 (2) (1988), pp. 210–41.

D. Levine, *Poverty and Society: the Growth of the American Welfare State in International Comparison* (New Brunswick: Rutgers University Press, 1988).

R. Levitas (ed.), *The Ideology of the New Right* (Cambridge: Polity Press, 1986).

J. Lewis (ed.), *Women's Welfare – Women's Rights* (Beckenham: Croom Helm, 1983).

M. Lombard, 'An Examination of Income Distributions in Australia 1983–89', Research Paper No. 340, School of Economic and Financial Studies, Macquarrie University, New South Wales, Australia, 1991.

M. Loney *et al.* (eds), *The State or the Market: Politics and Welfare in Contemporary Britain* (London: Sage, 1987).

J. Longue, 'And We Dreamed of a Just Society', *Scandinavian Studies*, 59 (2) (1987), pp. 129–41.

P. G. Macarthy, 'Justice Higgins and the Harvester Judgement', in J. Roe (ed.), *Social Policy in Australia* (Sydney: Cassell, 1976).

J. Mack and S. Lansley, *Poor Britain* (London: Allen and Unwin, 1985).

V. Mackie, 'Equal Opportunity in an Unequal Labour Market: the Japanese Situation', *Australian Feminist Studies*, 9 (1989), pp. 97–109.

H. Macmillan, *Tides of Fortune 1945–1955* (London: Macmillan, 1969).

A. Mama, 'Black Women, the Economic Crisis and the British State', *Feminist Review*, 17 (1984), pp. 21–35.

A. Mama, 'Violence Against Black Women: Gender, Race and State Responses', *Feminist Review*, 32 (1989), pp. 30–48.

David Marquand, 'The Irresistible Tide of Europeanisation', in S. Hall and M. Jacques (eds), 1989.

T. H. Marshall, *Social Policy* (London: Hutchinson, 1965).

J. Martin and C. Roberts, *Women and Employment* (London: Department of Employment/Office of Population Censuses and Surveys, 1984).

N. Maruo, 'The Developments of the Welfare Mix in Japan', in R. Rose and R. Shiratori (eds), 1986.

K. Marx and F. Engels, *The German Ideology* (Moscow: Progress Press, 1976).

K. Marx and F. Engels, *Manifesto of the Communist Party* (Moscow: Progress Press, 1968).

R. Miliband, *The State in Capitalist Society* (London: Weidenfeld and Nicolson, 1969).

R. Miliband, 'Reply to Nicos Poulantzas', in Robin Blackburn (ed.), *Ideology in Social Science Readings in Critical Social Theory* (Bungay, Suffolk: Fontana/Collins, 1973).

R. Miliband, *Marxism and Politics* (Oxford: Oxford University Press, 1977).

V. Milligan, 'The State and Housing: Questions of Social Policy and Social Change', in A. Graycar (ed.), 1983.

G. Milne, 'University Enrolments Up Despite Tertiary Tax', *Sydney Morning Herald*, 6 April 1989, p. 8.

P. Minford, 'The Role of the Social Services: A View from the New Right', in M. Loney *et al.* (eds), 1987.

Ministry of Finance, *The Swedish Budget 1989/1990* (Stockholm: Swedish Parliament, 1989).

Ministry of Labour, *Labour Market and Labour Policy in 1986* (Stockholm: Swedish Government's Printing, 1988).

R. Mishra, *Society and Social Policy* (London: Macmillan, 1977).

R. Mishra, *The Welfare State in Crisis* (Brighton: Wheatsheaf, 1984).

J. Mitchell, 'Reflections on Twenty Years of Feminism', in J. Mitchell and A. Oakley (eds), *What Is Feminism?* (Oxford: Blackwell, 1986).

J. Mitchell, 'Women and Equality' in A. Phillips (ed.), 1987.

J. Moore, 'Japanese Industrial Relations', *Labour and Industry*, 1 (1) (1987), pp. 140–55.

A. Murie, 'Housing and the Environment', in D. Kavanagh and A. Seldon (eds), 1989.

N. Naffine, 'Law and Feminism', *Work in Progress* (Canberra: Research School of Social Sciences, 1990), pp. 9–10.

National Labour Market Board (NLMB), *Equality in the Labour Market* (Stockholm: National Labour Market Board, 1989).

Y. Noguchi, 'Overcommitment in Pensions: The Japanese Experience', in R. Rose and R. Shiratori (eds), 1986.

A. Oakley, *Subject Women* (Oxford: Martin Robertson, 1981).

H. O'Connor, 'Feminism and the State', *Women and Work*, 12 (1) 1990 (Canberra: Department of Employment, Education and Training), p. 3.

J. O'Connor, *The Fiscal Crisis of the State* (New York: St Martin's Press, 1973).

J. O'Connor, *Accumulation Crisis* (Oxford: Basil Blackwell, 1984).

C. O'Donnell and P. Hall, *Getting Equal* (Sydney: Allen and Unwin, 1988).

OECD, *OECD Economic Surveys 1986/1987: Australia* (Paris: OECD, March 1987).

OECD, 'The Future of Social Protection', *OECD Social Policy Studies*, No. 6 (1988).

C. Offe, *Contradiction of the Welfare State* (London: Hutchinson, 1984).

S. Olsson, 'Decentralisation and Privatisation: Strategies Against a Welfare Backlash in Sweden', in R. Morris (ed.), *Testing the Limits of Social*

Welfare: International Perspectives on Policy Changes in Nine Countries (Hanover: University Press of New England, 1988).

S. Olsson, 'Social Welfare in Developed Market Countries: Sweden', in J. Dixon and R. P. Scheurell (eds), *Social Welfare in Developed Market Countries* (London and New York: Routledge and Kegan Paul, 1989).

C. Oppenheim, *A Tax on All the People: The Poll Tax* (London: CPAG, 1987).

E. Øyen, 'The Muffling Effect of Social Policy', *International Sociology*, 1 (3) (1986), pp. 271–82.

J. Pahl, *Money and Marriage* (London: Macmillan, 1989).

E. Papadakis and P. Taylor-Gooby, *The Private Provision of Public Welfare* (Brighton: Wheatsheaf, 1987).

E. Papadakis, *Attitudes to State and Private Welfare: Analysis of Results from a National Survey* (Sydney: Social Policy Research Centre, 1990).

J. Parker, *Social Policy and Citizenship* (London: Macmillan, 1975).

G. Pascall, *Social Policy* (London: Tavistock, 1986).

C. Pateman and E. Gross, *Feminist Challenges* (Sydney: Allen and Unwin, 1987).

C. Pateman, 'Feminist Critiques of the Public/Private Dichotomy', in A. Phillips (ed.), 1987.

D. Pearce, 'Women, Work and Welfare: The Feminisation of Poverty', in K. W. Feinstein (ed.), *Working Women and Families* (Beverly Hills, CA: Sage Publications, 1979).

G. Persson, *The Scandinavian Welfare State: Anatomy, Logic and Some Problems*, Discussion Paper No. 7, Suntory – Toyota International Centre for Economics and Related Disciplines (London: London School of Economics, 1986).

A. Phillips (ed.), *Feminism and Equality* (Oxford: Basil Blackwood, 1987), pp. 103–27.

J. Pierson, 'Aboriginal Power and Self-Determination in Adelaide', in M. Howard (ed.), *Aboriginal Power in Australian Society* (St Lucia: University of Queensland Press, 1982).

F. Piven and R. Cloward, *Regulating the Poor: The Functions of Public Welfare* (New York: Pantheon Books, 1971).

F. Piven and R. Cloward, *Poor People's Movements* (New York: Pantheon Books, 1977).

R. Plant, *Community and Ideology* (London: Routledge and Kegan Paul, 1974).

C. Pond, 'Introduction' in C. Sandford, C. Pond and Robert Walker, *Taxation and Social Policy* (London: Heinemann, 1980).

M. Poster, *Critical Theory of the Family* (London: Pluto Press, 1978).

N. Poulantzas, *Political Power and Social Classes* (London: New Left Books, 1973a).

N. Poulantzas, 'Problems of the Capitalist State', in Robin Blackburn (ed.), *Ideology in Social Science: Readings in Critical Social Theory* (Bungay, Suffolk: Fontana/Collins, 1973b).

A. R. Prest and N. A. Barr, *Public Finance in Theory and Practice*, 7th edn (London: Weidenfeld and Nicolson, 1985).

J. Rawls, *A Theory of Justice* (Oxford: Oxford University Press, 1985).
J. Raymond, *Bringing Up Children Alone*, Issues Paper No. 3 Social Security Review (Canberra: Department of Social Security, 1987).
M. Reddin, 'Occupation, Welfare and Social Division', in C. Jones and J. Stevenson (eds), *The Year Book of Social Policy in Britain 1980–1981* (London: Routledge and Kegan Paul, 1982).
A. Rees, *T. H. Marshall's Social Policy*, 5th edn (London: Hutchinson, 1985).
S. Ringen, 'Direct and Indirect Measures of Poverty', *Journal of Social Policy*, 17 (3) (1988).
S. Rintoul, 'Black Diggers Faced War on Homefront', *Weekend Australian*, 11–12 August 1990, p. 3.
C. Ronalds, *Affirmative Action and Sex Discrimination* (Sydney: Pluto Press, 1987).
G. Room, *The Sociology of Welfare* (Oxford: Basil Blackwell, 1979).
H. Rose, 'Re-reading Titmuss: The Sexual Division of Welfare', *Journal of Social Policy*, 10 (4) (1981).
H. Rose, 'Heart, Brain and Hand: A Feminist Epistemology for the Natural Sciences', *Signs*, 9 (1) Autumn (1983a), pp. 73–90.
H. Rose, 'Women, Work and Welfare in the World Economy', in C. Baldock and D. Goodrick (eds), (1983b).
R. Rose and R. Shiratori, *The Welfare State East and West* (New York: Oxford University Press, 1986).
R. Rose, 'The Dynamics of the Welfare Mix in Britain', in R. Rose and R. Shiratori (eds) (1986).
R. Rose, 'Divisions that Unite Britain', in D. Kavanagh and A. Seldon (eds) (1989).
M. Ruggie, *The State and Working Mothers: A Comparative Study of Britain and Sweden* (Princeton, NJ: Princeton University Press, 1984).
E. Ryan and A. Conlon, *Gentle Invaders: Australian Women at Work* (Ringwood, Victoria: Penguin, 1988).
E. Ryan, 'Japanese Women at Work', *Inkwel*, 3 Sept.–Oct. 1990, pp. 9–11.
W. Ryan, *Blaming the Victim: Ideology Serves the Establishment* (New York: Random House, 1971).
W. Sanders, 'The Politics of Unemployment Benefit for Aborigines', in D. Wade-Marshall and P. Loveday (eds), *Employment and Unemployment* (Darwin: North Australia Research Unit, 1985).
C. Sandford, C. Pond and R. Walker (eds), *Taxation and Social Policy* (London: Heinemann, 1980).
L. Sargent (ed.), *The Unhappy Marriage of Marxism and Feminism: A Debate on Class and Patriarchy* (London: Pluto Press, 1981).
A. S. Sassoon (ed.), *Women and the State: the Shifting Boundaries of Public and Private* (London: Hutchinson, 1987a).
A. S. Sassoon, 'Women's New Social Role: Contradictions of the Welfare State' A. S. in Sassoon (ed.) 1987b.
M. Sawer (ed.), *Australia and the New Right* (Sydney: Allen and Unwin, 1982).

M. Sawer, 'From the Ethical to the Minimal State: State Ideology in Australia', *Politics*, 18 (1) (1983), pp. 26–35.

M. Sawer (ed.), *Programs for Change* (Sydney: Allen and Unwin, 1985).

M. Sawer, *Sisters in Suits* (Sydney: Allen and Unwin, 1990).

M. Sawer and M. Simms, *A Woman's Place: Women and Politics in Australia* (Sydney: Allen and Unwin, 1984).

H. Scott, *Working Your Way to the Bottom: The Feminisation of Poverty* (London: Pandora Press, 1984).

J. Scutt, *Even in the Best of Homes: Violence in the Family* (Ringwood, Victoria: Penguin, 1983).

A. Seldon, *Agenda for Social Democracy* (London: Institute of Economic Affairs, 1983).

R. Sharp and R. Broomhill, *Short Changed: Women and Economic Policies* (Sydney: Allen and Unwin, 1988).

R. Sharp and R. Broomhill, 'Women and Government Budgets', *Australian Journal of Social Issues*, 25 (1) (1990), pp. 1–13.

S. Shaver, 'The Non-government State: The Voluntary Welfare Sector', paper delivered to Social Policy in the 1980s Conference, Canberra, 28–30 May 1982.

S. Shaver, 'Comment on Fraser', *Thesis Eleven*, 17 (1987), pp. 107–10.

A. Sinfield, 'Analyses in the Division of Welfare', *Journal of Social Policy*, 7 April (1978), pp. 129–56.

A. Sivanandan, *A Different Hunger: Writing on Black Resistance* (London: Pluto Press, 1982).

B. Sköldebrand, 'Employee and Owner – Convertibles', Working Paper H 24, Swedish Centre for Working Life, Stockholm (1989).

K. Skrede, 'Occupational and Industrial Distribution in the ECE Region – Part I', paper presented at Seminar on the Economic Role of Women in the Economic Commission for Europe (United Nations), Vienna, October (1984a).

K. Skrede, 'Occupational and Industrial Distribution in the ECE Region – Part II', paper presented at Seminar on the Economic Role of Women in the Economic Commission for Europe (United Nations), Vienna, October (1984b).

V. Smith, 'The Circular Trap: Women and Part-time Work' in A. S. Sassoon (ed.), 1987.

R. Spånt, 'Wealth Distribution and its Development in Sweden – with an International Comparison', Report for the Swedish Commission on Wage-earners and Capital Growth (Stockholm, 1979/80).

A.-C. Stahlberg, *Lifetime Redistribution of Social Insurance in Sweden* (Stockholm: The Swedish Institute for Social Research, 1988).

P. Steinfels, *The Neoconservatives* (New York: Simon and Schuster, 1982).

G. Stephenson, 'Taxes, Benefits and the Redistribution of Incomes', in C. Sandford, C. Pond and R. Walker (eds), 1980.

F. Stilwell, *The Accord and Beyond* (Sydney: Pluto Press, 1986).

A. Summers, *Damned Whores and God's Police* (Ringwood, Victoria: Penguin, 1975).

P. L. Swan and M. S. Bernstam, 'Support for Single Parents', in M. James (ed.), 1989.

Swedish Institute, 'Fact Sheets on Sweden: Child Care in Sweden', Stockholm, April 1987.

Swedish Institute, 'Fact Sheets on Sweden: Equality Between Men and Women', Stockholm, September 1989.

Swedish National Board of Health and Welfare, *The Social Services in Sweden* (Stockholm: NBHW, 1988).

T. Tachibanaki, *Non-wage Labour Costs: Their Rationale and Economic Effect*, Discussion Paper No. 19, Suntory – Toyota International Centre for Economics and Related Disciplines (London: London School of Economics, 1987).

H. Takayama, 'The Main Track at Last', *Bulletin*, 1 May 1990, pp. 74–5.

P. Thane, *The Foundations of the Welfare State* (London: Longman, 1982).

Awa Thiam, *Black Sisters Speak Out: Feminism and Oppression in Black Africa* (London: Pluto Press, 1978).

E. P. Thompson, *The Making of the British Working Class* (Harmondsworth: Penguin, 1968).

N. Thorogood, 'Race, Class and Gender: the Politics of Housework', in J. Brannen and H. Wilson (eds), 1987.

T. Tilton, 'Why Don't the Swedish Social Democrats Nationalise Industry?', *Scandinavian Studies*, 59 (2) (1987), pp. 142–66.

R. Titmuss, *Commitment to Welfare* (London: Allen and Unwin, 1968).

R. Titmuss, 'The Social Division of Welfare: Some Reflections on the Search for Equity', in *Essays on 'The Welfare State'* (London: Allen and Unwin, 1974).

A. Touraine, *The Voice and the Eye – An Analysis of Social Movements* (Cambridge: Cambridge University Press, 1981).

P. Townsend, *Sociology and Social Policy* (London: Allen Lane, 1975).

P. Townsend, *Poverty in the United Kingdom: A Survey of Household Resources and Standards of Living* (Harmondsworth: Penguin, 1979).

P. Townsend and N. Davidson (eds), *Inequalities in Health* (Harmondsworth: Penguin, 1982).

P. Townsend, P. Phillimore and A. Beattie, *Health and Deprivation: Inequality in the North* (London: Croom Helm, 1988).

B. Turner, *Equality* (London: Tavistock, 1986).

United Kingdom, Parliament, *Caring for People: Community Care in the Next Decade and Beyond* (London: HMSO, 1989).

J. Vandamme (ed.), *New Dimensions in European Social Policy* (London: Croom Helm, 1985).

A. Vandenberg, 'Uncommon Drama in the Swedish Riksdag', *Australian Society* (April) 1990, pp. 33–4.

C. Vellekoop-Baldock, *Volunteers in Welfare* (Sydney: Allen and Unwin, 1990).

J. Vogel, L.-G. Andersson, U. Davidson and L. Hall, *Inequality in Sweden* (Stockholm: Statistics Sweden, 1988).

C. von Otter, 'Workers' Attitudes to Worker Participation in Capital

Accumulation – A Critical Appraisal', (Stockholm: The Swedish Center for Working Life, 1985).

K. Waerness, 'Caring as Women's Work in the Welfare State', in H. Holter (ed.), 1984.

R. E. Wagner, *The Public Economy* (Chicago: Markham, 1973).

J. Wajcman and S. Rosewarne, 'The "Feminisation" of Work', *Australian Society*, 5 (9) (1986), pp. 15–17.

S. Walby, *Patriarchy at Work* (Oxford: Basil Blackwell, 1986).

A. Walker, 'Social Policy, Social Administration and the Construction of Welfare', *Sociology*, 15 (2) (1981), pp. 225–50.

M. Waring, *Counting for Nothing: What Men Value and What Women are Worth* (Wellington: Allen and Unwin, 1988).

J. Watanuki, 'Is There a "Japanese-type Welfare Society?"', *International Sociology*, 1 (3) (1986), pp. 259–70.

E. Waters, 'Sex and Semiotic Confusion', *Australian Feminist Studies* 12 Summer (1990), pp. 1–14.

S. Watson (ed.), *Playing the State: Australian Feminist Interventions* (Sydney: Allen and Unwin, 1990).

B. Wertheimer, *We Were There: The Story of Working Women in America* (New York: Pantheon Books, 1977).

P. Westen, 'The Empty Idea of Equality', *Harvard Law Review*, 95 (3) (1982), pp. 537–88.

L. Wheeler, 'War, Women and Welfare', in R. Kennedy (ed.), *Australian Welfare: Historical Sociology* (South Melbourne: Macmillan, 1989).

D. M. White, *The Philosophy of the Australian Liberal Party* (Richmond: Hutchinson, 1978).

C. Whitehead, 'Fiscal Aspects of Housing', in C. Sandford, C. Pond and R. Walker (eds), 1980.

P. Wilenski, *Public Power and Public Administration* (Sydney: Hale and Iremonger, 1986).

P. Wilenski, 'Dilemmas for Democrats', *Australian Society*, 3 (1) (1984), pp. 12–18.

H. L. Wilensky and C. N. Lebeaux, *Industrial Society and Social Welfare* (New York: The Free Press, 1965).

H. L. Wilensky, *The Welfare State and Equality* (Berkeley: University of California Press, 1975).

H. Wilensky, 'Taxing, Spending and Backlash: An American Peculiarity?', *Taxing and Spending*, July (1979), pp. 6–11.

D. Willetts, 'The Family', in D. Kavanagh and A. Seldon (eds), 1989.

F. Williams, *Social Policy: A Critical Introduction* (Cambridge: Polity, 1989).

R. Williams, *Keywords* (Glasgow: Fontana/Croom Helm, 1976).

J. V. Wills, 'An Exposure of Labour Exchanges', *Solidarity*, September 1913. Document reproduced in J. R. Hay, *The Development of the British Welfare State 1880–1975* (London: Arnold, 1978).

E. Wilson, *Women and the Welfare State* (London: Tavistock, 1977).

K. Wiltshire, *Privatisation: The British Experience; An Australian Perspective* (Melbourne: Longman Cheshire, 1987).

Women's Bureau, Department of Employment, Education and Training, *Women and Work*, 12 (3) (Spring) 1990.

A. Yeatman, *Bureaucrats, Technocrats, Femocrats: Essays on the Contemporary Australian State* (Sydney: Allen and Unwin, 1990).

N. Zacharova and A. Posadskaya, 'Economic Reform and Women's Status in the USSR', paper presented to the European Forum of Socialist Feminists, Gothenburg, 24–6 November 1989.

Index

Abel-Smith, B.   125, 236
able-bodied   25
abortion   49, 51, 223
Abramovitz, M.   24, 235, 236
ABS (Australian Bureau of
    Statistics)   124, 125, 12–28,
    200, 236
absolute poverty   *see* poverty
Accord, Prices and Income   98,
    182
accumulation   21, 105, 114
Acker, J.   206, 236
ACTU (Australian Council of
    Trade Unions)   187
advanced capitalist societies/
    democracies   22, 41, 186,
    229
Aerated Waters Award 1912   172
AFDC (Aid to Family Dependent
    Children)   101, 124, 197
affirmative action   34, 48, 62,
    187, 190, 217–22, 224
Affirmative Action Act   220
Africa   58
age/ageism   25, 45, 52, 60, 81,
    182, 188, 230
ageing population   108, 214 (*see
    also* caring)
age pensions   81, 90, 101–2, 107,
    112, 124
age of retirement   165
agricultural enclosure   77, 111
agricultural reform, Sweden   111

Allardt, E.   77, 110–13, 117, 236
alternative economic strategies
    187
Altman, D.   15, 236
Amos, V.   26, 236
anti-collectivism   42–5
anti-discrimination policy   34, 48,
    187, 190, 217–22, 224, 229
anti-nuclear marches   186
anti-racist critique (perspective)
    42, 49–52, 53, 65
apprenticeships   200
Ardener, Edward   3, 236
Arbitration Reports   171–2
Asia   58
Asians   90, 91, 93
Atkins, S.   89, 220, 236
ATP (Swedish social insurance
    scheme)   112
Austria   74, 137, 156, 183–4
Australia   6–7, 14, 25, 32, 35, 43,
    52, 56–8, 62, 64, 73–6, 78, 86,
    89–99, 100–1, 104, 106, 109,
    111–12, 119, 122, 124–7,
    130–1, 134, 137–9, 146, 150,
    153–4, 156–7, 163–4, 165–6,
    168–74, 178, 181–2, 188,
    193–5, 198–211, 213, 215–22,
    227–30, 235
Australia Parliament   184, 236
Australian Aborigines and Torres
    Strait Islanders   50, 52, 58,

Australian Aborigines *cont.*
   90–2, 94, 95, 163, 166, 172,
   193, 220–21
Australian Liberal (conservative)
   Party   44–5, 57, 88
Australian Labor Party   44, 90–1,
   97, 182
Australian left   16
Australian, The   139

Bacchi, C.   218–19, 235, 236
backlash   10, 17, 95, 117, 146,
   155, 223 (*see also* tax revolt)
Balbo, L.   223, 236
Baldock, C.   24, 49, 50, 236
Banks, O.   15, 48, 173, 235, 236
Barr, N. A.   145–6, 150, 165, 248
Barrett, M.   31, 48, 49, 50, 193,
   235, 236–7
basic wage   92, 98
Beattie, A.   126, 250
bedroom snooping   32
Beggs, J.   207–8, 237
Belgium   35, 74, 124, 126, 129,
   137, 149
Bell, D.   2, 237
Bello, W.   50, 237
Beltram, G.   130, 237
benefit/disbenefit   30, 154–8
Bergmark, A.   61, 237
Bernstam, M. S.   60, 250
betterment/worsement   30
Beveridge, Lord   40, 46, 83–4,
   167–8, 228
Bhavnani, K.   50, 51, 237
Bismarck   80
Björklund, A.   204–5, 237
Black Americans   58, 104, 106,
   190, 217–18
Black Death   78
Black feminism   50–1, 71
Black Power   186
Black Report   126
Black women   25, 125
Blackburn, R.   248
Blacks   42, 50, 85, 157, 186, 217–18
blaming the victim   54
Boer War   79

Boolsen, M. W.   179, 237
Boston Women's Health
   Collective   49, 237
Bradbury, B.   97, 237
Bramley, G.   85, 237
Brandeis, Justice Louis   44
breadwinner (worker) role   71,
   160, 162, 167–70, 188, 190,
   193
Brents, P. G.   102, 243
Britain   *see* United Kingdom
British Royal Commission on
   Taxation of Profits and
   Income, 1955   149
Brannen, J.   237
British welfare state   *see* welfare
   state
Broomhill, R.   182, 221, 249
Brownmiller, S.   49, 237
Bryson, L.   31, 178, 198, 207, 237
Burdekin, B.   157, 237
Bureau of Women's Affairs   211
bureaucracy   178–80, 189
Burns, A.   193, 237–8
Bush, President G.   14

Cabinet submission, implications
   for women   221–2
Calmfors, L.   113, 238
Canada   43, 50, 56, 73–4, 99, 111,
   134, 137, 147, 149, 195, 201,
   205, 213
capital accumulation   11, 21, 47,
   105, 114
capitalism   17–18, 181, 183, 217
   internationalisation of   75
   and patriarchal structure   25,
   50, 171
   and racial structure   25, 50
capitalist economic system   48,
   63, 70, 97, 122, 160, 181, 183,
   232–3
capitalist society/ies   25, 46, 48,
   160, 181, 229, 232
caring
   for the aged   108–9, 115, 160,
   214–15
   caring about   177, 212

caring for 177, 212
caring labour 21, 49, 179,
207–15, 224, 232–3
devalued 225, 232
disbenefits of 28, 225, 232
family care 107–9, 172, 207–11
as invisible work 212
men and 169, 177–80
private caring 213
public caring 213
women and 28, 108–9, 160,
211–15
see also child care
Carson, E. 78, 238
Carter, J. 237
Cass, B. 19, 24, 37, 49, 64, 143,
152, 206, 236, 238, 244
Castells, M. 15, 186, 238
Castles, F. 63, 76, 90–1, 94, 97,
111, 188, 235, 238
Cawson, A. 22, 47, 180–1, 238
centralised wage determination
206
Chamberlain, Joseph 47
charity 56, 60, 99, 105, 166,
209–11
gifts to 153–4
Chartists 80
child care 38, 106, 115, 118, 172,
178, 197, 202–3, 207–11, 220
child benefits/allowance 86, 107,
115, 122
child maintenance 194
child rearing, cost of 207
Choo, C. 95, 235, 238
churches 105, 181
citizenship 6, 48, 53–7, 63, 65–7,
88, 97, 164, 180–5, 216, 223
civil disorder and welfare 102,
105
Clarke, J. 242
class 4, 29, 47, 52, 161, 181
action 218
sex 49
relations 54, 224, 226
welfare and 26
working-class power (male)
22, 81, 181, 183, 206

Close, P. 202, 238
Cloward, R. 102, 105, 247
Cockburn, C. 171, 238
Cole, T. 83, 235, 238
collective bargaining 22, 76, 113,
206, 229
collectivisation of ownership 114
colonisers 25, 33, 119
Commission of Inquiry into
Poverty 58
community 31, 108
community care 178, 213
community charge 85, 144–5
Conlon, A. 168, 171–2, 235, 248
Connell, R. W. 17, 24, 26,
176–7, 186, 191, 222, 235, 238
Connolly, W. 26, 238
consciousness-raising 26
consensus/conflict 46–7
Conservative Government (UK)
12, 88, 183
conservatism/ives 16, 40, 43–5,
56–7, 79, 85, 105, 106, 108
Cope, J. M. 145–6, 148–9, 238
corporatism 22, 98, 114, 167,
180–5, 216
defined 180–1
tripartite 180
Coser, L. A. 10, 104, 235, 238
Coulson, M. 50, 51, 237
Coultan, M. 85, 238
Court, P. 17, 24, 26, 186, 191,
222, 235, 240
Cox, J. 97, 238
Critcher, C. 242
crisis of the state 9–17, 29, 74,
179, 183–5, 187, 226, 229
Croft, S. 178, 238
Crosland, A. 122
cross-national trends Ch. 3 *passim*
Cuba 72
cultural provisions 33, 35, 64,
154
Curthoys, A. 196, 238
Curtin, John 91
custody rights 191

Dahlberg, A. 171–4, 239

Dale, J.   24, 48, 53, 65, 169, 235, 239
Dalley, G.   207, 212, 235, 238
Dalziel, R.   164, 239
Danish Statistics   204, 239
data collection processes   37, 72–3, 111–21, 121, 132–3, 155–7
Davidson, N.   64, 250
Davidson, U.   251
Deacon, D.   174, 239
decentralisation   116, 118
defence policy   34, 37, 154
Deleeck, H.   16, 35, 64–5, 124–6, 128, 129, 131, 134, 138, 149, 151, 239
democracy   16
Denmark   14, 74, 81, 94–5, 110, 114, 117, 128, 137, 151, 178–9, 202, 204, 210
dependence, legitimate   196–200, 223
dependency levels   194–6, 205
dependency, wife   19, 174, 194–6, 223
dependent spouse allowance   107, 152–3, 169
demystification   3, 26
deregulation   105
   of finance sector   75, 87, 118
   of labour markets   76, 91
   of product markets   75, 87
Dethlefs, W.   237
Digby, A.   47, 78, 80, 82, 197–98, 235, 239
Dilnot, A.   150, 239
disability, people with   15, 62, 134, 159, 187, 190, 220–1, 230
disability pension   101–12, 115, 124, 140
disbenefit/benefit   30, 54
discourse
   conservative   16, 40, 43–5, 56–7, 79, 85, 105–6, 108, 187
   conventional   19, 33–6, 67, 99, 123, 159, 226
   defined   3–4

dominant (hegemonic)   3, 26, 38, 47, 73, 99, 123, 159, 232
dominant economic   36–9, 123, 187 (*see also* liberalism)
   individualist   42–5, 52, 54–5, 63–4, 99, 106, 219
   normative/political   39–52
   political economic   42, 46–7, 53
   political nature of   3–4
   social reformist   42–3, 45–6, 53–4, 55, 63
   status quo and   6, 67, 154–5
   on welfare   33–6, 123
   see also anti-racist critique
distribution of power and resources   1, 35, 37–8, 53, 97, 120, 131
distribution of state welfare   121–58
distribution, struggle over   15
diswelfare, diswelfare state   31
domestic labour   *see* household labour
domestic violence   49
dominant groups/race   47, 67
   white males   4, 188, 219, 226
Dominelli, L.   78, 86, 235, 239
Doyle, J.   97, 237
dualised society   157
Duke, V.   12, 239
Dworkin, A.   49, 239

earnings, men's and women's compared   174, 205–7
Eastern Europe   10, 11, 13, 17–18, 229–30, 232
ecological challenge   45
economic boom/prosperity   2, 56, 84
economic dependency   174–5, 194–6
economic individualism   *see* economic liberalism, individualism
economic liberalism   *see* liberalism
economic policy   34
economic rationalism   76, 178–9,

223 (*see also* economic liberalism)
Economist, The 72–3, 107
Edgell, S. 12, 239
education 20, 21, 33–4, 107, 128–9, 197, 199, 207–8
  apprenticeship 200
  benefit to higher-class males 61, 64, 125, 128–9, 188
  free elementary 82
  of girls 200
  rights to 191
  technical 200
  tertiary 200
education allowance 149
Edwards, A. 20, 23, 24, 159, 235, 239
Edwards, M. 192, 239
egalitarianism 162
Einhorn, E. 73, 95, 117, 235, 239
Eisenstein, H. 48, 239
Eisenstein, Z. 48, 57, 239
Elinson, E. 50, 237
Elsik, Edward 100
Elston, D. 50, 239
employee tax for welfare 95, 117
employer tax for welfare 115, 117–18, 133–5
Employers Confederation (Sweden) 116, 133
employment conditions 91–2, 97
employment exchanges (offices) 80, 112
employment training programmes for women 197–8
employment for women 190–9, 201–7
Engels, F. 185, 189, 246
environment 34, 38–9, 67, 73, 232
environmental movement 33, 186
EPAC 35–7, 239
Equal Employment Opportunity Act 220
equal opportunity 48, 61–2, 65, 141, 173, 187, 190, 216, 229

Equal Opportunities Commission 220
equal outcome 61, 191
equal pay 92, 169, 173, 191, 205
Equal Pay Act 220
equal rights 48, 50
Equal Rights Amendment 48
equality, relative 9
equality policies 190–1, 217–22
equity 16, 35
  horizontal 55, 63–5, 69, 83, 125, 152
  vertical 55, 63–6, 69, 88, 125, 133
escalator effect 9
Esping-Andersen, G. 12, 13, 56, 63, 110, 113, 115–17, 128, 130, 133, 137, 235, 239–40
ethnic group/s 4, 15, 17, 52, 54, 182, 187, 229, 229–30, 234
ethnicity 29, 190
European Court 89, 220
European Economic Community 17, 89, 179, 230
Evans, E. 77, 78, 170–71, 240
Evatt Research Centre 12, 16, 180, 240
exchange value 39
excluded groups 102

Factory Acts 170–1
factory inspection 112
familism 193
family 25, 49, 53, 56, 99, 101, 162, 165
  Afro-Caribbean families 193
  aged, desire to live with 214
  effect on work patterns 206–7
  female headed 97, 192–3
  patriarchal 85–6, 105, 109, 190
  role as defining 165–70
  sole parent 97, 192–3
  welfare 107, 108, 214
family allowance 83, 93, 169
Family Endowment Society 169
family income supplement 97, 193
family wage 71, 167–70

Farrer, A.   130, 194, 240
female household heads   192–4
feminisation of poverty   *see*
    poverty
feminisation of work   201
feminist/m
    Black feminism   50–2, 71
    conservative   48
    liberal   48, 53, 65, 219, 224
    literature   5, 24, 26, 34
    Marxist   48–9
    radical   49, 216, 224
    second wave   212, 223–4
    socialist   48–9, 51, 53, 216
    theory/perspective   4, 23–9, 42,
        47–9, 49–52, 186
    white middle class   50, 219, 230
    and race   4, 24–5, 42, 49–52,
        186
feminist awareness typology   23
feminists   16–17, 186
femocrat   222
finance systems   38, 232
Finch, J.   153, 178, 207, 235, 240
Finland   50, 74, 111, 116, 137
Firestone, S.   49, 240
First Home Owners' Scheme   96
First World   17, 18, 50
fiscal crisis   21–2, 74, 179, 183–5,
    187, 226, 229
fiscal welfare   *see* welfare; tax
    concessions
Flora, P.   15–16, 83, 235, 240
football hooliganism   37
Ford Foundation   99
foreign policy   34
Foster, P.   24, 48, 53, 65, 169,
    235, 238
Foucault, Michel   3–4, 25, 226,
    240
France   33, 74–5, 109, 134, 148,
    193, 205
franchise, male   81
Franzway, S.   17, 24, 26, 186,
    191, 222, 235, 240
Fraser, N.   49, 65, 101–2, 105,
    118, 160, 163, 166, 194, 197,
    211, 235, 240

French Revolution   80
Friedman, M.   43–4, 57, 240
Friedman, R.   43–4, 57, 240
friendly societies   81, 164
fringe benefits   141–2 (*see also*
    welfare, occupational)
fruit-pickers' case   172
Fuery, M.   135, 137, 240
functionalist position   21
Funder, K.   207, 240

Galbraith, John Kenneth   15
Galper, J. H.   56, 103, 235, 240
Gamble, A.   88, 240
Gans, H.   54, 240
Garraty, J.   79, 240
GATT (General Agreement on
    Tariffs and Trade)   75, 148
gays   15, 106, 186, 187
Giddens, A.   18, 26, 241
Gittens, D.   192, 241
gender   19, 23–9, 43, 52, 66, 122,
    124, 159, 170, 181, 185, 186,
    226, 229
    composition of parliament
        163–4, 217
    profile   183
    sub-text   160
George, David Lloyd   82
George, S.   50, 59, 78, 240
George, V.   22, 24, 40–3, 157,
    235, 240–1
Germany (East and West)   15–16,
    18, 33, 74, 80–1, 83, 114, 134,
    137, 148, 184, 193, 195, 201,
    204–5, 216
Gershuny, J.   150, 241
Glazer, N.   14, 102–3, 241
Glezer, H.   204, 241
global structures   14, 18, 230
Golding, P.   78–79, 241
Goldthorpe, J. H.   154–5, 241
Goodin, R.   64, 82, 235, 241, 245
Goodrick, D.   50, 236
Gospel of Matthew   134
Gough, I.   20–2, 35, 46, 64, 70,
    79, 88, 132, 186, 235, 241

government (collective)
  expenditure 36
  cuts to 1, 74, 76, 101–2, 104–5,
    116, 119, 122, 130, 155, 157,
    179–80, 189, 213, 218, 223
  externalities 37
  indivisible (non-excludable)
    37–8
Government Expenditure Plans
  1990–91 147
government receipts 73–4
government subsidies 32
Graham, H. 177, 192, 193–4,
  212, 241
Gramsci, A. 30
Graycar, A. 35, 37, 52, 241
Grichting, W. L. 53, 241
Grimes, S. 200, 241
Great Depression 56, 99, 228
Great Society programme 58, 61,
  102, 105, 129, 187 (*see also*
  War on Poverty)
Greece 74
Grimes, S. 200
gross domestic product 35, 38–9,
  67, 73–4, 157
  growth in 39
gross national product 72, 82,
  151
Groves, D. 178, 207, 235, 240
Gruen, F. 156, 241
guest workers 25
Gunasekera, M. 138, 242
Gunnarrson, E. 101, 113, 194,
  242

Habermas, J. 11, 22, 186, 242
Hadler, R. 148, 242
Hall, L. 251
Hall, P. 173, 203, 211, 235, 247
Hall, S. 16, 52, 187, 242
Hanish, T. 141, 244
Hanks, P. 163, 242
Hanson, R. 100–1, 104, 124, 17,
  235, 242
Harding, A. 35, 36, 64, 124, 127,
  242
Harris, R. 16, 43, 57, 60, 242

Hartmann, H. 48, 242
Harvester case 91, 168
Haveman, R. 129, 242
Hawke Labor Government 64,
  86, 93, 97–8, 152, 181, 230
Hayek, F. A. 57, 242
health
  aged 100, 107
  benefits to higher classes 64,
    126
  child 82
  insurance 80, 164
  private insurance 94
  scheme, Australia 93
  school health checks 80
  services 20, 33–4, 36, 106–7,
    115, 125
  USA scheme 100
  women's 49, 221, 224
Healy, D. (Chancellor of
  Exchequer) 144
hegemony 2
Heidenheimer, A. 15–16, 83,
  124, 150–51, 235, 240, 242
Henderson, D. 10–14, 75, 147,
  188, 206, 242
Hendessi, M. 50, 242
Hernes, H. M. 17, 65–6, 115,
  164, 179, 182–3, 190, 196, 216,
  235, 243
heterosexism 25
Hewitt, M. 209, 243
Hewitt, T. 167, 243
Hicks, J. R. 148
Hindess, B. 24, 243
Hiroshi, T. 141, 243
history
  of British welfare state 77–89
  importance of 14, 18, 26
  and racism 49, 93
  of welfare 15–16, 69
Hobson, B. 174, 194–96, 205–06,
  243
Holland *see* Netherlands
Holloway, J. 186, 243
Holt, H. 179, 237
Holter, H. 48–9, 243, 251
homelessness 157

homemaker role   162, 167–70, 172, 190, 196
home-work   172
Hooks, B.   25, 26, 51, 243
horizontal/vertical equity   *see* equity
Horowitz, D.   99, 243
House of Commons   81
household economy (system)   39, 70–1
household heads   *see* female
household labour (householding)   38–9, 190, 201, 215, 224
housing
    Australian Aborigines   95
    benefits from   125, 126–8, 147
    housing purchase/ownership   96, 128, 147, 151
    privatisation of   12–13, 86, 16, 128
    public   20, 33–4, 46, 64, 82, 95, 101, 117, 126–7, 147
    purchase allowance   96, 127
    renting   95–7, 127
    tax deductions and   34, 96, 117, 127, 151–2
Howe, I.   10, 104, 235, 238
humanism/humanist values   40–43
Hunter, E.   193, 243

Iceland   74
ilfare/ill-being   30
immigrants, immigration   25, 51, 86, 94, 111, 115, 157, 221
imperialism   50, 61
imputed rent   96, 127, 151
income
    defined   148–9
    distribution   35, 72, 98, 113, 125
    family   192
    inequality   98, 112
    loss from child rearing   207
    of sole female parent   193–4
    unreported   151
income security   33, 45, 49, 69, 92 (*see also* social security)

income transfer payments   64, 124, 182
indigenous people   25, 33, 50, 229
individualism   42–5, 52, 55, 63–4, 66, 99, 102, 104, 106, 137, 219
indivisible (non-excludable) expenditures   37–8
industrial conciliation and arbitration   91
infant mortality   209
informal (underground) economy   39, 150
inequality   40
    and capitalism   184
    cross-national   17
    de facto   66
    ideology of   122–4, 129, 154, 233
    north/south   126, 157–58, 159, 230
    of power, status and resources   58, 131
    redress for   36
    types of   2, 52
Institute of Public Affairs, London   56, 60
Interdepartmental Committee on Physical Deterioration   80
intermittent employment   206–7
international accounts (statistics)   38–9, 67, 232
international comparisons of welfare state   70–6, 100
International Women's Year and Decade of Women   50
international perspective
    on racism   49–52
    value of   5, 17–18, 67, 230
International Monetary Fund   14, 75
interventionist state   9, 13, 15, 105, 120, 186–9, 222, 229, 231
intra-national struggles   *see* race
Inuit   50
Iraq   14
Ireland   74
Ironmonger, D.   39, 96, 243

Isle of Man 163
Israel 156, 193
Italy 74, 133–4

Jacques, M. 16, 187, 242
James, M. 57, 243
Jamrozik, A. 35, 37, 39, 52–3, 60, 142, 202, 241–2
Japan 6–7, 14, 33, 36, 43, 71–6, 106–10, 119, 124, 134, 141, 163, 193, 201, 204, 210, 213–14, 227, 235, 243
Japanese Quarterly 141
Jencks, C. 64, 129, 243
Jenkins, J. C. 102, 243
Jessop, B. 180, 244
JET (Jobs, Education and Training Programme) 198
Johnson, President Lyndon 58, 102
Jones, C. 248
Jones, M. 95–6, 235, 244
Jordan, B. 14, 19, 53, 131, 157, 184, 235, 244
Jordan, L. 201, 244
Joseph, G. 51, 235, 244
juridical-administrative-therapeutic state apparatus 166

Kahn, A. 36, 244
Kaim-Caudle, P. 100, 102, 104, 244
Kalleberg, A. 141, 244
Kamerman, S. 36, 192, 193–4, 244
Kanter, R. M. 176, 244
Kavanagh, D. 244, 246
Kay, J. A. 153, 244
Kearns, D. 162, 244
Keens, C. 19, 37, 64, 143, 152, 244
Kemeny, J. 127, 244
Kendig, H. 215, 244
Kennedy, President John 102, 217
Kerr, H. 12, 78, 238, 244
Kerschgens, E. 18, 201, 244

Kewley, T. H. 90, 93, 244
Keynesian economics 46, 86, 102
King, M. A. 153, 244
Kinley, D. 50, 237
Knocke, W. 115, 244
Kolodney, D. 99, 243
Korpi, W. 12, 13, 56, 63, 110, 113, 115–17, 128, 130, 133, 137, 235, 239–40
Krever, R. 139, 244
Kristol, I. 103, 244

labour force *see* workforce
labour market policy 36, 107, 112, 114, 199
labour market, primary/secondary 157, 197, 223, 225
labour market programmes for women 197
labour market, restructuring 201, 203
labour unions (movement) 22, 88, 98–9, 111, 136, 180–5, 188, 221
laissez-faire 13, 15, 41, 48, 52, 87, 106, 120
land rights 50, 186
law and order 15, 37–8, 41, 154, 231
Lawson, N. 14, 57, 86, 241, 245
LDCs (least developed countries) 50, 58
Le Grand, J. 12, 36–7, 57, 64, 85, 122, 125, 126–9, 131, 235, 237, 241, 245
Lebeaux, C. N. 20, 56, 70, 103, 251
legitimacy/legitimation 11, 21–2, 47, 65, 80, 129, 186, 189
Leira, A. 202–3, 210, 245
Lekachman, N. 98, 245
less eligibility 78
Lever-Tracy, C. 203, 245
Levine, D. 80, 99, 100, 245
Levitas, N. 10, 13–15, 57, 235, 245
Lewis, J. 49, 235, 245

liberal democratic state   22, 41,
    162, 186, 216, 223
liberal feminism   *see* feminist
liberal theory and patriarchal
    welfare state   161–4, 186,
    216, 219
liberalism   16, 40, 106, 223
    economic (market)   13, 40–5,
        75, 84, 91, 99, 108, 113, 116,
        119, 120, 130, 137, 155,
        178–9, 188, 206, 223–4, 227–8
    New Deal   44, 57, 100, 102,
        105
    political   40–3, 65, 79, 130, 216,
        227–8
    small 'l' (humanist)   40, 44, 56,
        65
life expectancy   72, 106, 160, 165
LO (Swedish national union
    federation)   114
Lombard, M.   98, 245
Loney, M.   245
Longue, J.   113, 235, 245
Low, W.   85, 237
Luxembourg Income Study
    194–6

Macarthy, P. G.   92, 245
Mack, J.   58, 245
Mackie, V.   141, 235, 245
Macmillan, Harold   87, 245
male workers' advantage   170–5
malestream writing/perspective
    47, 102, 159
Mama, A.   25, 245
Maoris   50
market   56, 57, 64, 70–1, 75, 91,
        106, 116–17, 179, 222, 233
    capital   75–6, 91
    labour   75–6
    product   75–6
market, development of   1, 9–10,
        13, 15–16, 22, 179–80, 188,
        228
market-orientated state   17, 75–6,
        89
Marquand, D.   89, 245

married man's allowance   *see*
    dependent spouse
married women, ban on
    employment   172
married women's employment
    see employment of women
Marshall, T. H.   46, 65, 79, 12,
    245
Martin, J.   202, 246
Maruo, N.   107–9, 214–15, 235,
    246
Marx, K.   1, 30, 171, 185, 189,
    226, 246
Marxism/ists   40–3, 46–8, 185–8
Marxism Today   187
materialist position   48
maternity allowance   91, 93
maternity leave   169, 203, 209
Matthew effect/principle   134,
    142, 154
McIntosh, M.   31, 50, 193, 235,
    237
means test   59, 60, 62, 83, 93,
        96–7, 107, 117, 122–3, 127,
        166, 211
Medicaid   101
Medicare, US health insurance
    100
Meidner Plan   114, 154
men's welfare state   *see* welfare
    state
middle class, use of services   113,
    121–158
Middleton, S.   78–9, 241
Miliband, R.   185, 233–5, 246
military/ism   14, 15, 79, 107, 166,
    216, 231
Mill, John Stuart   14
Milligan, V.   96, 246
Milne, G.   200, 246
miners' strike   84, 188
Minford, P.   16, 45, 56, 86, 246
Minister for Employment,
    Education and Training
    198–9
Ministry of Finance, Sweden   10,
    118, 246

Ministry of Labour, Sweden 203, 205, 246
Ministry of Social Security 83
minority group 15
Mishra, R. 10, 15–16, 22–3, 35–6, 41–2, 46, 53–4, 131, 183–4, 187, 235, 245
Mitchell, J. 65, 224, 245
modernisation 107, 197
Moore, J. 141, 235, 246
motherhood
 and Black women 51, 125
 ideology 31, 202, 212
Mowbray, M. 31, 178, 207, 237
multiculturalism 4
Murie, A. 157, 246
muted groups 3–5, 162, 186, 189, 191, 229

Naffine, N. 152, 246
nation and race 25, 49–52
national accounts (statistics) 38–9, 232
National Assistance Act (UK) 1948 83
National Association for Promotion of Social Science 209
National Insurance Acts (UK)
 1911 81, 165, 209
 1946 83
National Health Service (UK) 1948 46, 83
National Labour Market Board (NLMB) 202, 204, 246
national liberation 186
nationalisation of industry 13, 86–7, 113
Native Americans 50, 58
NATO 216
neo-Marxist perspective 40–3
Netherlands, the 33, 71, 73–4, 114, 124, 126, 129, 134, 137, 156, 195–6, 202, 205, 213
New Deal 44, 82, 100, 102
'new left' 14, 187, 227
New Right 7, 13, 15, 16, 41, 43–5, 54, 63, 69, 72, 74, 77, 85, 90, 100, 103, 106, 115–16, 129, 145, 187, 218, 228
'new times' 16
New Zealand 6, 14, 50, 57, 73, 75, 89–91, 131, 134, 163, 164, 227–8
newspapers, development of 79
Noguchi, Y. 14, 107, 235, 246
non-decision 3, 5
non-government state/sector 177, 182, 213
Nordic states, countries 6–7, 14, 65, 71–6, 110–19, 128, 137, 179 (*see also separate country entries*)
north/south issue *see* inequality
Norway 50, 63, 72–4, 110, 116, 117, 128, 137, 156, 184, 195, 202–3, 210, 213, 219, 227–8
nursing 172–3, 177–8, 200, 201, 213

Oakley, A. 49, 246
OASDHI (Old Age, Survivors, Disability and Health Insurance) 100–1, 124, 137, 138
occupational segregation 170–5, 200, 213, 218
occupation welfare *see* welfare
O'Connor, H. 206, 246
O'Connor, J. 11, 21–2, 47, 105–6, 186–7, 235, 246
O'Donnell, J. 173, 203, 211, 235, 247
OECD 10–14, 36, 57, 72–6, 87, 96, 98, 118–19, 127–8, 133, 147, 150, 152, 155, 158, 174, 188, 194–6, 204, 206, 228, 230, 247
Offe, C. 10, 11, 22, 70, 180–1, 187, 199, 235, 247
Office of Federal Contract Compliance 21–8
Olsson, S. 14, 34, 35, 55, 112, 116, 118, 128, 129, 167, 235, 247

Omnibus and Budget
    Reconciliation Act, 1981   197
OPEC   14
Oppenheim, C.   85, 247
opportunity costs of government
    outlays   38
organisations and gender structure
    176–67, 183–5
Oxford English Dictionary   43
Øyen, E.   94, 247

Pacific Islanders   92, 93
Pahl, J.   192, 247
Papakadis, E.   12, 13, 57, 84, 95,
    125, 127, 128, 136, 137, 235,
    247
Papua   93
parental leave   115, 169–70
parenting, shared   219
Parker, J.   41, 60, 247
Parmar, P.   26, 236
part-time employment   141, 157,
    169, 202–4, 206 (*see also*
    women's work)
Pascall, G.   42, 200, 220, 22, 235,
    247
Pateman, C.   28, 65, 162, 186,
    191, 247
paternalistic egalitarianism   45
paternity leave   169–70, 204 (*see
    also* parental leave)
patriarchy   4, 48–9, 54, 78, 197
pay-roll tax   115, 117–18, 135
peace   186, 225
Pearce, D.   192, 247
Pearson, R.   50, 239
peasants, role   77, 110–1
pensions
    Act, 1908   81
    Act, 1946   83
    earnings-related   124
    flat rate   84, 88, 93, 97, 124–5,
        131, 134, 166
    and social control   32
    sole/single parent   32, 83, 160,
        192–3, 198
    support for public   136–7
    widows/survivor   197

Persson, G.   124, 235, 247
Phillimore, P.   126, 250
Phillips, A.   246, 247
Pierson, J.   15, 247
Piven, F.   102, 105, 247
Plant, R.   31, 248
political economic perspective
    42, 46–7, 53
political economy   21
political liberalism   *see* liberalism
poll tax   85, 144–5
Pond, C.   27, 144, 146, 148–9,
    248, 250
poor
    culture of   79
    impotent, war casualities,
        shiftless   79
    rural   77
    'undeserving'   15, 55, 61, 78,
        81, 102, 110
Poor Laws   54, 55, 57, 77–8, 81,
    82, 103, 170
pornography   49
Portugal   33, 74
Posadskaya, A.   201, 219, 252
positive discrimination   59, 61–2
post-industrial society   2
post-welfare state   231
Poster, M.   196, 248
post-war settlement/consensus
    43, 84, 86–9, 228
Poulantzas, N.   47, 185, 248
poverty   40, 54
    Aboriginal   95
    absolute   55, 57–9, 69
    child   97
    feminisation of   101, 192
    line   96–7, 192, 194
    within marriage   192
    prevention of   206
    rediscovered   58
    relative   55, 57–9, 65, 69, 89
    traps   62
    among sole parents   193–4
    War on Poverty   58, 61, 102,
        105, 129
    women's   192
Prest, A. R.   145–6, 150, 165, 248

Prices and Income Accord *see* Accord
private *see* public/private
private insurance 112, 118, 125
private personal pensions 84, 93, 135
private (personal, economic) wage 34–5, 98, 107–8, 174
privatisation in public enterprise 13, 15, 75, 87, 91, 155
privatisation in Scandinavia 12, 116–18, 137
professions 178, 181, 183
progress, myth of 2, 32–3, 74
proletarianisation 196–200, 224–5
property rights for married women 48, 191–2
protective legislation 170–5
protest of propertied class 114
public administration 37–8, 118
public (social) assistance 101–6, 112
Public Expenditure White Paper, 1979 147
public/private domains 28, 107, 162, 179, 191, 219
public safety 37
public service/sector work 136, 174, 183, 218
public welfare 20, 70

quotas (affirmative action) 218

race 23–9, 42–3, 52, 66, 122, 124, 161, 185, 186, 190, 226, 229–30
 defined 28
 and intra-national struggles 50–1
 non-dominant 4–5, 19, 28, 36, 46, 49–52, 54, 229, 234
 and oppression/discrimination 2, 298, 49–54, 62, 86, 90–2, 100, 134, 217, 220
Race Relations Act 220
Racial Discrimination Act 220

racial group/s 15, 17, 119, 182, 187
racism 28–9, 49–52, 93
rape 49
rape crisis centres 49, 177, 221, 224
Rathbone, Eleanor 169
rationing 60, 62
Rawls, J. 162, 248
Raymond, J. 194, 248
Reagan, President Ronald 14, 100–1, 104–5, 131, 157, 226–27, 230
recreational provision 35, 64, 154
Reddin, M. 135, 137, 248
redistribution to richer 89, 117, 122, 126
redistribution through public sector 113, 119–20, 124
Rees, A. 83–4, 248
refuges 177, 224
relative autonomy of the state 47, 185–8
relative poverty *see* poverty
reluctant collectivism 40
repatriation benefits 166, 181, 198 (*see also* welfare)
reproduction 34, 49, 53, 65
reproduction of workforce 21
reproductive technology 225
residual/ism 15, 83, 92, 97, 101, 104–5, 116, 123
restrictions on women's work *see* protective legislation
restructuring *see* labour market
retirement age 165
revenue raising 143–54
revolt of the rich 15
right to control fertility 51, 191
rights 14, 41–2, 44, 46, 48, 50–1, 54, 56, 58, 61–3, 115, 191, 222
Ringen, S. 58, 248
Rintoul, S. 167, 248
roads and highways 37
Robinson, R. 12, 57, 235, 245
Rockefeller Foundation 99
Ronalds, C. 190, 221, 248
Room, G. 23, 40, 42, 63, 248

Roosevelt, F. P.   100, 102, 217
Rose, H.   19, 24, 53, 132–3, 178, 187, 192, 232, 248
Rose, R.   99, 106, 107, 157, 168, 235, 248
Rosewarne, S.   201, 251
Ruggie, M.   209–10, 235, 248
Ryan, E.   168, 171–2, 204, 235, 248
Ryan W.   54, 248

safety-net   45, 55
Sami people   50, 111, 115
Sanders, W.   92, 249
Sandford, C.   248–9, 250
Sargent, L.   48, 249
Sassoon, A. S.   188, 235, 249
Sawer, M.   10, 15, 17, 43, 45, 48, 57, 90., 163–4, 174, 217–18, 221, 249
Scandinavian countries   46, 65, 110, 133, 151, 179, 185, 216–17, 235 (*see also* Nordic)
Scandinavian (Swedish) model   137
Scott, H.   192, 249
Scutt, J.   49, 249
Second World   17
segregation   *see* occupational
Seldon, A.   16, 43, 57, 60, 242, 244, 246, 249
selective/universal   16, 55, 59–63, 101, 112–13, 123, 129–31, 194, 210, 230
self help   81
SERPS (State Earnings Related Pension Scheme)   84, 88, 135
service occupations   213
servicemen   82, 181
settlement   *see* post-war
sex class   49
Sex Discrimination Act   220
sexism   24, 45
sexual discrimination   89, 122, 218, 220
sexual division of labour   21, 212
sexual preference   190, 230

shareholding   87, 140, 145
Sharp, R.   182, 221, 249
Shaver, S.   166, 177, 182, 213, 249
Shiratori, R.   99, 106, 107, 235, 248
Simms, M.   90, 163–4, 244, 249
Sinfield, A.   19, 20, 37, 53, 249
Sivanandan, A.   52, 249
skewed, tilted, balanced organisations   176
skill   201
Sköldebrand, B.   140–1, 249
Skrede, K.   200, 213, 249
Smith, V.   203, 210, 250
social assistance   *see* public assistance
social democracy   40–3, 106, 119, 184
social insurance   64, 81, 100, 102
social integration   63, 105, 129
social movements   105, 186
social policy, defined   34, 179
social reformist perspective   42–3, 45–6, 53, 63
social security   20, 34, 69, 107
Social Security Act, 1986   84
social services   33, 34
social solidarity   113, 115, 117, 129 (*see also* social integration)
social wage   6, 35, 46, 64, 91, 97–9, 108, 131, 181
   defined   34–5, 182
social welfare
   defined   33–4
   stigma and   27, 56, 61, 83, 143, 166, 167
   see also welfare
social work   33
socialisation of industry   113
socialisation system   70
socialist/m   41, 80, 106, 113, 227
   Fabian   43–4, 57
sociological approach/perspective   23–9, 230–3
south/north   *see* inequality
South America   58
Soviet Union   11, 201, 219, 230

Spain 33, 73–5
Spånt, R. 121, 155–6, 250
spinners 171, 173
subsidies to business 32
Supplementary Benefit/Income
 Support 83, 135
Stahlberg, A.-C. 124, 250
state
 capitalist 87, 185–8, 232
 communist 6
 corporate 22–3, 114, 180–5,
  216
 crisis of 9–17, 21, 29, 74, 179,
  183–5, 187, 226, 229
 fascist 6
 as guarantor of freedom 43
 intervention/s 5, 9, 13, 15, 17,
  19, 102, 105, 119–20, 121,
  125, 160, 178, 189, 222, 229,
  231
 interventionist 9, 13, 15, 105,
  120, 186–88, 222, 231
 interventions and New Right
  412, 54, 105, 223, 227–9
 legitimacy of 11, 21–2, 47, 65,
  80, 129, 186, 189
 liberal democratic 65
 masculinity of 176–7
 militaristic 6
 minimal 44, 178, 223
 'nanny state' 16, 227
 non-government state 177,
  182, 213
 non-intervention 5, 105
 patriarchal 87, 175–7, 185,
  187, 188–9, 215–17
 politics of 4, 215–17
 racist 87, 187, 188–9
 reduction of 1, 74, 76, 101–2,
  104–5, 116, 119, 122, 155, 157
 relative autonomy of 47, 185–8
 unions and 98, 180–5, 188
 women's power in 215–17
Statute of Labourers 78
Steinfels, P. 57, 250
Stephenson, G. 144, 250
Stephenson, J. 248

stigma 32, 54, 60–2, 83, 112–13,
 135, 143, 160, 166–7
Stilwell, F. 98, 250
structural adjustment 75
Summers, A. 164, 250
superannuation 93–4, 135–9, 188
supra-national bodies 230
Surrey 146–77
Swan, P. L. 60, 250
Sweden 6, 10, 13, 50, 60, 63,
 74–7, 90, 101, 104, 106,
 109–19, 129–30, 133–5, 137,
 140, 151, 154–6, 163, 166,
 169, 171, 173–5, 183–4,
 193–6, 200–11, 213, 217–22,
 227–30
Swedish Commission on Wage-
 earners and Capital Growth,
 155
Swedish Institute 169, 200–1,
 203–4, 211, 220, 250
Swedish National Board of Health
 and Welfare 115, 250
Swedish Social Democratic Party
 90, 104, 112–13, 116, 184
Swedish welfare ministries 33–4
Switzerland 72–4, 96, 135, 137,
 195, 202
Sydney Morning Herald 194

Tachibanaki, T. 132, 133–4, 141,
 250
Takayama, H. 163, 201, 210, 250
targeting welfare benefits *see*
 selective
Taylor-Gooby, P. 12, 13, 57, 84,
 125, 127–8, 136–7, 235, 247
tax revolt 10, 94–5, 101, 102,
 117, 146, 155
taxation
 allowances for dependants
  152–3
 avoidance 13, 150
 capital gains 64, 96, 127
 comprehensive income tax
  149, 231
 concessions (exemptions) 34,
  37, 75, 96, 143–54

taxation *cont.*
  concessions for private pensions
    35, 93, 136–9
  consumption (value added) 75,
    146
  as disincentive 145
  expenditure/exemption
    146–8, 232
  fairness of 145–7
  and gifts to charity 153–4
  and housing 151–2
  income 35, 148–9
  and informal economy 38
  as instrument of social policy 144
  international changes 75–6
  marginal rates 145–6
  minimisation 113, 150
  PAYE 95
  personal income tax 75
  progressive/ity 64, 113, 145–6,
    152, 155
  reduction of top rates 87
  regressive 144
  threshold 145–6
  of wages and salaries 95
taxation as welfare 20
telecommunications system 232
Temple, Archbishop 83
Thane, P. 20, 77, 81, 83, 107,
    144, 164–5, 235, 250
Thatcher, Margaret 13, 16, 23,
    43, 58, 84–5, 88, 125, 128,
    131, 136, 144, 150, 157,
    226–7, 230
Thiam, Awa 50, 250
Third World 17, 38, 49
Thompson, E. P. 77, 111, 250
Thorogood, N. 192, 193, 250
Tilson, John, Republican 99
Tilton, T. 113, 114, 250
Title VII of Civil Rights Act 218
Titmuss, Richard 7, 19, 20, 30,
    46, 53, 61, 63, 110, 121, 122,
    131, 133, 142, 178, 232, 250
Touraine, A. 186, 250
town planning 34, 82
Townsend, P. 58, 60, 63, 64,
    126, 250
transport 34, 125–6, 154, 197

Treaty of Rome 89
Turner, B. 66, 235, 251
typing/typist 173, 210

unemployment/unemployed 71,
    77, 79, 89, 182, 204–5
  benefits 80, 101–2, 112, 198
  insurance 166
  long-term 89
  voluntary 86
unions *see* labour unions
United Arab Emirates 72
United Kingdom 12–14, 32, 35,
    44–6, 50–1, 57–8, 62, 64,
    73–89, 101, 107, 109–12, 119,
    124, 127–8, 131, 133–5,
    145–7, 150–4, 157, 163–5,
    168–9, 170, 173, 178–9,
    180–1, 183–4, 186, 188,
    192–5, 199, 201–2, 204–11,
    213, 215–22, 227–30, 235
United Kingdom Parliament
    213, 251
United Nations, comparison of
    welfare states 72–3, 107
United Nations System of
    National Accounts 38
United Way of America 99
universal provision 92, 115, 123,
    129–31, 210
universal/selective *see* selective
universal suffrage 90
universalism 17, 5, 59–63, 64, 84,
    115, 129–31, 162, 164, 191,
    210
  false 26
urban social protests 186
USA 6–7, 13–14, 23, 25, 32–3,
    36, 43–4, 48, 50–1, 56, 54–7,
    61–2, 71–6, 82, 95, 99–106,
    109, 111, 119, 124, 127, 131,
    133–4, 137, 146–7, 151,
    153–4, 157, 163–5, 174, 180,
    186, 190, 193–5, 197, 201–11,
    213, 216–18, 227–30, 233–5

Vandamme, J. 179, 251
Vandenberg, A. 14, 113, 119,
    251

Vellakoop-Baldock, C. 177–8,
213, 251
Vietnam 103, 186
Vogel, J. 202, 251
voluntary work 177–9, 213
von Otter, C. 114, 251
voting rights 48, 90, 163, 191

Waerness, R. 213, 251
wage earners' welfare state 6, 76,
89–99, 156, 172
wages and conditions, regulation
of 91, 97–8, 206
Wagner, R. E. 148, 251
Waine, B. 210, 244
Wajcman, J. 201, 251
Walby, S. 170–1, 173, 251
Walker, A. 53, 251
Walker, R. 248, 249, 250
War on Poverty 58, 61, 102, 105,
129
Waring, M. 34, 38, 73, 179, 235,
251
Watanuki, J. 107, 108–9, 124,
141, 235, 251
Waters, E. 219, 251
Watson, S. 186, 251
wealth distribution 97, 121,
155–7
Webbs, S. and B. 61
welfare
bifurcated/dual system 100–6
broadened discourse 25–9, 59,
121–58, 226–34
cheats 79
classical form 33, 34, 36, 53
comprehensive definition of
154–8
contradictory effects of 31–3
definition 4
fiscal 7, 19, 35–7, 59, 64, 69,
93, 121, 132, 143–55, 188,
223, 231
as human face of capitalism 21
institutional 55–7, 58–9, 65,
71, 88, 100, 113 115–16, 213
literature 2–3
men and 164–7
middle-class support for 63,
94, 98, 115, 230
narrowly defined 4–5, 23–5,
30–3, 53–4
occupational 7, 19, 35–7, 59,
64, 69, 89, 93, 107–8, 121,
131–42, 155, 157, 188, 223,
231
repatriation 166–7, 198
residual 55–7, 71, 77, 83, 88,
92, 97, 101, 104–5
selective 16, 55, 59–63, 101,
194, 230
social 7, 19, 27, 53, 60, 69, 70,
188
traditional form 33
universal 55, 59–63, 65, 92,
115, 123, 129–31, 210, 230
and vertical equity 64, 88
and the wealthy 53, 155
working class and 64, 191
Welfare I and Welfare II 103–4,
welfare society 108
welfare state
Australian 89–99
beneficiaries of 121–58
British 6–7, 40, 77–89
crisis of 9–17, 29, 74, 179,
183–5, 187, 226, 229
defined 36
differentiated 183–4
gendered 180–5
German 16
institutional 55–7, 58–9, 65,
69, 100, 115, 129–31, 213
integrated 183–4
international comparisons 70–6
Japanese 106–10
laggard 76, 90, 99, 106
as male class politics 161, 188,
224
men's 159–89, 235
and national wealth 71–2
Nordic 110–9
as pacifier 22
reluctant 72
reversible/vulnerable 94, 97,
129–31
and Second World War 82
socialist 16

welfare state *cont.*
  Swedish provision   110–19
  USA   99–106
  wage earners'   6, 76, 89–99,
    156, 172
  women's   190–225, 235
  see also state
welfare wars   228
well-being   33, 39, 66, 106, 232
Wertheimer, B.   164, 251
Westen, P.   219, 251
Western advanced capitalist states 18
Wheeler, L.   166–7, 181, 198, 251
Whiggish view of history   2
White, D. M.   44–5, 251
White Australia policy   92
Whiteford, P.   97, 237
Whitehead, C.   152, 251
Whitlam Labor Government   44,
    93–4, 97
'who benefits?'   1–8, 29, 33,
    69–70, 76, 99, 122, 124–58,
    226, 232
  poor *v.* better-off   1–8, 27–8,
    32–3, 67, 122, 124–58
Wilding, P.   22–4, 40–3, 235, 241
Wilenski, P.   15, 17, 91, 233, 251
Wilensky, H. L.   20, 23, 70,
    102–3, 235, 251, 252
Willetts, D.   84–5, 183, 252
Williams, F.   23–5, 34, 42, 159,
    235, 251
Williams, R.   30, 252
Wills, J. V.   80, 252
Wilson, E.   34, 48–9, 53, 190,
    209, 252
Wilson, G.   237
Wilson Labour Government   98,
    184
Wiltshire   12, 252
Winter, D.   125, 131, 245
women
  and biology   26
  Black   24–5, 38, 49–52
  of colour   49–50, 102
  and corporatism   180–5
  as dependants   168, 174
  disadvantage of   62, 100–1,
    109, 115, 119, 134, 205–7

and employment   190
and family role   165
gains made by   106, 187
and poverty   48, 49
and rights to control own body
    51
as sole parents   97, 101, 125,
    160, 193
and superannuation   136–9
as welfare recipients   36, 160
white   25–6, 49
as workers   196–9, 201–5
women's budget statements   221
Women's Bureau   203–6, 252
women's economic position
    174–5, 192–6
women's health collectives/
    services   49, 177, 221, 224
Women's Liberation
    Movement   49, 224
women's movement   173, 213,
    218–19, 222, 224
women's reproductive labour   38,
    49, 53, 65
women's welfare state   *see* welfare
    state
women's work (labour)   38–9,
    49, 67, 141
work incentives, ethic   60, 76–7,
    103, 105, 109
worker role   164 (*see also*
    breadwinner)
worker's compensation   82, 92,
    100, 112
workfare   32, 104, 157, 197
workforce, fitness for   79
workforce participation rates
    196–7, 201–5
working class   22, 64 (*see also*
    class)
working hours   141, 157, 169,
    202–04
worsement/betterment   30

Yeatman, A.   4, 16, 30, 222, 235,
    252
Youth Training Scheme   86, 199

Zacharova, N.   201, 219, 252

herbal
ANTIVIRALS

STRENGTHEN YOUR IMMUNITY NATURALLY

Sorrel Davis

Healthy Living Publications
SUMMERTOWN, TENNESSEE

Library of Congress Cataloging-in-Publication Data

Names: Davis, Sorrel, author.
Title: Herbal antivirals : strengthen your immunity naturally / Sorrel Davis.
Description: Summertown, Tennessee : Healthy Living Publications, [2017] |
   Includes bibliographical references and index.
Identifiers: LCCN 2016057763 (print) | LCCN 2016059583 (ebook) | ISBN
   9781570673443 (paperback) | ISBN 9781570678547 (ebook)
Subjects: LCSH: Herbs—Therapeutic use. | Herbals. | Antiviral agents.
Classification: LCC RM666.H33 D425 2017 (print) | LCC RM666.H33 (ebook) | DDC
   615.3/21—dc23
LC record available at https://lccn.loc.gov/2016057763

We chose to print this title on responsibly harvested paper stock
certified by The Forest Stewardship Council®, an independent
auditor of responsible forestry practices. For more information,
visit us.fsc.org.

MIX
Paper from
responsible sources
FSC® C005010

Cover and interior design: John Wincek
Stock photography: 123 RF

Printed in the United States of America

Book Publishing Company
PO Box 99
Summertown, TN 38483
888-260-8458
bookpubco.com

ISBN: 978-1-57067-344-3

22 21 20 19 18 17   1 2 3 4 5 6 7 8 9

Disclaimer: The information in this book is
presented for educational purposes only. It
isn't intended to be a substitute for the medical advice of a physician, dietitian, or other
healthcare professional. Please note that herbal
remedies taken orally may interact with
medications that are broken down by the liver.
If you take these medications, ask your doctor
before using herbal remedies.

Preface 4

1 Understanding Viruses 6

2 Common Human Diseases Caused by Viruses 11

3 Symptoms of Viral Infection and Standard Treatments 21

4 Tips to Prevent Viral Infections and Strengthen Immunity ... 30

5 Understanding Influenza 43

6 Mosquito-Borne Viruses 51

7 Herbal Antivirals and Immune Boosters 58

AMERICAN GINSENG 61
ANDROGRAPHIS 65
ASIAN GINSENG 70
ASTRAGALUS 74
BAIKAL (CHINESE) SKULLCAP 78
BARBERRY 82
ECHINACEA 86
ELDERBERRY 92
LEMON BALM 96
LICORICE 100
PEPPERMINT 105
SIBERIAN GINSENG 112
TEA 118

Glossary and Notes 126
Resources 131
Index 132

PREFACE

T he human body is home to a wide and wild assortment of microorganisms, including viruses. They all have adapted to the human biological system and found ways to survive and thrive. It's estimated that millions of distinct types of viruses exist, although only about five thousand have been identified and described in detail. Virtually every ecosystem on our planet contains these minute life forms. The branch of science that deals with the study of viruses is known as virology, and it's an area of specialty within the field of microbiology.

Viruses are responsible for a variety of diseases in plants and animals. The ones we're most familiar with—measles, mumps, and polio—affect only humans, and although they once posed major health concerns, they now occur only incidentally due to the widespread use of vaccinations in children. However, diseases caused by other viruses, such as acquired immune deficiency syndrome (AIDS) and the human immunodeficiency virus (HIV), for which vaccines have not yet been developed, remain ongoing global concerns.

The fundamental nature of viruses was first discovered a little over a century ago from a disease found in tobacco, now known to be caused by the tobacco mosaic virus. The study of plant viruses has since played an important role in the study of human viruses, and more than nine hundred plant viruses have been identified and described.

Infectious viral diseases constitute a major health problem worldwide. Controlling these diseases is the focus of constant scientific efforts because of the body's resistance to known antiviral agents. One very promising approach is the development of antiviral products derived from natural sources, notably herbs.

Traditional herbal medicines are made from naturally occurring, plant-derived substances that have had minimal or no industrial processing. They have been used for millennia to treat illnesses within local or regional healing practices. Traditional herbal medicines are presently receiving significant attention in global health approaches and discussions. For example, in China, traditional herbal medicine played a prominent role in the strategy to contain and treat severe acute respiratory syndrome (SARS), and about 80 percent of African populations use some form of traditional herbal medicine. The market for medicinal herbal products around the world exceeds $60 billion annually, and interest in and public funding for international research of traditional herbal medicines is growing.

Herbs contain a wide variety of diverse phytochemicals, and some of these plant chemicals have been found to have natural antiviral properties that can either help stop a viral infection from progressing or shorten the duration or severity of symptoms. Herbal options have ignited the attention of researchers because viruses don't mutate in the presence of phytochemicals. This means the viruses are far less likely to develop resistance to herbal medicinals, so patients can use them repeatedly to fight a variety of infections and health conditions. Moreover, herbal antivirals generally have fewer or milder side effects than pharmacological options.

Unfortunately, at this time there simply aren't viable alternatives to vaccines to prevent the vast majority of serious or life-threatening viral infections, and there are still many known viruses (as well as new and emerging ones) for which no vaccine has yet been developed. However, because of a growing public outcry regarding concerns about vaccines and a groundswell of mistrust for the pharmaceutical industries that produce them and the regulatory agencies that oversee them, there's an urgent call to develop feasible options.

Every body is unique and has its own specific needs, and there will surely be times when it's not wise for you to treat an illness that's beyond the capacity of a natural solution. Use herbal antivirals with care, especially when it comes to children or if you're pregnant or trying to become pregnant, breastfeeding, using alcohol, or taking drugs of any kind, or have been diagnosed with or are being treated for any medical condition or disease. Always consult with your physician or healthcare provider when in doubt or before trying an herbal antiviral or natural medicinal.

If you want to better understand how viruses proliferate, learn how to protect yourself and your loved ones from viral infections, or are on a quest to find natural, drug-free solutions that may strengthen your immune system and minimize the symptoms and duration of an infection, I invite you to read on. I hope this book will provide the answers you are seeking.

Sorrel Davis

Understanding Viruses

> There is nothing so patient, in this world
> or any other, as a virus searching for a host.
>
> MIRA GRANT, *COUNTDOWN*

Hiding in Plain Sight

But however secure and well-regulated civilized life may become, bacteria, proto-
zoa, viruses, infected fleas, lice, ticks, mosquitoes, and bedbugs will always lurk
in the shadows ready to pounce when neglect, poverty, famine, or war lets down
the defenses.

Hans Zinsser (1878–1940), American physician, bacteriologist, and prolific author

V iruses, believed to be the most abundant biological entities on
Earth, are microscopic organisms that replicate inside the
cells of living hosts, including humans and other animals, plants,
and bacteria. Viral infections begin when proteins on the surface of
a virus particle, known as a virion (a complete virus particle that is
the extracellular infective form of a virus), bind to specific receptor
proteins on the surface of host cells. The distribution of these receptor molecules on host cells determines the cell preference of the
virus. For example, a cold or flu virus will target cells that line the
respiratory tract (airway and lungs), and a foodborne virus will target cells in the digestive tract (stomach and colon). The human
immunodeficiency virus (HIV) that causes acquired immune deficiency syndrome (AIDS) specifically attacks T lymphocytes (T cells),

which are white blood cells that fight infection and disease and are a vital component of a healthy immune system.

Putting Viruses to Work

An inefficient virus kills its host. A clever virus stays with it.

James Lovelock, independent scientist, environmentalist, and futurist

When it comes to viruses, most studies have focused on those that cause infection and disease. Yet recent research indicates that certain viruses, known as symbionts, may actually be of value to us. In fact, some viral entities are beneficial in helping to fight off invading microbes and can destroy a spectrum of harmful bacteria, thereby providing protection to humans and other living organisms. Viruses are valuable in aiding a number of microbiological metabolic processes, including decomposition. What's more, specific viruses are being investigated as constructive tools in modern medicine. Of particular note is the role viruses have played in evolution as an important means of horizontal gene transfer, helping to increase genetic diversity.

Through virology, the study of viruses, researchers have found several additional uses for these unique organisms. Here are just some of the most significant ways viruses are being used to our advantage:

Agriculture. Genetic engineering methods can be used to make modified genomes that can be carried into plants using viruses as vehicles, potentially leading to more productive transgenic food sources.

Bacteriophage therapy. Bacteriophages, believed to be the most numerous and prolific viruses on Earth, are highly specific virions that can target, infect, and destroy pathogenic bacteria when correctly selected. They are essential tools in molecular biology and have been researched for their therapeutic capabilities.

Biological studies. In research focused on molecular and cellular biology, viruses are being used to investigate and manipulate the function of cells.

Cancer prevention and treatment. Modification of the genes of cells, known as gene therapy, has been under investigation in plants and animals for a number of years. This process involves the introduction of genes with desired functions, such as the ability to correct defective or nonoperational genes into cells. This research looks promising for aiding cancer prevention and treatment in human populations.

Genetics research. Viruses have been used extensively in the study and understanding of genes, DNA replication, and immunology, as well as the management of inherited diseases, cancers, and genetic engineering.

Medicine. Viruses are being used in medical research as carriers that transport required material for the treatment of a disease to various target cells.

Nanotechnology. Nanotechnology deals with microscopic particles, which are used in biology, genetic engineering, and medicine. With the aid of nanotechnology, viruses can be used as carriers for genetically modified sequences of genomes to the host cells.

Vaccines. Live and weakened viruses have been used extensively for decades to inoculate people against numerous diseases, such as chickenpox, measles, and polio. When introduced into a healthy individual, the virus helps the immune system set up defenses against it, thereby preventing the disease it could cause. Vaccines using selected proteins of a virus (known as subunit vaccines; see page 26) have also been used to protect against liver cancer from hepatitis B and cervical cancer from human papillomavirus (HPV).

Anatomy and Life Cycle of a Virus

Most people think of viruses as parasites, but they aren't parasites at all. An organism has to be considered alive to be classified as a parasite. Viruses don't do any of the things living organisms do. They don't grow, they can't move on their own, and they don't metabolize. They don't even have cells. But the one thing a virus is very good at is reproducing. When it finds a suitable host cell, it attaches itself and injects its DNA through the cell's plasma wall. The virus's genes are transcribed into the host cell's DNA, and the host cell's genetic code is rewritten. Whatever its job was before, its new job is to do nothing but produce copies of the original virus, usually until it's created so many that the cell bursts open and spreads the infection.

Christian Cantrell, author of *Containment, Kingmaker,* and *Equinox*

Viruses vary in shape, from simple to complex, and are about one hundred times smaller than the average bacterium. A virus has three primary parts:

1. **Nucleic acid.** This is the core of a virus. It contains deoxyribonucleic acid (DNA) or ribonucleic acid (RNA), which holds all the information for the virus that makes it unique and helps it multiply.
2. **Capsid.** This is the protein coating that covers and protects the nucleic acid.
3. **Envelope.** Consisting of a lipid (fatty acid) membrane, the envelope covers the capsid. Many viruses don't have an envelope; these are known as naked viruses.

Because viruses are incapable of surviving on their own, they must locate host cells in which they can multiply. A virus enters the body from the environment (air, soil, or water) or other individuals (via the nose or mouth or any breaks in the skin) and seeks cells to infect. Most infecting viruses follow a basic pattern called the lytic cycle, during which a virus overtakes a cell and uses the cellular machinery of its host to reproduce. Copies of the virus fill the cell until the cell bursts, or lyses, killing the cell and releasing viruses to infect more cells. The following is the standard life cycle of a virus:

1. **Adsorption:** A virus particle (virion) attaches to a host cell.
2. **Entry:** The virion injects its DNA or RNA into the host cell.
3. **Takeover:** The invading DNA or RNA takes over the cell and recruits the host's enzymes.
4. **Replication:** The cellular enzymes start making new viruses.
5. **Assembly:** The viruses created by the cell come together to form new virions.
6. **Release:** The newly formed (progeny) virions kill the cell so they can break free, or lyse, search for new host cells, and begin the process again.

When viruses break the cell and spread elsewhere, it's called a lytic infection. Eventually, if the host's immunity is effective, the virus-infected cell may be killed by the host, leading to an interruption of the virus cycle and a resolution, or cure, of the infection. However, this is not true for all viral infections.

Some viruses persist in the cell without damaging it and make the cell a carrier. So although the host may appear to be cured, the infection endures and can spread to other potential hosts. Furthermore, symptoms of the infection may reappear at a later time, after this period of latency or remission, as with human immunodeficiency virus (HIV).

Viral Transmission

I pictured myself as a virus or a cancer cell and tried to sense what it would be like.

Jonas Salk (1914–1995), American medical researcher and virologist
who developed the first successful polio vaccine

Viruses cannot exist on their own, so in order to survive they need to spread to another host. This may be necessary because the original host has either died or eliminated the infection. Some important routes of viral transfer include the following:

- Animal bites (rabies)
- Fecal-oral (coxsackievirus, hepatitis A, polio, rotavirus)
- Insects (dengue virus, yellow fever)
- Respiratory (cold viruses, influenza viruses, measles, mumps, rubella)
- Sexually (hepatitis A, herpes 1 and 2, human papillomavirus/HPV, human immunodeficiency virus/HIV)
- Skin contact (HPV/warts)
- Transplacental (cytomegalovirus, HIV, rubella)

In order to spread, viruses must survive the immune system of their hosts. There is a special category of viruses called opportunists that cause disease only when the host's immune system is deficient in some way, such as with acquired immune deficiency syndrome (AIDS).

Some viruses can induce chronic infection. This occurs when a virus replicates over the entire remaining life of the host, regardless of the host's defense mechanisms, as with hepatitis B and hepatitis C infections. Individuals with chronic infections are considered carriers, and they will be reservoirs of the infectious virus as long as they live. In regional populations with a high percentage of carriers, the disease is deemed endemic.

Viral transmission may be vertical (from mother to child) or horizontal (from individual to individual). Horizontal infection, the most common means of viral propagation, can take place through the exchange of blood (as with a transfusion), the exchange of body fluid (as with sexual activity), or the exchange of saliva (as with kissing or shared eating utensils). Additionally, horizontal infection can occur via contaminated food or water, respiration of viruses dispersed in air or gases, or through animal or insect vectors, such as mosquitoes. How quickly a viral disease spreads depends on a number of factors, most significantly population density and sanitation.

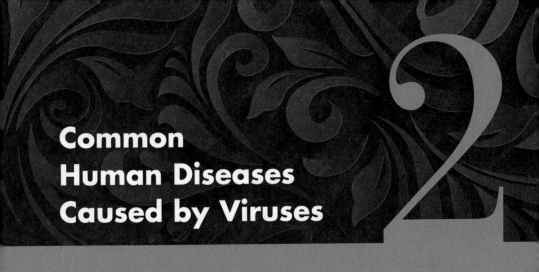

Common Human Diseases Caused by Viruses

In the event that I am reincarnated, I would like to return as a deadly virus, in order to contribute something to solve overpopulation.

PRINCE PHILIP QUOTED IN *DEUTSCHE PRESSE AGENTUR*, AUGUST 1988

Concerns of Global Proportions

The very word "virus" began as a contradiction. We inherited the word from the Roman Empire, where it meant, at once, the venom of a snake or the semen of a man. Creation and destruction in one word.

Carl Zimmer, American author and columnist

The spread or outbreak of a viral infection in a community is termed an epidemic. A pandemic occurs when there is a worldwide epidemic. The 1918 Spanish flu outbreak was such a pandemic. It was caused by an unusually severe and deadly influenza A virus. Most of the victims were healthy young adults, in contrast to the immunocompromised and elderly individuals who are the more typical targets of epidemics. The Spanish flu killed around one hundred million people, or at least 5 percent of the world's population in 1918. Today HIV is considered pandemic, with an estimated thirty-nine million people now living with the disease worldwide.

There are many good reasons to be concerned about dangerous viruses and to take precautions against the ones that can do us harm. Here are just some of the many diseases viruses are responsible for in humans:

Astrovirus. Human astrovirus infection primarily causes gastroenteritis, with the chief symptoms being abdominal pain, diarrhea, and loss of appetite. Although astrovirus mainly impacts young children worldwide, elderly people, institutionalized patients, and immuno-compromised individuals have also been affected by it. The illness is generally mild, self-limiting, and of short duration, with a peak incidence in the winter. The usual mode of transmission is fecal-oral, but contaminated water and food have also occasionally been implicated.

Chickenpox. This highly contagious infection mostly affects children. It's caused by the varicella-zoster virus (see "Shingles," page 19) and is spread through coughing, sneezing, or contact with body secretions. The primary symptoms are a mild fever and a skin rash with itchy, inflamed blisters.

Common cold. The common cold is caused by a viral infection located in the nose. It could also involve the bronchial tubes, ears, and sinuses. The signs of a common cold often include cough, hoarseness, nasal obstruction, runny nose, sneezing, sore or scratchy throat, and usually mild symptoms, such as chills, headache, and general malaise. Most colds last only two to three days, but more severe infections may last up to two weeks. A cold is a milder illness than the flu, although mild cases of the flu may be similar to colds. There are over one hundred different cold viruses. Rhinoviruses are the most significant, as they are responsible for at least one-half of all colds.

Dengue fever. This mosquito-borne disease is the leading cause of illness and death in the subtropics and tropics. Although dengue fever rarely occurs in the continental United States, it is endemic in Puerto Rico and in many popular tourist destinations in Latin America, the Pacific islands, and Southeast Asia.

Ebola. Ebola, a virus of the family *Filoviridae*, genus *Ebolavirus*, was first discovered in 1976 near the Ebola River in what is now the Democratic Republic of the Congo. Since then, outbreaks have appeared sporadically in several African countries. Previously known as Ebola hemorrhagic fever, Ebola is a rare and deadly disease caused by infection with one of the four Ebola virus species that cause disease in humans (a fifth species has caused disease in nonhuman primates but not in humans). The viruses are transmitted through direct contact with infected blood or body fluids, including but not limited to breast milk, feces, saliva, semen, sweat, urine, and vomit, as well as objects (such as needles and syringes) that have been contaminated with body fluids from a person who is sick with Ebola or the body of a person who has died from Ebola. Although Ebola isn't transmitted through the air, droplets of respiratory or other secretions from a person who is very sick with Ebola could make others sick.

Foodborne illness. Foodborne viral infections have been on the rise, due in part to changes in food processing and consumption patterns that have led to global availability of high-risk foods. As a result, vast outbreaks brought on by contamination of food from a single food handler or at a single source have occurred with greater frequency in recent years. The most common methods of transmission are direct (person-to-person) and indirect (via food, water, or objects/surfaces contaminated with virus-containing feces or vomit). People can be infected without showing symptoms and still transmit the virus to others. The populations most susceptible to serious illness and death from foodborne illnesses are the elderly and people with compromised or weakened immune systems. While certain foods have traditionally been implicated in foodborne virus outbreaks, almost any food item can be involved if it has been handled by an infected person.

Hand, foot, and mouth disease. Usually affecting infants and children younger than five years of age, hand, foot, and mouth disease can sometimes occur in adults. It's caused by viruses that belong to the genus *Enterovirus*, including coxsackieviruses, echoviruses, enteroviruses, and polioviruses. The disease usually starts with a fever, reduced appetite, sore throat, and a general sense of not feeling well. One or two days after the fever starts, painful sores, called herpangina, can develop in the mouth. A skin rash with red spots and sometimes blisters may develop on the palms of the hands and soles of the feet. The rash may also appear on the buttocks, elbows, genital area, or knees. Some infected individuals, especially young children, may get dehydrated if they aren't able to swallow enough liquids because of painful mouth sores. Others, particularly adults, may show no symptoms at all, but they can still pass the virus to others. The viruses that cause hand, foot, and mouth disease can be found in an infected person's nose and throat secretions (such as nasal mucus, saliva, or sputum), blister fluid, and feces. The disease may be spread to another person through close personal contact (such as through kissing), the air (through coughing or sneezing), contact with feces, and contact with contaminated objects and surfaces (such as touching a contaminated doorknob and then touching the eyes, nose, or mouth). Although uncommon, it's possible to get the disease by swallowing recreational water, such as water in a swimming pool, if it's contaminated with feces from an infected person and is not properly treated with chlorine.

Hepatitis A. Hepatitis A is a liver disease caused by the hepatitis A virus. The virus is primarily spread when an uninfected, unvaccinated person ingests food or water contaminated with the feces of an infected person. The disease is closely associated with unsafe water, inadequate sanitation, and poor personal hygiene. Unlike hepatitis B and C (see below), hepatitis A infection does not cause chronic liver disease and is rarely fatal. Nevertheless, it can cause debilitating symptoms and fulminant hepatitis (acute liver failure), which is associated with high mortality. More typically, however, the illness is mild, with symptoms such as abdominal discomfort, fever, nausea, and malaise.

Hepatitis B. Hepatitis B is a liver infection caused by the hepatitis B virus. It's transmitted via blood, semen, or another body fluid, such as through sexual contact; sharing needles, syringes, or other drug-injection equipment; or from mother to baby at birth. Although hepatitis B is usually an acute, short-term illness in adults, it can become a long-term, chronic disease, particularly in children. About 90 percent of infected infants become chronically infected compared with only 2–6 percent of adults. Chronic hepatitis B can lead to serious health issues, such as liver cancer or cirrhosis. The best way to prevent hepatitis B is by getting vaccinated.

Hepatitis C. Hepatitis C infects the liver and is caused by the hepatitis C virus. It is transmitted person-to-person through contaminated blood, typically by sharing needles or other equipment to inject drugs. Many infected individuals might not be aware they're infected because they aren't clinically ill or their symptoms are mild. But for 70–85 percent of infected people who become symptomatic, hepatitis C is a long-term, chronic disease than can result in serious health problems, including death. There currently is no vaccine for hepatitis C. The best way to prevent getting infected is to avoid behaviors that can spread the disease, especially injecting drugs.

Herpes. Herpes is a group of several viruses that infect humans. Diseases caused by the herpes viruses include cold sores around the mouth or face, genital herpes (affecting the anal area, buttocks, or genitals), chickenpox (see page 12), and shingles (see page 19). Herpes viruses are spread by direct contact between people by way of body fluids, through the air, and through contaminated objects and surfaces. The virus can be dangerous in newborns and in people with weakened immune systems. Some infected individuals have no symptoms; others get sores near the area where the virus has entered the body. These sores turn into blisters, become itchy and painful, and then crust over and heal. Most infected people have outbreaks several times a year, with frequency and severity diminishing over time. Prescription drugs are available to help the body fight the virus, decrease symptoms, and lessen outbreaks.

Human immunodeficiency virus (HIV). HIV is the virus that causes acquired immune deficiency syndrome (AIDS). The virus attacks the immune system, which eventually allows other diseases to infect and proliferate in the body. HIV can be spread through blood, breast milk, semen, and vaginal fluid. AIDS is the final stage of HIV infection, during which the body can no longer defend itself. There currently is no cure for HIV or AIDS. However, with proper treatment and support, people infected with HIV may be able to live long and healthy lives.

Human papillomavirus (HPV). Human papillomavirus is the most common sexually transmitted disease (STD). The US Centers for Disease Control and Prevention states that nearly all sexually active men and women get HPV at some point in their lives. There are hundreds of different strains of HPV, some of which cause no ill health effects. Other strains of the virus can cause genital warts and cancer, including cancer of the anus, neck, penis, throat, vagina, or vulva. HPV is spread through anal, oral, or vaginal sex with someone who has the virus, and it can be transmitted even when an infected person shows no signs or symptoms of infection. There is no way to know who has HPV and who will develop cancer or other illnesses from the virus. People with weakened immune systems (including individuals with HIV or AIDS) may be less able to fight off HPV and more likely to develop complications from it. Most people with HPV don't know they're infected and never develop symptoms or health problems from the virus. Some people find out they have HPV when they get genital warts. Women may discover they have HPV if they receive an abnormal Pap test result during a routine screening for cervical cancer. But many people only find out they're infected after they've developed a serious illness from HPV, such as cancer. The best way to prevent HPV is to get vaccinated.

Influenza. The influenza virus, commonly known as the flu, is spread by inhaling droplets that have been coughed or sneezed out by an infected person or by having direct contact with an infected person's respiratory secretions. Symptoms start one to four days after infection and can begin suddenly, with chills or fever as the first indication. Many people feel so ill, weak, and tired that they remain in bed for days. The most common complication of the flu is pneumonia, and people at the highest risk are children under the age of four, adults over the age of sixty-five, individuals with chronic medical disorders (especially those that affect the heart, lungs, or immune system), and people with diabetes mellitus. The standard recommended methods of prevention are annual vaccinations and, for some patients, antiviral drugs. For more information about influenza, see chapter 5, page 43.

Japanese encephalitis. This mosquito-borne virus produces the disease Japanese encephalitis, which is the leading cause of vaccine-preventable encephalitis in Asia and the western Pacific. It can cause severe symptoms in humans but is not transmitted between them. Most infections are asymptomatic or result in only mild symptoms. However, a small percentage of infected individuals develop encephalitis (inflammation of the brain), with symptoms that include sudden onset of headache, high fever, disorientation, tremors, convulsions, and coma. About one in four cases are fatal. Preventive measures include protecting against mosquito bites (see page 56) and getting vaccinated.

Measles. Measles is a highly contagious virus that lives in the nose and throat mucus of an infected person. It can spread to other people through coughing and sneezing. In addition, the virus can survive for up to two hours in an air space where the infected person coughed or sneezed. If other people breathe the contaminated air or touch an infected surface and then touch their eyes, nose, or mouth, they can become infected. Measles is so contagious that if one person has it, 90 percent of the people close to that person who are not immunized will also become infected. Early symptoms include cough, fever, red eyes, runny nose, and sore throat, followed by a rash that spreads over the body. Infected people can spread measles to others from four days before through four days after the rash appears. Measles can be serious in all age groups, but children younger than five and adults older than twenty are more likely to suffer from complications, including diarrhea, ear infections (which could result in permanent hearing loss), encephalitis (swelling of the brain), pneumonia (infection of the lungs), and even death. Measles may cause pregnant woman to give birth prematurely or have a baby with low birth weight.

Mumps. Mumps is a contagious disease transmitted person-to-person through respiratory secretions. Most people with mumps will have swelling of the salivary glands, which causes puffy cheeks and a tender, swollen jaw. Other symptoms may include fever, headache, muscle aches, tiredness, and loss of appetite. There's no specific treatment for mumps. Serious complications from mumps, such as hearing loss, are rare. Mumps was common in the United States until vaccinating against it became routine. Since then, the number of cases has dropped dramatically and the odds of contracting mumps are low. However, mumps outbreaks still occur in the United States, and the illness is common in many parts of the world. For that reason, the Centers for Disease Control and Prevention still recommends getting vaccinated against mumps.

Poliomyelitis. Commonly known as polio, poliomyelitis is an acute, communicable disease caused by an enterovirus in the *Picornaviridae* family. The virus is transmitted person-to-person by oral secretions or fecal material from an infected person. Most poliovirus infections cause asymptomatic viral replication that is limited to the alimentary tract. However, following an incubation period of seven to ten days, about 24 percent of those infected develop clinical signs, such as fever, headache and sore throat (considered minor symptoms). Paralytic (paralyzing) poliomyelitis is experienced in fewer than 1 percent of poliovirus infections. In the most severe cases, polioviruses attack the motor neurons of the brain stem, reducing breathing capacity and causing difficulty in swallowing and speaking. Without respiratory support, this type of infection (known as bulbar polio) can result in death. Polio can strike at any age, but it mainly affects children under three. The death-to-case ratio for paralytic polio is generally 2–5 percent among children and up to 15–30 percent for adults (depending on age). It increases to 25–75 percent with bulbar involvement. At one time poliovirus infection occurred throughout the world, but a global polio eradication program led to the elimination of polio in the Western Hemisphere in 1991 and a dramatic reduction of poliovirus transmission worldwide. In 2012 only 223 confirmed cases of polio were reported globally, and polio was endemic in only three countries.

Rabies. The rabies virus is contracted through wounds (such as scratches from an infected animal) or by direct contact with mucosal surfaces (such as a bite from an infected animal). Once inside the body, the virus replicates in the bitten muscle and gains access to the central nervous system, where a majority of the clinical symptoms manifest as acute encephalitis (inflammation of the brain) or meningoencephalitis (inflammation of the membranes of the brain and the adjoining cerebral tissue). The incubation period averages two to three months, and if intensive treatment is not sought, death occurs within two weeks after the appearance of clinical symptoms. In more than 99 percent of all cases of human rabies, the virus is transmitted via dogs. Rabies is most common in people younger than fifteen, although all age groups are susceptible.

Rubella. Rubella is an acute, contagious viral infection. Although generally mild in children, the illness has serious consequences in pregnant women, causing miscarriage, congenital defects known as congenital rubella syndrome (CRS), or fetal death. When a pregnant woman is infected with the rubella virus early in the pregnancy, there is a 90 percent chance the virus will be passed on to the fetus. Infants with CRS may excrete the virus for a year or longer. Children with CRS can suffer eye and heart defects, hearing impairments, and other lifelong disabilities, including autism, diabetes mellitus, and thyroid dysfunction. The rubella virus is transmitted by airborne droplets when infected people sneeze or cough. Humans are the only known host. The highest risk of CRS is in countries where women of childbearing age do not have immunity to the disease, either through vaccination or from having had rubella.

Severe acute respiratory syndrome (SARS). SARS is a serious form of pneumonia caused by a member of the coronavirus family of viruses (the same family that causes the common cold) and was first identified in 2003. Infection with the SARS virus causes acute respiratory distress (severe breathing difficulty) and sometimes death. SARS is transmitted when someone infected with the virus coughs or sneezes, spraying infected droplets into the air, and someone else breathes in or touches these particles. The SARS virus may live on hands, tissues, and other surfaces for up to six hours in these droplets and for up to three hours after the droplets have dried. The live virus has also been found in the stool of people with SARS, where it has been shown to live for up to four days. Moreover, the virus may remain active for months or years when the temperature is below freezing.

As with the common cold, it may be possible to become infected with SARS and then get sick again (reinfected). Symptoms usually occur within two to ten days after coming in contact with the virus, and people with active symptoms of illness are contagious. However, it isn't known how long a person may be contagious before or after symptoms appear. The primary symptoms are chills, cough, difficulty breathing, fever, headache, and muscle aches. Lung problems may worsen during the second week of illness. Less common symptoms include diarrhea, dizziness, nausea, vomiting, runny nose, and sore throat. People who are thought to have SARS should be checked right away by a healthcare provider and be kept isolated in the hospital. The death rate from SARS is between 9 and 12 percent of those diagnosed. In people over age sixty-five, the death rate is higher than 50 percent. The illness is generally milder in younger people.

Shingles. Shingles is caused by the varicella-zoster virus—the same virus that causes chickenpox (see page 12). An infection of shingles results in a burning, painful rash. While the rash can occur anywhere on the body, it most often appears as a single strip of blisters that wraps around either the left or the right side of the torso. After a person has had chickenpox, the virus lies dormant in nerve tissue near the spinal cord and brain. Years later, the inert virus may reactivate as shingles. Although shingles isn't a life-threatening condition, it is exceedingly painful. Vaccines can help reduce the risk of shingles, but they don't fully prevent it. Early treatment can help shorten a shingles infection and lessen the chance of complications.

West Nile virus. A mosquito-transmitted virus causes most incidences of West Nile infection. The majority of people infected with West Nile virus either don't develop symptoms or have self-limiting minor ones, such as body aches, fatigue, fever, and mild headache. However, some people can develop a life-threatening illness from the virus that includes inflammation of the brain or spinal cord. Acute symptoms, such as disorientation, fever, seizures, severe headache, and sudden weakness or partial paralysis, require immediate medical attention. Exposure to mosquitoes where West Nile virus exists increases the risk of getting infected.

Zika virus. Zika virus is a mosquito-borne viral infection that primarily occurs in tropical and subtropical areas of the world but has recently emerged in the United States. Transmission of the virus through sexual contact and blood transfusions has also been reported.

Most people infected with Zika virus have no symptoms, while others report mild fever, muscle pain, and rash. Additional symptoms may include conjunctivitis, headache, and general malaise. The illness is usually mild, with symptoms lasting from several days to a week. Severe disease requiring hospitalization is uncommon, and deaths from Zika are very rare. Zika virus infections during pregnancy have been linked to miscarriage and can cause microcephaly, a potentially fatal congenital brain condition, in the fetus. Zika virus also may cause neurological disorders, such as Guillain-Barre syndrome (a rare autoimmune disorder that can cause paralysis and even death), in children as well as adults. There is also evidence that adult brain cells critical to learning and memory are susceptible to the Zika virus, and this may be just one of several lingering effects. Researchers studying the virus agree that the more they uncover about it, the scarier it becomes. A few different Zika vaccines are currently in development or are being tested, but it could take several years before one is ready for use outside of a clinical trial.

Because Zika can cause devastating birth defects in babies born to women who were infected with the virus during pregnancy, the Centers for Disease Control and Prevention (CDC) recommends the following preventive measures:

- Pregnant women should not travel to any area where Zika virus is spreading.

- Pregnant women who must travel to one of these areas should talk to their doctor beforehand and strictly follow steps to prevent mosquito bites (see page 56) during their trip.

- Women trying to become pregnant, as well as their male partners, should consult with their doctor before traveling to these areas and strictly follow steps to prevent mosquito bites (see page 56) during their trip.

- Zika virus can be spread by a man to his sexual partners for many months after he's been infected. Genetic material from the virus has been found in semen six months after infection, in blood and urine many days after infection, and in saliva several months after infection. Men who have lived in or traveled to an area where Zika is prevalent and who have a pregnant partner should either use condoms or not have sex (vaginal, oral, or anal) during the pregnancy. The Centers for Disease Control and Prevention recommends that men infected with Zika wait at least six months after their symptoms appear before trying to father a child.

Symptoms of Viral Infection and Standard Treatments

How is it that you keep mutating and can still be the same virus?

CHUCK PALAHNIUK, *INVISIBLE MONSTERS*

Bacterial versus Viral Infections

If an alien visited Earth, they would take some note of humans, but probably spend most of their time trying to understand the dominant form of life on our planet—microorganisms like bacteria and viruses.

Nathan Wolfe, American virologist and director of Global Viral

People are often confused about the difference between viruses and bacteria. Bacteria are single-celled microorganisms that thrive in many different types of environments. Some varieties thrive in extreme cold or heat; others reside in our intestines, where they help digest food. Most bacteria are either beneficial or benign and cause us no harm. However, there are exceptions, of course. Some of the illnesses caused by bacteria include strep throat, tuberculosis, and urinary tract infections.

In some cases it may be hard to determine whether a bacterium or virus is the cause of symptoms. Many ailments, such as diarrhea, meningitis, and pneumonia, can be caused by either type of microbe. Also, both types are spread in similar ways: through the air (coughing and sneezing); contact with infected people (especially through kissing and sex); contact with contaminated surfaces, food, or water;

21

and contact with infected creatures, including insects (such as fleas and ticks), pets, and livestock. Moreover, either type of microbe can cause acute (short-lived) infections, chronic infections (those that last for weeks, months, or a lifetime), and latent infections (those that may not cause immediate symptoms but can reactivate over a period of months or years and cause symptoms later on).

Viral infections come with a host of symptoms ranging from mild to severe that may vary depending on the type of virus, the person's age and overall health, and which part of the body is affected. Symptoms of a viral infection may include any of the following:

Mild symptoms:

- Chills
- Coughing
- Diarrhea
- Fever
- Headache
- Muscle aches
- Rash
- Runny nose
- Sneezing
- Vomiting
- Weakness

More severe symptoms:

- Back pain
- Confusion
- Dehydration
- Impaired bladder function
- Impaired bowel function
- Loss of sensation
- Neck stiffness
- Paralysis of the limbs
- Personality changes
- Seizures
- Sleepiness that can progress into coma or death

Because it's not always easy to determine whether an infection is bacterial or viral, antibiotics have frequently been prescribed to treat comparable symptoms, even though antibiotics are powerless against viruses. Overuse and inappropriate use of antibiotics has contributed to the creation of resistant and virulent bacterial strains that are invulnerable to different types of antibiotic medications.

Viral infections are difficult to treat because viruses live inside the body's cells, which "shield" them from medicines, which usually move through the bloodstream. Antibiotics, which are effective against bacterial infections, don't work for viral infections, such as the common cold or flu. Over the past two decades, several medications that treat viral infections have been developed, but novel antiviral drugs are still in short supply. These medicines are more difficult to develop than antibacterial drugs because antivirals can damage host cells where the viruses reside. Currently there are more antiviral pharmaceuticals for HIV than for any other viral disease, and this has helped transform an infection that was once considered a death sentence into a manageable chronic condition. However, these drugs do not cure HIV infection; instead, they stop the virus from multiplying and prevent the progress of the disease. Although new drugs are needed to combat other epidemic viral infections, viruses in general are notoriously difficult drug targets because they rapidly mutate and adapt themselves to develop resistance to the drugs used to combat them.

Immunity

My immune system has always been overly welcoming of germs. It's far too polite—the biological equivalent of a Southern hostess inviting y'all nice microbes to stay awhile and have some artichoke dip.

A. J. Jacobs, journalist and author

Immunology is a complex subject far beyond the scope of this book, but a rudimentary understanding of how the immune system functions is necessary when discussing the prevention and treatment of viral infections. Immunity is the body's ability to discriminate between indigenous (those that reside naturally in the body) and foreign (invading) microbes, known as antigens, and develop specific substances (called antibodies) that fight off a single foreign organism or group of related organisms.

Antigens can either be live (as with viruses and bacteria) or inactivated. Once the immune system identifies antigens, its primary purpose is to mount a defense against them. This defense is called the immune response and usually involves the production of protein molecules by B lymphocytes (antibodies known as immunoglobulins), also known as B cells, and of specific cells, including T lymphocytes (also known as T cells, or cell-mediated immunity), whose function is to facilitate the elimination of foreign substances. Although B cells and T cells work differently, they share a mutual objective to defend the body against invading microbes, such as viruses and bacteria. They are specialized in how they do this, recognizing an invader by the shape of specific foreign antigen molecules on its surface. The immune system can make B cells and T cells to match any surface antigen, so only certain B cells and T cells react to a specific invader. These cells then multiply to produce a large number of identical cells ready to attack the same invader. Generally speaking, live antigens usually produce the most effective immune responses. However, an antigen does not necessarily have to be alive to be recognized by the immune system and produce an immune response.

There are two basic mechanisms for acquiring immunity: active and passive. Passive immunity is the transfer of protective substances (antibodies) produced by a human or animal to another human or animal. Passive immunity generally provides effective but temporary protection against some infections, but that protection can wane within a few weeks or months. The most common form of passive immunity is that which an infant receives when antibodies are transported across the placenta during the last one to two months of pregnancy, allowing the infant to have the same antibodies as its mother. These antibodies will protect the infant from certain diseases for up to one year.

Active immunity is the body's first line of defense. It entails stimulating the body's natural immune system to produce an antigen-specific response. Once the adaptive immunity has confronted an invading microbe, the immune system "remembers" it. The immune system can then provide a more permanent form of immunity that may last many years or even a lifetime by creating specific antibodies against that particular invading strain. This is called humoral immunity.

One way to acquire active immunity is to survive an infection from the disease-causing form of the organism. While exceptions (such as malaria) exist, in general, once people recover from an infectious disease, they will have lifelong immunity to that disease. The persistence of protection for many years after the infection is known as immunologic memory. Following exposure of the immune system to an antigen, certain cells continue to circulate in the blood and also reside in the bone marrow for many years. Upon reexposure to the antigen, these memory cells begin to replicate and produce antibodies very rapidly to reestablish protection.

Another way to produce active immunity is through vaccination. Vaccines often produce an immune response similar to that produced by the natural infection, but they don't subject the recipient to the disease and its potential complications. Many vaccines also produce immunologic memory similar to that acquired by having the natural disease.

While anyone can contract an infectious disease, the people who are most likely to get sick are those whose immune systems aren't working properly. The following factors can reduce a person's immunity:

- Acquired immune deficiency syndrome (AIDS)
- Certain types of cancer or other disorders that affect the immune system
- Human immunodeficiency virus (HIV)
- Steroids or other medications that suppress the immune system, such as antirejection drugs for a transplanted organ

In addition, medical or health factors, such as implanted medical devices, malnutrition, and extremes of age (very young or very old), may predispose a person to infection. A few types of infection have been linked to a long-term increased risk of cancer:

- Helicobacter pylori is linked to peptic ulcers and stomach cancer.
- Hepatitis B and hepatitis C have been linked to liver cancer.
- Human papillomavirus (HPV) is linked to cervical cancer.

There are also a number of factors that can influence a person's immune response to vaccination, such as the presence of maternal antibodies, nature of the antigen, dose of the antigen, route of administration, and presence of an adjuvant (a substance added to enhance the immunogenicity of the vaccine). Age, coexisting disease, genetics, and general health may also affect the recipient's immune response.

Vaccine Basics

Without equity, pandemic battles will fail. Viruses will simply recirculate, and perhaps undergo mutations or changes that render vaccines useless, passing through the unprotected populations of the planet.

Laurie Garrett, author, senior fellow for global health at the Council on Foreign Relations, and expert on global health systems, chronic and infectious diseases, and bioterrorism

T here are two basic types of vaccines: live attenuated and inactivated. The different characteristics of live and inactivated vaccines determine how the vaccine is used. Live attenuated (weakened) vaccines are created in a laboratory by modifying a "wild" disease-producing virus or bacterium. The organism that results retains the ability to replicate and produce immunity without causing the actual disease. When a live attenuated vaccine causes "symptoms," the symptoms are usually much milder than those caused by the natural disease and are referred to as an adverse reaction or adverse event (see "Concerns about Vaccines," page 27). To produce an immune response, live attenuated vaccines must replicate (grow) in the vaccinated person. A relatively small dose of the virus or bacteria is administered, which replicates in the body and creates enough of the organism to stimulate an immune response.

The immune response to a live attenuated vaccine is virtually identical to the response produced by a natural infection. The immune system doesn't differentiate between an infection with a weakened vaccine virus and an infection with a wild virus. Live attenuated vaccines produce immunity in most recipients with a single dose, except for vaccines administered orally. The more similar a vaccine is to the disease-causing form of the organism, the better the immune response to the vaccine. In rare instances, live attenuated vaccines may cause severe or fatal reactions as a result of uncontrolled replication of the vaccine virus in a recipient with immunodeficiency.

Live attenuated vaccines usually need to be refrigerated to retain their potency. If a vaccine needs to be shipped overseas and stored by healthcare workers in developing countries that have limited refrigeration, a live vaccine may not be the best choice.

Inactivated vaccines are produced in a laboratory by growing the virus in culture media and then deactivating it with heat and/or chemicals. Because these vaccines are not alive, they cannot replicate. The entire dose of antigen is administered in the injection; however, inactivated vaccines always require multiple doses. The first dose generally doesn't produce protective immunity but rather "primes," or prepares, the immune system. A protective immune response develops after the second or third dose. Inactivated vaccines cannot cause disease from infection, even in people who are immunodeficient.

In contrast to immunization with a live vaccine, which prompts an immune response that closely resembles a natural infection, the immune response to an inactivated vaccine is mostly humoral, meaning there is little or no resulting cellular immunity. Antibodies that fight inactivated antigens will diminish with time, and some inactivated vaccines may require periodic supplemental doses to increase, or boost, antibody concentrations.

Genetic engineering technology may also be used to produce vaccine antigens. Known as recombinant vaccines, they contain only a fraction of the pathogenic organism. Often they are synthetic peptides that represent the protein component that induces an immune response, but they can also consist of protein subunits (antigens) that use recombinant protein expression technologies. Most of the newer vaccines under investigation today are based on such purified recombinant proteins or subunits of antigens. However, just a few genetically engineered vaccines are currently available in the United States, including vaccines for hepatitis B, human papillomavirus (HPV), and influenza.

There have been key advancements with other types of vaccines that use innovative new technologies, such as nucleic acid–based vaccines, which encode the antigens of interest with ribonucleic acid (RNA) or deoxyribonucleic acid (DNA) and which elicit immune responses similar to those induced by live attenuated vaccines. Synthetic, self-amplifying vaccine platforms are another novel advancement. This approach uses a nonviral vaccine delivery system, avoiding the limitations of cell cultures. Both of these technologies offer a number of advantages: greater immunogenicity, safety, and purity, along with ease of production, manipulation, and administration.

Concerns about Vaccines

For each illness that doctors cure with medicine, they provoke ten in healthy people by inoculating them with the virus that is a thousand times more powerful than any microbe: the idea that one is ill.

Marcel Proust (1871–1922), French novelist

T here are a number of misconceptions about vaccinations, as well as a variety of reasons people have reservations about them either for themselves or for their children. Opposition to getting vaccinated may be rooted in fear; religious, moral, ethical, or philosophical objections; or concerns about the efficacy or safety of vaccines. Some people believe that vaccine-preventable diseases don't pose a serious or actual health threat or that the diseases vaccines target are often relatively harmless, thereby making vaccines unnecessary.

A small number of people can't be vaccinated because of severe allergies to the components in vaccines. There is also a small percentage of people who don't respond to vaccines and another small group of individuals who are too ill to get vaccinated. These groups are susceptible to vaccine-preventable diseases, and their only hope of protection is that the people around them are immune and can't pass these diseases on to them. The following diseases can be prevented by vaccination (note that smallpox, one of the worst scourges in human history, no longer exists outside the laboratory, thanks to a vaccine):

Chickenpox	Pertussis (whooping cough)
Cholera	Pneumococcal disease
Diphtheria	Poliomyelitis
Haemophilus influenzae type b (Hib)	Rotavirus
Hepatitis A	Rubella (German measles)
Hepatitis B	Shingles (herpes zoster)
Human papilloma infection	Smallpox
Influenza	Tetanus
Measles	Tuberculosis
Meningococcal disease	Typhoid fever
Mumps	Yellow fever

Like prescription drugs, vaccines are pharmaceutical products, and although they are designed to protect us from disease, they can cause side effects the same as any medication. A possible side effect resulting from a vaccination is known as an adverse event. Most side effects from vaccinations are mild, such as soreness, swelling, and redness at the injection site. Some vaccines are associated with achiness, fever, or rash. Although serious side effects are rare, they may include seizures or life-threatening allergic reactions.

Each year more than ten million vaccinations are given to American babies who are one year old and younger. During the first year of life, a significant number of infants suffer serious, life-threatening illnesses and medical events. It's also during this period that congenital conditions may become evident. Based on chance alone, many babies will experience a medical event in close proximity to an immunization, so it's often difficult to determine whether the event is directly related to the vaccination.

In 1990 the US Food and Drug Administration and the Centers for Disease Control and Prevention set up the Vaccine Adverse Event Reporting System (VAERS) to monitor, analyze, and investigate voluntarily reported adverse events that might be associated with immunization. Each year about thirty thousand events are reported to VAERS, and of these, 10–15 percent describe serious medical events that resulted in hospitalization, life-threatening illness, disability, or death.

Because reporting adverse events to VAERS is elective, serious side effects, such as those that require hospitalization, are far more likely to be reported than minor ones, such as swelling at the injection site. But not all adverse events, reported or unreported, are in fact caused by a vaccination, as they may be related to other factors or circumstances and the timing may simply be coincidental. The challenge, then, is being able to make that determination. Complicating matters further, not every serious health problem that occurs after a vaccination is caused by the most recently received immunization. Different vaccines are associated with different vaccine reactions that can occur within various time periods following a vaccination.

The controversy about vaccinations is unlikely to end anytime soon, despite how many safety studies are conducted or how many individuals or parents come forward with claims that they or their children were irreparably harmed by vaccinations. Regardless of where you stand on the issue, the following facts are important to bear in mind:

1. All fifty US states require vaccinations for children entering public schools, even though no mandatory federal vaccination laws exist.

2. All fifty US states issue medical exemptions for vaccinations, forty-eight states (excluding Mississippi and West Virginia) permit religious exemptions, and nineteen states allow an exemption for philosophical reasons.

3. Between 1988 and 2015, over 17,028 petitions were filed with the National Vaccine Injury Compensation Program. Over that period of twenty-seven years, 14,602 petitions were adjudicated, with 4,687 of those cases determined to be compensable, and 9,915 cases that were dismissed.

4. The Centers for Disease Control and Prevention estimated that 732,000 US children were saved from death and 322 million cases of childhood illnesses were prevented between 1994 and 2014 due to vaccination.

5. In 1855, Massachusetts passed the first US state law mandating vaccinations for schoolchildren, followed by New York in 1862, Connecticut in 1872, Indiana in 1881, and Arkansas in 1882.

6. Anaphylaxis (a severe allergic reaction), the most common side effect of inoculation, occurs in one per several hundred thousand to one per million vaccinations.

Be aware that no matter how healthy you are or how well you eat and take care of yourself, your immune system will not be able to protect you from every communicable disease. This is especially important when traveling to a foreign country where water safety and sanitation standards are questionable. Use common sense, and always weigh any risk of getting vaccinated versus the risk of contracting a potentially serious, chronic, debilitating, or life-threatening infection.

Tips to Prevent Viral Infections and Strengthen Immunity

4

We live in a dancing matrix of viruses; they dart, rather like bees, from organism to organism, from plant to insect to mammal to me and back again, and into the sea, tugging along pieces of this genome, strings of genes from that, transplanting grafts of DNA, passing around heredity as though at a great party.

LEWIS THOMAS, *THE LIVES OF A CELL*

Realistic Options

As a child, my family's menu consisted of two choices: take it or leave it.

Buddy Hackett (1924–2003), American comedian and actor

Is it possible to enhance our immunity? Can herbs, vitamins, or probiotics help the immune system fight off disease? What about diet and exercise?

While the immune system does a pretty remarkable job of defending against disease-causing microorganisms, it sometimes fails and viruses or bacteria invade and cause us to become ill. Is it possible to thwart this process by making the immune system stronger?

Although the notion of improving our immunity against infection is intriguing, our ability to achieve this has proved difficult for a number of reasons. First, researchers still don't fully understand the intricacies and interconnectedness of the immune system, which, because it's a system and not a single entity, requires harmony and overall balance. And second, there are no scientifically proven direct connections between what we eat, supplementation, and enhanced immunoprotection. Nonetheless, that doesn't mean these potential and promising links shouldn't be studied. In fact researchers have long been exploring the effects of lifestyle, habits, and other factors, such as age, diet, exercise, and psychological stress, on the human immune response, but they don't yet have any concrete answers.

For many viral infections that remain a tremendous threat to humans, such as coronavirus, dengue fever, Ebola virus, human immunodeficiency virus (HIV), and severe acute respiratory syndrome (SARS), there currently are no vaccines or effective conventional medicines available. Consequently, there's a dire need for natural and alternative solutions and preventive therapies to fill the gap. We know that traditional herbal medicine, dietary strategies, and other natural approaches have been used successfully to treat various illnesses, including viral infections, for centuries in many cultures worldwide. Preliminary scientific research on a number of herbal preparations and natural compounds has shown promising results for both inhibiting and fighting a range of milder, less serious viruses, with the added benefit of enhancing overall immune function.

Natural antivirals are appealing for several reasons. Although overuse of antibiotics and antivirals has been responsible for the creation of hard-to-treat, drug-resistant strains of "superbugs," viruses and bacteria typically don't develop defenses to or mutate in the presence of natural remedies. Natural alternatives also can help heal and fortify the immune system while generally avoiding the unpleasant side effects often caused by drugs. Many natural remedies are inexpensive, easy to take, and readily available.

Please be aware that natural alternatives can't take the place of conventional approaches for serious or potentially life-threatening viral infections, and medical attention should always be sought immediately if you experience any of the following:

- Animal or human bite
- Cough lasting more than seven days
- Difficulty breathing
- Fever lasting longer than five days

- Fever over 106.7 degrees Fahrenheit
- Rash
- Severe headache with fever
- Shortness of breath
- Sudden vision problems
- Swelling
- Symptoms lasting more than seven days
- Symptoms that severely worsen

Smart Lifestyle Strategies

Take care of your body. It's the only place you have to live.

Jim Rohn (1930–2009), American entrepreneur, author, and motivational speaker

I t's important to set the record straight about how the immune system fights off harmful microbial invaders and how you can help it operate at its best. If you didn't have a properly functioning immune system, simply brushing your teeth would introduce enough harmful bacteria into your bloodstream to be deadly. Fortunately, your immune system protects you from these microscopic everyday interlopers. Even though you aren't aware of it, your immune system is constantly devouring bacteria and preventing viruses from invading your cells. Like your digestive, cardiovascular, and respiratory systems, the immune response is a natural, self-activating process you can't control. However, there are a number of things you can do to give it a helping hand. When it comes to immunity, the best line of defense is a good offense. Every part of the body, including the immune system, functions optimally when augmented by wise lifestyle choices. While there's no foolproof way to avoid all dangerous microbes and the illnesses they cause, there are many habits we can incorporate into our daily lives to bolster our immunity and help ward off infection:

- **Get sufficient vitamin D.** Vitamin D is not actually a vitamin but a fat-soluble steroid hormone precursor that has profound effects on innate immunity. Vitamin D is unique in that it can be both ingested (via foods that are fortified with it) and synthesized by the body with exposure to the sun. It is then converted by the liver and kidneys to a form the body can use. Current research shows that vitamin D activates the innate immune system, stimulating the immune response and helping the body to naturally disable viruses.

■ **Practice good hygiene.** Keep germs at bay, stop infections before they begin, and avoid spreading infections to others by adopting good personal hygiene habits. It's easy to do if you follow these simple measures:

- Wash your hands with soap and water frequently (see page 41), especially before preparing food and after using the bathroom.
- Cover your mouth and nose with a tissue when you sneeze or cough, or cough into your elbow rather than your hand.
- Wash and bandage all cuts. Serious cuts and animal or human bites should be examined immediately by a doctor.
- Do not pick at scabs or wounds that are healing. Doing so allows germs to enter.

■ **Avoid touching your face.** Viruses are frequently spread by first coming in contact with a contaminated surface (those touched by infected people) and then transferring the virus to the face, especially the eyes, nose, and mouth.

■ **Eat a diet rich in fresh fruits and vegetables.** Fresh fruits and vegetables, especially those with deep pigmentation, are rich in natural antioxidants and micronutrients that help strengthen the immune system, reduce oxidative stress in the pathogenesis of viral infection, and stimulate the immune response.

■ **Irrigate the nasal passages.** Use a neti pot or similar nasal irrigation device to help wash pollutants out of nasal tissues.

■ **Exercise regularly.** Just like a nutritious diet, exercise can contribute to overall health and thereby to a strong and resilient immune system. Exercise may contribute even more directly by promoting good circulation, which allows the cells and substances of the immune system to move freely through the body, do their job efficiently, and remove waste products effectively.

■ **Don't smoke, and avoid secondhand smoke.** Nicotine, one of the main constituents of cigarette smoke, suppresses the immune system. In addition, there are thousands of toxins present in cigarette smoke that can affect immune cells by either impairing their proper function or altering immune cell count. Even light or intermittent smoking is associated with numerous health risks:

- Cataracts
- Chronic bronchitis
- Chronic obstructive pulmonary disease (COPD)
- Delayed or difficult conception in women
- Emphysema
- Esophageal cancer
- Heart disease
- Increased frailty in older men and women
- Low sperm count in men
- Lung cancer
- Pancreatic cancer
- Premature death from cardiovascular disease
- Respiratory tract infections
- Slower recovery from torn cartilage and other injuries
- Stomach cancer
- Weakened aorta (aortic aneurysm)

- **Minimize stress.** Chronic stress is the response to emotional pressure suffered by individuals for prolonged periods. While stress is subjective and difficult to measure in scientific studies, chronic stress (as opposed to trauma or acute stress that triggers the fight-or-flight response) is associated with general immuno-suppression and a detrimental effect on a larger number of components of the immune system. (For more about stress, see page 39.)

- **Get adequate sleep.** Sleep and the circadian rhythm exert a strong regulatory influence on immune function. Sleep deprivation manifests as immunodeficiency characterized by an enhanced susceptibility to infection and even a reduced immune response to vaccinations.

- **Drink alcohol in moderation (if at all).** Drinking too much alcohol weakens the immune system, making the body an easier target for infection and disease. Chronic drinkers are more likely to contract diseases such as pneumonia and tuberculosis.

Even drinking a large amount of alcohol on a single occasion will decrease the body's ability to ward off infection for up to twenty-four hours.

- **Immunize.** Regardless of where you stand on the matter, many serious infections can be prevented by vaccinations. While some common side effects, such as a sore arm or a low-grade fever, may occur, vaccines are generally safe and effective. Consult your healthcare provider regarding your current immunization status. If you plan on traveling, especially if you'll be traveling to questionable areas or outside the country, make sure to get any additional immunizations as necessary or required.

- **Follow food-safety protocols.** Although most cases of food poisoning are not life threatening, a few may lead to serious medical conditions, such as kidney failure or meningitis. Most cases of food poisoning can be prevented by preparing and storing foods properly at home. The following precautions will help destroy germs that are already present in the foods you buy and help you to avoid introducing new ones:

  - Wash your hands with soap and water (see page 41) before and after each time you handle a raw food.
  - Rinse all fruits and vegetables under running water before cooking or serving them.
  - If you eat animal products, use different cutting boards for meats and plant foods and always store and cook animal products safely (see meatsafety.org).
  - Defrost frozen foods only in the refrigerator or in the microwave.

- **Travel safely.** If you are planning a trip, ask your physician if you need any immunizations. Discuss your travel plans with your healthcare provider at least three months before you leave.

  - If you are traveling to an area where insect-borne diseases are present, take and use an insect repellent containing DEET. In most tropical regions, mosquitoes can carry dengue virus, Japanese encephalitis, malaria, yellow fever, and numerous other serious infectious viruses and bacteria. See page 56 for additional tips on how to prevent mosquito bites.
  - In many parts of the United States, ticks in meadows and woods carry Lyme disease or other diseases.

- Avoid getting any unnecessary shots, immunizations, or even tattoos abroad. Needles and syringes, including disposable ones, are often reused in some parts of the world.

- **Drink clean water.** Some countries do not follow stringent standards of water safety and purification. If you have any doubt about the food or water during your travels, take these precautions:

  - Do not consume ice while traveling. Freezing does not kill all infectious microbes.

  - Drink only bottled beverages, such as soft drinks or water, that have secure caps.

  - Avoid fruit juices, as they may contain impure local water.

  - Boil all tap water before drinking or drink only bottled water that has a secure cap.

  - Use bottled or boiled water to brush your teeth.

  - Do not eat uncooked vegetables, including lettuce or other salad greens.

  - Peel or cook all fresh fruit. Do not eat fresh, uncooked fruit that you haven't peeled yourself.

  - Do not consume dairy products, because the milk may not be pasteurized.

  - Regardless of where you are, do not drink untreated water from lakes and streams, as it can contain disease-causing organisms from human or animal waste. If you must drink the water, bring it to a rolling boil for at least one full minute to help minimize the chance of infection.

- **Practice safe sex.** The only sure way to prevent sexually transmitted diseases (STDs) is to not have sexual intercourse or other types of sexual contact. The next best option is to follow these safer-sex guidelines:

  - Engage in sexual relations with only one partner who has been tested and who is having sex only with you.

  - Use a latex or polyurethane condom or a female condom every time you have intercourse.

  - For oral sex, use a latex or polyurethane male condom or a female condom.

  - For anal sex, use a latex or polyurethane male condom.

Healthy Skepticism, Healthy Habits

The chains of habit are too weak to be felt until they are too strong to be broken.

Samuel Johnson (1709–1784), English poet, essayist, moralist, and novelist

Despite many products on store shelves claiming to boost or support immunity, there are few, if any, scientific studies to back up these assertions. Actually, the idea of attempting to boost the cells of the immune system is incredibly complicated because there are so many different types of cells in the immune system that respond to various microbes in diverse ways. It's also questionable from a scientific perspective: Which cells should be boosted and to what number? So far, scientists don't have the answer. They do know, however, that the body is continually generating immune cells and produces many more lymphocytes (small white blood cells, B cells and T cells, that are responsible for immune responses and play a large role in defending the body against disease) than it can possibly use. These extra cells are removed through apoptosis, a natural process of cell death that may happen before the cells are involved in any direct action or after a battle is won. No one knows how many cells are needed for peak immunity or what the best mix of cells is for the immune system to function at its optimum level. However, we do know that the body can be more or less susceptible to disease and infection depending on a variety of factors, although some of the factors we've always believed influenced immunity may actually not have any effect on it at all.

AGE AND IMMUNITY

As we age, the immune response seems to weaken, contributing to more infections, inflammatory diseases, and cancer. Although some people age with few health problems, many studies have concluded that the elderly are more likely to contract infectious diseases and more likely to die from them than younger people. Worldwide, influenza, respiratory infections, and particularly pneumonia are the leading causes of death in people over sixty-five.

Although scientists don't fully understand why this happens, they have observed that this increased risk correlates with a decrease in T cells, possibly caused by the thymus atrophying with age and producing fewer T cells to fight off infection. Some researchers are interested in whether bone marrow becomes less efficient at producing the stem cells that give rise to the cells of the immune system.

A decrease in the immune response to infection has been demonstrated by older people's response to vaccines. Studies have shown that influenza vaccines are less effective for people over age sixty-five compared to healthy children over the age of two. Despite this reduced efficacy, flu and pneumonia vaccinations have significantly lowered the rates of sickness and death in older people compared to elderly individuals who haven't been vaccinated.

Nutrition and immunity in older people have been positively correlated, particularly with regard to a condition known as micronutrient malnutrition, which is common in the elderly. Micronutrient malnutrition is a deficiency of certain essential vitamins and trace minerals that are usually obtained from the diet or via supplementation. This condition is attributed to the fact that older people tend to eat smaller amounts of food and often have limited variety in their diets. It's possible that vitamin-mineral supplements may help older people maintain a healthier immune system. Older people should discuss this option with a physician who is well versed in geriatric nutrition. Although some supplements may be beneficial for older people, the wrong ones or the wrong dosages could have serious repercussions for this age group, especially for people who are ill or who are taking prescription, over-the-counter, or herbal medications.

COLD TEMPERATURES

Although most of us grew up following our parents' admonition to wear a jacket when it's chilly outside or we'll catch a cold, researchers so far haven't found any actual connection between normal exposure to moderately cold temperatures and an increased susceptibility to infection. In fact, the majority of health experts concur that the reason colds and flu spike during winter is because more people are spending time indoors, in enclosed spaces and in closer contact with other people who can more readily pass along their germs. A group of Canadian researchers who reviewed hundreds of medical studies on the subject and even conducted some of their own research concluded that moderate cold exposure has no detrimental effect on the human immune system.

EXERCISE

Although it might seem too good or simplistic to be true, regular exercise is the easiest and most effective way to fend off infection as well as lower the risk of colon cancer, diabetes, heart disease, and high blood pressure. Hundreds of studies confirm this finding and have demonstrated that exercise not only can help most people feel better but also can help them live longer. Just be sure to start and maintain an exercise program that is tailored to your physical abilities, interests (so you'll stick with it), and lifestyle.

HERBS AND OTHER SUPPLEMENTS

The shelves of natural food stores and vitamin shops are packed with bottles of pills and herbal preparations that claim to enhance or support immunity. Although some natural preparations and herbal mixtures have been found to alter or improve certain components of immune function (see chapter 7, pages 58–125), there's minimal evidence they can actually bolster immunity to the point of protecting against or preventing serious infectious diseases. Demonstrating whether an herb can ward off infection is a highly complicated matter, mainly because scientists are yet unable to determine whether an herb that seems to raise the levels of antibodies in the blood is actually doing anything beneficial in terms of overall immunity from disease in general, let alone from specific diseases.

NUTRITION

Scientists have long acknowledged that people who are impoverished and malnourished are more vulnerable to infectious diseases. However, there are relatively few studies on the effects of nutrition on the human immune system and even fewer studies on the effects of nutrition and the development of diseases.

There is some laboratory evidence that micronutrient deficiencies, such as deficiencies of copper, folic acid, selenium, zinc, and vitamins A, B_6, C, and E, may affect immune responses. Although the impact of these changes on human health needs further investigation, studies regarding micronutrients and immunity appear promising. However, researchers are still exploring the immune-boosting potential of a number of different nutrients. In the meantime, if you are concerned about micronutrient deficiencies in your diet, taking a daily multivitamin-mineral supplement may be helpful, but taking megadoses of a single nutrient likely will not be.

STRESS

A wide assortment of ailments, including headaches, hives, insomnia, upset stomach, and even heart disease, have been linked to the consequences of psychological and emotional stress. The relationship between stress and immune function continues to be studied by various types of scientists, but it has not yet been a major focus of research for immunologists.

Exploring a connection between stress and the immune system presents some troublesome research challenges. For starters, stress is elusive: it's difficult to define and varies from individual to individual. What one person considers stressful may not be for someone else. Beyond that, stress levels are almost impossible to measure. There's no way for scientists to know if the subjective assessment of the amount of stress a person is experiencing is accurate. Scientists can only measure empirical factors that may reflect stress, such as blood pressure, heart rate, and respiration, but even these may have other causes and therefore may not objectively indicate stress levels.

Most researchers exploring the relationship between stress and immunity are studying chronic (persistent) rather than acute (short-lived or sudden) stress to determine the effects of ongoing stress on the immune system. But experiments of this nature are challenging to perform on people because a great many factors can affect the measurements being taken, making the studies tough to control and the findings unreliable.

Avoid Catching and Spreading Viruses

I love you. I hate you. I like you. I hate you. I love you. I think you're stupid. I think you're a loser. I think you're wonderful. I want to be with you. I don't want to be with you. I would never date you. I hate you. I love you. . . . I think the madness started the moment we met and you shook my hand. Did you have a disease or something?

Shannon L. Alder, inspirational author

The old adage "an ounce of prevention is worth a pound of cure" is certainly true when it comes to viral illnesses. While it's not possible at this time to prevent all viral infections, there are steps each of us can take right now to reduce our chances of contracting a severe infection and of spreading viruses to others. At the top of the list is washing your hands.

Handwashing is among the most effective ways to protect yourself and those around you from getting sick and spreading the microbes that cause illness. In fact, handwashing is as close to a do-it-yourself "vaccine" as you can get. The following five steps (wet, lather, scrub, rinse, dry) explain in detail the correct way to wash your hands:

STEP 1: WET

Wet your hands with clean, running water (warm or cold).

STEP 2: LATHER

Apply soap and create a lather by rubbing your hands together. Be sure to also lather the backs of your hands, between your fingers, and under your nails.

STEP 3: SCRUB

Scrub your hands for at least twenty seconds. To ensure you're scrubbing long enough, hum the "Happy Birthday" song twice, from beginning to end.

STEP 4: RINSE

Rinse your hands well under clean, running water (warm or cold).

STEP 5: DRY

Dry your hands using a clean towel or paper towel or air-dry them.

Regular handwashing, done correctly, particularly before and after certain activities, is one of the best ways to avoid getting sick and prevent spreading germs to others. Plus it's quick and easy. Handwashing is especially critical at the following key times:

- Before, during, and after food preparation
- Before eating food
- Before and after caring for someone who is ill
- Before and after treating a cut or dressing a wound
- After using the toilet
- After changing diapers or cleaning a child who has used the toilet
- After blowing your nose, coughing, or sneezing
- After touching an animal, animal feed, or animal waste
- After touching garbage

Although washing your hands with soap and water is the most effective way to remove germs, if you don't have access to soap and water, you can use an alcohol-based hand sanitizer that contains at least 60 percent alcohol. An alcohol-based hand sanitizer can quickly inactivate many types of microbes when used correctly, but it will be less effective if an insufficient amount is used or if it is wiped off before it has dried. It's also important to note that hand sanitizers can't remove or inactivate all types of germs. They may not be able to remove chemicals, pesticides, or heavy metals and are not as effective when hands are heavily soiled or greasy. Alcohol-based hand sanitizers are safe when used as directed, but they can cause alcohol poisoning if a person swallows more than a couple of mouthfuls. Always keep hand sanitizers out of the reach of young children. Follow these steps when using a hand sanitizer:

1. Apply a sufficient amount of the sanitizer to the palm of one hand (read the label to learn the correct amount).
2. Rub your hands together.
3. Rub the sanitizer over all surfaces of both hands, including the backs and between the fingers, until your hands are dry.

Understanding Influenza

5

The Common Enemy

Disease could wipe out an army quicker than any battle.

George R. R. Martin, *A Dance with Dragons*

T he influenza virus causes the illness known as influenza, commonly called the flu. Even if you've never had any other viral infection that you're aware of, there's a very high chance you've had the flu at least once—or probably several times—in your life so far. Four major flu pandemics have occurred in the last century: in 1918, 1957, 1968, and 2009. The 1918 pandemic was the most serious and manifested at the end of World War I. Between fifty million and one hundred million people died, which was more than the total number of people killed in the war.

All four pandemics were caused by different types of influenza viruses that had been introduced to humans from animals. This is why scientists are on the lookout for any new flu viruses that might be able to infect humans and cause high levels of illness or death. Even if a virus is not considered especially serious or life-threatening, large numbers of people taking off sick from work or school can have significant, far-reaching economic repercussions.

43

There are four types of influenza viruses: A, B, C, and D. Human influenza A and B viruses cause seasonal epidemics nearly every winter in the United States and vary in severity depending on the strain of the virus prevalent that year. However, the emergence of a new or very different influenza type A virus has the potential to cause a flu pandemic. Type A viruses are capable of infecting animals, although it's more common for humans to suffer the ailments associated with this type of infection. Wild birds commonly act as the hosts for the type A virus. Type B influenza viruses are found only in humans. Often causing a less severe reaction than type A influenza viruses, type B viruses can still be extremely harmful even though they don't cause pandemics. Influenza type C infections generally result in a mild respiratory illness and are not believed to cause epidemics. Influenza D viruses primarily affect cattle and are not known to infect or cause illness in people.

Although all pandemics are important to study, seasonal flu is particularly crucial. That's because hundreds of millions of people around the world are infected with flu annually, and hundreds of thousands die. The influenza vaccine is of value, but it needs to be modified almost every year to keep up with the evolution of the flu virus.

We contract the flu when we breathe in air containing contaminated droplets produced when an infected person coughs or sneezes. When people get the flu, they typically feel miserable for seven to ten days after being infected and then recover. However, some people develop serious complications, such as pneumonia, and some people even die from it. The groups at the highest risk of complications from flu are infants, people over the age of sixty, and individuals of any age who have heart disease, lung disease, or other chronic diseases, such as diabetes, that compromise the immune system. In addition to causing severe pneumonia, influenza can also weaken the lungs, allowing dangerous bacteria to proliferate and cause bacterial pneumonia, even in healthy young adults. Once we're exposed to a particular strain of influenza, we're immune to that strain for life. However, new strains emerge each year to which we have no immunity, making flu a relentless global health challenge.

Prevention Tips

Only cells that had been transformed by a virus or a genetic mutation had the potential to become immortal.

Rebecca Skloot, *The Immortal Life of Henrietta Lacks*

D espite the prevalence of flu each year, there are a number of steps you can take to avoid getting infected or infecting others:

- **Wash your hands.** See page 41 for detailed instructions.

- **Keep your distance.** The flu is most readily transmissible when you're within three feet of someone who has it. That's about the distance large particles in a sneeze can travel before hitting the ground.

- **Use common sense.** Don't hug people who are obviously sick. Avoid drinking from a glass or sharing plates and utensils that were used by a sick person. Don't touch your face, especially your eyes, nose, or mouth, after touching a possibly contaminated surface. Regularly disinfect surfaces that are touched often, including doorknobs, faucet handles, and light switches.

- **Wear a face mask.** If you're in a high-risk group and can't avoid coming in close contact with people who may be infected with the flu, wear a surgical face mask. These are readily available at most pharmacies. Face masks can help stop droplets from being spread by the people wearing them. They also keep splashes or sprays from reaching the mouths and noses of the people wearing them. However, they are not designed to protect against breathing in the aerosols of very small particles that may contain viruses and are generally best used by healthcare workers and when in the presence of an infected person. They will not offer much, if any, protection in public places and will be ineffective if they're loose or if you have facial hair (such as a beard or mustache).

- **Protect others.** Don't go to work, school, or social gatherings if you have the flu, even if your symptoms are mild or have just begun, as that is the time when flu is often the most contagious.

- **Get vaccinated.** A vaccine is developed annually to fight the strains of influenza virus that are prevalent that year. A healthy immune system may be insufficient to protect you from getting infected, even if you have immunity from other (prior) influenza strains. The Centers for Disease Control and Prevention recommends that nearly everyone six months of age and older get a flu shot every year. There are two ways that flu vaccines are administered: injection and nasal spray. An injection can be given to most people unless they're severely allergic to eggs, allergic to any ingredient in the vaccine, or allergic to the vaccine itself. Some people with Guillain-Barré Syndrome (a severe, paralyzing illness, also called GBS) should not get the flu vaccine; talk to your doctor before getting vaccinated if you have a history of GBS. The nasal spray should only be used by healthy individuals ages two to forty-nine who are not pregnant. Side effects from flu vaccines are generally uncommon and mild, such as a slightly sore arm, low-grade fever, or rash.

Symptoms, Diagnosis, and Treatment Options

The doctor tells the patient he has very bad flu. The patient says he wants a second opinion. The doctor says, "OK, you're ugly too."

Anonymous

SYMPTOMS

Flu symptoms generally emerge between one and four days after a person is exposed to the virus, an interval known as the incubation period. Although symptoms can vary greatly from strain to strain and from person to person, fever is common and gradually rises over the first day of the illness. The flu typically lasts for five to seven days, but some people feel tired for several weeks after recovery. The following are common symptoms of the flu:

- Chills
- Cough
- Fatigue
- Fever or feeling feverish

- Headache
- Muscle aches
- Sore throat

DIAGNOSIS AND TREATMENT

Antibiotics are ineffective against the flu because the illness is caused by a virus not a bacterium (antibiotics only fight bacterial infections). However, if the flu has led to a bacterial infection of the sinuses or lungs, antibiotics might be prescribed by your physician. Also, if you are at a high risk for complications from the flu, your doctor may prescribe an antiviral drug, such as amantadine (Symmetrel), oseltamivir (Tamiflu), rimantadine (Flumadine), or zanamivir (Relenza), within twenty-four hours of the onset of symptoms to lessen the length and severity of the illness. Tests are rarely used to diagnose flu; diagnosis is typically based on a patient's symptoms. The best treatments for the flu include the following:

- Drink plenty of clear liquids.
- Drink warm fluids to soothe a sore throat.
- Humidify the air; moist air can ease breathing difficulties.
- Rest.
- Take nonsteroidal anti-inflammatory drugs (NSAIDs), such as ibuprofen or naproxen, to relieve pain and fever.

CAUTIONS

- Call your doctor immediately or go to the emergency room if you have trouble breathing.
- Contact your doctor if you have a fever that doesn't subside after four days.
- Never give aspirin to infants or children or anyone under the age of twenty-one because of the risk of Reye's syndrome, a rare but serious condition that causes swelling in the liver and brain.

What's Bugging You?

Disease may be defined as a change produced in living things in consequence of which they are no longer in harmony with their environment.

William Thomas Councilman, *Disease and Its Causes*

We often don't know whether the bug we've got is the flu or something else. The table on page 48 will help you sort out what you have and how to treat it.

Separating Flu Facts from Fiction

Seasonal flu is now a pandemic that lasts for years and years because you've got so many people that it's jumping back between northern and southern hemispheres and moving itself around the world. By the time it gets back to where it started, it's changed sufficiently so that people are no longer immune.

Nathan Wolfe, American virologist and director of Global Viral

Having the flu can be a pretty miserable experience. Unfortunately, there's no shortage of poor advice and misinformation about how to deal with it. Be aware that many popular beliefs about the flu and common recommenda-

Is It the Flu or Something Else?

	ALLERGY	COLD	FLU	SINUSITIS
SYMPTOMS				
Bad breath or bad taste in the mouth	✗	✗	✗	✔
Contagious stage	✗	During the first 3 days of symptoms	1 day before symptoms develop and 5–7 days after becoming sick	Possibly contagious depending on the cause
Cough	✗	Mild	Severe	Mild
Facial pain or pressure	✗	Mild	✗	✔
Fatigue or weakness	✗	Mild	Severe	Mild
Fever	✗	Low-grade possible; less common in adults	High (100–102 degrees F or higher); lasts 3–4 days	Low to moderate
General course	Chronic or seasonal	Symptoms usually last for about 1 week	Gradual improvement over 2–5 days; may feel run down for 7–10 days or longer	Acute (10–14 days); subacute (4–8 weeks); chronic (8 weeks or longer); recurrent (several attacks in a year)
Headache	✗	Mild	Severe	Mild
Itchy eyes/scratchy throat	✔	✗	✗	✗
Muscle aches	✗	Mild	Severe	Mild
Nasal discharge	Watery	Watery	Thin	Thick; discolored
Sneezing	✔	✔	✗	✗
Sore throat	✗	✔	✔	✗
TREATMENT				
Antibiotics	✗	✗	✗	✔
Antihistamines	✔	✔	✗	✗
Antivirals	✗	✗	Sometimes	✗
Decongestants	✔	✔	Sometimes	✔
Fluids	✗	✔	✔	✔
Inhaled steam	✗	✗	✗	✔

tions for treating symptoms are simply wrong, and following the advice of these folk tales can sometimes be downright dangerous.

MYTH: The flu is the same as a bad cold.

FACT: *The symptoms of flu are similar to those of a bad cold, such as a runny nose or sore throat, sneezing, coughing, and hoarseness. But the flu is much more serious and severe than a cold. In the United States alone, at least thirty-six thousand people die from the flu each year and more than two hundred thousand are hospitalized because of it.*

MYTH: The flu can't be spread by someone who doesn't have any symptoms.

FACT: *About 25 percent of people infected with the flu virus feel fine and have no symptoms, but they nevertheless are just as contagious as someone who is symptomatic.*

MYTH: You can catch the flu by going out in cold weather without a coat or by sitting near a drafty window.

FACT: *The only way you can catch the flu is by being exposed to the influenza virus. Because flu season coincides with cold weather, people often associate the illness with chilly temperatures and drafty environments, but these factors are completely unrelated to the flu.*

MYTH: Feed a fever, starve a cold. Or is it feed a cold, starve a fever?

FACT: *Whether you have the flu or a cold, you need more fluids, especially if you have a fever. Although you may not have much of an appetite when you're sick, there's no reason to increase or decrease the amount of food you eat. Poor nutrition or hunger pangs won't help you recover any faster and may only make you feel weaker and more lethargic.*

MYTH: Chicken soup will speed your recovery from the flu.

FACT: *Hot liquids can help soothe a sore throat and will provide much-needed fluids, but chicken soup has no other special attributes that can help combat the flu.*

MYTH: You can contract influenza from the flu vaccine.

FACT: *The flu vaccine is made from an inactivated virus that cannot transmit infection. People who become ill after receiving a flu vacci-*

nation were going to get sick regardless, because the vaccine can take one to two weeks before it starts providing protection. Nevertheless, people often assume that because they got sick shortly after getting vaccinated, the shot was responsible for their illness.

MYTH: Healthy people don't need to be vaccinated.

FACT: Although the flu vaccination is routinely recommended for individuals with chronic illness, nearly everyone can benefit from being vaccinated, even people who are healthy. Current guidelines recommend that children ages six months to nineteen years of age, pregnant women, and anyone over the age of forty-nine be vaccinated annually. Additionally, the flu shot is suggested for healthy people who might spread the virus to others who are particularly susceptible. It's especially advisable that healthcare workers get an annual flu vaccination to protect their patients.

MYTH: A flu vaccination is all you need to protect yourself from the flu.

FACT: There are several things you can do to protect yourself during flu season in addition to being vaccinated: avoid contact with people who have the flu (see "Prevention Tips," page 45), wash your hands frequently (see page 41), and consider taking antiviral medications or herbal antivirals (see chapter 7, pages 58–125) if you were exposed to the flu prior to getting vaccinated.

MYTH: It's not necessary to get a flu shot every year.

FACT: The flu virus mutates (changes) every year, so last year's vaccination won't work against this year's influenza strain. It's important to get vaccinated annually to ensure immunity against the current year's strains that are most likely to cause an outbreak.

Mosquito-Borne Viruses

If you think you're too small to have an impact,
try going to bed with a mosquito.

ANITA RODDICK (1942–2007), FOUNDER OF THE BODY SHOP

The Bite That Bites

Mosquitoes are the greatest mass murderers on planet Earth.

Katherine Applegate, American author of books for children and young adults

The Division of Vector-Borne Diseases, a branch of the US Centers for Disease Control and Prevention, strives to protect the country from bacterial and viral diseases transmitted by mosquitoes, ticks, and fleas. While some of these diseases have long been present in the United States, others have recently emerged, including some of the world's most destructive ones. Increasingly, these diseases have become serious threats to human health. Their proliferation is attributable, in large part, to environmental changes and globalization. These vector-borne scourges are among the most complex of all infectious diseases to prevent and control.

Mosquitoes cause more human suffering than any other life form. Each year over one million people worldwide die from mosquito-borne diseases. Not only can mosquitoes carry diseases that infect humans, but they also transmit several diseases and parasites that can afflict dogs and horses, including dog heartworm, Eastern equine encephalitis, and West Nile virus. In addition, mosquito bites can trigger severe skin irritation through an allergic reaction to the mosquito's saliva, which is what causes the red bump and itching that typically accompany a bite. Mosquito-vectored diseases include a number of viruses, filarial (parasitic) diseases (such as dog heartworm), and protozoan diseases (such as malaria).

There are nearly two hundred types of mosquitoes in the United States and thousands of species of mosquitoes around the world. However, just two species are extremely efficient at transmitting flaviviruses, the viruses that cause a number of serious human diseases, including chikungunya, dengue, yellow fever, and Zika. They are *Aedes aegypti* (Linnaeus), also known as the yellow fever mosquito, and *Aedes albopictus* (Skuse), also known as the Asian tiger mosquito. Dengue viruses are endemic throughout territories of the United States, including American Samoa, Guam, Northern Mariana Islands, Puerto Rico, and the US Virgin Islands. However, only sporadic outbreaks of dengue occur in the continental United States. Globally, dengue fever is the most common arboviral disease, with 40 percent of the world's population living in areas with dengue virus transmission.

Most recently, outbreaks of locally transmitted dengue have occurred in Florida, Hawaii, and Texas. In 2014 twelve cases of locally acquired chikungunya infections were reported in Florida. Although once common in the United States, yellow fever has not caused locally transmitted outbreaks since 1905. However, it circulates in the tropical forests of Latin America, and periodically travelers who are infected with it return to the United States.

In 2015 Zika outbreaks were reported in the Western Hemisphere, with local transmission occurring in Central and South America, the Caribbean, and Mexico. In 2016 Zika virus was, for the first time, reported in the United States. It is expected that Zika transmission will continue to increase throughout these regions, including the United States. Local outbreaks have occurred and will continue to occur as a result of virus importation by infected, viremic travelers. In addition, any viremic travelers visiting or returning to parts of the United States could initiate local virus transmission.

Only 20–25 percent of people infected with dengue or Zika develop symptoms, but 80–90 percent of those infected with chikungunya develop fever, rash, or severe joint pain. Furthermore, the symptoms often continue long after the body has rid itself of the virus. The first report of chikungunya in the Western Hemisphere was in 2013, when the virus was found in St. Martin in the Caribbean. Since then it has spread throughout the Western tropics, transmitted mostly by tropical *Aedes aegypti* mosquitoes. In 2015 chikungunya virus disease became a nationally notifiable condition, with a total of 896 reported chikungunya virus disease cases in the United States and a total of 237 reported cases from US territories.

There is a safe and effective vaccine against yellow fever, but none currently exists for chikungunya, dengue fever, or Zika, although one is currently in development for Zika. Therefore, the prevention or reduction of transmission of these viruses is completely dependent on the control of mosquito vectors as well as limiting person-mosquito contact (see "Prevention Tips," page 56). The only upside to the expansion of these diseases is that pharmaceutical companies and the medical establishment might be prompted to more seriously focus on the development of preventive and therapeutic treatments for the viruses that cause them, which, until recently, have largely been ignored.

Yellow Fever Mosquito

How to spell *Aedes aegypti,* the world's one-stop, viral-disease-transmitting mosquito: T-R-O-U-B-L-E.

T. K. Naliaka, international author of fiction adventure books

The yellow fever mosquito, *Aedes aegypti* (Linnaeus), can only survive in warmer climates. It is native to sub-Saharan Africa and was most likely brought to the New World by slave traders in the 1500s. As its common name suggests, *Aedes aegypti* is the primary vector of yellow fever, a disease prevalent in Africa and tropical South America, but the mosquito often emerges in temperate regions during summer months and has been a nuisance species in the United States for centuries. During the Spanish-American War, US troops suffered more casualties from yellow fever transmitted by *Aedes aegypti* than from enemy fire.

Aedes aegypti was a common vector in Florida until the invasion of *Aedes albopictus,* the Asian tiger mosquito, which arrived by way of Texas in 1985. Since then, the population of the yellow fever mosquito has declined dramatically in Florida, but it still thrives in urban areas of South Florida.

Aedes aegypti are small, dark mosquitoes with white lyre-shaped markings and banded legs. They prefer to bite indoors and primarily bite humans. They thrive in highly populated urban areas where there's close contact with people. Because they're container-inhabiting mosquitoes, they can use natural habitats (such as tree holes or plant axils) or artificial receptacles that hold water (such as birdbaths, buckets, cemetery vases, drainage ditches, empty drums, unused flowerpots, discarded tires, untreated swimming pools, saucers or plates under potted plants, tin cans, clogged rain gutters, ornamental fountains, and water bowls for pets) to lay their eggs. This species has also been found in underground collections of water, including open or unsealed septic tanks, storm drains, and wells. *Aedes aegypti* are extremely common in areas lacking piped water systems and depend greatly on stored or stagnant water containing organic material (such as algae or decaying leaves) for breeding sites. They prefer dark containers with wide openings located in the shade.

Although male and female adult *Aedes aegypti* feed on the nectar of plants, the females primarily feed on human blood in order to produce eggs, and they are active during the daytime. About three days after feeding on blood, the female mosquito lays her eggs inside a container just above the water line. The eggs, laid over a period of several days, are resistant to desiccation (exposure to dryness) and can survive for an extended period of six or more months. When rain floods the eggs with water, the larvae hatch. The larvae generally feed on algae, small aquatic organisms, and particles of plant and animal material in the water-filled containers. The full cycle from egg to adult can occur in as little as seven to eight days. The life span of adult mosquitoes is about three weeks. Egg-production sites are usually within homes or in close proximity to them. *Aedes aegypti* cannot survive the winter in the egg stage in colder climates.

While many mosquitoes bite at dawn, dusk, or night, *Aedes aegypti* bites primarily during the day. Sneaky and resilient, this species is most active for approximately two hours after sunrise and for several hours before sunset, but it can bite at night in areas that are well lit. People may not be aware they're being bitten because the mosquito approaches from behind and bites the ankles and elbows. This technique prevents people from swatting the mosquito and has earned it the nickname "the sneak-attack mosquito." *Aedes aegypti* greatly prefers to bite humans, but it has also been known to bite dogs and other domestic animals, primarily mammals.

The following maps provide a comparison of where *Aedes aegypti* and *Aedes albopictus* live. Although both can transmit Zika virus, *Aedes aegypti* is especially good at doing so in the United States. (Graphic by the US Centers for Disease Control and Prevention.)

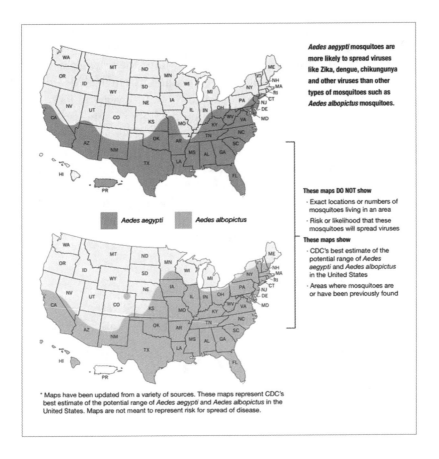

Aedes aegypti mosquitoes are more likely to spread viruses like Zika, dengue, chikungunya and other viruses than other types of mosquitoes such as Aedes albopictus mosquitoes.

These maps DO NOT show
· Exact locations or numbers of mosquitoes living in an area
· Risk or likelihood that these mosquitoes will spread viruses

These maps show
· CDC's best estimate of the potential range of Aedes aegypti and Aedes albopictus in the United States
· Areas where mosquitoes are or have been previously found

Aedes aegypti   Aedes albopictus

* Maps have been updated from a variety of sources. These maps represent CDC's best estimate of the potential range of Aedes aegypti and Aedes albopictus in the United States. Maps are not meant to represent risk for spread of disease.

Asian Tiger Mosquito

Mosquitoes remind us that we are not as high up on the food chain as we think.

Tom Wilson, American author and illustrator

Aedes albopictus, commonly known as the Asian tiger mosquito, reflects the flashy stripes on its body. It can transmit the same viruses as *Aedes aegypti* and, like its relative, thrives in human habitats and feeds aggressively on people. However, it can survive year-round in much cooler climates.

Although *Aedes aegypti* is perhaps better at transmitting diseases than *Aedes albopictus*, that may be changing. Starting in the 1960s, *Aedes albopictus* expanded its native range beyond Asia. Permanent breeding populations now exist in the United States, living as far north as New Jersey and Connecticut, and throughout much of Europe. In the northern part of their range, Asian tiger mosquitoes lay eggs in the fall, but the eggs don't develop and hatch until the warmer weather arrives in the spring. In addition to expanding its range, *Aedes albopictus* has been adapting over the past thirty to fifty years to its newly occupied habitats, allowing more and more of the mosquitoes to survive. This is particularly worrisome, because in order for an epidemic of mosquito-borne disease to take hold, a certain density of mosquitoes is necessary so the virus can rapidly jump from one host to another before the hosts' immune systems kill off the virus. Since Asian tiger mosquitoes are reaching a critical density for disease transmission in certain areas of their expanded range, they're primed to become a scourge both in the United States and in Europe.

Prevention Tips

He who cures a disease may be the skillfullest, but he that prevents it is the safest physician.

Thomas Fuller (1608–1661), English historian

Whether you're staying at home or traveling abroad, preventing mosquito bites is the best way to reduce the risk of mosquito-borne diseases. Mosquitoes can be found in many different environments, and you may not always be aware that you've been bitten. In some areas, mosquito activity can be year-round. The following steps will help you prevent mosquito bites:

Apply repellents. Use DEET, picaridin (a chemical repellent sold under the trade names Bayrepel and Saltidin), oil of lemon eucalyptus (a plant-based repellent also known as PMD), or IR3535 (a synthetic insect repellent) only on exposed skin and/or clothing as directed on the product label. Do not use repellents under clothing. If repellent is applied to clothing, wash the clothes before wearing them again.

Adults and children (age two months and older) should use a repellant containing 25–30 percent DEET. Repellents with DEET should never be used on children under two months of age. After returning indoors, wash off the repellent with soap and water.

According to the US Centers for Disease Control and Prevention, insect repellents containing DEET or picaridin work better than other products. Studies have shown that oil of lemon eucalyptus works as well as low concentrations of DEET.

Cover up. Wear long pants, long-sleeved shirts, socks, and shoes if you must be outdoors when mosquitoes are most active. Use mosquito netting over infant carriers, cribs, and strollers.

Discard. Recycle or properly dispose of barrels, bottles, broken appliances, buckets, cans, cookware, drums, old tires, and other items that aren't being used and can harbor stagnant water.

Drain. Drain standing water from birdbaths, coolers, empty flowerpots, garbage cans, house gutters, pool covers, toys, wagons, wheelbarrows, or any other containers in which rain or sprinkler water has collected.

Empty and clean. At least twice a week, empty, clean, and scrub birdbaths and any water bowls for pets that are kept outdoors. Empty plastic swimming pools when they're not in use. Dump the water from saucers or overflow dishes under potted plants and flowerpots. If empty containers or large objects, such as boats or old appliances, must be stored, they should be covered, turned over, or placed under a roof that doesn't allow them to fill with water.

Fill. Fill tree holes and other cavities in or around plants and garden areas with sand or soil.

Investigate. Look for and drain hidden bodies of water near your home, such as clogged drains, manholes, septic tanks, and wells.

Report. Call the health authorities when you detect large or unusual numbers of mosquitoes.

Screen. Install window and door screens to keep out mosquitoes. If you already have window and door screens, make sure they're in good condition and are securely attached.

Shield. Protect boats and other open vehicles from rain by using tarps that don't accumulate water. Cover rain barrels with tight screening so mosquitoes can't enter.

Herbal Antivirals and Immune Boosters

The Maxims of Medicine

Before you examine the body of a patient,
Be patient to learn his story.
For once you learn his story,
You will also come to know
His body.
Before you diagnose any sickness,
Make sure there is no sickness in the mind or heart.
For the emotions in a man's moon or sun,
Can point to the sickness in
Any one of his other parts.
Before you treat a man with a condition,
Know that not all cures can heal all people.
For the chemistry that works on one patient,
May not work for the next,
Because even medicine has its own
Conditions.
Before asserting a prognosis on any patient,
Always be objective and never subjective.
For telling a man that he will win the treasure of life,
But then later discovering that he will lose,
Will harm him more than by telling him
That he may lose,
But then he wins.

SUZY KASSEM, *RISE UP AND SALUTE THE SUN: THE WRITINGS OF SUZY KASSEM*

The Need for Safe Alternatives

A mistake that a lot of people make, and I've been guilty of this as well, is that we assume that just because something is natural it is therefore safe, and ergo, good for us. I like to point out that cobras are natural too, but I don't want to kiss one.

Steve Bivans, *Be a Hobbit, Save the Earth: The Guide to Sustainable Shire Living*

Viral infections play a vital role in human diseases. Moreover, a number of difficult-to-cure and complex syndromes, including Alzheimer's disease, type 1 diabetes, and liver cancer, have been associated with viral infections. Particularly problematic are the epidemic outbreaks caused by emerging and reemerging viruses, such as dengue virus, influenza virus, measles virus, severe acute respiratory syndrome (SARS) virus, West Nile virus, and Zika virus. These outbreaks have been primarily attributed to rapid urbanization and the rise in global travel. For many of these viruses, vaccines and effective antiviral therapies are not yet available, so eradicating the diseases spread by them remains a daunting task. As a result, there is an urgent need to discover effective, affordable, novel antivirals to manage and control viral infections when vaccines and standard therapies for them are lacking. Even for viruses for which effective immunization and antiviral drugs exist, their efficacy is hampered by the potential development of drug-resistant viral mutations.

The Potential of Herbal Antivirals

A weed is a plant whose virtue is not yet known.

Ralph Waldo Emerson (1803–1882), American essayist, lecturer, and poet

The nascent research on herbal medicines to combat viruses and viral infections is still quite limited, but establishing the antiviral mechanisms of natural agents has helped identify where and how they interact with the viral life cycle, including viral entry, replication, assembly, and release, as well as specific virus-host interactions. Although several herbs have demonstrated antiviral capacity or potential, there currently are no known herbs or herbal components that can actually protect us from acquiring a viral infection. The only reliable preventive measure at this time is virus-specific vaccination. However, there are comparatively few vaccines in relation to the extensive number and variety of viruses we're up against, and only a limited number of pharmaceuticals and medical therapies available to treat a viral infection.

Fortunately, herbs and herbal products provide excellent sources of biodiversity for discovering novel antivirals and developing effective protective and therapeutic strategies against viral infections. Medical researchers have acknowledged that natural, plant-based products, which generally inhibit viruses from mutating, are ripe for such discoveries. Combatting infection with herbal antivirals encompasses a two-pronged approach:

1. Stimulate the immune system so it will produce more immune cells, thereby strengthening the immune system overall and, in turn, enhancing immunity to decrease the duration of an infection and reduce the severity of symptoms.

2. Disrupt the replication of a virus so it cannot survive.

A number of herbs and their components have been observed in laboratory studies to possess robust antiviral activity. These discoveries can help in the development of natural antivirals for humans, but the research is still preliminary. Much additional exploration is needed in order to define and characterize the bioactive ingredients in these natural agents, determine their underlying mechanisms, and assess their efficacy, suitable dosages, appropriate delivery systems, and potential applications for antiviral treatments. Equally important, additional studies must also examine the possibility of combining conventional therapies with herbal antivirals because multitarget therapies could help decrease the risk of generating drug-resistant viruses. Once these discoveries are made, there is no doubt that herbal products will play an important, ongoing role in the development of innovative antiviral combatants and treatments.

Getting Started with Herbal Antivirals

All right, calm down! Maybe I like alternative medicine because it's been in use for more than six thousand years. After all that time, they have to know what they're doing.

Robin Cook, *Intervention*

T his chapter examines a variety of herbs that have been shown in laboratory studies to contain active antiviral components. These natural substances are safe when used as directed and don't have many of the negative side effects commonly associated with pharmaceuticals and vaccinations. Equally important, viruses can't build up resistance to these herbal therapies the way they can to pharmaceuticals. Many herbal antivirals are only available as extracts or supplements or are most potent in these forms, while others can be purchased in their raw or dried forms from which you can make your own capsules, extracts, or tinctures (see "Glossary and Notes," page 126). Being armed with these natural solutions is particularly important in light of the many viruses for which no vaccines or pharmaceutical treatments currently exist.

Please continue reading to begin exploring the bounty of traditional and modern herbal antivirals and immunity boosters that are available to you today!

Safety Precautions for Using Antiviral Herbs

The United States Food and Drug Administration (FDA) does not strictly regulate herbs and supplements. Consequently, there is no guarantee of the strength, purity, or safety of these products, and their effects may vary from batch to batch and brand to brand. Always read product labels carefully. If you have a medical condition or are taking other drugs, herbs, or supplements, speak with your doctor or a qualified healthcare provider before starting a new therapy. Consult a healthcare provider immediately if you experience side effects. Herbs and supplements that work on the liver may interact with pharmaceutical drugs that are broken down by the liver. If you are taking any type of medication, talk with your doctor before using herbal treatments and supplements.

American Ginseng

Much virtue in herbs, little in men.

Benjamin Franklin (1706–1790), one of the Founding Fathers of the United States
and a leading author, inventor, statesman, and diplomat

OVERVIEW

The term "ginseng" refers to either American ginseng (*Panax quinquefolius*) or Asian ginseng (*Panax ginseng*), which is also known as Korean ginseng (see page 70). Both types belong to the genus *Panax* and contain ginsenosides, the active chemical substances believed to give the herb its primary medicinal properties. However, these two types of ginseng contain different types of ginsenosides and in different concentrations. Eleuthero (*Eleutherococcus senticosus*), commonly called Siberian ginseng (see page 112), is distantly related to ginseng but doesn't contain ginsenosides.

One of the most popular herbs in the United States, American ginseng has traditionally been used by Native Americans to treat headache, fever, indigestion, and infertility. Wild American ginseng is in such high demand that it has been declared a threatened or endangered species in several US states. As a result, it tends to be quite expensive. Today American ginseng is primarily grown on farms to protect the wild herb from being overharvested.

Laboratory research has demonstrated that American ginseng is effective in strengthening the immune system by bolstering the performance of cells that play a role in immunity. This improvement in immune function could potentially help the body fight off infection and disease, including helping to prevent colds and flu or decreasing the intensity and duration of symptoms. Additional studies show that American ginseng has antioxidant capacities as well as therapeutic potential for treating inflammatory diseases. The herb is also considered an adaptogen, a substance that helps the body normalize when it's under mental or physical stress.

Researchers have found that American ginseng possesses potent anticancer properties and has been shown to inhibit tumor growth. Studies indicate that both the berries and root of American ginseng can help lower blood sugar levels in people with type 2 diabetes and also prevent diabetes-related complications, such as retinal and functional cardiac changes, by helping to reduce stress. To avoid hypoglycemia (low blood sugar), always take American ginseng with food, even if you don't have diabetes.

PRIMARY EFFECTS

American ginseng has the following key actions on the body:

- Adaptogenic
- Antiviral
- Immunostimulant
- Regulates blood sugar levels
- Regulates cholesterol levels
- Tonic

PLANT DESCRIPTION

Both American and Asian ginseng are light tan and have gnarled roots with stringy shoots that resemble a human body. In fact, the word "ginseng" is derived from a Chinese term that literally translates as "man root," designated as such because of the herb's appearance. American ginseng products are made from the root and the long, thin offshoots called root hairs. The leaves of American ginseng grow in a circle around a straight stem. Yellowish-green, umbrella-shaped flowers grow in the center and produce red berries. Wrinkles form around the neck of the root and indicate the plant's age. This is important because the herb will be not be ready for medicinal use until it has grown for about six years.

AVAILABLE FORMS

American ginseng is available in the following forms:

- Capsules
- Dried root
- Fresh root
- Liquid extract
- Powder
- Standardized extract
- Tablets
- Tincture

Read product labels carefully to make sure you're getting the type of ginseng you want. For American ginseng, look for *Panax quinquefolius*. It may also be combined with other herbs.

USAGE AND PRECAUTIONS

American ginseng is considered safe when taken by mouth and used for short periods. Doses of 100–3,000 milligrams per day have been reported as safe for up to twelve weeks, as well as single doses of up to 10 grams. For preventing upper respiratory infections, such as the common cold or flu, a specific American ginseng extract called CVT-E002, sold under the brand names Afexa Life Sciences and Cold-FX, has also been used safely for up to four months.

Although side effects when using American ginseng are rare, they may include the following:

- Anxiety
- Breast pain
- Diarrhea
- Euphoria
- Headache
- Hypertension (high blood pressure)
- Insomnia
- Nosebleed
- Restlessness
- Vaginal bleeding
- Vomiting

Do not give American ginseng to children unless under a doctor's supervision. Women who are pregnant or breastfeeding should not take American ginseng. If you are being treated for or have a history of any of the following conditions, do not take American ginseng or products containing it without first consulting with your physician:

- Acute illness of any kind
- Bipolar disorder
- Breast cancer
- Hormone-sensitive conditions
- Hypertension (high blood pressure)
- Hypotension (low blood pressure)

If you have surgery scheduled, stop taking American ginseng at least one full week prior to your procedure. American ginseng can lower blood glucose levels and create problems for patients fasting before surgery. Also, American ginseng may act as a blood thinner, increasing the risk of bleeding during or after the procedure.

DRUG INTERACTIONS

Avoid American ginseng and products containing it except under a doctor's supervision if you are taking any of the following medications or drugs, as the herb may increase, decrease, or counteract their effects, or cause the drug to build up in the body:

- Alcohol
- Anticoagulant (blood thinner) drugs, herbs, or supplements
- Antidepressants
- Antipsychotic medication, especially drugs for bipolar disorder and schizophrenia
- Aspirin
- Caffeine
- Diabetes medication
- Hypoglycemic agents (oral)
- Insulin
- Monoamine oxidase inhibitors (MAOIs)
- Morphine
- Stimulants, including amphetamines

Andrographis

OVERVIEW

Andrographis (*Andrographis paniculata*), also known as kalmegh and "king of bitters," is an herbaceous annual in the family *Acanthaceae*. It is native to India and Sri Lanka and is widely cultivated in southern and Southeast Asia, where it has long been used in the traditional herbal medicine practices of those regions. The earliest reported uses of andrographis were for digestive problems, fever, immune stimulation, inflammation, liver complaints, snakebites, and many types of infection ranging from dysentery to malaria. Although the roots of andrographis were sometimes utilized for herbal treatments, today the leaves and flowers are more frequently used for medicinal purposes. In fact, the leaves of *Andrographis paniculata* have been a part of Indian folk medicine (Ayurveda) for centuries. Traditional Chinese and Thai herbal medicine have used andrographis mostly for its "bitter" properties, as a treatment for digestive problems, and as a remedy for a variety of fever-inducing illnesses. The herb has been used in Scandinavia for about thirty years and is popular as a curative for upper lung infections and the flu.

Andrographis is often prescribed by herbal practitioners for a wide assortment of ailments: digestive complaints (colic, constipation, diarrhea, intestinal gas, stomach pain), liver problems (enlarged liver, jaundice, liver damage caused by medications), infections (cholera, gonorrhea, HIV/AIDS, leprosy, malaria, pneumonia, rabies, sinusitis, syphilis), and various skin conditions. Some alternative practitioners also prescribe andrographis for allergies, bronchitis, coughs, sore throat, and upper respiratory complaints. The herb is sometimes used to treat atherosclerosis and prevent diabetes and heart disease.

A surprising number of these traditional and contemporary uses have been validated by modern scientific research. In clinical trials, andrographis extract has been studied for use as an immunostimulant in upper respiratory tract infections and to treat human immunodeficiency virus (HIV) infection. There is also strong evidence to suggest that andrographis effectively reduces the severity and duration of certain types of lung infections and may have therapeutic potential as a general anti-inflammatory agent and treatment for chemically induced liver damage. Andrographis has been studied in human clinical trials for the flu and familial Mediterranean fever (a hereditary inflammatory disorder). Early research indicates that the herb's anti-inflammatory effects may play a therapeutic role in the treatment of intestinal disorders with inflammatory associations, such as Crohn's disease and ulcerative colitis.

The major constituents in andrographis are compounds known as andrographolides. These bitter constituents are believed to have immune-stimulating, anti-inflammatory, and liver-protective actions and may stimulate bile secretion. The most widely tested andrographis product is Kan Jang, made by Swedish Herbal Institute. This product contains standardized andrographis extract combined with eleuthero (see "Siberian Ginseng," page 112) and has been shown in double-blind clinical trials to reduce symptoms of the common cold. Andrographis has also proven helpful in combination with antibiotics in the treatment of dysentery, an intestinal infection with severe diarrhea, and has shown promise for treating chronic viral hepatitis.

PRIMARY EFFECTS

Andrographis has the following key actions on the body:

- Adaptogenic
- Antiallergenic
- Anti-inflammatory
- Antimicrobial
- Antipyretic (prevents or reduces fever)
- Antiviral
- Astringent
- Carminative (relieves flatulence)
- Choleretic (increases the secretion of bile)
- Digestive tonic
- Diuretic
- Emmenagogue (increases menstrual flow)
- Emollient
- Febrifuge (reduces fever)
- Gastric tonic
- Hepatoprotective (protects the liver)
- Hypocholesterolemic (lowers blood cholesterol)
- Hypoglycemic (lowers blood sugar)

- Hypotensive (lowers blood pressure)
- Immunostimulant
- Liver tonic

PLANT DESCRIPTION

Andrographis paniculata is an erect annual herb that grows to a height of one to three and a half feet. It is native to China, India, and Southeast Asia and is widely cultivated in Asia. The square stem has wings on the angles of new growth and is enlarged at the nodes, while small white flowers with purplish-rose spots are displayed on a branching panicle. The plant produces yellowish-brown seeds, and all parts have an extremely bitter taste. The aboveground portion of the plant is harvested in the fall.

AVAILABLE FORMS

Andrographis is available in the following forms:

- Capsules
- Dried leaves (for tea)
- Liquid extract
- Powder
- Standardized extract
- Tablets
- Tea bags
- Tincture

Andrographis may be combined with other herbs in certain formulations. Kan Jang (made by Swedish Herbal Institute) is available with andrographis alone or in combination with eleuthero derived from *Eleutherococcus senticosus* (Siberian ginseng; see page 112).

USAGE AND PRECAUTIONS

Although side effects with using andrographis are uncommon, they may include the following:

- Diarrhea
- Fatigue
- Headache
- Loss of appetite
- Rash
- Runny nose
- Vomiting

In rare instances, when used in high doses or for extended periods, andrographis might cause serious allergic reactions, a bitter or metallic taste in the mouth, elevation of liver enzymes, swollen lymph glands, or other side effects. These haven't been reported in people using whole andrographis or standardized extracts in the recommended amounts.

Some people develop intestinal upset when taking andrographis. If this occurs, decrease the amount taken or take it with meals. As with all bitter herbs, andrographis may aggravate heartburn and ulcers.

Andrographis should be avoided by pregnant women, as there is evidence that andrographis taken orally during pregnancy may cause miscarriage. There is insufficient evidence about the safety of andrographis during breastfeeding. Andrographis may be safe for children when taken orally for brief periods. It has been administered safely to children in combination with other herbs for up to one month. Do not give andrographis to children unless under a doctor's supervision.

Animal research suggests that andrographis could interfere with fertility in both men and women. It should therefore be avoided by men trying to father a child or women trying to become pregnant.

Andrographolides, the active chemical in andrographis, might slow blood clotting, increase the risk of bleeding, and worsen bleeding disorders. A few of the medications that slow blood clotting include aspirin, clopidogrel (Plavix), dalteparin (Fragmin), diclofenac (Cataflam, Voltaren, and others), enoxaparin (Lovenox), heparin, ibuprofen (Advil, Motrin, and others), naproxen (Anaprox, Naprosyn, and others), warfarin (Coumadin), and many others. Taking andrographis along with medications that also slow clotting may increase the chances of bruising and bleeding. Andrographis should be avoided if you are taking anticoagulant or antiplatelet herbs or supplements, such as angelica, clove, danshen, garlic, ginger, ginkgo, or *Panax ginseng* (see page 70), among others.

Andrographis seems to decrease blood pressure. Taking andrographis along with medications for high blood pressure may cause your blood pressure to drop too low.

Andrographis appears to be safe for adults when taken in appropriate doses by mouth for short periods. It also appears to be safe when taken in products that combine andrographis extract and Siberian ginseng (*Eleutherococcus senticosus*; see page 112), as in Kan Jang, for up to three months.

Research suggests that andrographis may reduce the severity and duration of symptoms in active infections if dosing is started within thirty-six to forty-eight hours after symptoms develop. Andrographis is generally available as capsules containing the dried herb or as standardized extracts containing 11.2 milligrams andrographolides per 200 milligrams of extract. A typical recommended dose is 500–3,000 milligrams of andrographis leaf taken by mouth three times daily.

The following are commonly suggested dosages for specific needs:

- For the common cold: Take Kan Jang (made by Swedish Herbal Institute), which contains a specific combination of standardized andrographis extract (standardized to contain 4–5.6 milligrams andrographolides) plus 400 milligrams of Siberian ginseng, three times daily. Start using Kan Jang within seventy-two hours of the onset of symptoms. Although some symptoms may improve after two days of treatment, it generally takes four to five days of treatment to obtain the maximum benefit.

- For the treatment of upper respiratory tract infection: Take 3–6 grams of andrographis (containing 48–500 milligrams of andrographolides), divided into three or four daily doses, by mouth for four to ten consecutive days. Alternatively, take 100 milligrams of KalmCold (a brand-name extract) by mouth twice daily after breakfast and after dinner for five days. Do not exceed the recommended amounts, as higher dosages may lead to serious side effects.

- For the prevention of upper respiratory tract infection: Take 200 milligrams of andrographis (two Kan Jang tablets) by mouth daily for three months. Do not exceed the recommended amounts, as higher dosages may lead to serious side effects.

- For ulcerative colitis: Take 400 milligrams of an extract containing 8–10 percent andrographis by weight three times daily for eight weeks. Alternatively, take 1,200–1,800 milligrams of an andrographis extract by mouth daily in three divided doses for eight weeks.

- For indigestion: Andrographis may be taken in the form of a tea. Use 1 teaspoon of the dried herb for each cup of hot water. Let the mixture stand for 10–15 minutes before straining and drinking. Sip the tea before or between meals.

The standard dose of *Andrographis paniculata* basic root extract is 2,000–6,000 milligrams. The root extract tends to have 1–2 percent andrographolide content, by weight, though up to 4 percent has been reported. Concentrated root extracts can have an andrographolide content of up to 30 percent. The standard dose for a concentrated extract is 200 milligrams.

If you are being treated for or have a history of any of the following conditions, do not take andrographis or products containing it without first consulting with your physician:

- Autoimmune diseases
- Bleeding disorders
- Hypotension (low blood pressure)

If you have surgery scheduled, stop taking andrographis or products containing it at least one full week prior to your procedure. Andrographis and andrographolides can lower blood glucose levels and create problems for patients fasting before surgery. Also, the herb may act as a blood thinner, increasing the risk of bleeding during or after the procedure.

DRUG INTERACTIONS

Avoid andrographis and products containing it except under a doctor's supervision if you are taking any of the following medications, as the herb may increase, decrease, or counteract their effects, or cause the drug to build up in the body:

- Anticoagulant (blood thinner) drugs, herbs, or supplements
- Antihypertensive drugs (high blood pressure medication)
- Antiplatelet drugs, herbs, or supplements
- Aspirin
- Ibuprofen
- Immunosuppressants

Asian Ginseng

Health is merely the slowest way someone can die.

Anonymous

OVERVIEW

Asian ginseng (*Panax ginseng*) is also known as Chinese or Korean ginseng; they are all the same plant but they're grown in different regions. American ginseng (see page 61) is related to this species but is native to North America. Asian ginseng has been used in traditional Chinese medicine for over five thousand years. It grows wild in the mountains of Manchuria, China, where it has been revered for its rejuvenating powers and is considered to be a symbol of divine harmony. Ginseng's benefits were first documented during China's Liang Dynasty (AD 220–589). Legend has it that early emperors used the herb as a general curative, a health-promoting food, and an ingredient in creams, lotions, and soaps.

Both Asian and American ginseng (see page 61) contain ginsenosides, the primary active chemical components in the herbs. The term "ginsenosides" was coined by Asian researchers, but the term "panaxosides" was chosen by early Russian researchers because Asian ginseng contains panaxans (glycans) as well as ginsenosides. Asian ginseng also contains B vitamins, flavonoids, peptides, polysaccharides, and volatile oils. The herb's immune-boosting properties may help the body fight off infection and disease and may reduce the risk of getting a cold or the flu or lessen the severity of symptoms and shorten the duration of the illness. Studies have found that ginseng increases the number of immune cells in the blood and improves the immune system's response to flu vaccines. Although Asian ginseng has been shown to exert direct antiviral effects by inhibiting viral attachment, membrane penetration, and replication, the herb's foremost antiviral activities are attributed to the enhancement of host immunity.

Korean red ginseng (KRG) is produced by repeated steaming and air-drying of fresh ginseng. Because of changes that occur in the herb's chemical constituents during the steaming process, KRG possesses greater pharmacological activity and stability than the fresh herb. In addition to having immune-modulating properties that may protect against the effects of microbial infections, KRG contains active anticancer and anti-inflammatory components.

Asian ginseng is also an antioxidant, which means it can help rid the body of free radicals that can damage DNA and contribute to cancer, diabetes, and heart disease. Several studies suggest that Asian ginseng slows down or stops the growth of tumors and that it may decrease LDL ("bad") cholesterol levels and increase HDL ("good") cholesterol levels. Preliminary research indicates it may improve the symptoms of heart disease.

People who take ginseng commonly proclaim feeling more alert, and research supports these anecdotal accounts that the herb improves mental performance. Asian ginseng is considered an adaptogen and is credited with helping the body cope with physical or mental stress. There have also been reports of improved energy, sleep, sexual stamina, personal satisfaction, and general well-being when taking Asian ginseng.

PRIMARY EFFECTS

Asian ginseng has the following key actions on the body:

- Adaptogenic
- Antiviral
- Immunostimulant
- Regulates blood sugar levels
- Regulates cholesterol levels
- Tonic

PLANT DESCRIPTION

Asian ginseng is similar in appearance to American ginseng (see page 61) and shares many of the same characteristics and healing qualities. The plant has a straight stem with leaves that grow in a circle around it. In the center are yellowish-green, umbrella-shaped flowers that produce red berries. The taproot of ginseng looks similar to the human body, with two "arms" and two "legs." In China the word for "ginseng" literally means "man root." Wrinkles around the neck of the taproot reveal the plant's age. Ginseng is not ready to be used medicinally until it has grown for about six years.

AVAILABLE FORMS

Asian ginseng supplements are made from the root of the plant and the long, thin offshoots called root hairs. White Asian ginseng is made from the dried, peeled root, and red Asian ginseng is made from the unpeeled root and is steamed before it is dried. Both types are available in the following forms:

- Capsules
- Dried, for making decoctions (boiling the root in water)
- Liquid extract
- Powder

Read product labels carefully to make sure you're getting the type of ginseng you want. For Asian ginseng, look for *Panax ginseng*. It may also be combined with other herbs.

USAGE AND PRECAUTIONS

Do not give Asian ginseng to children. The use of *Panax ginseng* in babies has been linked to poisoning that can be fatal, and the safety of *Panax ginseng* in older children is not currently known.

People who have high or low blood pressure or autoimmune disease (such as rheumatoid arthritis, lupus, or inflammatory bowel disease) should not take Asian ginseng without a doctor's authorization and supervision. Individuals with bipolar disorder should avoid Asian ginseng, as it may increase the risk of mania. Pregnant women shouldn't take Asian ginseng because it may increase the chance of vaginal bleeding, and one of the chemicals in *Panax ginseng* has been found to cause birth defects in animals. Women who have a history of breast cancer should not use Asian ginseng.

Because Asian ginseng can naturally increase energy, if it is taken in high doses or is combined with caffeine, it may cause excitability, insomnia, irregular heartbeat, nervousness, restlessness, or sweating. Alcohol interacts with *Panax ginseng* and may affect how quickly the body rids itself of the alcohol. Do not take *Panax ginseng* orally for more than six months, as it may have hormone-like effects that could be harmful with longer use.

The most common side effect of Asian ginseng is trouble sleeping (insomnia). Uncommon side effects that have been reported include liver damage, dangerous allergic reactions, and a severe rash called Stevens-Johnson syndrome. Other possible side effects, though rare, may include the following:

- Anxiety
- Breast pain
- Diarrhea
- Dizziness
- Euphoria
- Headache
- Hypertension (high blood pressure)
- Hypotension (low blood pressure)
- Itching
- Loss of appetite
- Menstrual problems
- Mood changes
- Nosebleed
- Rash
- Vaginal bleeding
- Vomiting

Adults should work with a doctor or healthcare provider familiar with herbal medicine to determine the right dose for their individual needs. Asian ginseng should not be used continuously. People in good health who want to enhance immunity, boost physical or mental performance, prevent illness, or increase resistance to stress should take Asian ginseng in cycles, with occasional breaks. Many experts recommend taking Asian ginseng every day for two to three weeks, then taking three weeks off before starting it up again.

For flu prevention, a common dose is 200 milligrams of *Panax ginseng* extract (G115) daily, starting four weeks prior to getting a flu shot and continuing for eight weeks after the injection. One gram of *Panax ginseng* extract three times daily for twelve weeks has also been used. Ginseng extract (G115) is a trademarked standardized extract made from the roots of the *Panax ginseng* plant. It's reputed to have a high level of safety and quality with efficacy guaranteed from capsule to capsule.

If you want to use Asian ginseng for an extended period, consult with your doctor or a trained expert in the field of botanical medicine. Stop taking Asian ginseng at least one full week prior to a scheduled surgery, as the herb may act as a blood thinner and increase the risk of bleeding during or after a procedure.

To avoid hypoglycemia (low blood sugar), always take Asian ginseng with food, even if you don't have diabetes.

DRUG INTERACTIONS

Avoid Asian ginseng and products containing it except under a doctor's supervision if you are taking any of the following medications or drugs, as the herb may increase, decrease, or counteract their effects, or cause the drug to build up in the body:

- Alcohol
- Angiotensin-converting enzyme (ACE) inhibitors
- Anticoagulant (blood thinner) drugs, herbs, or supplements
- Antidepressants
- Antihypertensive drugs (high blood pressure medication)
- Antipsychotic medication, especially drugs for bipolar disorder and schizophrenia
- Caffeine
- Calcium channel blockers
- Diabetes medication
- Immunosuppressants
- Insulin
- Monoamine oxidase inhibitors (MAOIs)
- Morphine
- Stimulants, including amphetamines

Astragalus

From the bitterness of disease man learns the sweetness of health.

Catalan Proverb

OVERVIEW

Astragalus (*Astragalus membranaceus*) is a perennial flowering plant in the *Fabaceae* family that is native to the grasslands and mountains of central and western Asia, principally in China, Korea, and Taiwan. Also known as *huang qi*, which literally means "yellow senior," astragalus is one of the fifty fundamental herbs used in traditional Chinese medicine (TCM). It has been revered as an essential tonic for more than two thousand years.

Studies have shown that astragalus has antiviral properties and stimulates the immune system, suggesting that it may help prevent colds and similar viral infections. Astragalus is an adaptogen, an herb that increases the body's endurance and resistance to a range of biological, chemical, and physical stressors. Adaptogens have been found to enhance the immune response, reduce inflammation, and stabilize blood sugar. They also help normalize the functioning of various body systems, particularly the adrenal and pituitary glands, by affecting the action of hormones.

The taproot of the astragalus plant contains antioxidants that protect cells from damage. It's used medicinally to support the immune system and to help prevent upper respiratory infections, lower blood pressure, treat diabetes, and protect the liver. Astragalus also has both antibacterial and anti-inflammatory properties and is sometimes used topically in ointments to increase blood flow to a particular area of the body and to speed wound healing.

Researchers in the United States have been taking a look at astragalus as a possible treatment for patients whose immune systems have been weakened or compromised. Studies show that astragalus supplements may assist immunocompromised individuals with speedier recovery and improved longevity. Because astragalus is an antioxidant, it may aid in the treatment of heart disease, helping to lower cholesterol levels and improve heart function. It's also a mild diuretic, meaning that it can assist the body with getting rid of excess fluid.

Astragalus is often used to treat symptoms of acquired immune deficiency syndrome (AIDS), allergies, anemia, colds, fibromyalgia, flu, human immunodeficiency virus (HIV), and upper respiratory infections, and to strengthen and regulate the immune system. It's also used in the treatment of symptoms caused by chronic fatigue syndrome, diabetes, high blood pressure, and kidney disease. Some herbal practitioners prescribe astragalus to fight certain viral and bacterial infections, to protect the liver, and as a general tonic.

While astragalus is popular in the West primarily as a supplement to aid sleep, improve energy, and enhance libido, in TCM it is often combined with other herbs to strengthen the body and help prevent disease. Although astragalus has few side effects, especially at low to moderate dosages, it will interact with a number of other herbs and prescription medications. Because the herb may stimulate the immune system, if you have an autoimmune disease, you should speak with your doctor before taking astragalus.

PRIMARY EFFECTS

Astragalus has the following key actions on the body:

- Adaptogenic
- Antiallergenic
- Antioxidant
- Antiviral
- Cardiovascular toner
- Diuretic
- Hepatoprotective (protects the liver)
- Immunostimulant
- Laxative
- Strengthens the gastrointestinal tract
- Tonic
- Vasodilator (widens blood vessels)

PLANT DESCRIPTION

Astragalus, also called milk vetch root, is the root of the perennial plant *Astragalus membranaceus*, a member of the pea family. Astragalus grows to a height of sixteen to thirty-six inches and has hairy stems with leaves made up of twelve to eighteen pairs of leaflets. The large yellow taproot contains the highest concentration of active constituents, and it's usually harvested for medicinal use from plants that are four to seven years old. Although there are several different species in the *Astragalus* family, *Astragalus membranaceus* is the only one used for medicinal purposes.

AVAILABLE FORMS

Astragalus root is available in the following forms:

- Capsules (standardized and nonstandardized)

- Injectable forms (for use in hospital or clinical settings in Asian countries)
- Ointment
- Tablets (standardized and nonstandardized)
- Tincture

USAGE AND PRECAUTIONS

Astragalus should not be taken by pregnant women, as research in animals suggests that it can be toxic to the mother and fetus. Evidence about whether astragalus is safe for women who are breastfeeding is lacking. There also is limited research regarding giving astragalus to children, so don't administer it to a child without first talking with the child's pediatrician or healthcare provider. According to TCM, astragalus should not be given to a child with fever because the herb may worsen the fever and cause it to last longer. Dosage should be determined by a pediatrician.

Because astragalus may stimulate the immune system, it could worsen symptoms of autoimmune diseases. Avoid astragalus if you have any immune-related conditions, such as lupus, multiple sclerosis, or rheumatoid arthritis.

At this time there is insufficient scientific information to determine an appropriate dosage range for astragalus. However, astragalus has been reported as usually safe for most adults when taken by mouth or intravenously. Doses taken orally of up to 30 grams per day for three months and 40 grams per day for two months have been reported as safe, as have 80 grams per day taken intravenously for one month.

In adults, the appropriate dosage and dosing schedule should be established by a physician. Dosing depends on a number of factors, including the condition being treated and the patient's age, health, and weight. For the best results, a standardized astragalus supplement is preferred. Astragalus appears to have few side effects at low to moderate doses. However, it does interact with several other herbs and prescription medications and has mild diuretic effects.

DRUG INTERACTIONS

Avoid astragalus and products containing it except under a doctor's supervision if you are taking any of the following medications, as the herb may increase, decrease, or counteract their effects, or cause the drug to build up in the body:

- Anticoagulant (blood thinner) drugs, herbs, or supplements
- Antihypertensive drugs (high blood pressure medication)
- Antiviral medication
- Diabetes medication
- Diuretics (water pills)
- Immunosuppressants
- Insulin
- Lithium

Baikal (Chinese) Skullcap

You know what they call alternative medicine that's been proved to work? Medicine.

Tim Minchin, Australian comedian, actor, composer, musician, and director

OVERVIEW

The term "skullcap" typically refers to one of two species in the same botanical family: Baikal (Chinese) skullcap (*Scutellaria baicalensis*) and American skullcap (*Scutellaria lateriflora*), also known as blue skullcap. Each type is used to treat different conditions, and the herbs are not interchangeable. Most scientific research has been done on Baikal skullcap.

Native to China and parts of Russia, Baikal skullcap, also known as Baical skullcap, Chinese skullcap, *huang qin*, and golden root, is one of the fifty fundamental herbs essential to traditional Chinese medicine and has been used in China for over two thousand years. Today Baikal skullcap is often prescribed by herbalists and alternative healthcare practitioners to treat acquired immune deficiency syndrome (AIDs), allergic rhinitis (hay fever), atherosclerosis, cancer, coughs, dermatitis, dysentery, fever, gastrointestinal infections, headaches, human immunodeficiency virus infection (HIV), inflammation, jaundice, kidney infections, seizures, upper respiratory infections, urinary tract infections, viral hepatitis, and other ailments.

The flavonoid baicalin is one of the primary active constituents in *Scutellaria baicalensis*. In a variety of studies, the antiviral effects of baicalin have been reported in numerous RNA viruses (viruses that have ribonucleic acid as their genetic material), suggesting that baicalin has broad antiviral activity. Research indicates that baicalin induces its antiviral effects by modulating the function of a protein that regulates the host's innate immune responses.

In laboratory studies, baicalin has demonstrated anti-influenza viral activity, both in vitro and in vivo. Antiviral effects of baicalin on dengue virus, hepatitis B virus, HIV-1 virus, herpes simplex virus-1 (HSV-1), and influenza A virus (IAV) have also been reported. Studies done on enterovirus 71 (EV71) showed that baicalin exhibits a strong antiviral effect on EV71 replication at early stages of infection, with high efficacy and low toxicity.

In traditional Chinese medicine, baicalin is used orally in combination with *shung hua* (ephedra) to treat upper respiratory tract infections. In combination with other herbs, Baikal skullcap is used to treat arthritis, attention deficit-hyperactivity disorder (ADHD), bronchiolitis (an inflammatory lung condition), hemorrhoids, and prostate cancer. Baikal skullcap is also used topically in ointment as a treatment for psoriasis.

PRIMARY EFFECTS

Baikal (Chinese) skullcap has the following key actions on the body:

- Antibacterial
- Anticancer
- Anticholesterolemic (prevents the buildup of cholesterol)
- Anti-inflammatory
- Antimicrobial
- Antioxidant
- Antipyretic (prevents or reduces fever)
- Antispasmodic
- Antiviral
- Astringent
- Diuretic
- Febrifuge (reduces fever)
- Haemostatic (prevents or stops hemorrhaging)
- Immunoprotective (protects the immune system)
- Neuroprotective (protects the nervous system)
- Sedative
- Strengthens the circulatory system
- Tonic

PLANT DESCRIPTION

Baikal skullcap (*Scutellaria baicalensis*) is native to China, Japan, Korea, Mongolia, and Russia, where it thrives on sunny, grassy slopes and grows well in dry, sandy soil. It's usually found in open locations that are between 350 and 8,000 feet above sea level. It grows from one to four feet in height and produces lance-shaped leaves and purplish-blue flowers. The herb's name is derived from the cap-like appearance of the outer whorl of its blooms. Its beige taproot is stout and slightly conical, and the roots are harvested for medicinal purposes in autumn or spring from plants that are three to four years old. Baikal (Chinese) skullcap is related to and resembles American skullcap, but they are two distinctly different plants.

AVAILABLE FORMS

Baicalin is available powdered or in capsules. Baikal skullcap root is available in the following forms:

- Capsules
- Dried, for making decoctions (boiling the root in water)
- Liquid extract
- Powder
- Tablets
- Tinctures

Read product labels carefully to make sure you're getting the type of skullcap you want. For Baikal (Chinese) skullcap, look for *Scutellaria baicalensis*. It may also be combined with other herbs.

USAGE AND PRECAUTIONS

Baikal skullcap may be safe when administered to children intravenously by a physician for a short period (no more than seven days). There is insufficient evidence about the safety of Baikal skullcap in children when used for longer periods. It is advisable for pregnant or breastfeeding women to avoid Baikal skullcap, as there is little reliable information about its safety for the fetus or infant.

Baikal skullcap should be safe for most adults when taken orally. A daily dosage of 250–500 milligrams of baicalin, taken in one or two doses, has been used safely in clinical trials lasting four to twelve weeks. Common side effects are drowsiness and a drop in blood pressure. There is limited information about other side effects from Baikal skullcap, but there have been some reports of fever and lung inflammation. However, these effects are thought to be due to allergic or hypersensitivity reactions in a small number of people.

Both Baikal (Chinese) and American skullcap can increase the sedative effects of drugs or herbs that have a sedating effect, including the following:

- Alcohol
- Anticonvulsants
- Barbiturates
- Benzodiazepines, such as alprazolam (Xanax) and diazepam (Valium)
- Catnip
- Insomnia drugs, such as eszopiclone (Lunesta), ramelteon (Rozerem), zaleplon (Sonata), and zolpidem (Ambien)
- Kava kava
- Tricyclic antidepressants, such as amitriptyline (Elavil)
- Valerian

Baikal skullcap should be avoided if you are taking anticoagulant or antiplatelet herbs or supplements, such as angelica, clove, danshen, garlic, ginger, ginkgo, or *Panax ginseng* (see page 70), among others. Note that garlic and garlic supplements may decrease the absorption of baicalin.

Baicalin might also lower blood sugar levels. If you have diabetes, watch for signs of hypoglycemia (low blood sugar) and monitor your blood sugar carefully, especially if you use Baikal skullcap in amounts larger than would normally be found as a seasoning in food. Baikal skullcap and baicalin may lower blood pressure, causing it to become too low in people who already have low blood pressure or who are on blood pressure medication.

If you are being treated for or have a history of any of the following conditions, do not take Baikal skullcap or products containing it without first consulting with your physician:

- Acute illness of any kind
- Bleeding disorders
- Diabetes
- Hormone-sensitive conditions
- Hypotension (low blood pressure)

If you have surgery scheduled, stop taking Baikal skullcap at least one full week prior to your procedure. Baikal skullcap can lower blood glucose levels and create problems for patients fasting before surgery. Also, Baikal skullcap may slow blood clotting, increasing the risk of bleeding during or after the procedure.

DRUG INTERACTIONS

Avoid Baikal skullcap or products containing it except under a doctor's supervision if you are taking any of the following medications, as the herb may increase, decrease, or counteract their effects, or cause the drug to build up in the body:

- Alcohol
- Anticoagulant (blood thinner) drugs, herbs, or supplements
- Antiplatelet drugs, herbs, or supplements
- Cholesterol-lowering drugs (statins)
- Diabetes medication
- Hypotensive drugs (low blood pressure medication)
- Insulin
- Lithium
- Sedatives

Barberry

Isn't it a bit unnerving that doctors call what they do "practice"?

George Carlin (1937–2008), American stand-up comedian, actor, social critic, and author

OVERVIEW

Barberry (*Berberis vulgaris*), also known as European barberry, is native to Europe, where it is often used as an ornamental shrub. It is also commonly grown in North America. Oregon grape (*Berberis aquifolium*), a close relative, is native to North America. Two other species, Indian and Nepalese barberry, are native to those respective regions and possess similar qualities.

Barberry has been used medicinally in Asia for about three thousand years. A staple in Indian folk medicine (Ayurveda) for centuries, it's been used to combat diarrhea, relieve heartburn, treat biliary disorders, reduce fever, stimulate appetite, enhance energy, and improve overall well-being. Berberine, an alkaloid also found in goldenseal (*Hydrastis canadensis*), is one of the chief active ingredients in the stem, root bark, and fruit of the barberry plant. In laboratory studies, berberine has been shown to stimulate and strengthen the immune system, and modern research has confirmed what herbalists have known for millennia—berberine has remarkable medicinal properties and has been proven effective in treating a variety of ailments.

Recent studies suggest that berberine has antioxidant and anti-inflammatory properties and may help prevent certain types of cancer. In addition, berberine has been used in China to treat white blood cell depression caused by chemotherapy or radiation treatments.

Berberine has demonstrated antimicrobial potential that could help with eradicating harmful bacteria and parasites. The aqueous (water-based) extract of barberry has beneficial effects on the cardiovascular system and may be useful in the treatment of hypertension (abnormally high blood pressure) and tachycardia (rapid heartbeat). The extract also has a positive effect on the nervous system, and its anticonvulsant properties may be of benefit in treating certain neuronal disorders, such as epilepsy and seizures. Barberry may also have hypotensive (the ability to lower blood pressure) and sedative effects. Berberine affects the smooth muscle that lines the intestines, and this property may aid digestion and decrease gastrointestinal pain.

Barberry may be an effective treatment for diarrhea, including diarrhea caused by bacteria-related food poisoning or contaminated water. Some studies suggest that barberry may improve symptoms faster than antibiotics, possibly due to the herb's astringent properties, but antibiotics may be more effective at destroying bacteria in the intestinal tract. Although barberry may help ease symptoms, it's best to take the herb along with prescribed antibiotics because of the serious consequences associated with bacterial diarrhea. Be aware that taking barberry with antibiotics may reduce the effectiveness of the drug, so talk with your doctor or healthcare provider before trying this combination.

In addition to possessing antiviral, antibacterial, and antifungal properties, barberry has demonstrated antiprotozoal effects, making it a valuable tool in fighting all types of gastroenteritis. It is specifically effective in inhibiting the growth of *Entamoeba histolytica* (the parasite that causes amebiasis, which includes dysentery), *Giardia intestinalis* (previously known as *Giardia lamblia*, the flagellate protozoan that causes giardiasis, a major diarrheal disease found throughout the world), and *Trichomonas vaginalis* (the tiny, anaerobic, flagellated protozoan parasite and causative agent of the sexually transmitted disease trichomoniasis). Barberry's actions are similar to common antiprotozoal medications but with the distinct advantage of having no side effects. The herb has even been used to treat malaria and leishmaniasis, a parasitic disease found in parts of southern Europe and the tropics and subtropics.

PRIMARY EFFECTS

Barberry has the following key actions on the body:

- Antimicrobial
- Antioxidant
- Antiparasitic
- Antiprotozoal
- Antiviral
- Cardiovascular toner
- Hypotensive (lowers blood pressure)
- Immunostimulant
- Neuroprotective (protects the nervous system)
- Sedative
- Strengthens the gastrointestinal tract

PLANT DESCRIPTION

Barberry is a bushy, perennial shrub with woody stems, ash-colored bark, and thorny branches that grows eight to ten feet high. Barberry flourishes in dry, sandy soil and prefers sunny locations. It blooms between April and June with bright yellow flowers that turn to drooping bunches of dark-red berries in the fall. The bark, berries, and root are all used for medicinal purposes. The cultivation of barberry is restricted in some areas, as it hosts and promotes stem rust, a scourge to cereal crops.

AVAILABLE FORMS

Barberry is available in the following forms:

- Capsules
- Dried root (which can be infused for tea)
- Liquid extract (standardized to contain 8–12 percent berberine)
- Ointment
- Tincture

USAGE AND PRECAUTIONS

Berberine, the active constituent in barberry, may interfere with liver function in infants and could worsen jaundice, a condition caused by too much bilirubin in the baby's system. Because barberry can cause uterine contractions and may trigger miscarriage, it should be avoided by pregnant women. Additionally, the berberine in the herb can pass from a mother's body into her unborn child through the placenta. Brain damage has developed in newborns exposed to berberine. Similarly, berberine, as well as other harmful chemicals in barberry, can be transferred to an infant through breast milk and might cause brain damage. Barberry is likely unsafe for children in certain dosages, and at this time there is insufficient evidence to establish a specific dose. Do not administer barberry to children without the direction and supervision of a pediatrician.

Dosages for adults should be determined by a physician or qualified healthcare provider. Do not take barberry for more than seven days without the approval and oversight of a doctor. Strong extracts may cause stomach upset, especially when used for longer periods.

Berberine, the active chemical in barberry, might slow blood clotting, increase the risk of bleeding, and worsen bleeding disorders. Berberine might also lower blood sugar levels. If you have diabetes, watch for signs of hypoglycemia (low blood sugar) and monitor your blood sugar carefully, especially if you use barberry in amounts larger than would normally be found as a seasoning in food. Berberine may lower blood pressure, causing it to become too low in people who already have low blood pressure or who are on blood pressure medication.

There is concern that berberine might prolong bleeding, depress the nervous system, and interfere with blood sugar control during and after surgery. Stop taking barberry at least two weeks prior to a scheduled surgical procedure.

Do not take barberry or products containing berberine if you have chronic respiratory problems or heart disease.

When recommended doses of barberry are used, side effects are unusual. With extremely high doses, kidney irritation, lethargy, low blood sugar, nosebleeds, skin and eye inflammation, and vomiting have been reported. Because barberry works on the liver and most medications are metabolized by the liver, the herb may alter the effects of medications. Additionally, a wide range of drugs, herbs, and supplements may interact with barberry; consult your physician or healthcare provider about potential interactions.

If you are being treated for or have a history of any of the following conditions, do not take barberry or products containing it without first talking with your physician:

- Bleeding disorders
- Chronic respiratory problems
- Diabetes
- Heart disease
- Hypertension (high blood pressure)
- Hypotension (low blood pressure)

DRUG INTERACTIONS

Avoid barberry and products containing it except under a doctor's supervision if you are taking any of the following medications, as the herb may increase, decrease, or counteract their effects, or cause the drug to build up in the body:

- Antibiotics
- Anticoagulant (blood thinner) drugs, herbs, or supplements
- Antihistamines
- Antihypertensive drugs (high blood pressure medication)
- Anti-inflammatory drugs
- Diabetes medication
- Diuretics (water pills)
- Hypotensive drugs (low blood pressure medication)
- Insulin
- Medications processed by the liver, such as celecoxib (Celebrex), diclofenac (Voltaren), fluvastatin (Lescol), glipizide (Glucotrol), ibuprofen (Advil, Motrin), phenobarbital, phenytoin (Dilantin), piroxicam (Feldene), and secobarbital (Seconal), among others
- Nonsteroidal anti-inflammatory drugs (NSAIDs), such as ibuprofen or naproxen

Echinacea

A bad cold wouldn't be so annoying if it weren't for the advice of our friends.

Kin Hubbard (1868–1930), American cartoonist, humorist, and journalist

OVERVIEW

One of the most popular medicinal herbs in the United States, echinacea is a perennial that's native to areas east of the Rocky Mountains; it's also grown in western states as well as in Canada and Europe. The genus name *Echinacea* is derived from the Greek *echinos*, which literally means "hedgehog" and refers to the appearance of the herb's spiny seed head. It was named by the eighteenth-century botanist Conrad Moench because the seed head reminded him of a hedgehog or sea urchin. Echinacea is also known as purple coneflower, coneflower, and American coneflower.

There is archaeological evidence that Native Americans used echinacea for more than four hundred years as a general curative and to treat burns, coughs, fever, infections, snakebites and other venomous bites and stings, sore throats, toothaches, and wounds. Once European settlers learned of the North American herb's many uses, they quickly adopted it as a remedy for colds and influenza and brought it back to Europe with them in the seventeenth century.

A group of doctors known as American Eclectics, who were prominent from 1830 to 1930, used botanical medicinals in their practices. The group became a leading force in bringing echinacea to the forefront of herbal medicine in the United States. Historically echinacea has been used to treat a broad range of ailments: blood poisoning, diphtheria, malaria, scarlet fever, and syphilis. After enjoying great popularity in the United States during the eighteenth and nineteenth centuries, the herb's useage waned during the twentieth century, due largely to the introduction of antibiotics. However, echinacea became increasingly popular in Germany at that time, and much scientific research on the herb has been conducted there. Echinacea regained its stature in the United States in the 1970s and '80s with the revival of herbal medicine. In the last fifty years, it has achieved worldwide popularity as an antiviral, antibacterial, and antifungal.

Echinacea has been found to stimulate the production of leukocytes, the white blood cells that fight infection. It also assists phagocytes, which are cells that engulf and absorb toxins so they can be removed from the body. The herb has a mild antibiotic effect, helping to protect cells from invading pathogens, such as viruses, bacteria, and fungi. Echinacea stimulates properdin, a protein present in the blood that helps the body control and prevent infection, and increases production of alpha- and alpha-2 gamma globulins, which prevent viral and other types of infections.

Today many herbalists recommend echinacea to prevent, minimize the symptoms of, or shorten the duration of colds, flu, and other infections based on the belief that the herb stimulates and strengthens the immune system to more effectively fight infection. Research on whether echinacea can help prevent or treat the common cold has been contradictory and controversial, and echinacea preparations tested in clinical trials have differed greatly, most likely due to which part of the plant was used, which species of the plant was used, and the concentration of specific active substances used in the studies. However, a review of fourteen clinical studies examining the effect of echinacea on the incidence and duration of the common cold found that echinacea supplements decreased the odds of getting a cold by 58 percent. If you want to try echinacea for this purpose, it's important to choose a high-quality product, use it as soon as the first signs of cold symptoms appear, and take multiple doses per day for the first several days. Talk to your healthcare provider regarding recommended products and dosages.

Results from a number of studies indicate the active substances in echinacea (alkamides, flavonoids, glycoproteins, polysaccharides, and volatile oils) may boost immune function and offer antiviral, antioxidant, and hormonal effects. These substances may also help to relieve pain and reduce inflammation. For this reason, professional herbalists, naturopaths, and other practitioners of alternative medicine regularly turn to echinacea to treat a variety of health conditions and infections: acquired immune deficiency syndrome (AIDS), allergic rhinitis (hay fever), anxiety, athlete's foot, candida (vaginal yeast infection), chronic fatigue syndrome, ear infections, human immunodeficiency virus (HIV), human papillomavirus (HPV), indigestion, migraine headaches, nose or throat infections, rheumatoid arthritis, sinusitis, swine flu, urinary tract infections, and warts.

Echinacea may be applied topically to treat abscesses, bee stings, boils, burns, eczema, gum disease, hemorrhoids, herpes simplex outbreaks, psoriasis, slow-healing wounds, snake and mosquito bites, and sun-related skin damage. It may also be used as an injection to treat vaginal yeast infections and urinary tract infections. One study suggests that echinacea extract may exert antiviral action on the development of recurrent cold sores caused by the herpes simplex virus when the herb is taken prior to an outbreak.

There are are nine known species of echinacea, but only three are typically used for medicinal purposes: *Echinacea angustifolia*, *Echinacea pallida*, and *Echinacea purpurea*. Although *Echinacea purpurea* is the type most commonly used, echinacea preparations may contain any one of these species or a combination of two or even all three of them.

PRIMARY EFFECTS

Echinacea has the following key actions on the body:

- Antiallergenic
- Antibiotic
- Antimicrobial
- Antiviral
- Bactericidal
- Collagen protectant
- Cytokine stimulant against tumor cells
- Immunostimulant
- Lymphatic tonic
- Wound healer

PLANT DESCRIPTION

The echinacea plant has tall stems and bears single pink or purple flowers. Its large central cone, which is actually a seed head, is either brown or purple and is surrounded by sharp spines that resemble a stiff comb (or angry hedgehog). The aboveground parts of the plant and deep, slender, black roots are used fresh or dried to make extracts, pressed juice, preparations for topical use, or tea.

The chemical composition of the upper portion and the root of *Echinacea purpurea* differ considerably. The aerial parts contain a greater concentration of polysaccharides, the substances known to stimulate the immune system. The roots have significant amounts of volatile oils. Although the combination of these active substances may be responsible for the herb's beneficial effects, when it comes to their antiviral potential and ability to boost the immune system, the aboveground portion is more effective. Because different products incorporate different parts of the echinacea plant, efficacy and potency may vary significantly from one product or brand to another. Whenever possible, select standardized extracts or products with a guaranteed potency, and only purchase those made by reputable companies that distribute their products through trustworthy channels, as some echinacea products may be contaminated with arsenic, lead, or selenium.

Echinacea is cultivated widely in both medicinal and ornamental gardens and propagates easily from seeds or root cuttings. However, because of its increasing popularity as an herbal supplement, echinacea is numbered among the top medicinal plants considered at risk by the Vermont nonprofit organization United Plant Savers (unitedplantsavers.org).

AVAILABLE FORMS

All three species of echinacea (*Echinacea angustifolia*, *Echinacea pallida*, and *Echinacea purpurea*) are available alone or in combination in the following forms:

- Capsules
- Extract
- Juice
- Ointment
- Tablets
- Tea
- Tincture

Echinacea is also available in products combined with other immune-boosting herbs and in vitamin and/or mineral supplements.

USAGE AND PRECAUTIONS

Although rare, echinacea may cause allergic reactions that can range from a mild rash to life-threatening anaphylaxis. People with allergies or asthma may be at increased risk for developing an adverse reaction. In particular, individuals allergic to plants in the daisy family (*Asteraceae* or *Compositae*) should not take echinacea without the supervision of a doctor.

When echinacea is taken orally, it may cause temporary tingling or numbing of the tongue. Additional minor side effects can include the following:

- Dizziness
- Dry eyes
- Nausea
- Stomach upset

Echinacea doesn't appear to increase the risk of birth defects or contribute to other pregnancy-related health concerns. However, until more-conclusive studies are conducted, it is advised that pregnant and breastfeeding women avoid using echinacea.

Do not give echinacea to children unless under a doctor's supervision. Always consult with the child's pediatrician or an herbal practitioner specializing in pediatrics to determine the proper dosage. Use only alcohol-free preparations for children.

For adults, take echinacea with food or a large glass of water. Do not ingest echinacea on an empty stomach. For general immune system stimulation at the onset of a cold, flu, upper respiratory infection, or urinary tract infection, take echinacea three times a day until symptoms improve. Do not take echinacea for longer than ten days.

A popular treatment for the common cold is 20 drops of *Echinacea purpurea* extract in water every two hours on the first day symptoms appear, followed by three times daily for up to ten days. An alternative treatment is taking 5 milliliters of the extract twice daily for ten days. Another option is to drink 1 cup of tea that contains multiple species of echinacea (such as Echinacea Plus by Traditional Medicinals) five or six times on the first day of cold symptoms, then decrease the dose by 1 cup per day over the next five days.

For slow-healing wounds, apply echinacea ointment as needed.

Taking echinacea along with caffeine may cause too much caffeine to build up in the bloodstream and may increase the risk of side effects, such as headache, jitteriness, and rapid heartbeat.

Echinacea may reduce the effectiveness of medications that suppress the immune system. Organ transplant recipients who must take immunosuppressant medications should avoid this herb. If you are being treated for or have a history of any of the following conditions, do not take echinacea or products containing it without first consulting with your physician:

- Acquired immune deficiency syndrome (AIDS)
- Autoimmune diseases
- Connective tissue disorders
- Diabetes
- Human immunodeficiency virus (HIV)
- Leukemia
- Liver disorders
- Multiple sclerosis
- Organ transplant
- Tuberculosis

DRUG INTERACTIONS

If you are taking any prescription drugs, including those used during surgery, such as anesthesia medications, you should talk to your doctor before using echinacea. Avoid echinacea except under a doctor's supervision if you are taking any of the following medications or drugs, as the herb may increase, decrease, or counteract their effects, or cause the drug to build up in the body:

- Caffeine
- Immunosuppressants

Elderberry

A cough is a symptom, not a disease. Take it to your doctor and he can give you something serious to worry about.

Robert Morley (1908–1992), English actor

OVERVIEW

Elderberry (*Sambucus nigra*) is native to Europe, Africa, and parts of Asia, but it has become widespread in the United States. *Sambucus canadensis*, also known as American black elderberry, is a species of elderberry native to a large area of North America east of the Rocky Mountains and south through eastern Mexico and Central America to Panama.

Elderberry flowers and fruit (berries) have been used in folk remedies for centuries in North America, Europe, western Asia, and North Africa and are widely used in herbal medicine today. Often referred to as "nature's medicine chest," elderberry is most recognized for its immune-supporting properties and its ability to fight viral and bacterial infections. In the early 1990s, elderberry extract was used to effectively treat flu symptoms during an influenza epidemic in Panama. Currently no satisfactory medication is available that can cure influenza types A and B, but elderberry extract, with its promising clinical trials, low cost, and absence of side effects, could potentially offer a safe treatment.

Elderberries are rich in vitamin C as well as anthocyanins, one of the most widely studied flavonoid categories. Anthocyanins, which have impressive antioxidant capacities and immunostimulant effects, are the water-soluble pigments responsible for the dark red-purple color found in certain flowers, fruits, and vegetables. The darker the berry, the more anthocyanins are present. Elderberries contain nearly four times the anthocyanins as other commonly consumed berries, outranking blackberries, blueberries, cranberries, and goji berries in total flavonoid content. The anthocyanins and other flavonoids in elderberry, including quercetin, are believed to account for the therapeutic actions of the plant's berries and flowers.

Elderberry has been used for centuries to treat wounds when applied to the skin. Some evidence suggests that chemicals in the berries and flowers may have anticancer and anti-inflammatory effects and may help reduce swelling in mucous membranes, including the sinuses, thereby relieving nasal congestion. Herbal practitioners often prescribe elderberry to treat the flu and other viral infections, reduce inflammation, and boost the immune system. The herb may also be prescribed to treat allergic rhinitis (hay fever), chronic fatigue syndrome, constipation, neuralgia (nerve pain), sciatica, and sinus pain, and to increase urine output and sweating. Elderberry is believed to help combat diabetes; research has shown that extracts of the flowers stimulate glucose metabolism and the secretion of insulin, which may help to lower blood sugar levels.

Sambucol brand products are based on a standardized black elderberry extract. These natural remedies have proven antiviral properties, especially against different strains of the influenza virus. In fact, Sambucol was shown to be effective in vitro against ten strains of the influenza virus. And in a double-blind, placebo-controlled, randomized study, Sambucol decreased the duration of flu symptoms to about three days. In addition to its antiviral properties, Sambucol elderberry extract and its formulations have been shown in studies to boost immune function by increasing inflammatory cytokine production, which benefits healthy individuals as well as people with a variety of diseases. Research also suggests that Sambucol could have immunoprotective and immunostimulant effects when administered to patients with acquired immune deficiency syndrome (AIDS), cancer, or human immunodeficiency virus (HIV) in conjunction with chemotherapy or related treatments.

Although there are several species of elderberry, *Sambucus nigra* and *Sambucus canadensis* are the ones typically used for medicinal purposes. Always use trusted preparations of elderberry because the raw and unripe fruit, as well as the bark, leaves, and seeds, contain a chemical related to cyanide, which is poisonous.

PRIMARY EFFECTS

Elderberry has the following key actions on the body:

BARK

- Diuretic
- Emollient (topical)
- Laxative
- Promotes vomiting (in large doses)

BERRIES

- Diaphoretic (promotes sweating)
- Diuretic
- Laxative

FLOWERS

- Anti-inflammatory
- Circulatory stimulant
- Diaphoretic (promotes sweating)
- Diuretic
- Expectorant
- Reduces phlegm

PLANT DESCRIPTION

Elderberry is a large, hardy, deciduous shrub that thrives in sunny areas in wet or dry soil and can reach heights of thirty feet. Its broad leaves grow in opposite pairs of five to seven leaflets and exude a distinctive aroma. The flowers are white and flat, topped with five primary rays. The berries turn from green to red to black, dark blue, or purple when ripe. The unripe (green and red) berries are toxic and should not consumed; only the ripe black, blue, and purple berries of elderberry are edible and are used for medicinal purposes. The elderberry plant flowers in May to July and produces berries between September and October.

AVAILABLE FORMS

Elderberry is available in the following forms:

- Capsules
- Dried flowers
- Liquid extract
- Lozenges
- Syrup
- Tincture

Dried elderflowers are usually standardized to at least 0.8 percent flavonoids. Sambucol brand black elderberry products are standardized to 38 percent elderberry extract for adults and 19 percent for children. Sinupret (made by Bionorica) syrup and tablets contain 18 milligrams of elderflowers.

USAGE AND PRECAUTIONS

Do not give elderberry or any product containing any part of the plant to children without the approval and supervision of a pediatrician. Herbal remedies containing elderberry should be avoided by pregnant and breastfeeding women, as there is insufficient information regarding their safety.

The flowers and fruit of the elderberry plant contain a mildly poisonous alkaloid that is destroyed by cooking; the leaves are also poisonous. Never use unripe or raw (uncooked) elderberries, as they may be toxic.

Elderflowers and elderberries occasionally cause allergic reactions. When used for short periods (up to five days) in appropriate dosages, elderberry appears to have few side effects.

Because elderberry may stimulate the immune system, consult with your doctor before using it if you have an autoimmune disease, such as lupus or rheumatoid arthritis.

A standard dose of Sambucol brand black elderberry extract for adults is 4 tablespoons per day for three days to treat symptoms of the common cold and flu. A standard dose of Sinupret (made by Bionorica) for adults is 2 tablets taken three times per day for bacterial sinusitis. To make elderberry tea, steep 3–5 grams of dried elderflowers in 1 cup of boiling water for 10–15 minutes. Strain before serving. Drink 1 cup of the tea three times per day.

DRUG INTERACTIONS

Do not use elderberry if you are taking medications to suppress the immune system, including corticosteroids, as the herb may reduce their effectiveness. Organ transplant recipients who must take immunosuppressant drugs should not use elderberry. Avoid elderberry and products containing it except under a doctor's supervision if you are taking any of the following medications, as the herb may increase, decrease, or counteract their effects, or cause the drug to build up in the body:

- Chemotherapy drugs
- Corticosteroids (such as prednisone)
- Diabetes medication
- Diuretics (water pills)
- Immunosuppressants
- Insulin
- Laxatives
- Theophylline (a drug used to treat asthma and other respiratory conditions)

Lemon Balm

Adam and Eve ate the first vitamins, including the package.

Edward Robinson Squibb (1819–1900), American physician, chemist, and pharmacist

OVERVIEW

Lemon balm (*Melissa officinalis*) is a citrus-scented, aromatic, perennial herb that's a member of the *Lamiaceae*, or mint, family. It's a soothing, sedative herb that can relieve tension and lift depression. Because of its proven calming effects, it has earned the nickname "herb of good cheer."

Lemon balm was used as far back as the Middle Ages to soothe anxiety, aid sleep, improve appetite, promote good digestion, relieve flatulence, and alleviate colic. Even before the Middle Ages, lemon balm was steeped in wine to lift the spirits, help heal wounds, and treat venomous insect bites and stings. The Greeks used lemon balm medicinally over two thousand years ago. Honeybees swarm to the plant, and their attraction to it inspired the genus name *Melissa*, the Greek word for "honeybee." The Romans introduced lemon balm to Great Britain, where it became a popular garden herb. The plant is now naturalized around the world, from North America to New Zealand. Today lemon balm is favored by herbalists for promoting relaxation, and it's often combined with other calming herbs, such as chamomile, hops, and valerian.

A number of studies suggest that topical ointments containing lemon balm may help treat cold sores caused by the herpes simplex virus by significantly decreasing redness and swelling, shortening healing time, and effectively preventing recurrence. Topical preparations have also been found to reduce the healing time of lesions caused by genital herpes. Studies suggest that lemon balm reduces the development of resistance in the herpes virus and blocks the attachment of the virus to the receptor sites of host cells, preventing the spread of infection. In preliminary studies, lemon balm in high concentrations has also exhibited activity against human immunodeficiency virus (HIV) infection.

Lemon balm contains volatile oils, including citral (geranial and neral), citronellal, eugenol, and linalool, along with a variety of chemical compounds, including flavonoids, polyphenols, rosmarinic acid, tannins, and triterpenoids. These biologically active constituents account for the herb's antiviral, antioxidant, and immune-boosting effects.

Lemon balm's lemony fragrance and flavor are largely attributed to citral and citronellal. However, other phytochemicals, including geraniol (which is rose scented) and linalool (which is lavender scented) also contribute to the herb's distinctive aroma.

Lemon balm supplements are made from the leaves of the plant. Essential oils derived from lemon balm leaves contain plant chemicals called terpenes, which play a primary role in the herb's calming effects. Both the terpenes and tannins in lemon balm are responsible for many of its antiviral effects. The eugenol in lemon balm calms muscle spasms, kills bacteria, and numbs tissues.

PRIMARY EFFECTS

Lemon balm has the following key actions on the body:

- Antibacterial
- Antidepressant
- Antihistamine
- Antispasmodic
- Antiviral
- Carminative (relieves flatulence)
- Diaphoretic (promotes sweating)
- Digestive stimulant
- Restorative for the nervous system
- Sedative
- Tonic

PLANT DESCRIPTION

Lemon balm grows in bushy clumps to about two feet tall or higher if not trimmed, and it branches out to about eighteen inches. It thrives in full sun or partial shade in moist, fertile soil from mountainous to coastal regions. The heart-shaped, deeply wrinkled leaves are heavily veined, with scalloped edges and square, velvety stems. The leaves range in color from dark green to yellow-green depending on the soil and climate in which the plant is grown, and they emit a pleasant lemony scent when rubbed or crushed. The tiny golden or white blossoms grow in the leaf axils and bloom from June through October. Lemon balm is a hardy, self-seeding plant and spreads easily in the proper soil conditions. The essential oil content is concentrated primarily in the top third of the plant.

AVAILABLE FORMS

Lemon balm is available in the following forms:

- Capsules
- Dried leaves (loose tea)
- Essential oil
- Extracts
- Tea bags
- Tinctures

Some topical creams containing high levels of lemon balm are available in Europe but not the United States. If lemon balm cream isn't available, the warm or cool brewed tea can be applied to the skin using cotton balls. Lemon balm is also available in homeopathic remedies.

Lemon balm combines well with the leaves of nettle (*Urtica dioica*) and peppermint (*Mentha piperita*), as well as the flowers of chamomile (*Matricaria chamomilla*).

USAGE AND PRECAUTIONS

Lemon balm leaves and flowers are used in medicinal remedies and are the most potent when freshly picked. The volatile oils will diminish in medicinal potency when the herb is stored. Freezing the freshly harvested herb is a good way to preserve the leaves for later use.

Do not give lemon balm orally to children unless under a doctor's supervision. Lemon balm may be used topically on children to treat cold sores. Speak with the child's pediatrician or healthcare provider regarding the appropriate dosage based on the child's age.

Pregnant and breastfeeding women should avoid using lemon balm, as there is insufficient evidence regarding its safety.

The sedative effect of lemon balm means that it can depress the central nervous system when given in high doses. Lemon balm might cause too much drowsiness if combined with medications used during and after surgery. Stop using lemon balm at least two weeks prior to a scheduled surgical procedure.

People with glaucoma should avoid using lemon balm essential oil because it may raise the pressure inside the eye.

In research, lemon balm has been used safely for up to four months. Do not take lemon balm longer than that because not enough is known about the safety of its long-term use.

When lemon balm is taken orally, it may cause some side effects, including the following:

- Abdominal pain
- Dizziness
- Nausea
- Vomiting
- Wheezing

For difficulty sleeping or to reduce bloating, flatulence, or indigestion, consult a knowledgeable healthcare provider for the specific dose that will best fit your needs. The following are some common dosages:

- Capsules: Take 300–500 milligrams of dried lemon balm three times daily or as needed.

- Tea: Put ¼–1 teaspoon of dried lemon balm leaves in 1 cup of hot water, or put 2 ounces of fresh lemon balm leaves in a heatproof container and add 2½ cups of boiling water. Steep for 10 minutes and strain. Drink 3–4 cups of the warm or chilled tea per day. The prepared tea will keep for two days stored in a sealed container in the refrigerator.

- Tincture: Take 60 drops of lemon balm daily.

- Topical: Apply a topical cream to the affected area three times per day or as directed by your healthcare provider.

- For cold sores or genital herpes sores: Steep 2–4 teaspoons of crushed lemon balm leaves in 1 cup of boiling water for 10–15 minutes. Cool and strain. Apply the tea with cotton balls to the sores throughout the day.

DRUG INTERACTIONS

Lemon balm should be used in lower doses when combined with other herbs, particularly those with a sedative effect, such as chamomile and valerian. Never take lemon balm when using alcohol or taking prescription sedatives, as it can intensify their effects.

Lemon balm has been reported to interfere with the action of thyroid hormones. Do not use lemon balm if you are taking any medication containing thyroid hormones.

Avoid lemon balm and products containing it except under a doctor's supervision if you are taking any of the following medications, as the herb may increase, decrease, or counteract their effects, or cause the drug to build up in the body:

- Barbiturates
- Human immunodeficiency virus (HIV) medication
- Sedatives
- Thyroid medication

Licorice

OVERVIEW

Licorice (*Glycyrrhiza glabra*) originated in the Mediterranean region and in central and southwest Asia and has been cultivated in Europe since the sixteenth century. A staple both in Eastern and Western medicine, licorice has been used to treat a variety of illnesses, from the common cold to liver disease. The medicinal benefits of licorice root have been studied extensively, and its use in traditional herbal medicine is well documented.

Glycyrrhiza is a Greek word meaning "sweet root." The glycoside glycyrrhizin, found in the root, is more than fifty times as sweet as sugar. The roots and rhizomes are the main medicinal parts of licorice, although glycyrrhizin, which is converted to glycyrrhizic acid when ingested, is credited with much of the medicinal action of licorice. However, nearly three hundred flavonoids and more than twenty triterpenoids (a class of chemical compounds) have been isolated from licorice. Recent studies have shown these compounds to possess numerous pharmacological effects, including antiviral, antimicrobial, anti-inflammatory, antitumor, and other beneficial effects.

In recent years many studies have confirmed the antiviral activity of glycyrrhizin, indicating potential novel roles for glycyrrhizin in the treatment of patients suffering from chronic hepatitis C, herpes simplex virus, human immunodeficiency virus (HIV), and viral myocarditis (inflammation of the heart muscle). Several studies have also shown the ability of glycyrrhizin to have a significant inhibiting effect on the influenza virus, making it a promising agent in the treatment of flu. One study revealed that glycyrrhizin was effective against coxsackievirus and enterovirus infections. The glycyrrhizin in licorice root has been shown to inhibit the expression of Epstein-Barr virus, which is associated with the development of certain cancers. The antiviral effects of glycyrrhizin appear to be the result of a combination of factors, including inhibiting virus gene expression and replication, reducing adhesion force and stress, enhancing host cell activity, and/or suppressing host cell apoptosis, among others.

Licorice is a demulcent, which means it relieves irritation of the mucous membranes in the mouth. It's also an expectorant, meaning that it helps eliminate phlegm. Not surprisingly, the root extract is a common component of many medicinal cough syrups and throat lozenges. Singers often chew licorice root to ease throat irritation and to strengthen their voices. Herbal practitioners may suggest whole licorice root for asthma, coughs, and other respiratory concerns.

The herb is an effective mild laxative and liver tonic and is used as an anti-inflammatory medicine for the treatment of arthritis. In combination with other herbs, licorice is used to treat muscle spasms. It also acts to reduce stomach acid and relieve heartburn. Other active chemical constituents in licorice root include asparagine, chalcones, coumarins, flavonoids, isoflavonoids, sterols, and triterpenoid saponins. Studies have shown that licorice stimulates the production of interferon, a protein that impedes viral replication and proliferation. The various forms of interferon are the body's most rapidly produced and important defenses against viruses.

The demulcent action of licorice root extract coats and soothes ulcerated tissue, making it a valuable ingredient in preparations for healing peptic ulcers. Because licorice has a beneficial effect on the endocrine system, it's useful in treating problems related to the adrenal gland, such as Addison's disease. Phytochemicals in the root act similarly to the adrenal cortex hormone aldosterone and also stimulate the body's natural secretion of this hormone.

Licorice has antibacterial effects and is beneficial in the treatment of hypoglycemia. This sweet herb also increases bile flow, and when added to the diet, it aids with lowering blood cholesterol levels and the rate of oxidation in cardiovascular tissue. Recent studies have shown that licorice is also cardioprotective. Additionally, the glycyrrhizin in licorice appears to inhibit the growth of cancer cells and induce apoptosis, or self-destruction, in the cells of human breast and prostate tumors. Topical licorice preparations are used for eczema and various types of skin conditions.

PRIMARY EFFECTS

Licorice has the following key actions on the body:

- Adaptogenic
- Antiallergenic
- Anti-inflammatory
- Antiviral

- Blocks tumor-promoting agents
- Cardioprotective (protects the heart)
- Demulcent (soothes mucous membranes)
- Hepatoprotective (protects the liver)
- Hormone balancing

PLANT DESCRIPTION

Licorice (*Glycyrrhiza glabra*) is a perennial with purple and white flowers that's native to the Mediterranean region and central and southwest Asia, where it still grows wild. It's widely cultivated for its sweet taproot that grows to a depth of four feet. Licorice is a hardy plant that thrives in full sun or partial shade and prefers rich, moist soil. It can reach heights of three to seven feet. The brown, fibrous, wrinkled root has yellow interior flesh and is covered with a tangle of rootlets that branch from the stolons. Licorice supplements are made from the roots and underground stems of the plant. The aerial parts of the plant are erect and branching with round stems that become somewhat angular near the top. The leaves are odd-pinnate, dividing into as many as eight pairs of oblong leaflets. Licorice blossoms in late summer. The blooms, which are similar to sweet pea flowers, grow in clusters forming in the angle where the stem joins the branch. The maroon seed pods are one to two inches in length and contain between one and six kidney-shaped seeds.

AVAILABLE FORMS

Licorice is frequently used in medicinal compounds along with other herbs. In traditional Chinese medicine it is used in a plethora of preparations because licorice tones down or masks the bitter taste of many herbal components and helps blend and harmonize mixtures.

Licorice products are made from the powdered or finely chopped dried root as well as liquid extracts. The taproot of three- to four-year-old plants is harvested in late autumn. Washed and dried, the root may be stored intact until it's needed for a preparation.

Some licorice extracts do not contain glycyrrhizin. These extracts, known as deglycyrrhizinated licorice (DGL), do not appear to have the undesirable side effects common to other forms of licorice. Some studies suggest DGL may be better for treating ulcers and may offer protection against ulcer formation when taken with aspirin.

Licorice is available in the following forms:

- Capsules
- Liquid extract
- Tablets
- Tea

To make a decoction (tea), combine 1 teaspoon of the dried root (powdered or finely chopped) with 1 cup of water and bring to a boil. Decrease the heat and simmer for 15–20 minutes. Strain. A standard dose is 3 cups per day. Prepare the decoction fresh daily.

To make a tincture, combine 1 part dried root (powdered or finely chopped) with 5 parts vodka or brandy in a glass container. Alternatively, use half alcohol and half water. Seal the container and let the mixture macerate in a dark location for two weeks. Shake the jar daily. Strain the mixture through cheesecloth and pour into a dark glass bottle. Seal tightly. The tincture will keep for up to two years. A standard dosage is 1–3 milliliters of the tincture three times per day.

Germany's Commission E, a governmental regulatory agency composed of scientists, toxicologists, physicians, and pharmacists, suggests a daily intake of licorice root of 5–15 grams of cut or powdered root, or dry extracts equivalent to 200–600 milligrams of glycyrrhizin. The World Health Organization (WHO) suggests a daily dose of 200–800 milligrams of glycyrrhizin.

USAGE AND PRECAUTIONS

Never give licorice tea to an infant or toddler. Older children who have a sore throat can chew a piece of licorice root or drink licorice tea. Do not administer licorice tea for more than one day without talking to the child's doctor. A pediatrician should determine the proper dose for the child.

Pregnant or breastfeeding women should not take licorice. Some studies suggest that taking licorice during pregnancy may increase the risk of stillbirth.

Adults who regularly take large amounts of licorice may elevate blood levels of the hormone aldosterone, which can cause serious side effects, including headache, high blood pressure, and heart problems. For people who already have high blood pressure, heart problems, or kidney disease, even small amounts per day can trigger these side effects.

Licorice that contains the active compound glycyrrhizin in large amounts may cause serious side effects, such as pseudoaldosteronism, a condition that can cause a person to become overly sensitive to a hormone in the adrenal cortex and may lead to fatigue, headaches, high blood pressure, and even heart attacks. It may also cause edema (water retention), which can lead to leg swelling and related problems. Another type of licorice, called deglycyrrhizinated licorice, or DGL, does not appear to have the same side effects and is sometimes used to treat canker sores, gastroesophageal reflux disease (GERD), and peptic ulcers.

Do not use licorice for longer than one week without talking to your doctor. Although dangerous side effects mostly happen with high doses of licorice or glycyrrhizin taken for more than three to four weeks, smaller amounts, especially when consumed for extended periods, may also cause problems, such as muscle pain or numbness in the arms and legs. To be safe, ask your healthcare provider to monitor your use of licorice and determine the dose that's right for you. If you're being treated for or have a history of any of the following conditions, do not take licorice or products containing it without first consulting with your physician:

- Diabetes
- Edema (fluid retention)
- Erectile dysfunction
- Heart disease
- Heart failure
- Hormone-sensitive cancers, such as breast, ovarian, prostate, or uterine cancer
- Hypertension (high blood pressure)
- Hypokalemia (low blood potassium)
- Kidney disease
- Liver disease

DRUG INTERACTIONS

Avoid licorice and products containing it or glycyrrhizin except under a doctor's supervision if you are taking any of the following medications, as it may increase, decrease, or counteract their effects, or cause the drug to build up in the body:

- Angiotensin-converting enzyme (ACE) inhibitors
- Anticoagulant (blood thinner) drugs, herbs, or supplements
- Antihypertensive drugs (high blood pressure medication)
- Corticosteroids (such as prednisone)

- Diabetes medication
- Diuretics (water pills)
- Hormone medication
- Insulin
- Laxatives
- Monoamine oxidase inhibitors (MAOIs)
- Oral contraceptives
- Medications processed by the liver, including celecoxib (Celebrex), diclofenac (Voltaren), fluvastatin (Lescol), glipizide (Glucotrol), ibuprofen (Advil, Motrin), phenytoin (Dilantin), piroxicam (Feldene), phenobarbital, and secobarbital (Seconal)

Peppermint

Children would beg for a peppermint drop each time he walked into town, and they'd follow behind, asking for a second and a third. When he died suddenly, while working late at his office, every boy and girl in the village reported smelling mint in the night air, as if something sweet had passed them right by.

Alice Hoffman, *Here on Earth*

OVERVIEW

Peppermint (*Mentha piperita*) belongs to the *Lamiaceae* family and grows throughout North America, Asia, and Europe. Native to Asia and Europe, peppermint is naturalized to North America and grows wild in moist, temperate areas. Some varieties are indigenous to Australia, South Africa, and South America. There are more than twenty-five species of true mint grown worldwide.

Peppermint is a natural hybrid of spearmint (*Mentha spicata*) and water mint (*Mentha aquatica*) and was first cultivated in England in the late seventeenth century. Today the United States produces about 75 percent of the world's supply of peppermint.

In laboratory tests, peppermint has been shown to kill certain viruses, bacteria, and fungi, suggesting that it has antiviral, antibacterial, and antifungal capacities. Aqueous extracts of peppermint have been shown to inhibit human immunodeficiency virus (HIV) through interference with viral entry without altering cell viability. Several additional enveloped viruses were similarly affected, suggesting that peppermint could be valuable in the treatment of HIV and other viral infections. The herb has also shown promise for combatting the viruses that cause herpes and influenza.

Peppermint has a time-honored history as a traditional medicinal. It has been valued as a remedy for dyspepsia since ancient Egyptian times; in fact, dried peppermint leaves were found in Egyptian pyramids dating back to 1000 BC. The ancient Greeks and Romans also used peppermint to soothe indigestion. In western Europe during the eighteenth century, peppermint held favor as a folk remedy for nausea, morning sickness, and vomiting, as well as a treatment for respiratory infections and menstrual disorders.

Peppermint is one of the most popular flavoring agents for a wide range of products, including candies, chewing gums, confections, cough drops, digestive aids, ice creams, liqueurs, mints, mouthwashes, teas, and toothpastes. It's also used to scent air fresheners, deodorants, detergents, lip balms, perfumes, soaps, and other cosmetics and personal care items. On top of that, it's included as an ingredient in many over-the-counter medications.

Therapeutically, peppermint is a cooling, relaxing herb that can help calm inflamed tissues, ease cramps and muscle spasms, and inhibit the growth of bacteria and microorganisms. It also has infection-preventing and pain-relieving properties. Highly valued by herbal practitioners and providers of both conventional and alternative medicine, peppermint is used to treat ailments of the immune system, circulatory system, digestive system, nervous system, respiratory system, and skin. The herb's calming effects can be helpful in treating anxiety, insomnia, restlessness, and stress.

When applied to the skin, peppermint helps to reduce sensitivity and relieve pain. Rubbed on the temples, across the forehead, and behind the neck, peppermint oil can help ease headaches and migraines by generating a cooling effect on the skin and relaxing the cranial muscles.

Peppermint is often suggested for the treatment of various digestive ailments, such as bloating, colic, diarrhea, gas, heartburn, loss of appetite, stomach cramps, and symptoms of irritable bowel syndrome. A tea made from the infused herb can stimulate the flow of digestive juices and the production of bile, a substance that aids the digestion of fats. This improves digestion, alleviates gas, eases colon spasms, relieves nausea, and calms motion sickness. When peppermint is taken after a meal, its effects help to reduce flatus and improve digestion by decreasing the amount of time the food is in the stomach. This explains the popularity of after-dinner mints.

The primary active ingredients in peppermint have antispasmodic properties and soothing effects on the gastrointestinal tract. Several studies support the use of peppermint for indigestion and IBS. Combinations of peppermint oil and other botanical medicines also have been studied as treatments for non-ulcer dyspepsia. In vitro studies show peppermint oil to be effective in relaxing the smooth muscle of the colon. However, peppermint oil has also been shown to relax the lower esophageal sphincter, which can cause gastroesophageal reflux or exacerbate gastroesophageal reflux disease (GERD). This finding has led to the widespread use of enteric-coated peppermint formulations, which bypass the stomach and upper GI tract unmetabolized, thereby facilitating their effect in the lower GI tract.

The medicinal parts of peppermint include flavonoids, phenolic acids, triterpenes, and volatile oil, all of which are derived from the whole herb. Nevertheless, peppermint is chiefly cultivated for its oil, which is extracted from the leaves of the flowering plant. Essential oil of peppermint contains the principal active ingredients of the plant: menthol, menthone, and menthyl acetate. Menthyl acetate is responsible for the herb's minty aroma and flavor. Menthol, the primary active ingredient, is found in the leaves and flowering tops of the plant. It provides the cool sensation that peppermint is best known for. The menthol content of the peppermint plant determines the quality of its essential oil, which varies depending on the climate and location in which the herb is grown. For example, American peppermint oil contains 50–78 percent menthol, English peppermint oil contains 60–70 percent menthol, and Japanese peppermint oil contains approximately 85 percent menthol.

Menthol is an effective decongestant and is often included as an ingredient in chest rubs to treat symptoms of the common cold. When menthol vapors are inhaled, nasal passageways are opened to provide temporary relief of nasal and sinus congestion.

As both a decongestant and an expectorant, peppermint is used to help treat many respiratory ailments, including asthma, bronchitis, coughs, and sinusitis. Not surprisingly, peppermint is a component of many cough preparations, including cough drops and syrups, not only because of its pleasant taste but also because its compounds help to ease coughs. Because menthol thins mucus, it acts as an expectorant that can help loosen phlegm and break up coughs. It's soothing and calming for pharyngitis (sore throat) and dry coughs and increases the production of saliva, which helps to suppress the cough reflex. A tea made from peppermint leaves can stimulate the immune system and relieve the congestion that accompanies colds, flu, and upper respiratory infections.

PRIMARY EFFECTS

Peppermint has the following key actions on the body:

- Analgesic (relieves pain)
- Antifungal
- Antinausea
- Antiparasitic
- Antiseptic
- Antispasmodic
- Antiviral
- Aromatic
- Carminative (relieves flatulence)
- Digestive tonic
- Increases sweating while cooling internally
- Relaxes peripheral blood vessels
- Relieves muscle spasms
- Stimulates bile secretion
- Topical anesthetic (but can also be a skin irritant)

PLANT DESCRIPTION

Peppermint (*Mentha piperita*) is an aromatic perennial plant that grows to a height of about three feet. It has light purple flowers and green leaves with serrated edges. The plant is harvested in the summer, shortly before it blooms, which is when the oil content in the leaves is the highest. Peppermint is always collected in the morning, before the afternoon sun desiccates the oil.

AVAILABLE FORMS

Peppermint is available in the following forms:

- Capsules
- Dried leaves (loose or in bulk)
- Essential oil (also called "pure peppermint oil")
- Fresh leaves

- Tablets
- Tea bags
- Tincture

Peppermint tea (loose in bulk or in tea bags) is prepared from the dried leaves of the peppermint plant and is widely available commercially.

Enteric-coated capsules, typically containing 0.2 milliliters of peppermint oil per capsule, are specially coated so the oil's therapeutic properties are released into the lower (small) intestine rather than the stomach. These enteric-coated pills are often used in the treatment of irritable bowel syndrome (IBS), diverticulitis, and other chronic digestive disorders.

Peppermint tincture contains 10 percent peppermint oil and 1 percent peppermint leaf extract in an alcohol solution. A tincture can be prepared by adding 1 part peppermint oil to 9 parts pure grain alcohol.

Mentholated creams or ointments should contain 1–16 percent menthol.

Note that peppermint extract used for culinary purposes is safe for ingestion, as it contains only a small percentage of the essential oil and only a few drops of the extract are used to flavor foods.

USAGE AND PRECAUTIONS

Do not give peppermint to an infant or a small child. Peppermint oil applied to the face of infants can cause life-threatening breathing problems. Additionally, peppermint tea may cause a burning sensation in the mouth. For digestion and upset stomach in older children, use 1–2 milliliters per day of peppermint glycerite that is specially formulated for children.

Peppermint oil should not be ingested except under the supervision of a physician or experienced healthcare provider, as it may cause an irregular heartbeat. Large internal doses of peppermint essential oil may result in kidney damage. Pure menthol should never be ingested, as it is poisonous and fatal in doses as small as one teaspoon.

Pregnant women with a history of miscarriage should use peppermint with caution. Large amounts of peppermint have emmenagogue (increases menstrual flow) effects and may trigger a miscarriage. Caution should be practiced by women who are breastfeeding their infants.

If peppermint essential oil is not used properly, it can cause dermatitis and other skin or allergic reactions.

Side effects may include the following:

- Allergic reactions
- Flushing
- Headache
- Heartburn
- Mouth sores
- Rash (with topical applications)

Peppermint oil capsules have been shown to be effective in treating lower intestinal disorders. Enteric-coated capsules should be swallowed whole and not crushed, broken, or chewed because peppermint oil can irritate the mouth, esophagus, and stomach. Tablets should be taken 30–60 minutes before meals on an empty stomach. Rare reactions to enteric-coated capsules may occur. These reactions include heartburn, muscle tremors, skin rash, and slow heart rate. Because of peppermint's ability to relax the smooth muscle of the GI tract, patients with hiatal hernia may experience worsening symptoms when ingesting preparations containing peppermint. Peppermint oil should not be administered to patients with heartburn or active gastric ulcers because symptoms may be exacerbated. The oil can decrease esophageal sphincter pressure and contribute to gastroesophageal reflux. Peppermint should not be used in conjunction with homeopathic treatments.

The following are common dosages for peppermint:

- Enteric-coated capsules: For irritable bowel syndrome (IBS), take 1 or 2 capsules, each containing 0.2 milliliters of peppermint oil, two to three times per day between meals. Alternatively, take 1 or 2 capsules of IBGard (by IM Health Science) 30 minutes before or after each meal for at least one month or as directed by your physician. IBGard capsules contain individually enteric-coated sustained-release microspheres of purified peppermint oil that is delivered quickly and reliably to the small intestine. IBGard has been shown in clinical trials to be effective in moderating or resolving the symptoms of IBS.

- Gallstones: Take 1 or 2 capsules, each containing 0.2 milliliters of peppermint oil, three times per day between meals.

- Itching and skin irritation: Apply mentholated cream or ointment no more than three to four times per day.

- Tea: Steep 1 teaspoon of dried peppermint leaves in 1 cup of boiling water for 10 minutes. Strain before drinking. Drink 1 cup four to five times per day between meals. Peppermint tea appears to be safe, even in large quantities. Peppermint tea may be used to relieve digestive ailments, migraine headaches, minor colds, and morning sickness, as well as many other conditions. Taken after a meal, the tea can help settle the stomach and improve digestion. To help relieve migraine headaches, drink 1–2 cups of the tea daily. For digestive disorders, drink 1 cup of warm peppermint tea with meals. For cough relief, drink 3–4 cups of warm tea throughout the day, sipping it every 15–30 minutes.

■ Tension headaches: Lightly coat the forehead with peppermint oil tincture and allow the tincture to evaporate.

When inhaled, peppermint oil can reduce fever, relieve nausea and vomiting, improve digestion, and soothe the respiratory system. Several studies have confirmed the oil's ability to enhance a person's sense of smell and taste and improve concentration and mental acuity. Peppermint oil can be inhaled, diffused into the air, included in topical preparations, or added to a therapeutic bath. Below are some common applications for the use of peppermint oil:

■ Digestion: Dilute several drops of peppermint oil in water and massage it into the stomach or abdominal area or rub the undiluted oil on the bottoms of the feet.

■ Headache: Put a few drops of peppermint oil on a cool, wet towel and place it on the forehead as a compress. Alternatively, massage a few drops of the oil into the neck, temples, and forehead.

■ Motion sickness: Put a few drops of peppermint oil on a tissue and inhale.

■ Steam inhalation for congestion relief: Put a few drops of peppermint oil in a large bowl of hot water. Cover your head with a towel, lean over the bowl, and inhale the steam.

■ Therapeutic bath: Put several drops of peppermint oil into tepid bath water to help relieve symptoms of digestive disorders, headache, nasal congestion, or menstrual cramps. Alternatively, fill a cloth or muslin bag with several handfuls of dried or fresh peppermint leaves and put the bag in the bathwater.

Use caution with peppermint oil, as it is highly concentrated and should be diluted with a neutral vegetable oil prior to topical use to prevent adverse reactions. Note that some people are allergic to peppermint and/or its essential oil. The oil may cause a skin reaction if the dosage is excessive. Always avoid contact with the eyes.

If you are being treated for or have a history of any of the following conditions, do not take peppermint or products containing it without first consulting with your physician:

- Achlorhydria (a stomach condition in which the stomach is not producing hydrochloric acid)
- Chronic diarrhea
- Gallstones
- Gastroesophageal reflux disease (GERD)
- Heartburn
- Hiatal hernia
- Hypertension (high blood pressure)
- Indigestion
- Organ transplant

DRUG INTERACTIONS

Avoid peppermint and products containing it or menthol except under a doctor's supervision if you are taking any of the following medications or drugs, as it may increase, decrease, or counteract their effects, or cause the drug to build up in the body:

- Antacids and other acid-reducing drugs (such as Pepcid, Prevacid, Prilosec, Nexium, Tagamet, and Zantac)
- Antihypertensive drugs (high blood pressure medication)
- Caffeine
- Cholesterol-lowering drugs (statins)
- Cyclosporine
- Diabetes medication
- Immunosuppressants

Siberian Ginseng

The art of medicine consists in amusing the patient while nature cures the disease.

Voltaire (1694–1778), French Enlightenment writer, historian, and philosopher

OVERVIEW

Siberian ginseng (*Eleutherococcus senticosus*), also known as eleuthero ginseng or eleuthero, has been used for centuries in Eastern countries, including China, Korea, Japan, and Russia, and is one of the most widely used herbs in the world. Despite being in the same botanical family as American ginseng (*Panax quinquefolius*, see page 61) and Asian ginseng (*Panax ginseng*, see page 70), and having a similar name, Siberian ginseng isn't the same plant and doesn't have the same chemical components. Siberian ginseng's active ingredients are a complex group of chemicals called eleutherosides, which differ from the ginsenosides found in the *Panax* varieties of ginseng. This variance in their active ingredients has sparked debate among herbalists about whether Siberian ginseng should even be considered a true ginseng at all.

Siberian ginseng supplements are made from the root of the plant because the root contains the richest concentration of eleutherosides. Eleutherosides are reported to stimulate the production of interferon (a protein that inhibits virus replication) and enhance natural killer cells and antibody activity. Among the herb's other constituents are chemicals called polysaccharides, which have also been found to boost the immune system and lower blood sugar levels in laboratory tests.

Siberian ginseng has been used in traditional Chinese medicine for over two thousand years to treat respiratory and other infections, including colds and flu, and increase energy, vitality, and longevity. The herb was also used as a folk remedy for hundreds of years in Eastern Europe. However, it was not until the 1940s that Siberian ginseng became popular in Russia and in other parts of Europe.

Until recently, most scientific research on the herb had been done in the former Soviet Union. I. I. Brekhman, a Russian physician, is credited with popularizing Siberian ginseng. After studying Korean ginseng in the 1940s, he documented some of its effects on the body and determined that the plant was an adaptogen. But because Korean ginseng was so expensive, Brekhman decided to explore the Russian forests to seek a less costly alternative. He discovered that Siberian ginseng was also an adaptogen and offered some of the same benefits as Korean ginseng, even though it had a different chemical composition.

Over the next thirty years, Siberian ginseng became the focus of many studies performed by scientists in the former Soviet Union. Many of the study results are still unavailable in English. However, those that have been translated, as well as more recent studies, have corroborated the benefits of Siberian ginseng. In the Soviet studies, the herb was found to increase the endurance and performance of athletes, and many famous Soviet Olympic champions included Siberian ginseng as part of their training regimens. In fact, the benefits of Siberian ginseng were so highly touted that Soviet astronauts took the herb into space with them instead of the amphetamines the American astronauts carried. Soviet scientists discovered that Siberian ginseng strengthened the immune system, and it was dispatched to highly stressed workers as herbal support. Siberian ginseng was also given to individuals who had been exposed to radiation after the Chernobyl nuclear accident.

Siberian ginseng is credited with having antiviral and immune-stimulating properties. It has been shown in several studies to reduce the severity and duration of colds when taken within seventy-two hours of the onset of symptoms. One study found that healthy people who took Siberian ginseng for four weeks had more T-cells, which may indicate that their immune systems were stronger. In a double-blind study of people with the herpes simplex virus type 2, which can cause genital herpes, participants had a reduced number of outbreaks when taking Siberian ginseng, and outbreaks that did occur were less severe and didn't last as long.

In many studies Siberian ginseng has been shown to improve physical endurance, oxygen uptake, recovery, and overall performance in a broad range of athletes, from runners to weight lifters. In patients with either low or high blood pressure, Siberian ginseng has been documented to normalize blood pressure. It has also been shown to reduce the general symptoms of stress, protect against gastric ulcers, boost immune system response, increase the activity of lymphocytes and killer cells in the immune system, enhance the body's overall resistance to infection, and fight the effects of toxic chemicals and radiation on the body, including the side effects of radiation used in the treatment of cancer.

Siberian ginseng is recommended as an overall strengthener for the body and the immune system. It is considered an effective herbal support for exhaustion, fatigue, and stress. Beyond that, the herb is used as an immune and energy booster for people suffering from chronic diseases, such as acquired immune deficiency syndrome (AIDS), chronic fatigue syndrome, fibromyalgia, human immunodeficiency virus (HIV), and lupus. Siberian ginseng is also used to assist patients with recovery from anxiety and depression.

PRIMARY EFFECTS

Siberian ginseng has the following key actions on the body:

- Adaptogenic
- Antiviral
- Immunoprotective (protects the immune system)
- Immunostimulant
- Regulates blood sugar
- Regulates cholesterol levels
- Tonic

PLANT DESCRIPTION

Siberian ginseng is a shrub native to the forests of southeastern Russia, northern China, Korea, and Japan. It grows to a height of about ten feet. The leaves of Siberian ginseng are attached to a main stem by long branches, and both the branches and stem are covered with thorns. Yellow or violet flowers grow in umbrella-shaped clusters, which turn into round, black berries in late summer. The root of the plant is used medicinally and is brown, woody, wrinkled, and twisted; it's also much more branched and hairy than other varieties of ginseng. Although Siberian ginseng can be grown from seed, it's a difficult plant to germinate. Nonetheless, Siberian ginseng is considered more adaptable than other ginseng varieties and matures more quickly, making it less expensive to cultivate.

AVAILABLE FORMS

Siberian ginseng is often formulated with other herbs and supplements, especially in products designed to alleviate fatigue or improve alertness. The quality of Siberian ginseng products tends to vary greatly. Tests of commercial products claiming to contain Siberian ginseng found that as many as 25 percent contained none of the herb and many were contaminated with ingredients not indicated on the label. Be sure to purchase Siberian ginseng only from reputable manufacturers.

Siberian ginseng is available in the following forms:

- Capsules
- Dried root (for tea)
- Fresh root (for tea)
- Liquid extract
- Powder
- Solid extract
- Tablets

Read product labels carefully to make sure you're getting the type of ginseng you want. For Siberian ginseng, look for *Eleutherococcus senticosus*. It may also be combined with other herbs.

USAGE AND PRECAUTIONS

Do not give Siberian ginseng to children. Siberian ginseng is generally considered safe for most adults when taken for limited periods by mouth. Although rare, some people can experience the following side effects, especially in high doses:

- Anxiety
- Confusion
- Drowsiness
- Headache
- Hypertension (high blood pressure)
- Insomnia
- Irregular heart rhythm
- Mood changes
- Muscle spasms
- Nosebleed
- Vomiting

A common dosage for Siberian ginseng root powder is 1–2 grams daily, taken in capsules or mixed with water or juice. Dosages should be divided and taken between meals, two or three times per day. The suggested dose for the liquid extract is 1–2 milliliters two times per day. Look for Siberian ginseng products that contain standardized percentages of eleutherosides. Although Siberian ginseng can be taken on an ongoing basis, it is generally recommended that for every three months of use, a break of two to four weeks should follow. Siberian ginseng is sometimes combined with other adaptogenic herbs, such as American ginseng, Asian ginseng, astragalus, and/or schisandra, to boost its effectiveness. The following are commonly suggested dosages for specific needs:

- For herpes simplex type 2 infections: Take Elagen, a brand-name product that is standardized to contain eleutheroside 0.3 percent, to reduce the frequency, severity, and duration of herpes simplex type 2 outbreaks.

- For the common cold: Take 400 milligrams of Kan Jang (by Swedish Herbal Institute), which contains a combination of Siberian ginseng plus a specific andrographis extract (see "Andrographis," page 65), standardized to contain 4–5.6 milligrams andrographolide, three times per day. Start using Kan Jang within seventy-two hours of the onset of symptoms. Although some symptoms may improve after two days of treatment, it generally takes four to five days of treatment to obtain the maximum benefit.

In general, side effects from Siberian ginseng are rare and more mild than those that occur with American and Asian ginseng. Mild diarrhea has been reported with its use, and insomnia may occur if it's taken too close to bedtime. Women who have a history of estrogen-sensitive cancers or uterine fibroids should consult their healthcare provider before taking Siberian ginseng because the herb may act like estrogen in the body. Siberian ginseng may lower blood sugar levels, raising the risk of hypoglycemia (low blood sugar). Because Siberian ginseng can boost immune function, it may interact with drugs taken to treat autoimmune diseases or drugs taken after organ transplantation.

If you are being treated for or have a history of any of the following conditions, do not take Siberian ginseng or products containing it without first consulting with your physician:

- Autoimmune diseases
- Diabetes
- Estrogen-sensitive cancers
- Heart disease
- Hypertension (high blood pressure)
- Inflammatory bowel disease (IBD)
- Insomnia
- Irritable bowel syndrome (IBS)
- Mania
- Mental illness
- Narcolepsy
- Organ transplant
- Schizophrenia
- Seizures
- Sleep apnea
- Uterine fibroids

DRUG INTERACTIONS

Avoid Siberian ginseng and products containing it except under a doctor's supervision if you are taking any of the following medications, as it may increase, decrease, or counteract their effects, or cause the drug to build up in the body:

- Angiotensin-converting enzyme (ACE) inhibitors
- Anticoagulant (blood thinner) drugs, herbs, or supplements
- Antihypertensive drugs (high blood pressure medication)
- Antipsychotic medication, especially drugs for bipolar disorder and schizophrenia
- Aspirin
- Barbiturates
- Corticosteroids (such as prednisone)
- Diabetes medication
- Digoxin
- Hormone medication
- Immunosuppressants
- Lithium
- Sedatives

Tea

"I don't want tea," said Clary, with muffled force. "I want to find my mother. And then I want to find out who took her in the first place, and I want to kill them."

"Unfortunately," said Hodge, "we're all out of bitter revenge at the moment, so it's either tea or nothing."

Cassandra Clare, *City of Bones*

OVERVIEW

Tea (*Camellia sinensis*) is the most widely consumed beverage worldwide, second only to water. It's also one of the most popular herbal infusions in existence—enjoyed regularly by over half the world's population. Studies suggest that tea, especially white or green tea, has many beneficial effects on human health, including antiviral, antibacterial, anticarcinogenic, antifungal, and cardioprotective activities.

Although several elements in fresh tea leaves are responsible for producing tea's desirable appearance, aroma, flavor, and health benefits, polyphenols are the most abundant and significant. Research indicates the antioxidant effects of polyphenols are even greater than those of vitamin C. These biologically active compounds give tea its astringent and somewhat bitter taste. Because polyphenols are derived from amino acids via sunlight, tea grown in the shade will have a smaller concentration of polyphenols and a higher concentration of amino acids. The bud and first leaf have the highest concentration of polyphenols, with the polyphenol levels decreasing in each leaf as you move down the plant. There are an estimated thirty thousand polyphenolic compounds in tea, but the group known as flavonoids are considered the most noteworthy in terms of health benefits. In the flavonoid group, flavanols, also known as tannins, are the most prevalent. There are several major flavanols (also known as flavan-3-ols) in tea: catechin, epicatechin, epicatechin gallate, epigallocatechin, epigallocatechin gallate (also known as EGCG), and gallocatechin. EGCG is the most active and most studied of the tea flavanols, which are sometimes collectively referred to as catechins. In addition to flavanols, tea flavonoids include anthocyanins, flavones, flavonols, and isoflavones, all of which contribute to the color, taste, and health attributes of tea.

Tea also contains alkaloids, including caffeine, theobromine, and theophylline. These provide tea's familiar stimulant effects. Ironically, L-theanine, an amino acid compound found in green tea, has been studied for its calming effects on the nervous system.

There are four primary varieties of tea: white, green, black, and oolong. They differ mostly in how they are processed. White tea is very minimally processed, which means that much less oxidation occurs than with other types of tea. When the tea buds are plucked, they are allowed to wither and air-dry naturally in the sun, or they are dried in a temperature-controlled outdoor or indoor setting. For more rapid withering and to quickly stop oxidation, some buds are dried using steam or are exposed to low heat. Minimal oxidation will occur even when the buds are allowed to dry naturally, but because there is less oxidation than with green and black teas, which undergo manual processing, white tea has a much lighter, sweeter, and more delicate flavor profile.

Green tea is produced by steaming or roasting the leaves as soon as they are picked. The leaves are then rolled and dried to remove any moisture. People in Asian countries more commonly consume green and oolong tea, but black tea is more popular in the United States. Black and oolong teas involve processes during which the leaves are fermented (black tea) or partially fermented (oolong tea). The longer the leaves are fermented, the lower the polyphenol content. Consequently, green and white teas, which undergo no fermentation, have the highest polyphenol content compared to other types of tea.

The medicinal history of green tea dates back five thousand years or more in China. In traditional Chinese and Indian medicine, practitioners have used green tea as a stimulant, a diuretic to increase urine output, and an astringent to control bleeding and help heal wounds. Other traditional uses of green tea include treating intestinal gas and indigestion, regulating body temperature, stabilizing blood sugar, improving heart health, and enhancing concentration and mental alertness.

The antiviral effects of green tea have been demonstrated against the Epstein-Barr virus, enterovirus, herpes simplex virus, human papillomavirus (HPV), influenza virus, rotavirus, tobacco mosaic virus, and human immunodeficiency virus (HIV). Tea and its active constituents appear to have both bactericidal (the ability to prevent infection by destroying bacteria) and bacteriostatic (the ability to prevent infection by inhibiting the growth or action of bacteria) effects. Moreover, the active compounds in tea have been shown to modify the antibiotic sensitivity of bacteria and to alter the expression of factors that determine bacterial virulence. Although the precise antimicrobial spectrum of tea is difficult to define because of wide variations in testing methods, the antibacterial effects of tea have been demonstrated against a number of microorganisms, including *Bacillus*, *Escherichia coli*, *Klebsiella*, *Pseudomonas aeruginosa*, *Salmonella*, *Shigella*, *Staphylococcus aureus*, and *Vibrio cholerae*.

The chemicals in green tea may help to treat genital warts, prevent or lessen the symptoms of colds and flu, and heal dermatologic conditions. What's more, green tea may play a role in preventing cognitive decline, Parkinson's disease, and osteoporosis. Studies show that drinking green tea is associated with a reduced risk of dying from any cause.

PRIMARY EFFECTS

Tea has the following key actions on the body:

- Antibacterial
- Anticarcinogenic
- Antifungal
- Antimicrobial
- Antiviral
- Astringent
- Cardioprotective (protects the heart)
- Carminative (relieves flatulence)
- Diuretic
- Stimulant

PLANT DESCRIPTION

All teas (excluding herbal teas, which are produced from a variety of different herbs or combination of herbs) are derived from the same plant, *Camellia sinensis*, which is cultivated in high-altitude areas or in countries where warm, rainy growing conditions abound. The tea plant is a type of evergreen bush, with glossy green leaves and small white or pink flowers. The plants can reach a height of forty feet or taller in the wild, but they're generally kept to a height of six feet or under on the tea plantations where they are grown in Argentina, Bangladesh, China, India, Indonesia, Japan, Kenya, Malawi, Pakistan, Sri Lanka, Tanzania, and Turkey.

Tea plants are harvested when they reach maturity after three to four years of growth. The young leaves and leaf buds contain the highest concentration of polyphenols.

AVAILABLE FORMS

White, green, black, and oolong teas are available loose or in tea bags and can be purchased at supermarkets, natural food stores, and gourmet or specialty tea shops. Tea is graded by leaf size; tea that contains whole leaves and leaf tips is considered the highest quality. Although all green tea is obtained from the *Camellia sinensis* plant, slight variations in tea processing (usually based on the way the tea is rolled) have created a number of varieties, such as Dragon Well (Longjing tea), gunpowder, Hyson, matcha, and sencha. There are also four main varieties of white tea, including Silver Needle (*Bai Hao Yin Zhen*), White Peony (*Bai Mu Dan*), Long Life Eyebrow (*Shou Mei*), and Tribute Eyebrow (*Gong Mei*), as well as a legion of oolong and black tea varieties. In general, tea varieties (whether white, green, black, or oolong) are based on the region of origin, season in which the tea is harvested, method and length of withering, and other types of processing.

Tea leaves can be stored for six months to a year in an airtight container, which will help the tea retain its flavor and prevent odors and moisture from being absorbed into the leaves. Here are some additional buying and storage tips:

- Purchase tea from a reputable company so you know how and when the tea was processed and packaged.
- Buy fresh tea in small quantities and put the date of purchase on the package so you know how long it's been in your pantry.
- Store tea in an opaque, airtight container. The longer or more frequently the container is opened, exposing the tea to oxygen,

the more the tea will absorb odors and moisture from the ambient air. Glass, tin, and aluminum containers are best. Plastic will transfer odors and chemicals to the tea leaves and impair the tea's flavor.

- Don't store tea in the same cupboard as aromatic foods, such as coffee or spices, because their flavors and aromas will leach into the tea leaves.

- Store tea in a cool, dark place and keep it away from heat, light, oxygen, and moisture. Light and heat can activate enzymes that will degrade the tea.

- Never store tea in the refrigerator or freezer. Tea is stable at room temperature because it's completely dry. Any contact with moisture can drastically shorten the shelf life of tea.

Tea is available in the following forms:

- Bottled liquid
- Capsules
- Dried leaves
- Liquid extract
- Powder
- Solid extract
- Tea bags

Most tea dietary supplements are sold as dried leaves in capsules or liquid extracts made from the leaves and leaf buds. Look for standardized extracts and supplements. On average, one cup of green tea contains 50–150 milligrams of polyphenols. The polyphenols in decaffeinated green tea products are more concentrated. Caffeine-free tea supplements are also available.

The concentration of caffeine in tea depends on numerous factors: plant varietal, age of the plant, age of the leaves, the region in which the plant was grown, length of the growing season, field conditions, soil nutrients, rainfall, and stress on the plant caused by pests. The final caffeine content may be further affected during the processing of the leaves. Also, how the tea is prepared will greatly influence how much caffeine ends up in the brewed tea. Factors that affect caffeine content include the amount of tea used, the water temperature, the brewing time, and whether the leaves are steeped in a tea bag or strainer or are loose. Overall, the larger the quantity of tea, the hotter the water, and the longer the steeping time, the more caffeine there will be per cup. Broadly speaking, there are 35–90 milligrams of caffeine per cup of tea as compared to 150–200 milligrams of caffeine per cup of coffee.

USAGE AND PRECAUTIONS

The most common method of preparing green tea is as an infusion. The tea is mixed with boiling water, steeped for several minutes, and then strained or removed from the infusion before drinking. Approximately 2 teaspoons of loose tea or a single tea bag should be used for each cup of boiling water. A strainer, tea ball, or tea infuser can be used to immerse loose tea into the boiling water before steeping and separating it. Alternatively, an infusion can be made by mixing loose tea with cold water, bringing the mixture to a boil in a tea-kettle or saucepan, and then straining the liquid before drinking it. The flavonoids—a type of bioactive plant chemical with antioxidant properties—are released into the water as the tea steeps. The longer the steeping time, the more flavonoids are released, although most will infuse into the water during the first five minutes of brewing. A longer steeping time also results in a higher caffeine content in the brewed tea.

Tea consumption by children has not been studied, so tea is not recommended for pediatric use. The US Food and Drug Administration includes tea on its list of "Generally Recognized as Safe" (GRAS) substances. However, pregnant and breastfeeding women should limit their intake of tea because of its caffeine content or use decaffeinated tea products instead, as they contain just small amounts of caffeine. Tea can pass into breast milk and cause sleep disturbances in nursing infants. Pregnant or breastfeeding women should check with their healthcare provider about drinking tea.

Tea can stimulate the production of gastric acid, so individuals with ulcers should avoid drinking tea for this reason. Because tea contains caffeine, it stimulates the central nervous system and, especially in larger quantities, can cause dizziness, heart palpitations, insomnia, irritability, loss of appetite, restlessness, tremor, and upset stomach. Caffeine overdose can cause diarrhea, headache, nausea, and vomiting. If you're drinking a large amount of tea and start to have abdominal spasms or begin vomiting, you may have caffeine poisoning. If your symptoms are severe, seek immediate medical attention.

For adults, 2–3 cups of green tea per day (for a total of 240–320 milligrams of polyphenols) or 100–750 milligrams per day of standardized green tea extract is a suggested dose, depending on the brand of tea or extract.

The tannin in tea can cause nausea when consumed on an empty stomach. It can also inhibit the absorption of nonheme iron. Individuals with iron-deficiency anemia who take iron supplements should avoid drinking tea several hours before and after taking supplements. Iron absorption can be increased by consuming foods rich in vitamin C, such as a slice of lemon, along with tea.

If you are being treated for or have a history of any of the following conditions, do not drink tea or use tea products without first consulting with your physician:

- Anemia
- Anxiety
- Bleeding disorders
- Diabetes
- Diarrhea
- Glaucoma
- Heart disease
- Hypertension (high blood pressure)
- Inflammatory bowel disease (Crohn's disease or ulcerative colitis)
- Irritable bowel syndrome (IBS)
- Kidney disease
- Liver disease
- Osteoporosis
- Psychological disorders
- Stomach ulcers
- Tremor conditions

DRUG INTERACTIONS

Avoid tea and tea products except under a doctor's supervision if you are taking any of the following medications or drugs, as tea may increase, decrease, or counteract their effects, or cause the drug to build up in the body:

- Alcohol
- Antiarrhythmics (drugs for abnormal heart rhythm)
- Antibiotics
- Anticoagulant (blood thinner) drugs, herbs, or supplements
- Antidepressants
- Antifungal drugs (oral)
- Antihistamines
- Antiplatelet drugs, herbs, or supplements

- Antipsychotic medication, especially drugs for bipolar disorder and schizophrenia
- Barbiturates
- Beta-blockers
- Caffeine
- Chemotherapy drugs
- Cocaine
- Contraceptive drugs
- Diabetes medication
- Disulfiram (Antabuse)
- Ephedrine
- Estrogen
- Heart medication
- Insulin
- Lithium
- Liver medication
- Monoamine oxidase inhibitors (MAOIs)
- Morphine
- Nicotine
- Sedatives
- Stimulants, including amphetamines
- Tranquilizers

GLOSSARY AND NOTES

Adaptogen. A natural substance that's believed to exert a normalizing effect on the body's autonomic processes and help the body adapt to stress.

Apoptosis. The death and elimination of cells that naturally occurs as part of an organism's normal growth or development, also known as "cell suicide" and "programmed cell death." Apoptosis plays a crucial role in developing and maintaining the health of the body by eliminating old cells, unnecessary cells, and unhealthy cells.

Arboviral disease. A disease transmitted by arthropods (invertebrate animals of the large phylum *Arthropoda*, such as crustaceans, insects, or spiders) to vertebrate hosts.

B lymphocytes (B cells). The precursors of T cells (see page 129), B cells are antibodies known as immunoglobulins that are produced in the bone marrow but leave the bone marrow and mature in the thymus.

Bactericide. A substance that's capable of destroying bacteria.

Bacteriophages. Viruses that infect bacteria and require a bacterial host in order to replicate themselves. Also known as phages or bacterial viruses, bacteriophages are made up of proteins that coat an inner core of nucleic acid—either deoxyribonucleic acid (DNA) or ribonucleic acid (RNA). Bacteriophages vary in structure, ranging from simple to elaborate and complex.

Bacteriostat. A substance that prevents bacteria from multiplying without destroying them.

Capsid. The protein coat or shell of a virus particle, surrounding the nucleic acid or nucleoprotein core.

Decoction. A tea preparation made from the hardy parts of a plant, including the bark, roots, and seeds. The plant parts are immersed in cold water, brought to a boil, and simmered for 15–60 minutes, depending on the desired potency.

Demulcent. A substance that relieves irritation of the mucous membranes in the mouth.

126

Endemic. A high percentage of carriers of a specific disease within a regional population.

Epidemic. The spread or outbreak of a viral infection in a community.

Expectorant. A substance that helps eliminate phlegm.

Extract, liquid. The foundation of nearly all herbal preparations, extracts separate ("pull," "draw," or "wash") the beneficial (medicinal) components of an herb from the inert fibrous parts by using a solution of alcohol and water or glycerin and water. Extracts come in two forms: liquid (also known as "fluid extracts") or solid (see below). Many people assume that liquid herbal extracts are superior to dry, or solid, herbal extracts, but this is not necessarily true. Each herb has its own unique properties, and which type of extract is best depends on the particular biochemical constituents and medicinal properties of the specific herb being extracted.

Extract, solid. A substance derived from mixing an herb with a solvent (usually a mixture of alcohol and water or glycerin and water) and then removing the solvent. Solid extracts may be soft (viscous) or dry (powdered), depending on the plant, part of the plant used, and the extraction process employed.

Flaviviruses. Any of a group of RNA viruses, mostly having arthropod (invertebrate animals of the large phylum *Arthropoda,* such as insects, spiders, or crustaceans) vectors, that cause a number of serious human diseases, such as dengue fever, hepatitis C, various types of encephalitis, yellow fever, and Zika virus.

Flavonoids. A group of water-soluble plant pigments that have antiviral and antioxidative qualities.

Glycosides. Any group of organic compounds that occur abundantly in plants and yield a sugar and one or more nonsugar substances on hydrolysis (the chemical breakdown of a compound caused by a reaction with water).

Influenza types A, B, C, and D. Human influenza A and B viruses are responsible for the seasonal flu epidemics that occur annually in the United States. Influenza A viruses are known to also infect a variety of other mammals, including nonhuman primates, cats, horses, mink, pigs, seals, and whales. Wild birds commonly act as the hosts for the type A virus. Type B influenza viruses are found only in humans. Responsible for about one-third of flu infections in the United States, they tend to cause a less severe reaction than type A viruses and don't cause pandemics (see page 128). Influenza type C infections generally result in a mild respiratory illness and are not believed to cause epidemics (see page 127). Nearly all adults have been infected with influenza C virus, which causes mild upper respiratory tract illness; lower respiratory tract complications are rare. There is no vaccine against influenza C virus. Influenza D viruses primarily affect cattle and are not known to infect or cause illness in people.

Infusion. A water-based tea made from the more delicate parts of a plant, such as the leaves and flowers, that employs the process of steeping rather than boiling to extract the beneficial components of the herb. To make an infusion, simply put the plant parts in a jar and cover them with cool, warm, or boiling water. Let the liquid sit for as long as you like. The longer the herb steeps, the more potent the tea will be. Typically herbal infusions made with alcohol or vegetable glycerin are referred to as tinctures (see page 129) or extracts (see page 127), and the difference between them is the amount of herb infused in the alcohol or glycerin.

In vitro. A study or process performed within a test tube, culture dish, or elsewhere outside a living organism.

In vivo. A study or process performed or taking place within a living organism.

Leukocytes. White blood cells that fight infection.

Ointment. A mixture of water (either plain or in the form of a tea) and oil (plain or infused with herbs) in a ratio of 1:4. This combination creates a cream that is easily absorbed into the skin and is very moisturizing.

Pandemic. A worldwide epidemic (see page 127).

Phagocytes. Cells that engulf and absorb toxins so they can be removed from the body.

Polyphenols. A generic term for biologically active compounds with antioxidant properties. Polyphenols all have similar ring-shaped chemical structures but differ in the number of rings and molecules attached to those rings. Polyphenols are grouped into four categories based on those differences: flavonoids, lignans, phenolic acids, and stilbenes.

Properdin. A protein present in the blood that helps the body control and prevent infection.

Standardized herbal extracts. An herbal extract that has one or more components present in a specific, guaranteed amount, usually expressed as a percentage. The purpose of standardization is to ensure the consumer is getting a product in which the active constituents are consistent from batch to batch. The practice of standardization evolved from the belief that isolated compounds are responsible for the action of an herb. It was based on the drug model of herbal medicine, a system used by scientists to identify the components of a plant that have known pharmacological activity in the body.

However, when scientists separate constituents from an herb, they may unintentionally disregard other components that may contribute to the activity of that component or to the overall efficacy of the herb. As a result, standardization isolates and concentrates a single component at the potential expense of other components that may be equally important, while also changing the balance of the herb's natural chemistry. Few, if any, medicinal herbs are known to have just a single function. Plants contain a complex blend of phytochemicals that likely have multiple functions and interactions. Furthermore, many herbal constituents are as yet unknown, and how they react in the body and interact with each other is not fully understood. Although a standardized extract may not provide the same spectrum of capabilities as the whole herb, research has nevertheless proven the efficacy of some of these concentrated extracts in terms of their specific biological activity and actions on the body.

Another type of standardization maintains the same spectrum of components as the whole herb but uses key constituents as identifying markers. These types of standardized extracts aren't necessarily more concentrated than the whole herb, but they're guaranteed to maintain a minimum potency of these specific markers.

Syrup. A syrup is made by adding a sweetener, such as agave nectar, honey, or maple syrup, to a highly concentrated tea in a ratio of 2:1.

T lymphocytes (T cells). White blood cells that fight infection and disease and are a vital component of a healthy immune system.

Tea. An herbal extract made by using water as the solvent. Although teas are by far the most popular and easy-to-make herbal preparation, they are also the least concentrated. However, ingesting herbal extracts in a tea is often ideal for chronic health conditions for which long-term yet mild exposure to an herb is preferable.

Tincture. Concentrated extracts made by putting chopped fresh or dried herbs into a jar and covering them with a solvent, such as alcohol or glycerin. The mixture is then sealed and set aside to macerate for several weeks. Most medicinal components of herbs are soluble in alcohol, so this method of preparation is considered to be very effective. Also, because alcohol is rapidly absorbed into the bloodstream, tinctures are the best preparations to use for acute illnesses. A tincture is considered 1 part herbs to 3 parts alcohol or glycerin. The average dose for any tincture is 10–30 drops in a small amount of water three times a day. This will vary depending on the herb and the condition being treated. With echinacea, use 30 drops during times of illness. Please note that children's doses are generally one-quarter of an adult dose.

Tonic. Herbs that have adaptogenic (see page 126) qualities and also enhance strength, increase vitality, and improve longevity.

Vector. An organism, typically a biting insect or tick, that transmits a disease or parasite from one animal or plant to another.

Virion. A complete virus particle that is the extracellular infective form of a virus outside a host cell, with a core of RNA or DNA and a capsid (the protein coat or shell of a virus particle that surrounds the nucleic acid or nucleoprotein core).

Whole herb. Products that contain all the constituents of the plant. The herb is either dried and put into capsules or processed and preserved in alcohol or another solvent.

A Modern Herbal
botanical.com

Centers for Disease Control and Prevention
cdc.gov

Chinese Herbs Healing
chineseherbshealing.com

Drugs.com
drugs.com

Encyclopedia of Herbal Medicine
altmd.com/Herbs-Supplements

Herbal Encyclopedia of Knowledge
cloverleaffarmherbs.com

HerbWisdom.com
herbwisdom.com

HRSA National Vaccine Injury
Compensation Program
hrsa.gov/vaccinecompensation/
index.html

Insight Medical Publishing
imedpub.com

International Medical Council
on Vaccination
vaccinationcouncil.org

Medical News Today
medicalnewstoday.com

MedlinePlus
nlm.nih.gov/medlineplus/druginfo/
natural

Merck Manual
merckmanuals.com

National Center for Biotechnology
Information, US National Library
of Medicine
ncbi.nlm.nih.gov

National Center for Complementary and
Integrative Health
nccih.nih.gov

National Institute on Alcohol Abuse and
Alcoholism
niaaa.nih.gov

ProCon.org
vaccines.procon.org

ScienceDaily
sciencedaily.com

ScienceDirect
sciencedirect.com

University of Maryland Medical Center
Complementary and Alternative
Medicine Guide
umm.edu/health/medical/altmed

US National Library of Medicine
nlm.nih.gov

Vaccine Adverse Event Reporting System
vaers.hhs.gov

WebMD Vitamins and Supplements Center
webmd.com/vitamins-supplements

Wellness Library: Foods, Herbs, and
Supplements
http://goo.gl/WUi6s6

World Health Organization
who.int

A

active immunity, 24
adaptogenic herbals, 62, 66, 71, 72, 75, 76, 101, 113, 115, 116
Afexa Life Sciences, 63
age, immunity and, 37–38, 44
AIDS (acquired immune deficiency syndrome), 4, 6, 10, 15, 25, 65, 75, 78, 88, 91, 93, 114
alcohol consumption, immunity and, 44
Alzheimer's disease, viral infection and, 59
American black elderberry, 92
American Eclectics, 87
American ginseng, 61–64, 70, 71, 72, 113, 116
American skullcap, 78, 81
andrographis, 65–70
anthocyanins, 92, 119
antigens, immunity and, 23–24, 25, 26, 27
Asian ginseng, 61, 62, 70–74, 113, 116, 117
Asian tiger (Aedes albopictus) mosquito, 52, 53, 54, 55–56
astralagus, 74–78
astrovirus, 12

B

baicalin, 78–79
Baikal (Chinese) skullcap, 78–82
barberry, 82–86
berberine, immunity and, 82–83
Brekhman, I.I., 113

C

cancer prevention, viruses to assist in, 7–8

CDC (US Centers for Disease Control and Prevention), 15, 17, 20, 28, 29, 45, 55, 56
cervical cancer, HPV (human papillomavirus) and, 25
chickenpox, viruses and, 12, 15
chikungunya virus disease, 52–53, 54
children, vaccines and, 27, 38, 50
children and/or infants, viruses and, 4, 12, 13, 14, 16, 17, 18, 20, 24, 28, 44
Chinese ginseng, 70
Chinese herbals/medicine, 63, 65, 70, 75–76, 77, 78, 79, 80, 81, 102, 113, 119
Chinese (Baikal) skullcap, 78–82
cold sores, herbals to treat, 96, 98, 99
cold sores, herpes viruses and, 14, 88
cold temperatures, infections and, 21, 38
Cold-FX, 63
colon cancer, viral infections and, 6
Commission E, 103
common cold, herbals to treat, 63, 66, 69, 88, 91, 95, 100, 107, 114, 116–117
common cold, viruses and, 12, 18, 19, 22, 48
coughing
  cautions about, 31, 33, 41
  herbals and, 65, 78, 87, 92, 101, 106, 107, 108, 111
  as symptom, 19, 22, 46, 48, 49
  viruses and, 12, 13, 16, 18, 19, 21, 22, 44
CVT-E002, 63

D

dengue fever/virus, 10, 12, 31, 35, 52, 53, 59, 79
DGL (deglycyrrhizinated licorice), 102, 104
diabetes, viruses and, 18, 44, 59

diarrhea, bacterial vs. viral, 21, 22
diet/nutrition, immunity and, 30, 31, 33, 38, 39
drinking water, immunity and, 36

E

Ebola, 12–13
echinacea, 86–92
EGCG (epigallocatechin gallate), 119
elderberry, 92–95
eleutherosides, 113
European barberry, 82
exercise, immunity and, 30, 31, 33, 38–39

F

FDA (U.S. Food and Drug Administration), 28, 61, 123
flavonoids, 71, 88, 94, 96, 100, 101, 107, 119, 123
flu. *See* influenza (flu)
food safety, immunity and, 35
foodborne illness/virus, 6, 13

G

GBS (Guillain-Barré syndrome), Zika virus and, 20
German measles (rubella), 10, 18, 28
ginseng, 61–64, 70–74, 112–118
ginsenosides, 61–62, 71
glycans (panaxans), 71
glycyrrhizin, 100, 101, 102, 103, 104
GRAS (Generally Recognized as Safe), 123

H

hand, foot, and mouth disease, 13–14
handwashing, to stop infections, 33, 35, 40–42, 45, 50
heart defect, rubella and, 18
hepatitis
  A, 10, 14, 28
  B, 8, 10, 14, 25, 27, 28, 79
  C, 10, 14, 25, 79, 100
  herbals and, 66, 78, 79, 100
herpes
  about, 14–15
  herbals to treat, 79, 88, 96, 99, 100, 106, 114, 116, 120

hosts and, 10, 79
  shingles and, 15, 19, 28
HIV (human immunodeficiency virus)
  about, 15
  drugs for, 23
  herbals and, 65, 75, 78, 79, 88, 91, 93, 96, 99, 100, 105, 114, 120
  host cells and, 6
  immunity and, 25
  life cycle, 9
  as pandemic, 11
  transmission, 10
  vaccine, lack of, and, 4, 31
HPV (human papillomavirus), 8, 10, 15, 25, 27, 88, 120
hygiene, immunity and, 14, 33, 35, 40–42, 45, 50

I

immunity
  about, 23–25
  active/passive, 24
  age and, 37–38, 44
  alcohol consumption and, 34–35
  antigens and, 23–24, 25, 26, 27
  berberine and, 82–83
  cold temperatures and, 38
  diet/nutrition and, 30, 31, 33, 38, 39
  drinking water and, 36
  enhancing/improving, 30–31, 37
  exercise and, 30, 31, 33, 38–39
  food safety and, 35
  HIV (human immunodeficiency virus) and, 25
  hygiene and, 14, 33, 35, 40–42, 45, 50
  lifestyle and, 32–36
  natural medicines and, 31–32, 39
  safe sex and, 36
  sleep and, 34
  smoking and, 33–34
  stress and, 31, 34, 39–40
  travel and, 35–36
  vaccines and, 8, 24, 25–29, 35, 45, 50
  viruses and, 8, 9, 10, 11, 12, 14, 15, 16, 18, 20, 56
  vitamins and, 30, 32–33, 38, 39
Indian medicine (Ayurveda), 65, 82, 119

Indian/Nepalese barberry, 82
influenza (flu)
  about, 16, 43–44
  aging adults and, 38
  antibiotics and, 22
  deaths and, 37, 38, 43, 44
  diagnosis & treatment, 46–47, 59
  herbals to treat, 62, 65, 66, 71, 73, 75,
    87, 88, 91, 92, 93, 95, 100, 108, 113,
    120
  hosts and, 6, 10
  myths about, 47–50
  other illnesses vs., 12, 47, 48, 49
  as pandemic, 11, 43, 44
  preventing, 44–46
  Spanish flu, 11
  symptoms, 46
  types of, 44
  vaccines and, 27, 28, 38, 44, 45–46,
    49–50

J
Japanese encephalitis, 16, 35

K
kalmegh (andrographis), 65
Kan Jang, 66
"king of bitters" (andrographis), 65
Korean ginseng, 70, 71, 113

L
lemon balm, 96–99
leukocytes, 87
licorice, 100–105
lifestyle, immunity and, 32–36
liver cancer/disease, viral infections and,
  8, 14, 25, 59
lungs, viruses and, 6, 16, 17, 44, 46
lymphocytes, 6, 23, 37, 114

M
malaria, 24, 35, 52, 65, 84, 87
malnutrition, 25, 38, 49
measles/rubella (German measles), 4, 8,
  10, 16–17, 18, 28, 59
mosquito-borne viruses
  about, 51–53

Asian tiger mosquito and, 55–56
  preventing, 56–57
  yellow fever mosquito and, 53–55
mumps, 4, 10, 17, 28

O
Oregon grape, 82

P
panaxans (glycans), 71
panaxosides, 71
pandemic(s), 11, 25, 43, 44, 47
passive immunity, 24
peppermint, 105–112
phagocytes, 87
phytochemicals, 5, 97, 101
polio (poliomyelitis), 4, 8, 10, 13, 17, 28
polyphenols, 96, 118–119, 121, 122, 123
pregnancy, viruses and, 18, 20, 24, 50

R
rabies, 10, 18
repellents, for mosquitoes, 56–57
RNA viruses, 78
rubella (German measles)/measles, 4, 8,
  10, 16–17, 18, 28, 59

S
safe sex, immunity and, 36
Sambucol, 93, 94, 95
SARS (severe acute respiratory
  syndrome), 5, 18–19, 31, 59
shingles, varicella-zoster virus and, 19
Siberian ginseng, 66, 67, 69, 112–118
skin, viruses and, 9, 10, 12, 13
sleep, immunity and, 34
smoking, immunity and, 33–34
STDs (sexually transmitted diseases), 10,
  15, 36, 83–84
stomach cancer, Helicobater pylori and,
  25
stress, immunity and, 31, 34, 39–40
Swedish Herbal Institute, 66

T
tannins, 97, 119, 123
tea, 118–125

terpenes, 97
travel, immunity and, 35–36
triterpenoids, 100

U

ulcers, viruses and, 25
United Plant Savers, 90

V

vaccine(s)
  as advantageous/safe & effective, 8, 35
  alternatives to, 5, 59, 61
  anatomy/life cycle of, 8–9
  Asian ginseng and, 71
  basics, 25–27
  concerns about, 27–29
  effectiveness, in older people, 38
  handwashing vs., 41
  immunity and, 8, 24, 25–29, 35, 45, 50
  inactivated, 26
  influenza (flu) and, 27, 28, 38, 44, 45–46,
    49–50
  Japanese encephalitis and, 16
  lack of and, 4, 14, 31, 53
  live attenuated, 25–26
  for mosquito-borne diseases, 53
  nucleic acid-based, 27
  recombinant, 26–27
  Salk, Jonas, and, 10
  shingles and, 19

synthetic, self-amplifying, 27
Zika and, 20
VAERS (Vaccine Adverse Event Reporting
    System), 28
varicella-zoster virus, 15, 19
virion(s), 6, 7, 9
viruses. *See also* specific herbals to treat;
    specific types of
  about, 4–5, 6–7
  anatomy & life cycle of, 8–9
  bacterial infections vs., 21–23
  as beneficial, 7–8
  epidemics/pandemics, 11, 59
  as global concern, 11
  handwashing to avoid, 40–42
  safe alternatives for, 59–61
  transmission of, 10
vitamins, immunity and, 30, 32–33, 38, 39

W

West Nile virus, 19, 59
WHO (World Health Organization), 103

Y

yellow fever, 52
yellow fever (*Aedes aegypti*) mosquito,
    52, 53–55

Z

Zika virus, 19–20, 52, 54, 55, 59

Book Publishing Co.

books that educate, inspire, and empower

Visit **BookPubCo.com** to find your favorite books on
plant-based cooking and nutrition, raw foods, and healthy living.

**Aromatherapy and
Herbal Remedies
for Pregnancy, Birth,
and Breastfeeding**
Demetria Clark
978-1-57067-328-3
$14.95

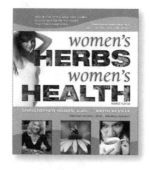

**Women's Herbs,
Women's Health**
*Christopher Hobbs, LAc
Kathi Keville*
978-1-57067-152-4
$24.95

**Herbal Healing
for Children**
Demetria Clark
978-1-57067-214-9
$14.95

**Oil of Oregano:
Nature's Antiseptic
and Antioxidant**
Barbara Schuetz
978-1-57067-329-0
$5.95

**Beauty
by Nature**
Brigitte Mars
978-1-57067-193-7
$19.95

**Native Plants,
Native Healing**
Tis Mal Crow
978-1-57067-105-0
$12.95

Purchase these titles from your favorite book source or buy them directly from:
Book Publishing Company • PO Box 99 • Summertown, TN 38483 • 1-888-260-8458

Free shipping and handling on all orders

To
the members of
Leicestershire Constabulary